COLLECTED WHEEL PUBLICATIONS

VOLUME 10

NUMBERS 132 – 151

BPE

BPS Pariyatti Editions

BPS Pariyatti Editions
An imprint of Pariyatti Publishing
www.pariyatti.org

Although this is an American edition, we have left any British spelling of words unchanged.

First BPS Pariyatti Edition, 2022
ISBN: 978-1-68172-160-6 (Print)
ISBN: 978-1-68172-161-3 (PDF)
ISBN: 978-1-68172-162-0 (ePub)
ISBN: 978-1-68172-163-7 (Mobi)
LCCN: 2018940050

Contents

WH 132 to 134 Touching the Essence
Bhikkhu Dhammapāla (Henry van Zeyst) 1

WH 135 The Message of the Saints
V. F. Gunaratna 75

WH 136 The Problem of Sin
P. M. Rao 103

WH 137 & 138 The Buddhist Wheel Symbol
T. B. Karunaratne 131

WH 139 Prayer and Worship
Francis Story 161

WH 141 to 143 Survival and Karma in Buddhist Perspective
K.N. Jayatilleke 187

WH 144 to 146 Schopenhauer and Buddhism
Bhikkhu Ñāṇājīvako 257

WH 147 to 149 The Wheel of Birth and Death
Bhikkhu Khantipālo 329

WH 150 & 151 Brāhmaṇism, Buddhism, and Hinduism
Lal Mani Joshi 369

Key to Abbreviations

A	Aṅguttara Nikāya	Paṭis	Paṭisambhidamagga
Ap	Apadāna	Peṭ	Peṭakopadesa
Bv	Buddhavaṃsa	S	Saṃyutta Nikāya
Cp	Cariyāpiṭaka	Sn	Suttanipāta
D	Dīgha Nikāya	Th	Theragātha
Dhp	Dhammapada	Thī	Therigātha
Dhs	Dhammasaṅgaṇī	Ud	Udāna
It	Itivuttaka	Vibh	Vibhaṅga
Ja	Jātaka verses and commentary	Vin	Vinaya-piṭaka
Khp	Khuddakapāṭha	Vism	Visuddhimagga
M	Majjhima Nikāya	Vism-mhṭ	Visuddhimagga Sub-commentary
Mil	Milindapañha	Vv	Vimānavatthu
Nett	Nettipakaraṇa	Nidd	Niddesa

The above is the abbreviation scheme of the Pali Text Society (PTS) as given in the *Dictionary of Pali* by Margaret Cone.

The commentaries, *aṭṭhakathā*, are abbreviated by using a hyphen and an "a" ("-a") following the abbreviation of the text, e.g., *Dīgha Nikāya Aṭṭhakathā* = D-a. Likewise the sub-commentaries are abbreviated by a "ṭ" ("-ṭ") following the abbreviation of the text.

The sutta reference abbreviation system for the four Nikāyas, as is used in Bhikkhu Bodhi's translations is:

AN	Aṅguttara Nikāya	DN	Dīgha Nikāya
MN	Majjhima Nikāya	Sn	Saṃyutta Nikāya
J	Jātaka story	Mv	Mahāvagga (Vinaya Piṭaka)
Cv	Cullavagga (Vinaya Piṭaka)	SVibh	Suttavibhaṅga (Vinaya Piṭaka)

Touching the Essence

Six Lectures on Buddhism

by

Bhikkhu Dhammapāla
(Henry van Zeyst)

WHEEL PUBLICATION NO. 132/133/134

From the Foreword to the First Edition

The nature of the radio lectures delivered by me was such that a more careful study of them was thought to be useful not only for the many who listened in at the time, but especially for all who were not in the same position.

The lectures, which form a series, touch upon the most essential parts of the Buddha's teaching: the Four Noble Truths, the three characteristics of *anicca, dukkha* and *anattā*, the doctrine of *kamma*, the *paṭicca samuppāda* and the deliverance of Nibbāna. The second part of the lecture on Soullessness, being of a more polemic nature, could not be broadcast for obvious reasons, but was delivered at the Y.M.B.A., Colombo, the original publishers of this series, under the caption: "Can the soul-idea be vindicated?"

The many questions that followed this and similar lectures are a proof of the great interest taken in Buddhism by the intellectual classes, if only the Norm is presented to them in a normal way which will satisfy their hunger for truth.

May this publication bring about, if not satisfaction, at least a whetting of their appetite!

Bhikkhu Dhammapāla
Udawatte Temple
Kandy
March 15th, 2487 (1944)

The Evolution of Truth

Aparutā tesaṃ amatassa dvārā
Ye sotavanto pamuñcantu saddhāṃ.

Open are the doors to the Deathless state;
You that have ears, send forth true faith!

Dhammacakkappavattana Sutta

With those solemn words the Buddha declared his intention to preach his noble teaching, "deep as a lake, hard to perceive, difficult to grasp, tranquil, sublime, beyond sophistry, abstruse, comprehensible (only) by the wise" (MN 26).

After having attained that "unsurpassable supreme Enlightenment," while the Master was seated at the foot of the goatherd's banyan tree at Uruvelā, he hesitated wondering whether it would be of any use to make his newly found truth known to the world. For "to mankind devoted to, intent on, and delighting in its attachments it is hard to understand this condition of things, their causal connection, their dependent origination, the cessation of all conditioned things, the rejection of every basis of rebirth, the waste of craving, dispassionateness, cessation, deliverance" (Mv 5).

But then also the thought came to him that there would be beings only slightly covered with the dust of worldliness, who not hearing the Norm would go to ruin, but hearing it might become knowers of the truth.

It was for the sake of those few that the Lord Buddha established at Benares in the Deer Park at Isipatana his Teaching supreme, "which cannot be overthrown either by monk or priest, by god or devil, or by anyone in the world" (MN 141).

It is in this first discourse that the Lord Buddha points out that Middle Path which alone can lead to Deliverance by the avoidance of both extremes.

Now, after more than 2,500 years, that same discourse is still applicable, word for word, because only a few have understood and seen, whose ears and eyes were only slightly covered with the dust of ignorance and lust.

The doors to the Deathless are opened wide still for everyone who cares to see.

But also the two extremes are there, more attractive than ever. One extreme is "being intent upon luxurious living in sensuous pleasures, which is despicable, vulgar, ordinary, base, leading to no good." It is the extreme of materialism, which sees but one origin, matter, and which strives but for one end, material well-being.

The other extreme is "being intent upon self-mortification which is painful, ignoble, leading to no good." It is the extreme of idealism, which sees but one reality, that of thought; and strives but for one end, the liberation of that thinking "self."

It was again at the end of the last century that scientific materialism and idealistic monism confronted one another as two independent modes of thought. Theoretically opposed like two extremes, they practically converge both in their starting point and in their goal. "Self" is their beginning and satisfaction is their end.

There is very little difference between the materialists, condemned by the Lord Buddha, the Epicureans of 300 BCE denying an external agency as the cause of matter and hence concluding that the highest good was pleasure, and the later materialists like Hobbes, or the Positivists like Comté and Stuart Mill, holding that only the sensuous can be an object of knowledge.

Though cautious thinkers have abandoned the attempt to explain the entire universe in terms of matter and motion—though the frank materialism of Moleschott (1852), relegating all the phenomena of life and mind to the changes of matter, is dead to all appearances—yet this scientific thinking had deep repercussions, the effects of which will long still be felt.

As soon as science became applied, human craving monopolized it for the sake of its own satisfaction. Inventions have been utilized for the increase of comfort. But increase of comfort has only led to desire for still more; and the desire for more has led and will always lead to conflict and conquest. "Over-civilization has brought us to a point where the work of getting food is so strenuous that we lose our appetite for food in the process of getting it" (Lin Yutang).

Life has become unnatural because it has become mechanized; man is reduced to the position of a cogwheel in a machine. Like a cogwheel is moved on and on by other, sometimes smaller, wheels, and thus by turning round and round merely passes on that movement to the next, thus man, to find his place in society must move on with society, and in his whirling round gets hold also of others, whom he drags along with him in the vortex of materialism.

Surely, that is "despicable, vulgar, ordinary, base, leading to no good."

The other extreme is idealism, which expresses itself in different ways. Yet at bottom they are outgrowths from one root—self.

Fichte in his subjective idealism held that it is the "I" alone who exists; all the rest is a modification of my mind. Schelling and Berkeley tell us in their objective idealism that all, including the "I," are mere manifestations of the Absolute. Finally Hegel informs us in his absolute idealism that only the relation between subject and object is real.

Has all this anything to do with the extreme against which the Buddha warned us when showing his Middle Path?

Addiction to self-mortification is merely the practical side of the speculation of idealism. In idealism the "self" is sublimated, with the natural consequence that the "self" must be liberated from matter; soul must be delivered from the bonds of the body. The passions of the body must be subdued even by force; body becomes the eternal enemy of the spirit which can only be overcome "by prayer and fasting" (Matt. 17: 21).

This kind of idealism will easily lead to pretension, simulation, deceit, hypocrisy; it is much more dangerous than materialism; for materialism may make a man bad and that is the end of it; but idealism will sublimate the evil and call it good; egoism becomes an eternal soul; killing becomes justice; nations are suppressed for the sake of freedom and God in heaven is thanked for a victory here on earth.

Thus idealism becomes fanaticism. Surely, that is "painful, ignoble, leading to no good." Between the two, not as a meeting-place, not as a compromise of the two extremes of materialistic self-indulgence and idealistic self-denial but "avoiding both" the Blessed One has found the Middle Path, a path not of mediocrity, but of the highest truth and attainment, "giving knowledge and wisdom," not in the wavering of speculation, not in the excitement of discussion, but "in tranquillity of mind and penetrative insight, leading to Enlightenment and Deliverance," enlightenment with regard to the real nature of things, deliverance from all suffering and its cause.

Thus the Noble Eightfold Path, though a path of earnest striving, unremitting endeavour, and perseverance till the end, can only be entered upon by right understanding of the Truth.

With this we arrive again at the old question, which remained unanswered 1900 years ago: "What is truth?" (John 18:38).

Truth is usually defined as the correspondence between the intellect and the object. The intellect, however, being the *act* of understanding, can increase. But increase and growth involve change. Thus even truth is subject to change. This is called *subjective* truth.

Of a purely *objective* truth we can know nothing, because any experience of it would make it subjective. Truth, therefore, is not something existing in itself, but is a mental experience. Now, that experience will not be the same in all.

No one expects a child of four to have the same religious notions as a college-student; and an adult's experience will be quite different again. There is growth in truth, and for that very reason it *cannot* be *proved*, but only be experienced. Proved can only be that which is static, has the nature of an entity.

Therefore, to understand that truth is a process, that truth is actuality, that is Right Understanding.

And what is actual? That all component things are sorrow-fraught. This is the First Noble Truth.

Birth is called suffering, because becoming itself is the manifestation of the aggregates, the condition sine qua non of all misery, and also the evil result of past dissatisfaction.

Decay is called suffering as the dwindling of vitality.

Death is called suffering as the dissolution of the aggregates.

Thus the arising as well as the passing away of the aggregates is a source of woe, the first as potential, the later as actual.

Sorrow is called suffering which results from loss of relations, wealth, health, virtue, or right understanding.

Lamentation is the suffering that finds expression in weeping and crying.

Pain is the suffering of bodily discomfort.

Grief is the suffering of mental disagreement.

Despair is the suffering of worry and mental unrest.

"To be associated with things one dislikes, to be separated from things one likes, not to get what one wishes—that also is suffering."

This together with the last two, viz. grief and despair represent the mental characteristic of suffering.

Finally and summarily "the five aggregates of clinging (*pañcu-padānakkhandhā*) are suffering," by which in one word are indicated the root and cause of all suffering, namely, clinging (*upādāna*).

This is the Second Noble Truth:

The source of all suffering is attachment, craving, clinging.

This craving takes one of three forms: craving for sense-pleasures, craving for permanent existence or eternalism, craving for no more existence or annihilationism.

The truth of this statement will at once become clear when it is considered (and this is the Third Noble Truth) that with the utter cessation of craving also suffering will come to an end. For, he who has no desires is always content. Contentment cannot be obtained in any other way, for desires are "unsatisfiable," likened unto a bare bone with which a dog cannot still its hunger, decaying flesh which is poisonous, a torch of straw borne against the wind which thus burns the hand of the bearer, borrowed goods which cannot be kept in possession.

Is it pessimism to consider pleasures as suffering? No, it is actuality! But to consider the satisfaction of the senses as real pleasure—that is sheer folly. In order to cure that folly, the fact of suffering is raised to the rank of a noble truth; for folly can only be cured by wisdom.

This shows again how Buddhist ethics or moral principles, like everything else in Buddhism, are based on a foundation quite different from morality in other religions.

Mental development is exactly what is needed for the development of morality. For, "when religion ceases to be wisdom, it becomes superstition overlaid with reasoning" (George Santayana).

In other religions good conduct is enough to become a saint: "If you have love, you have perfected the law," said St. Paul to the Ephesians.

According to later reformers like Luther, faith alone is enough for salvation.

But in Buddhism real virtue is impossible without the foundation of reason. The truth must both be experienced and understood.

To experience suffering surely can be done by any being endowed with feeling; that, however, does not prevent a possible return.

Understanding therefore is necessary of the real nature of the evil and of its cause. When properly understood suffering will be seen as an effect of action which must have been evil to produce such a bad effect. When thus understood in connection with action, it becomes living like actuality itself. No longer passive fate but active *kamma*, which means self-responsibility.

Action is not finished with action and it is just that which makes life so terribly actual.

At every moment I am reaping the fruit of the past; at every moment I am sowing the seed for the future.

Is there then no escape possible, no salvation? There is! And the escape lies along the Noble Eightfold Path, of which Right Understanding is the first step. Like knowledge of a disease is the chance for a cure, thus understanding the cause-and-action of suffering is the beginning of Deliverance.

This understanding should be accompanied by the right intention. It should express itself in word and deed, in practical daily life, in perseverance and in mind control.

Thus should suffering be comprehended, the cause of suffering eradicated, the cessation of suffering realized and the path leading to the cessation of suffering developed. For, the knowledge of the truths must be translated into function, if ever the task will be accomplished.

This is the Noble Path that avoids the two extremes of materialism under all its disguises and of idealism with all its false decorations.

It is the Path of Actuality that leads to Reality. Only having realized this Path with knowledge and insight, the deliverance of mind is steadfast, the last life is reached, rebirth no more waits.

And how did the five monks to whom this first sermon was preached receive it? What was their reaction? "All received it with joy."

Yet, only of one it is said that his eyes opened to the truth; and he reflected: "Whatsoever is of the nature of arising that is also subject to cessation."

No rapt enthusiasm, no utterance of admiration, but the deep tranquillity of a lake without ripple, reflecting the pure light of the sun.

Cessation—that is it where the Path leads to Cessation, not of being, for there is no permanent soul to cease, but cessation of *arising* (*bhava-nirodha* = *Nibbāna*). Thus cessation is not a doctrine of rationalized suicide, not of annihilation, and hence it does not lead to asceticism. Only in one sense does the Buddha admit to be an annihilationist, namely, in so far as he teaches the annihilation of the passions, of evil inclinations, of craving.

To reach this sublime state of perfection there is only one way, the way of renunciation. To renounce is to give up, to let go, to abandon, to discard. And its object is all that has the appearance of being. To be is an affirmation of self, of permanency. Hence all morality which strives to perpetuate self or soul is a subtle kind of selfishness, hence immorality. And the more subtle and sublimated, rationalized and idealized it is, the more dangerous and the more difficult also to escape from it.

Here no rectification of thought will suffice, but only the stilling of thought. No argument can solve this problem; for the more words we use, the greater the chances for misunderstanding. Only one thing is to be done: just ceasing.

And in ceasing we will cease. In letting go we shall arrive. In giving up we shall obtain. For, that which we abandon is the burden of sorrow; that which we discard is the fetter of self. And thus renunciation becomes freedom, relief, deliverance, a foretaste of Nibbāna.

This doctrine of cessation, so characteristic in the Buddha's teaching, is the natural outcome of his discovery that all our suffering is due to our own craving. If craving is suffering, then renunciation must be happiness.

In the renunciation of self the clouds of ignorance clear up, for in the light of non-self (*anattā*) things are seen in their true impermanent nature. In the renunciation of self all distinction between self and others disappears and love becomes truly universal. In the renunciation of self all fear becomes impossible, for fear is the child of delusion and attachment. "When pleasures vanish of their own accord they end in keen anguish for the mind; but when relinquished by one's own will they produce infinite happiness proceeding from tranquillity" (*Vairāgya Sataka*).

While leading his ascetic life Prince Siddhartha had to leave his five companions to find enlightenment all by himself. Only after having purified himself from this attachment was he able to attain what he had sought up to now in vain. Perfect in renunciation, pure in detachment, with insight in truth, he could return to his former companions without running risks of being defiled by their ignorance and craving, "unaffected by good and bad alike, even as a lotus fair to water gives no lodgement" (Sn 6).

Thus also the mind has to detach itself from the five senses of the body. Purified in detachment, enlightened by the truth, the mind can give guidance to the impressions in the five senses, and thus lead experience up to full realization.

Then all feelings and perceptions will be conceived as impermanent, then they will lead to dispassion (*virāga*), to cessation of craving (*taṇhā-nirodha*). Thus forsaking them one will cling to nothing in the world, and without worry one will attain Deliverance for oneself. Then one will know: "Destroyed is the possibility of rebirth, led is the holy life, done is what had to be done, nothing more for this life."

Then truly it may be said: "Oh death! Where is thy sting? Oh grave, where is thy victory?" Then shall be brought to pass the saying that is written: "Death is swallowed up in victory" (1 Cor. 15:55). Not because this corruptible shall have put on incorruptibility, not because this mortal shall have put on immortality, but because no death can sadden, where no more birth occurs.

Thus set the Master rolling the Wheel of Righteousness "excellent in the beginning through its foundation on morality, excellent in the middle through its development of calm and insight, excellent in the end through its termination in Nibbāna" (Vism II 7–2).

> *Svākkhāto bhagavatā dhammo, sandiṭṭhiko, akāliko,*
> *ehipassiko, opanayiko, paccattaṃ veditabbo viññūhī.*
>
> Well-proclaimed is the Teaching of the Blessed One to be realized in this life, yielding fruit immediately, inviting investigation, leading up to Nibbāna, to be attained to by the wise, each one for himself.
>
> *Seyyathāpi bho Gotamo nikkujjitaṃ vā ukkujjeyya,*
> *paṭicchannaṃ vā vivareyya,*
> *mūḷhassa vā maggaṃ ācikkheyya,*

andhakāre vā telapajjotaṃ dhāreyya
cakkhumanto rūpāni dakkhinti.

As one with might
could set aright
what had been overturned.
As one has shown
what was unknown.
(what still had to be learned).
To men astray
he told the way,
(to truth he gave the key.)
Into the night
he brought a light,
so that all men could see.

Like these waves of sound spread and roll on and contact you all, may thus the thoughts of loving-kindness which permeated these words reach you too and set vibrating in your hearts and minds similar thoughts, so that there may be peace even in war, love amidst hate, freedom from lust in a world of craving, freedom from suffering in an ocean of misery!

May all living beings be happy!

Soullessness

Netaṃ mama, nesohaṃ asmi, na meso attā.

This is not mine, this I am not, this is not my self.

Anattalakkhaṇa Sutta (Mv I 6, 38-47)

There are some great primary questions that lie at the bottom of every religious system and which form the seed of religious development, upon the answer to which depends the nature of any religious philosophy. These questions have been puzzling mankind from time immemorial and they will be troubling him for ever more to come, because, though the answers to those weighty questions have been as numerous as there are different religions, they have been unable to satisfy the thinking mind.

The reason for the "unsatisfactoriness" of all these answers—and we may safely predict that any future trial to find a new solution to those problems will be equally unsuccessful—lies in the fact of the intrinsic impossibility to formulate an answer. Any answer is beside the point because those "weighty" questions are based upon misunderstanding. All of them begin to assume the existence of the very thing they want to prove; in other words they beg the question, or in more philosophical terminology they are guilty of the sophism called "*petitio principii.*"

Some of those questions are: Whence am I? Whither do I go? How do I know myself? What happens to me after death? How came I (or life) into this world? How does this world enter into me, into my consciousness? Is the soul the same as the body or not?

These and similar questions are sometimes said to be of vital importance, but then only to those who choose to enquire into them, like children will make a vital problem of the discovery, that a round peg does not go into a square hole. But a person with reason and insight will see at once that it does not fit. Not the peg or the hole, but the child is wrong here. So also not the play of world-events, but only those who put such questions are to blame.

It will be seen that there should be one question prior to all those enquiries, upon which depends the very possibility of further questioning, namely: Is there anything at all which deserves the designation of "I"?

The method followed by the Buddha in solving this question is the most scientific. He does not base his doctrine on logic, for by doing so one ought to presuppose the reality of the thinking subject as standing outside the process of thinking, as a witness or rather as a judge.

That which is not logical in reasoning will be either illogical or a-logical.

Illogical is that which is contrary to logic. Such is faith, belief, acceptance on the authority of someone else without being able even to ascertain the existence of such an authority.

Logic in reasoning, as is said, cannot solve the difficulty, because it presupposes that which it is out to prove; hence it becomes a sophism: *petitio principii.*

Only one kind of logic can help here, the logic of events; only this kind of logic is beyond sophistry and on this a-logical basis the Buddha has grounded his teaching of "soullessness."

The logic of events, of facts, the doctrine of actuality can be understood not by argumentation but by actual analysis.

Whatever we know of the body is known in its parts and in its entirety as subject to change. Within seven years even the smallest particle has been replaced. Composed of the four elementary qualities of extension, cohesion, caloricity and vibration, the ultimate insubstantiality of all so-called solid matter is evident.

The relative qualities of hardness and softness, the occupation in and of space, are due to the elementary duality of extension (*paṭhavi*). It is the element of cohesion (*āpo*) which makes the many parts adhere intrinsically and to one another, and thus prevents an aimless scattering about or disintegration, thus giving rise to the idea of a "body." Caloricity (*tejo*) depends on vibration (*vāyo*) for by increased vibration the temperature rises and when the temperature is lowered, the vibration too is reduced in speed so that gases liquefy and liquids solidify.

Matter being thus reduced to mere qualities and forces which are in a constant state of flux, there certainly no permanent entity can be discerned.

Is not there, however, present a something which supports the qualities, which is the possessor of the attributes, which as a substance stands under them all, upholds them all and unites all phenomena?

Dimensions, form, place, colour, action, even material might change, yet is not there a something which remains unaltered?

A table may be round or square, have three or four legs, have any colour and be made of wood or iron—yet for all that, it remains a table. Is there then not a something independent from the phenomenon?

Independent from all attributes there is naught, no substance, no substratum, no entity, not even the idea or concept! For it is impossible even to think of an object without any qualities. The qualities together form the object. The qualities, the phenomena may change, but then the object also changes.

A carpenter can make a round table from a square one, still it remains a table. But that is not the entity that has persisted, but only the idea thereof, namely, the concept of an object suitable to lay out meals, to keep smaller articles on, to do writing work, to play games, etc. Yet that idea is dependent on certain conditions, e.g., a flat top; for if *that* would be removed even the *idea* of table cannot remain connected with the remainder. Substance therefore is a mere concept, has no existence except in a worldling's imagination. When science bends more and more to the opinion that all so-called solid matter is merely a form of energy, advocated by scientific materialism or as some prefer to call it, *energism*, that is only admitting in different words the ultimate insubstantiality of all so-called solid matter.

The view that matter or the body is the real self or ego-entity must lead to the doctrine of annihilationism (*uccheda-diṭṭhi*), the perishing of that "self" at the disintegration of the body.

The view of the persistence of a self after the breaking up of the body (*sassata-diṭṭhi*) will therefore find another more permanent seat for that self, namely, the mind.

The biologist Haeckel and the chemist Ostwald were the real pioneers of this modern revolt against traditional metaphysics. Yet in the *anattā* doctrine of the Buddha a substance-like entity either in matter or mind, underlying and supporting the phenomena was most categorically denied twenty-five centuries ago.

Yet matter shows more permanency than thought. If thus the body cannot be held to be a permanent entity, still less so can the mind be said to be an everlasting soul or self.

"Better were it, O monks," said the Lord Buddha (S II 94), "that the untrained average man should conceive this body composed of the four primary elementary qualities as soul, rather than the mind. And why? The body is seen to persist for a year or two ... for a generation or even for a hundred years ... while that which is called consciousness, that is mind, that is intelligence, arises as one thing, ceases as another, both by night and by day."

Feelings (*vedanā*) are of three kinds, pleasant, unpleasant or neutral. Now feeling is mental, for if contact is not mentally perceived, no concept of feeling will be formed. Can this mental action of sensation be said to be the self? Or is the perception (*saññā*) of this sensation the self? But then if a pleasant sensation makes place for an unpleasant feeling one would have to admit that the "self" has changed.

There is, however, an experience which gives the impression that there is something which remains the same even though sensations, impressions, perceptions, concepts change. That remaining, unchanging entity is called the soul. Now it is clearly not our duty to disprove any statement which is made without sufficient ground. On him who puts the thesis rests also the burden of the proof. Otherwise: "*Quod gratis asseritur, gratis negator*"—"What is gratuitously asserted may be gratuitously rejected."

A so-called direct proof for the existence of a soul as a permanent entity to be distinguished from changing modes of action is the firm conviction that, though thoughts and actions change, yet the thinker and the doer remain the same.

In refutation it must be said that often the most firm and universal conviction cannot prove a fact. For, conviction is feeling, sentiment, emotion, but proof requires reason. The general conviction of many centuries that this earth was the centre of the universe, even the ecclesiastical condemnation of Copernican astronomy, for upholding which Galileo had to undergo dire penalties and Giordano Bruno was burnt at the stake, could never change the fact that this earth is a minor planet turning round the sun which is only a star not of the first brilliancy. Conviction is no proof.

But even if we let this pass for argument's sake, we cannot admit that the thinker and doer remain the same, for it is exactly by thoughts that we change our mind, by actions that we change our habits.

If that change does not always come all of a sudden and for that reason is less conspicuous, yet the change is not less real for that. Actions cannot be separated from the doer, cannot exist purely as such. There cannot be *walking* without a body that walks. If therefore the action changes, the so-called actor must change at the same instant. Thus the "I" is identified with the action. It is only that "I," which can walk, and sit, and think, and eat, and sleep. But that "I" is not a permanent, unchanging entity; it is identified with the action, is the action itself, and thus changes with the action. "I" cannot stay at home, while "I" go out for a walk.

It is the conventional language which has spoilt the purity of conception, though in some cases even the language has remained pure enough as, e.g., in the intransitive form of impersonal verbs; e.g., it rains. Who rains? What rains? Simply: *it* rains, meaning rain rains. Likewise the concept should not be: I think, but thought thinks.

The fact that conventional language uses the terms "I" and "mine" may be advanced in support of the human conviction; but that does not make that conviction any truer than our way of speaking of sunrise and sunset.

The individual, conventionally called "I" or "self," is a mass of physical and psychical elements without a soul behind them, without a soul inherent in them, the elements themselves being a mere flux (*santāna*), a continuity of changes without identity.

The Sāṅkhyas too believed in constant change, but a change of the same substratum, eternal matter.

The assemblage of impermanent elements, however, does not require a permanent entity to keep them together. The very presence of an unchanging substance would prevent any change in the phenomena dependent on it.

In postulating a mythical, permanent, unchanging entity, as the possessor of changing qualities, one merely assumes that the existence of which had to be proved. A single moment of existence *has* no qualities, but it *is* those qualities.

Matter does not *have* extension, cohesion, temperature, vibration, but it merely *is* all that, and without that it is not. Mind, likewise, is not an entity, but a function, consciousness is thought, and it arises when certain conditions are present: the object, the sense-organ, the proper attention. Thus a thought arises not as the action of a thinking subject, but conditioned by, originating from, dependent on other states. And as such it will be again the condition to, the origin of, the *raison d'etre* of further states—in ceasing passing on its movement, thus giving the impulse to new arising.

"Mind arises from a cause; and without assignable conditions consciousness does not come about" (MN 8). Then the Lord Buddha further explains in the *Mahātaṇhāsaṅkhaya Sutta* that consciousness is conditioned by the objects, i.e., thought arises in dependence on objects presented to the sense organs. If the object is a visible shape and is presented to the eye, then, dependent on those conditions, a thought may arise which is called in this case eye-consciousness, as fire derives its name, wood-fire, grass-fire, from the fuel applied.

Without fuel, however, no fire, without objects and organs, no thought can arise. Becoming is according to the stimulus (lit. food) and when that stimulus ceases, that which has become also ceases.

Void is this of self, or what is belonging to a self.

(MN 43, Mahā Vedalla Sutta)

The teaching of *anattā* does not proclaim that there is no individuality, no self, but only that there is no permanent individuality, no unchanging self.

Personality or individuality is according to Buddhism not an entity, but a process of arising and passing away, a process of nutrition, a process of combustion, a process of grasping.

This individuality has no permanent existence, as a wave in the ocean is only existent as a process, and in rolling on makes itself, and destroys itself.

Yet the individuality of consciousness, though not a permanent entity or soul, is neither a merely physical process. It is a process of grasping. Like fire can only burn as long as it lays hold of new fuel, thus the process of individuality is a constant arising, an ever-renewed laying hold of the objects of its craving, a process of grasping.

It is craving which causes the friction between sense-objects and sense-organs; and from that friction leaps up the flame of new *kamma* which in ignorance will not be extinguished, but in grasping lays hold of fresh material, thus keeping alive the process of burning.

> All is a burning, O monks! The eye is burning, form is burning, eye consciousness is burning, eye contact is burning. And whatever feeling arises dependent on that contact, that also is burning, burning with the fire of lust, the fire of hate, the fire of delusion." (Mahā Vagga, 1 20.2)

As long as that fire is kept aflame, there will be the delusion of "self," there will be the craving to perpetuate that individual self, so that it becomes a something rather than a function, an entity rather than a condition, a soul which sharply separates man from the animals, which have no souls worth saving.

Thus in the ultimate sense this deluded affirmation of self as a permanent soul is craving which says: "This is mine" (*etaṃ mama*); it is pride which says: "This am I" (*eso ahaṃ asmi*); it is the erroneous view which says: "This is my soul" (*meso attā*).

The error is rooted in craving and pride—craving for happiness and bliss, pride which cannot acknowledge defeat. Where the wrong view of an everlasting soul is thus connected with craving for permanency and bliss, there the teaching of soullessness must necessarily follow from the teaching that all things are impermanent and unsatisfactory.

If there were in this body a soul, if feeling or perception, mental differentiations or consciousness were the real self, then the body would not be subject to ill, the mind would not be subject to distress; for if they were the real self, they would be in a position to order: "Let this be so, let this not be so!" If then the body and the mind are impermanent and for that reason sorrow fraught, one is not justified in thinking: "This is mine; this am I; this is my soul!"

Few there are in the world who identify this perishable body with a permanent entity or soul. On the other hand there are many who maintain that the mind or one of its functions, like sensation, perception, mental differentiations or consciousness are identical with an individual, permanent soul, or that those functions possess such a soul-entity, or that they contain in their action such a permanent self, or, finally, that they are contained by or in a soul.

There are many who even now try to prove the existence of a soul. It is maintained by them that the changing mind and character are supported by an unchanging soul. This supposed soul escapes all observation, even though there may be some awareness of thought and action. A direct proof of this existence of a permanent soul is universally admitted to be impossible; it cannot be known directly in itself. What, however, cannot be known directly in itself, might be known sometimes indirectly from its working. If an effect can be observed, we may legitimately conclude to the existence of a cause. And the nature of the effect proves to some extent the nature of the cause. There is no need to put one's finger in the fire to find out whether the fire is hot. One can readily conclude to the heat of the fire, if the temperature of the water increases, while being placed over the fire.

Similarly, a permanent soul, if it would be existent, must produce effects according to its nature. Now a being in order to be permanent, as the soul is supposed to be, cannot be material, because matter is composed, and what is composed is also decomposable, that is, impermanent. Hence the permanent soul should be immaterial. This is fully admitted even by the strongest adherers to the soul theory. Indeed they claim the soul to be spiritual.

But if the soul is immaterial, its working must be immaterial also, and its existence and functioning should be independent from matter.

Around this turns the whole argument in favour of or in disproof of the existence of a soul. This independence from matter is attempted to be proved in various ways. We shall consider and refute them one by one.

The first alleged proof is taken from *external evidence,* namely, the opinion of all men. If all people agree upon one point, it is said to be the voice of nature, which cannot err. It is said that all people at all times were convinced of a continued existence after death. Now this argument loses its very foundation, because not all men believe in a soul. One sixth of the world's population is Buddhist and denies the existence and the very idea of a soul; further there are millions of atheists and scientific men who have lost all faith in God, soul and religion, who have turned completely materialists, who, even if some of them accept the existence of a substance underlying the phenomena, will consider this to be of a purely material substance dependent on, and perishing together with, the coexisting form; further still, even the majority of the so-called believers are so only in name, for they contradict their faith by their deeds whenever they commit a mortal sin, thus condemning their souls to eternal damnation for the sake of a short-lived satisfaction, which they certainly never would do, if they really believed in an eternal soul.

Thus there remains only a very small minority who really and actually believe in their soul. And they can certainly not claim to echo the voice of nature. For their conviction is not even a natural growth of mental development, but rather a remnant of the childish submission in their youth to the dogmatic interpretation by ecclesiastical authorities. This kind of blind faith, which, enforced upon the child, remains sometimes a habit in uneducated adults, is in reality the crudest form of religion, hardly to be distinguished in degree from the superstitious practices of primitive tribes.

But, moreover, what is this voice of nature? It is nothing else but the collection of individual opinions, as a nation is the collection of persons, born and living in the same country. If one individual can err, so can two or three, or a thousand, or a million, and even all.

The fact of general opinion, even of the whole human race, should never be overestimated. In the past we have seen how the strongest convictions have finally crumbled so that they now seem ridiculous to us.

Yet in their days people have made even the sacrifice of their lives for convictions, generally disbelieved then, but now equally generally accepted; which is only another way or saying that general opinion has changed.

Only 400 years ago the mass of civilized humanity laboured under the delusion that the sun goes daily round the earth; that this earth forms the centre of the universe. Copernicus stood practically alone opposing not only what was then said to be common sense, but also divine revelation and the authority of the Bible. Galileo was jailed and by threat of torture compelled to disavow his former opinions, because his telescope contradicted the Bible. Because Giordano Bruno dared to draw some inferences from the Copernican theory contrary to the Scholastic Philosophy of the church based on Aristotle, he was excommunicated and handed over to the secular authorities with a recommendation of a "punishment as merciful as possible and without shedding of blood," the atrocious formula for burning alive. He perished in the flames, turning his eyes away from the crucifix that was held up to him, the victim of theological stupidity and self-applauding intolerance—the martyr for freedom of thought.

It was and still is the common daily testimony of the sense of sight of every being that the sun does move round the earth. And yet, that sense of sight, that common sense, that general opinion, that divine revelation, that biblical authority, is clearly mistaken and false.

The same happens even nowadays and might happen ever and ever again. What was only yesterday proved by science and tested in practice is overthrown today by some newer theories equally proved and tested and universally accepted ... till tomorrow some more advanced theories are brought forward, explaining the same facts quite differently, but more logically and more according to the truth.

Does truth change? If by truth is meant (as it is defined in philosophy) the harmony between consciousness and the known object, then truth will change with any increase or decrease of knowledge; then there will be degrees of truth, of objective truth in which the object becomes better known, or of subjective truth in which knowledge becomes clearer. If truth, on the other hand, is taken in itself, it must be said to have no existence at all; for if an object is not related to any knowing mind, in which would then exist its truth?

Moreover, we usually call a thing true if it corresponds with the idea we have formed of it; but our ideas themselves, according to which we judge the truth of things, are formed from impressions of those selfsame objects.

Thus it will be seen that a general or even universal agreement of opinion is no sign of proof of the truth.

To say then that the voice of nature, if there would be any such thing, cannot err is neither induction, i.e., a conclusion from individual experience to a general truth or principle, nor deduction, i.e., an application of a universal characteristic to individual cases. It is merely bad logic based on sentiment rather than on reason.

In this way we have disposed of external evidence in favour of the soul-idea in two ways, namely, in so far as we have shown that the existence of a soul is not the universal opinion, and even if it were so, it would prove nothing.

It may be true that all people at all times believe in existence after death; even we Buddhists accept this doctrine; but existence after death does not involve a *permanent* existence after death, nor the existence of a permanent soul. Even the Hindus, who believe in transmigration of soul as opposed to the soulless rebirth in Buddhism, do not really believe in individual, permanent souls; for according to *Vedānta* the soul after transmigration through many lives in *saṃsāra* will be reunited, reabsorbed in Brahman, from where it was emanated in the beginning of its wandering. There its individual existence will have come to an end.

External evidence thus having failed, we come to a whole series of arguments alleged to be proofs from *internal evidence.*

Internal evidence means evidence that manifests itself not directly in its existence, but only indirectly through the manifestation of action. Thus, e.g., when a car tyre goes flat we may safely conclude that there must be a hole somewhere in the tube, even if we cannot discern it with the eye. For, if there were no hole, the air could not have escaped.

Similarly from the working of the intellect we may draw some conclusions with regard to the nature of the intellect.

Everything is received according to the nature of the receiver. Water, e.g., takes the shape of the glass tumbler in which it is contained. Colours can only be perceived by the sense organ of sight; sound only by the ear, etc.

Now the mind is said to have *universal* or *general* ideas. Though John Locke, the English philosopher of the 17th century, in his doctrine of ideas, maintained that universal ideas stand for individual objects that are real in the context of experience, this would be a proof for the materiality of universals rather than for anything else. There will be, however, very few supporters of the soul-theory if any, to support this opinion, for, if universal ideas stand for individual objects, they would cease to be universal. And that is exactly our point of view. Berkeley, though a Bishop of the Church of England, and an Idealist in the fullest sense, thought rightly that all ideas are particular; things or objects as presented are individual; they are given together with the relations, each of which may be described by concrete reference to the presented object or event. There is no such thing as shape apart from objects possessing shape, nor colour apart from things having colour, or any idea of motion except as bodies moving (*Principles of Human Knowledge*). The idea of a triangle is dependent on the knowledge of various types of triangle. The idea of colour has no reality, cannot be thought of except as red, or blue, or white, etc. Universality has no meaning apart from the relationship of particulars. An idea is general only in so far as it stands for particulars of the same kind. We speak about humanity. It is true this idea maintains even though individuals die and are born, even though after a hundred years the whole human race has been renewed. But still the idea is only possible as a collective noun through knowledge of individuals. Thus the idea is based on, and derived from, material experience and therefore cannot be said to be immaterial. A proof that the so-called universal or general ideas are based on a material foundation can be obtained from the fact that, if the material experience is insufficient or wrong, the so-called general ideas will suffer from the same deficiency. The first Europeans, e.g., who landed in Africa created a panic by their mere appearance, because they were not considered to be human beings. Clearly the idea of a particular colour had crept into the idea of a human. Only when experience grows, ideas become enlarged, so that the most general or universal idea is dependent on the largest amount of individual, particular experience which is always material.

If, therefore, universal ideas do not contain anything immaterial, the intellect itself cannot be said to be immaterial. Thus even if there would be a soul, we might conclude from its material action that it too would be material. But material is composed; hence it is also decomposable or impermanent.

A second refutation can be drawn up from the major premise that everything is received according to the nature of the receiver. Now it is beyond doubt, and everyone will have to admit it for himself, that the mind has many times very material and materialistic ideas, thoughts of lust and hate, of profit and comfort.

Those thoughts must come from a material source. Now, if the soul is said to be that source, then it is a very material soul, indeed; decomposable also, because material, and hence impermanent, and no soul at all.

Another argument from internal evidence to prove the existence of an immaterial, permanent soul is taken from the fact that the mind seems to have *immaterial concepts* like unity, truth, virtue, justice. Those concepts, however, are not truly immaterial, as they have been derived from material experience. The idea of unity arose only when, after counting for a long time with beads or beans, we were able to substitute units for those objects. Unity is nothing but uniformity from a certain point of view, while the differences are intentionally overlooked. Even unity and order in nature, on which science has built its laws and axioms, have no real existence, but are based on experiment and observation, hence thoroughly material, and can be overturned by new observation and experiment.

Even a thousand scientific experiments do not definitely prove a fact and make it a law, but one single experiment can upset the law and prove its invalidity.

As physical phenomena do not follow an absolutely rigorous necessity, but permit a contingency, incalculable like chance, so the mind does not follow any fixed law. Though conditioned and influenced, its choice cannot be predicted; thus the alleged perfect regularity, uniformity, necessity of things is a mental fiction, a proof of the possibility of mental aberration in its lack in actuality rather than of immateriality.

Likewise truth, virtue, justice, etc., are only ideas resulting from associating different experiences; they are dependent on education, and that is not even a sign of reason, still less of immateriality. For even a dog can learn to do many things and finally come to "understand" that putting up his right paw means a piece of cake. Education, which is nothing but mental training, brings ideas together; and once they are associated, the point of connection might become hidden in the subconscious mind. The real connection being forgotten or suppressed, the mind will try to establish an artificial link, which is called rationalization. If ideas like virtue and justice were really immaterial and permanent they ought to remain the same and unaltered in different times and climes. But the association of ideas depends on acquired learning and cannot be therefore an inherent natural action of a permanent soul. Thus a Christian who keeps two wives is guilty of bigamy and considered as very immoral. But a Muslim can be very virtuous in the legal possession of many more than two. That morality changes is a truism. Not so very long ago slavery was deemed right, encouraged by the state, sanctioned by the church, but that way of thinking has given place to a morality which judges slavery to be wrong, because it assigns higher values to human personality. A few hundred years ago any father had the absolute right of life and death over his own children; nowadays we have laws even for the prevention of cruelty against animals. The moral laws which prevail here in *Kāmaloka* do not hold good in *Brahmaloka*. Thus these few examples show that abstract ideas like virtue, justice, and morality are very much impermanent and can therefore not be the expressions of a permanent soul.

But then, the mind can conceive *essential* ideas, it is said, expressing the intrinsic nature of things, such as definitions comprising the common genus and the specifying difference. These are said to be unchangeable and can therefore only be conceived by an unchangeable, permanent entity or soul. Definitions are said to originate from Socrates, while Plato built up a system of eternal ideas. But definitions have as little reality about them as a mathematical problem. They may be useful or even necessary for logical distinctions, but they cannot be said to be either permanent or impermanent, because they are mere mental fiction.

Definitions, essential ideas, so-called eternal principles are all based on material experience and exist only in particulars. It is the very nature of essence to be particularized. It is true that we try to separate the idea of man from this or that individual. But at once we find it impossible for the essential idea to exist separately, and equally impossible to unite it with the individual, as we do not see any relation. This unnatural and illogical position arises from the mistake that we tried to separate the two: essence only exists in particulars. Thus they are not unchangeable in this sense, that the objects to which they refer and on which they depend are changeable and impermanent. The particulars are material; so are therefore definitions and essences, abstractions and universals.

The last arrow on the bow of internal evidence from the intellectual powers is the *reflex idea.* In reflection thought becomes the object of thought. And here certainly, say the upholders of the soul-idea, is nothing material. According to Buddhism the mind is classed as a sense, the internal sense, and thus we have two sources of ideas: sensations which have come through the external sense-doors, eye for sight, ear for sound, nose for odour, tongue for taste and the whole body for touch—and sensations furnished by the mind of its own operations, reflections. Thus reflection is the knowledge of perceived sensations. When sensations are material and are perceived in material sense organs, how then can the knowledge thereof become at once immaterial? Reflex ideas are also experienced in animals; they too show to have memory, attachment, and revenge. Yet nobody will maintain that animals have an immortal soul, for never yet has a dog been baptized to save his soul from eternal damnation. But if animals can have reflections without a permanent soul, why should a soul be postulated in the case of humans?

There is separate from the intellect another power in man which is the subject of much controversy, and that is the will.

The supporters of the soul-theory try to make the working of the powers of the will dependent on the soul they imagine, and like for the intellectual powers they claim the will-power to be immaterial, because it strives, they say, not only after material and particular good things, but for the absolute good. This is not true, because the absolute good cannot be known; would it be known, it would cease to be absolute and become relative. What cannot be known cannot be desired or willed for, and such a general object cannot have any attractive power. No man can love the most beautiful woman in the world without knowing her, though this is still rather material. One always strives for some particular good which is always material. "'Immaterial objects' do not exist"; this is a mere phrase containing a contradiction in terms.

It is maintained, however, that some will-objects are unchangeable, e.g., it is always good to respect one's parents. But if that respect would include even obedience with regard to evil, it would no longer be good, and thus no fitting will-object.

Whatever is good or bad is only so with respect to its good or bad effect. *Kamma* is only *kusala* if there is a *kusala vipāka*. And as the effect or the result is always particular, a concrete instance, the action and volition must be of the same kind.

From this follows a last objection, namely, the freedom of the will. In inorganic matter we see an absolutely rigid determinism towards a certain end, but in similar circumstances man remains free and master over his actions, which clearly show his superiority over and independence from matter. Thus if the will is free, that is, independent, it must be immaterial and then also permanent.

The discussion on the freedom of will is usually opened from the wrong perspective. For, whether one accepts the freedom of the will or rejects its independence, in both cases the will is taken as an entity, as something existent, be it free or be it bound.

Will, however, can neither be said to be free, nor bound, because it is non-existent. It merely arises whenever there is the possibility of a choice. If there is nothing to choose from, there can be no question of willing. On the other hand, the possibility of choosing shows the presence of two opposites or more. The possibility to choose what is evil shows that the action is conditioned and influenced, and therefore not free.

Even if one chooses to do what one *knows* to be harmful to oneself, there will still be some motives that brought about that choice. E.g., knowing that association with certain people will bring one to excessive drinking and gambling and other actions that bring about financial difficulties, deterioration of health, and the ruin of family-happiness, yet one might seek that company because one lacks the moral strength to break with them.

To show one's courage, to imagine one's independence are sufficient subconscious motives to influence and determine one's choice against the better dictates of reason and common sense. Even one's pride might not allow one to go back on a previous decision, even if it is perceived as harmful.

If there were no attraction, no inducement, no motive, equilibrium would have been established already and no choice would take place.

Thus volition arises only when a choice becomes possible. If there is a choice possible, there will be attraction and repulsion that influence the choice and make it not free. If there is no choice, then, of course, there is no will at all, but determinism and no freedom whatever. When we, therefore, must admit that this inducement and coercion are never absent, we must also conclude that will is never free.

As we can only strive for one end which we see and understand as best we can according to our limited capacities, so we can only choose those means which seem to us the best under given circumstances. The reasons that induce us to choose a certain means may differ in different people according to their understanding; but, though the line we follow may differ, we all follow the line of least resistance.

To speak about "free will" contains really a contradiction, which is carefully avoided in our Buddhist psychology. For "free will" would indicate the existence of a will prior to, and independent from, a choice, while "will," which is but another and milder word for "craving," does not exist separately, but only arises in dependence on contact and feeling: "*phassa paccayā vedanā—vedanā paccayā taṇhā.*" Where contact and feeling cease, no craving can arise.

This teaching is not the same as the Psychological Determinism of Leibniz and Herbart, in so far that the doctrine of *kamma* is not fatalism. *Kamma* is volition (*cetanā*), said the Lord Buddha; but volition itself is based on consciousness that is continually arising and passing. It is this consciousness fettered by craving which is ignorance; but freed from the fetters (*saṃyojana*) and defilements (*kilesa*) it is Deliverance or Nibbāna. Freed from craving there is pure insight, and no more volition, no more *kamma*. Thus our real freedom lies not in the will, but to be without will.

Thus we have then disposed of all the so-called proofs in favour of a permanent soul.

Some Western scholars in Oriental languages, though not scholars in the teachings expressed therein, yet venture to offer their criticism on this most essential point in the Dhamma. They will explain "no-self" as "self" in the following way: When the Buddha speaking of the components of the aggregates of clinging (*pañcupadānakkhandhā*) said of each separately: "That does not belong to me; that am I not; that is not my self," what else could he mean but that the self or soul exists separate from them? To which we answer: Had the Buddha stated simply and directly that there is no permanent ego-entity, he would have given the impression of siding with the Annihilationists against the Eternalists. Well, both schools of thought were wrong and the Buddha wanted to show to both their wrong. Therefore, without saying that life comes to a complete end at death, which is the teaching of Annihilationism, he merely analyzed the so-called being and whatever he found of matter or of mind, he did not find a soul there.

Could he have taught us the doctrine of no-self (*anattā*) more explicitly and more impressively?

Whatever there be, "that does not belong to me; that am I not; that is not my self" (*netaṃ mama, nesohaṃ asmi, na meso attā*).

Personality was described by the Bhikkhunī Vajirā as a bundle of aggregates, thus a stream of successive states without abiding entity.

There is then no sound basis for the assertion that the soul is distinct from the body or mind. If, therefore, one maintains that the soul is immortal, one must equally predicate that body and mind are immortal, which is clearly absurd.

Human soul cannot be distinct from human life, and human life collapses together with the body, just like animal life and body.

What remains? The influence of good or bad deeds, which will cause another life on the same basis of good or bad.

There is no soul, there is no self, no permanent "I" or ego-entity. But there is a flux, a process of life, of action and reaction, which rises and falls like the waves of the ocean. Those waves will come to rest, that process will come to a stop, when all desires are stilled, because "I" is an expression of selfishness, of craving. When craving has gone, no "I" will be left.

If the teaching of the Lord Buddha is rightly said to be beyond sophistry (*atakkāvacara*) it is never *more* so than with regard to the teaching of soullessness (*anattā*). For, any reasoning, even the purest logic, will presuppose the ego in thinking, as Descartes did: "I think therefore I am—*Cogito ergo sum*."

"Soullessness" cannot be proved with reason, as darkness cannot be seen by bringing in a light. Darkness can be experienced only when all light is quenched. Likewise "soullessness" can only be realized when all selfishness is excluded. When the craving of "mine" and the pride of "I" have vanished, then also the error of self (*sakkāya-diṭṭhi*) cannot arise.

But when there is no more thought of self, disgust will be felt, leading to dispassion on the Path of Sainthood; and this detachment will produce the sweet Fruit of Emancipation with the knowledge of attainment that "the possibility of rebirth is extirpated, lived is the holy life, done is what had to be done, beyond this there is none."

The load of life laid low,
The precious price is paid;
The waves of well and woe
of stormy stream are stayed.
The direst duty's done,
A tenfold tiger tamed;
The weary war is won,
The timeless term obtained.

It is significant that after hearing the first discourse of the Buddha only one of the five disciples understood and even he could only *enter* the Path to Holiness. A fuller explanation of the Truth was necessary. But after hearing this second discourse, the *Anattalakkhaṇa Sutta*, all five attained the highest perfection of *Arahatship*.

"Soullessness" is indeed a *lakkhaṇa*, a distinguishing mark, the essential characteristic of the Truth. For with self all morality is immorality, but without self good and bad alike are transcended in the pure deliverance of heart and mind, in the freedom from all attachment or lust, from all aversion or hate, from all ignorance or delusion.

May the understanding of soullessness grow in us through the practice of unselfishness!

"May we come unto this darkness which is beyond the light of mere reason; may we without seeing and without knowing, see and know that which is above vision and knowledge, through the realization that by not seeing and by not knowing we attain true vision and knowledge" (Dionysius, the Areopagite). May in the realization of non-self all beings be happy!

Joy and Sorrow

Dukkhañc'eva paññāpemi dukkhassa ca nirodhaṃ

One thing only do I teach:
Woe and how its end to reach.

(MN 22, Alagaddūpamasutta)

In this saying the Lord Buddha has summed up the whole of his noble teaching, laid down its essential features, and indicated the line of thought and action, which we, his disciples, ought to follow, if we too wish to attain what so many have attained before us, and what all of us are striving for, Buddhists and non-Buddhists, knowingly or unknowingly—the attainment of the highest and purest bliss.

The very fact that we all are striving for greater happiness shows that the degree of happiness in our possession is not satisfactory, that that degree of happiness is not even considered as good. We do not strive for what is better, but for the best. The best, however, is not better than the good, but it is the good that we have recognized as such. And after having recognized it, all the rest cannot even compete; it becomes simply evil, and as such it is rejected, whatever other name we may give to it.

Because the good is not attained, the quest of the good involves striving, struggle. Hence it is that even the vaguest idea of happiness contains an element of no-more-struggle, no-more-striving, attainment, equilibrium, rest. It is the eternal rest we all are seeking.

"The night keeps hidden in its gloom the search for light;
The storm still seeks its end in peace, with all its might."

(Rabindranath Tagore)

Rest is the natural goal of all action; and all action, because it is non-attainment, is dissatisfactory: *dukkha*. As life is action, actuality, non-attainment, striving, it is also impermanent. Hence life is sorrow-fraught, because it is impermanent.

To see that there is suffering in the world is not such an extraordinary discovery. The greatness of the Buddha's insight, however, lies in the fact that he realized that *everything* is suffering;

in other words he saw not merely that there was suffering in life, but he realized that life itself is suffering.

Thus suffering is actuality and as such it forms the foundation of the Buddha's teaching. This does not make Buddhism pessimistic. It has merely to be accepted as a fact, as the truth, as actuality. There is nothing to be unhappy about the fact of *dukkha,* but there is something to be learned from that fact. Indeed, the whole of Buddhism is dependent on it. Here in suffering lies the origin of Buddhism, and in the deliverance from suffering its culmination.

Even if Buddhism would teach the universal fact of suffering without showing at the same time the deliverance thereof, still it could not be said to be pessimistic; it would be stating the truth without exaggeration. But pessimism is an exaggeration towards the dark side. It would be pessimistic to state that no deliverance from, no cessation of suffering were possible. But the Buddha said: "As there is in the mighty ocean but one taste, the taste of salt, thus there is in my teaching but one taste, the taste of Deliverance" (Udāna).

So stands Buddhism marked, not as a pessimistic religion, a religion of sorrow and sadness, but as leading to the purest happiness and joy, because it teaches the deliverance from sorrow.

But in order to be delivered from sorrow, we must first understand what sorrow is.

Like the idea of happiness is linked up with eternal rest, so the idea of unhappiness is based on restless change. It is the teaching of change, of transience, of impermanence: *anicca,* which makes us understand all as suffering: *dukkha.*

To see the world as a continual flux, to see its dynamic nature, its perpetual impermanence, should not seem to be so very difficult to people who are used to discriminate. Yet most of those who even scientifically accept universal impermanence make a double exception, thereby breaking down their own logic. First of all there are those who are firmly convinced of the impermanent nature of all things, but who maintain at the same time an underlying substance that unchangingly supports the ever-changing phenomena. Secondly there are those who place themselves outside the field of observation, thus imagining to judge the phenomena objectively, as if they were the only fixed point in this raging ocean of change.

No, there is no exception to the law of nature that all component things are transient: *sabbe saṅkhārā aniccā.*

But why should suffering always be the result of impermanence? Not all separation is bound up with sorrow.

The rays of the setting sun part with the landscape, clouds are dispersed by the blowing wind, yet there is no suffering. Only that separation, only that transience, which is experienced through the delusion of self is experienced as sorrow. But when there is no "self," when soullessness, *anattā*, is not only known but also realized, then there will still be transience, but no more sorrow. And transience too will be no more when all component things are decomposed.

Sorrow thus depends on transience, and on the misconception of "self." As long as "self" is not understood as a misconception, as a delusion, as an act of ignorance, so long also impermanency will not be understood as suffering. Here nothing can be learned by argument. Here nothing can help, but to pass, over and over again, through the crucible of suffering and thus to learn by experience. This is the meaning of *saṃsāra*. It is our egoism that makes us suffer, and suffer direly all the more, because we suffer in ignorance.

The fact of suffering is admitted by all, but it is not by all understood in the same way.

There are some (like the Hindus) who do not see sorrow as real, but as an illusion; it is an illusion indeed to see sorrow as an illusion, not as real. There are others (like the Christians) who admit the widespread fact of sorrow in human life, but they consider it as a divine favour: "Blessed are the sorrowful." It is the sickly effect of an overworked imagination.

There are others again (like the Moslems) who do not see much evil in the world at all and submit to it fatalistically. It is contrary to actuality.

But in Buddhism sorrow is not accepted as a blessing in disguise, but as an evil to get rid of; sorrow is not an illusion, but real enough, though it is dependent on ignorance; sorrow is not to be submitted to, but to be overcome. And Buddhism alone teaches how to overcome in a final victory which needs not to be fought again, because it teaches how to uproot the evil and cut down the root by the overcoming of craving, through which alone an escape from "self," from sorrow and transience is possible. If the breadth and the depth of a religion may be measured by the keenness of its analysis of evil and by the appropriateness of the salvation that it offers, then certainly the prize should go to Buddhism. For, when sorrow is identical with life, the only solution lies in no-more-rebirth. But rebirth and all the evil resulting therefrom will occur as long as there is the will to live.

Thus that will to live, that desire to be, that lust to enjoy, that craving to possess, that clinging to keep, has to be rooted out so that it will not grow again.

"Through not understanding the Noble Truths of Suffering, its origin, its cessation and the way to its cessation, we have been wandering in this beginningless *saṃsāra*, both you and I," said Lord Buddha (Parinibbāna Sutta).

It is ignorance that leads to rebirth, i.e., to sorrow; thus it is in knowledge that the great problem of life and death must be solved. To understand that decay, disease, death, sorrow, lamentation, grief, woe and despair are unsatisfactory does not require much understanding indeed. But to understand that birth is suffering, it is necessary to know that birth is not only the physical process in which a living being appears in this world, but also the mental conception that is followed by craving. It is the birth of the defilements (*kilesajāti*): greed, hate, delusion, pride, false belief, scepticism, sloth, agitation, unscrupulousness and recklessness of consequences. It is the birth of actions (*kammajāti*) that will give rise to effects (*vipākajāti*). Understood in this way, any existence is evil, for it is arisen from craving and offers fresh fuel for ever-renewed craving. But to understand that life itself with all its beauty and joy is suffering, one must have tasted and understood the impermanency of life. Experience and understanding both are necessary. For if transience is only experienced, it might well become a new source of fresh delight which keeps away the boredom and the tedium of constant and unchanging beauty and joy. Is not the sea made beautiful by the rise and fall of her waves? Do not the different seasons add to the attraction of nature? Does not a change of food add to better appetite, a change of climate to better health?

But the fact that our craving ever wants a new supply of new delights must lead to disappointment, because the supply is not always at our command. Not to understand this is ignorance of the First Noble Truth of the universality of sorrow. To miss this point is to miss the whole of Buddhism. No introduction, no argument can be of any use. He who finds happiness in suffering, who is satisfied with what he has, will never seek beyond. The understanding, the realization of sorrow, of life as sorrow, is a growth of insight. No fruits can be expected of a seedling; growth is necessary and development, till at the proper season from the fading blossom of transience, will ripen the fruit of understanding.

What matters it, if that fruit be bitter in taste, as long as it cures the chronic disease of craving? Sorrow, if recognized as a by-product of "self," may become the means, may open the road to Deliverance, as the proper diagnosis of an illness is the first step, the chance for a cure.

But the sorrow, the suffering, on which the Lord Buddha based his doctrine of actuality and deliverance, is more than pain-laden affections. The five aggregates of clinging (*pañcupadānakkhandhā*), the psycho-physical composition of mind and body (*nāma-rūpa*) itself is said to be sorrow. Thus suffering is both bodily and mental; it is the imperfection inherent in life, whatever form that life may take.

A certain amount of happiness may fill the emptiness within to some extent, but that craving, like an abysmal emptiness, will never be fulfilled. Before the cup is full to the brim, it has sprung a leak at the bottom. Hence that constant thirst resulting from that fleeting happiness. When the object of craving is within reach for a moment, that craving becomes clinging (*taṇhā-paccayā upādāna*); but clinging is impossible because all is impermanent (*anicca*).

Even if one finds some little happiness through satisfying one's desire, does this mean that complete satisfaction will give complete happiness? Because a thirsty man gets satisfaction in drinking water, everlasting bliss is not found in being drowned.

It is the want that makes one strive for satisfaction, but if that satisfaction is obtained, the need for it is no longer felt, and it is not wanted anymore.

Even the satisfaction bears in itself the seed of fear and discontent, fear owing to its uncertainty, discontent over its impermanence, which is even hidden in the folds of smiling lips, while it leaves one afterwards emptier than ever before.

The satisfaction of a want is not a final satisfaction; it seems only to create a new want instead.

Modern civilization has made much progress and given to man many comforts. But those very comforts have only made life more complicated; easier communications have made the problems and quarrels of families those of nations. It is like an attempt to reach the horizon; the harder one strives, the greater is the disappointment for not getting nearer the goal.

But why then is the goal unattainable?

It is because the goal exists not in reality but is only the mind's fiction. Not by striving, but by bringing the mind at peace, by giving up even the idea of self, is it possible to attain that rest and equilibrium which form the foundation and essence of happiness.

But the striving, which is involved even in the attainment of states of spiritual absorption (*jhāna*), is attended with great difficulties and is known as the distressful path (*dukkha-paṭipadā*). It would be interesting to draw a comparison here with what mediaeval spiritual authors have called "the dark night of the soul."

Thus *dukkha* is not only bodily pain (*kāyika dukkha*) and mental distress (*cetasika dukkha*), that is physical and psychological suffering—it is also the ethical, religious experience as opposed to bliss and even the difficulty encountered in the process of attaining that bliss. Nay, even joy and delight itself are called sorrow-fraught: "*nandi pi dukkhā*": not merely because joy and delight are not lasting, but far more because delight is a fetter (*nandi-saṃyojana*) which will prevent the attainment of perfect freedom.

Though delight is thus shown as a source of sorrow, yet sorrow, well understood, can become a source of happiness. Here especially lies the greatness of the Buddha's teaching—that it shows the deliverance from sorrow and also from pleasure, which leads to sorrow.

Like the knowledge of an illness, though painful in itself, may be the reason why one consults a doctor, who finally cures the disease—similarly the understanding of all life as suffering will be the driving force to seek a remedy. And as of all religious teachers only the Buddha has pointed out *all* life as sorrow-fraught, it is natural that to him we turn in confidence.

Confidence is not the same as faith. For faith is in things that cannot be known; knowledge destroys faith and faith destroys itself, for it is based on that which it cannot know. Faith is defined (by Pope Pius X) as a real assent of the intellect, thus condemning those Modernists holding that faith is merely a blind feeling about religion in the subconscious.

Voltaire said: "The proof of faith is that it is unintelligible." "Faith is to believe in something which your reason tells you cannot be true, for if your reason approved of it, there could be no question of blind faith" (Edwin Montagu).

Confidence, however, is not a mental acceptance of that which cannot be known; it is an assured expectation, not of an unknown beyond, but of what can be tested and experienced and understood by everyone for oneself (*paccattaṃ veditabbo viññūhi*). It is the confidence a student has in his teacher who explains in the classroom the inverse square law of gravitation as stated by Newton. But if the student has heard something of the relativity-theory of Einstein, he will not implicitly believe his teacher and his textbook, but reserve his judgment till the time that he will be able to investigate for himself.

Likewise a student of Buddhism will have confidence in the Teacher, because his teaching can be tested and ought to be tested. As a doctrine of actuality Buddhism cannot attach any value to blind submission. No possible good can follow from the neglect of use of the very sense which lifts man sky-high above his surroundings, the use of reason. But when, walking on the path, one sees the light grow while proceeding, one may safely continue in confidence and yet investigate the path step for step. It is that confidence which is the immediate fruit of the understanding of sorrow: *dukkhupanisā saddhā*. And it is that same confidence which gives already that first taste of the happiness towards which all striving is moving. It is the joy (*pāmojja*) of having found a possibility to escape from this round of birth, suffering and death; the increase of that joy will become sheer delight (*pīti*) only to make place for a serene tranquillity (*passaddhi*) and that sense of security, equilibrium, the bliss of well-being (*sukha*), which is the very opposite of that sense of insecurity, unbalanced striving, which is sorrow-fraught (*dukkha*).

When this tranquillity and sense of security have been obtained through the experience and understanding of suffering, the vicissitudes of life will no longer be able to create disturbances in the peace of mind.

Concentration of mind (*samādhi*) will become a second nature; and in that natural peacefulness things will be seen in their real nature, not coloured by likes or dislikes, not disfigured by passions, not hazed by ignorance, like objects seen at the bottom of a rippleless lake of clear water.

It is with this knowledge and insight into the real nature of things (*yathābhūtañāṇadassana*) that the golden mean can be attained, when exaggerated enthusiasm is cooled down, thus preventing the disillusion of the idealist; on the other hand preventing also the other extreme which makes life materialistic, mechanical and sombre.

By seeing things as they really are, valueless trifles will not be treated as occurrences of the highest importance, which tend to make life unnecessarily complicated.

It will leave room for a sense of humour in which we may laugh even at ourselves, for it is the sense of actuality which gives the sense of humour, in which the world is seen but as the world:

"a stage where every man must play a part. "

(Merchant of Venice)

"a tale told by an idiot, full of sound and fury,
signifying nothing."

(Macbeth, V. 5)

It is the lack of this insight that creates worry, a resultant of craving. The world puts all its "self" in every action, and thus the reaction is so keenly felt. Indeed, *dukkha* has no existence apart from taṇhā. This world is merely the shadow of truth, for the world as we know it is only the reaction of our contact and thus the reflection of our "self." The more of "self" we have put in, the greater will be the reaction—thus we make our own sorrow and suffering. But for all that it remains a reaction all the same, a shadow, a reflection of "self."

"The world is a comedy to those who think,
A tragedy to those who feel."

(Horace Walpole)

We all can enjoy even the most terrible misery as long as it is painted upon a piece of canvas; then we can appreciate the skilfulness of the artist, the exquisiteness of forms, the beauty of colours, hardly being moved by the represented misery. The reason is that it is not "real," by which we mean that we do not take part in it, there is no "self" in it, and we are mere spectators.

Thus we are mere spectators in this picture palace of the universe. Even if we see ourselves acting on the screen, we know that that is no real self who suffers or rejoices. It is mere acting.

> All the world's a stage,
> And all the men and women merely players.
> They have their exits and their entrances;
> And one man in his time plays many parts,
> His acts being seven ages.
>
> (*As You Like It*, II 7)

This sense of humour may seem rather grim now and then, as if mocking at what is holiest and dearest, at life itself. It is the grin of a skull which can look at life from the other side of the grave. Thus he who perceives and understands sorrow and the emptiness of sorrow, he perceives also a sense of the human comedy.

Through understanding the real nature of things, through understanding the nature and origin of sorrow and suffering, i.e., of actuality—weariness, repulsion, disgust (*nibbidā*) arise which can only lead to passionlessness, dispassion (*virāga*), the detachment from world and self, from matter and mind, which is the real freedom and release (*vimutti*) for which we all are striving. Detachment, indeed, is not a morbid asceticism which aims at mortification of the flesh, or at subjection of the mind, but it should grow from understanding as necessarily as a flower in due season from a well-developed plant. It is the knowledge of things as fearful (*bhaya-ñāṇa*) and the knowledge of things as dangerous (*ādīnava-ñāṇa*), the understanding of the evil of conditionality (*saṅkhāra-dukkha*) and of the evil of changeability (*vipariṇāma-dukkha*), which make craving and clinging impossible, because the object is no longer seen as one worthy to possess, but rather as one causing disgust. Craving for, and attachment to, disgusting states or things is impossible; and thus it is that the realization of suffering, so far from being pessimistic, leads to the deliverance from all suffering and even to the deliverance from a possible return.

Once a misconception is realized as such, it cannot be reinstated, but clarity of insight will lead to purity of virtue (*sīla-visuddhi*), the first of the seven stages of purity on the way to Nibbāna.

Virtue thus purified will further purify the mind with further progress on the Path of Holiness, till finally the fruit of Sainthood (*arahatta-phala*) is obtained, where a final death with no more rebirth will make an absolute end to all suffering, happy (*sukha*) because free from all sorrow, desirable (*subha*) because free from all desires, which are the causes of sorrow, eternal (*dhuva*) because free from becoming and rebirth which result in decay and death.

May all attain to that birthless, deathless state, the supreme deliverance of heart and mind, Nibbāna.

The Process of Life

Kammaṃ satte vibhajati yadidaṃ hīnapaṇītatā.

Kamma makes the distinction between different grades of beings.

Where life's entirety can only be comprehended as an unsatisfactory process of change, the natural question will arise how this proceeding takes place. If this process is not only change and unsatisfactory (*anicca-dukkha*) but also a mere process of change without an entity to pass on from change to change (*anattā*), it will be asked what is it then that changes, what is it that suffers and passes on that suffering, what is it that proceeds?

In a previous lecture we have seen already that Buddhism does not deny the individuality of the process, but merely the permanency of an individual.

Individual processes are differentiated and this is caused by *kamma*.

Beings are said to be owners of their deeds (*kammasaka*), for whatever we have of other possessions cannot be said to be ours in such an intimate degree as the actions, the deeds, which have produced this very existence and life. Of nothing else but our action, our *kamma*, can we be called owners in such an absolute sense, as over nothing else we have such absolute power of disposing.

We are called heirs to our deeds (*kammadāyāda*) for in the reaction we inherit the full consequences of our actions, so that whatever we are and in whatever condition we are, we must see therein the effect of past causes, the fruit of previously sown seed.

It is from action, from *kamma*, therefore, that we take our origin (*kammayoni*), so that *kamma* is compared with the mother's womb from where this life arose.

We are linked to *kamma* so closely, as family ties (*kamma-bandhu*) that cannot be broken.

But also we have in *kamma* our greatest protection (*kam-mapaṭisaraṇā*), so that we need not rely upon any external agency as long as our deeds are good and pure.

"Whatever deed they do, either noble or evil, they become heirs to that."

(Dasadhammasutta, AN 10)

Kamma (=*karma* in Sanskrit) cannot be comprehensively dealt with under one chapter heading, for all the truths and conclusions derived therefrom are centred in and emanating from the *kamma* doctrine.

To understand *kamma*, one must first study the mind by which *kamma* is produced: and that is Psychology. The effects of this mind-production can be deduced to some extent by reason and experience: and that is Logic. Further, *kamma* leads to rebirth, renewed existence: and that is Ontology. Finally the moral aspect of skilful and unskilful action should lead to the overcoming of all *kamma*: and that is Ethics. Thus we see how this one word covers the whole of Buddhist Philosophy.

When analyzing a thought-unit (*cittuppāda*) into seventeen thought-moments (*cittakkhaṇa*), one will meet with some mind-impressions (*manosamphassa*), which are so weak (*paritta, atiparitta*) that they hardly disturb the subconscious stream (*bhavaṅga-sota*). But if an impression is strong enough (*mahanta*) to arrest the subconscious stream, thus not merely knocking at the sense doors, but actually forcing an entrance, gate-crashing, only then will full apperception (*javana*), consciousness in the full sense, arise.

Only now arises the possibility of forming new *kamma*. Thus we see that though *kamma* means action (from *karoti*: he acts), it is an action of the mind, therefore a thought, an active thought. Here our character is formed and hence the Buddha calls *kamma* our inheritance and our parent. When physical elements are added to, and combined with others, something new emerges from that composition. Similarly, when psychical action is added to psychical results previously obtained, new life, new character will be produced.

Kamma thus is action, mental action; yet not all action of the mind or of the body is *kamma*.

Action will be present as long as there is existence, because existence is not static, but a process; and a process must proceed. The very existence of the senses consists in activity. As a flame cannot exist without consuming, its very nature being combustion, so the senses cannot exist without activity.

To understand this it will be good to remember that in Buddhist philosophic terminology the senses are not understood merely as the material organs. Each sense is considered as threefold: (1) the material base (subject), (2) the material object, (3) the appropriate connection. "If the subjective eye is in good order, and if external matter (e.g., visible form) comes into focus, but if there is no appropriate bringing together, then the corresponding species of consciousness (i.e., eye-consciousness) does not come into manifestation. But if the subjective eye is in good order and if external matter comes into focus, and if there is also the appropriate bringing together (conjunction), then the corresponding species of consciousness manifests itself" (MN 28).

Thus if one of three conditions is wanting, no consciousness arises, and there will be no sense-activity. This is meant when it was said that the very existence of the senses consists in activity.

It is not the mere contact between subjective organ and external object that constitutes the activity. Not the wick drenched in oil produces the flame. After analyzing a poem into lines, each line into words, each word into letters, we still cannot say that those letters compose the poem: for, only when set in a particular order they will form words and sense; out of order they are sheer nonsense. Thus an individual can be analyzed into corporeality, sensations, perceptions, differentiations and conceptions. Yet the mere heaping up of those aggregates would not constitute a living process in the sense of growth, of development, of *kamma*-formations. For even in an Arahat are present all those aggregates; but in him is missing that which binds them together in activity: craving.

Like the mind of the poet gave order to the letters which thus received life, so does craving set the aggregates in working order; and rebirth is the effect. Who only considers the formation of the letters will never be able to read and understand the poem. Thus he who only analyes the body in anatomy, or the mind in psychology, will never be able to read, understand and solve the problem of *kamma*, i.e., of life as craving.

If body or mind is conceived as a thing complete in itself, identical with itself, as an isolated self-contained entity, it becomes absolutely impossible to explain the interaction of different subjects upon one another. As long as the process of life is cut up into artificial segments, each of them considered as something static, it is impossible to conceive the whole as a process in which all is seen in its natural connection.

As long as one is concerned with analyzing individuality into the five aggregates of existence (*pañcakkhandha*), one might consider a person as a rounded off whole of mind and matter (*nāma rūpa*), isolated in so far as he is not another (*na ca añño*). But things become different as soon as one is concerned no longer with the component parts, but with the process of its growth, *kamma*.

One can consider a tree in itself, composed of leaves, fruit, twigs, branches, bark, wood and further characteristics. Those peculiarities make a tree what it is, that individual tree and not another one. But all those peculiarities and component parts of the individual have come there by a process of growth; and in this process of growth the individual can no longer be isolated (*na ca so*).

Kamma is a process of action, mental action, mental action with craving.

"Cetanaṃ ahaṃ bhikkhave kammaṃ vadāmi."

"I say, O monks, that kammic action is volition."

In this process of volitional activity the aggregates of an individual are not parts of a whole, but forms of action, modes of grasping.

As action with volition, *kamma* does not come in the field of observation, except through its effect. This effect is the reaction (*vipāka*). It is somewhat incorrect to call this reaction old action (*purāṇa kamma*) for, if action is past, it is no more action, no process of actuality.

Yet to some extent the action is continuing its process in the reaction, which is entirely dependent on that previous action. It is with a view on the inherent connection of condition and effect that both will always belong to the same class. In dependence on the desirability or non-desirability of the effect, its cause is called either skilful (*kusala*) or unskilful (*akusala*).

From the fact that thus *kamma* is always either moral or immoral, it must be clear that *kamma* is the very opposite of fate, with which it is sometimes confused. For fate has nothing to do with morality, as it is a predetermining power (real or imaginary) that fixes one's destiny with disregard of action, good or bad.

Fate interferes with the working of cause and effect in so far as it produces results which are not caused by corresponding acts. As a denial of cause and effect fate must be dismissed as a mere fiction.

The undesirable effect of *akusala kamma* in some conditions cannot be altered, but has merely to be outlived.

Take as illustration a man who has borrowed a hundred pounds from his master in order to marry. The feast being over, he finds himself incapable of repaying the debt. If the master is kind-hearted, he might not confiscate his property, but say, e.g., that his servant can pay him off with his work, one day counting for one pound. In that case a hundred days will be needed before the accounts are squared, before the servant can begin to earn again something. During that period no new acquisition can be made, but his previous possessions remain his all the same.

Somewhat similarly *akusala kamma* can effect a rebirth in such a state of misery that no new *kusala* action can be done there. This undesirable effect has simply to be outlived, "till the last penny of the debt is paid." When the effect of that unskilful action is exhausted, like a cloud which has shed all its rain, then naturally like the sunshine, the previously accumulated good tendencies will produce their good effects (*kusala vipāka*). This can happen at any time whenever the opportunity is favourable. It is *this* accumulated *kamma* (*katatta kamma*) that can become indefinitely effective (*aparāpariya vedanīya kamma*). If, however, it would miss the opportunity to become effective, it would become "dead," unproductive (*ahosi kamma*).

This unproductiveness is the only escape from this repeated round of rebirth (*saṃsāra*). From this possibly unproductive *kamma* one can clearly understand that Buddhism is neither an absolutely rigid law of cause and effect, where every seed must produce its fruits, nor fatal predetermination, nor blind chance.

"There are these three sources of irrational views," it is said in the Aṅguttara Nikāya (Tikanipāta, Mahāvagga 61), "which are questioned, investigated and abandoned by the wise who follow the hereditary traditions—three sources of irrational views which establish themselves in the denial of *kamma*: (1) there are some who believe that all is a result of acts in previous lives; (2) there are others who believe that all is the result of creation by a Supreme Ruler; (3) there are others again who believe that everything arises without reason or cause. But then if a person becomes a murderer, a thief, an adulterer, etc., if this would be due to past actions, or made by the creation of a Supreme Ruler, or if this would happen by mere chance, then one would not be responsible for evil action."

Kamma is the very opposite of all these irrational views, because it is action itself; and upon each new action depends all further effects. If that action produces results and that depends on other actions—those results will correspond to their cause. Any other view is unproved, unprovable, illogical, irrational, untenable.

"Karma avoids the superstitious extreme, on the one hand, of those who believe in the separate existence of some entity called the soul; and the irreligious extreme, on the other, of those who do not believe in moral justice and retribution" (*Buddhism*, Prof. T. W. Rhys Davids, p. 103).

What we are and that we are, are not mere chance; it is not rigid determinism either, for that would leave unexplained the differences in faculties and modes of life. As a scientific law, be it physical or biological, is clearly not a law with binding force, but only a description of a way of action, constant as far as our observation goes—similarly the law of *kamma* is not a necessity of causality where every action must produce its effect. Laws are like grammatical rules for a language, which have always some exceptions and might become modified in time through the progressive use of that language. Similarly an effect of a certain action cannot be predicted, because there are so many factors present which through their influence might support, impede, modify or even destroy the effect altogether. Not causality, but conditionality!

Though we speak of causality as the foundation of Buddhism, we should not take it in too strict a sense. As in science so in daily life everything is based on cause and effect—what would be the chaos in the kitchen, if one day the salt were no longer salt! Yet modern physics sees the need of a certain free play for chance or fate, so that natural laws are not determinate and uniform for each individual case, but for the average. In the same way we cannot always speak of causation, but rather of *condition*, which has not such a rigid meaning and corresponds more faithfully to the Pāli:

paccayā, as it is used in the last book of the *Abhidhamma*, the *Paṭṭhāna*, the Book of Origination.

If we pay attention to the operative force (*kicca*), *kamma* is fourfold.

Reproductive or generative *kamma* (*janaka kamma*) is that action which acts again in the combination of mind and matter (*nāma rūpa*) or in other words the plant that gives fruit, the cause that produces effects (*vipāka*). Once having reproduced itself, this kind of *kamma* is lost in its effect and cannot generate, germinate again. It is, so to say, a transformation, if that term be understood properly, i.e., not in the sense of an entity, but of a process of growth. Like the seed from which a plant has grown cannot germinate again, because it has no more existence, but lives in the plant, so this reproductive *kamma* is exhausted in the act of generating. Yet the effect produced may make itself known during very long periods and many lives. It will always be, however, of the same kind as the generating *kamma* force.

During this course of process new actions, called supporting *kamma* (*upatthambhaka kamma*), may maintain the effects of previous actions or even intensify them, thus leading from good to better, or from bad to worse. On the other hand, counteractive action (*upapīḷaka kamma*) may interfere with the working out of the effects of reproductive (*janaka*) action, weakening, modifying, impeding its potential energy, thus making good effects less good and evil effects less evil. If this kind of counteraction is so strong as to completely annihilate the effects of previous *kamma*, it is called destructive *kamma* (*upaghātaka kamma*). This fourfold division according to the operating forces or function is the most important for the proper understanding of *kamma*. For, if all action would be reproductive, an escape from the effects would not be possible and the faring on through this round of repeated rebirths (*saṃsāra*) would be endless. Only because action can counterbalance action, and thus nullify the otherwise unavoidable result, deliverance is a possibility.

The possibilities of supporting, counteracting or annihilating the good or evil effects of action that would have been normally reproductive depend entirely on the potential efficacy of the interfering activity. Thus there are four possibilities of producing effects (*pākadāna*).

Weighty *kamma* (*garuka kamma*) is that kind of action, the effects of which cannot be counterbalanced. They are fixed as to their consequences for good or for bad. Fixed in good results (*sammatta niyatā*) are, e.g., the four paths (*ariya magga*) in the quest of Nibbāna inevitably establishing the state of exemption from a miserable rebirth. Fixed in bad results (*micchatta niyatā*) are the five crimes which find retribution in a miserable rebirth without delay, i.e., immediately on the disintegration of the aggregates of existence (*ānantarika kamma*), namely, matricide, parricide, murder of an Arahat, wounding of a Buddha, causing a schism in the Sangha. Sometimes we find also "wrong views" (*micchā-diṭṭhi*) mentioned as such a crime. In that case "wrong views" means the extreme perversity of opinion, disregard even of the law of causality and moral retribution, and not mere disbelief, resultant from lack of knowledge. Thus it will be seen that, only in rare occasions, *kamma* will be of such a nature that nothing else can influence it.

It is logically the very last thought of a lifespan which decides the immediately following rebirth; therefore it is called death proximate (*āsanna*) *kamma*.

Thought giving rise to thought, as a flame sets all burning which it can lay hold of—and the last thought of a lifetime being extremely weak owing to the failing physical conditions under which it arises—this last dying thought will lack the power to influence or modify for better or for worse and thus it will give rise to the relinking consciousness (*paṭisandhi viññāṇa*) according to its own nature. And so it happens that this one single last thought determines a whole coming life. Usually, of course, it will be one's habitual mode of thinking that will prevail, when in dying all resistance has been reduced to a minimum. This habitual (*āciṇṇa*) *kamma* is one's tendency for good or bad, formed through numerous repeated actions during one's life. It is extremely improbable—though not impossible—that in one's dying hours one should be able to break the fetters of habit forged during a whole lifetime. But even if this would happen through force of external conditions, e.g., relations reminding the dying man of a certain good action done many years ago, this would not mean that all the other actions have become ineffective.

The *kamma*, which through force of circumstances cannot express itself, may do so at any time when conditions are more favourable. Till then it is said to be accumulated (*kaṭattā*).

Take for example a miser. The energy of his whole life having been directed towards the hoarding of wealth, he has made avarice his habitual *kamma* (*āciṇṇa*). Thus most likely his last thought will be one of craving for, and attachment to, his possessions, and of regret to be unable to take his wealth with him. If he dies with suchlike thoughts, no other rebirth can be expected but in the planes of "unsatisfiable" desire (*petayoni*). But it may happen that through kindly influence of relations his last thoughts are directed towards nobler ideals, thus resulting in a happy rebirth owing to his good death-proximate (*āsanna*) *kamma*. As, however, the cause of this good effect was only his one last thought, the fruits thereof may very soon be exhausted, and then the habitual *kamma* of the miser which was temporarily suspended as accumulative (*kaṭattā*) *kamma* will get the upper hand. This exhaustion of proximate *kamma* may be an explanation of the death of embryos and infants.

The reverse might happen equally well, in which case a last thought of worry, e.g., temporarily suspends the natural consequences of a very virtuous life, as it is said to have happened in the case of Queen Mallikā, whose subsequent life in a state of misery lasted only for seven days.

Other kammic thoughts can become effective only in the second birth, in which case they are called subsequently effective (*upapajja vedanīya kamma*). If such a thought does not get the opportunity then, it becomes inoperative (*ahosi kamma*). Weaker even than this kind is the initial stage, the first moment of a thought-unit, which also becomes ineffective (*ahosi*), unless it can produce an effect in that life itself (*diṭṭha dhamma vedanīya kamma*). *Kamma* which is so strong that it can produce an effect at any other than the above-mentioned births is called indefinitely effective (*aparāpariya vedanīya kamma*).

Properly classified, *kamma* is thus:

A. According to function (*kicca*):
    1. Reproductive (*janaka*)
    2. Supportive (*upatthambhaka*)
    3. Counteractive (*upapīḷaka*)
    4. Destructive (*upaghātaka*)

B. According to the strength of effect (*pākadāna*):
1. Serious (*garuka*)
2. Death-proximate (*āsanna*)
3. Habitual (*āciṇṇa*)
4. Accumulative (*kaṭattā*)

C. According to the time of taking effect (*pākakāla*):
1. Effective in this very life (*diṭṭha dhamma vedanīya*)
2. Effective in the next life (*upapajja vedanīya*)
3. Indefinitely effective (*aparāpariya vedanīya*)
4. Ineffective (*ahosi*)

D. According to the spheres of effect (*pākaṭṭhāna*):
1. Unskilful in the spheres of sense (*akusala-kāmāvacara*)
2. Skilful in the spheres of sense (*kāmāvacara kusala*)
3. Skilful in the spheres of form (*rūpāvacara kusala*)
4. Skilful in the formless spheres (*arūpāvacara kusala*)

"If anyone says, O monks, that a man *must* necessarily reap according to (all) his deeds, in that case there is no religious striving possible, nor is there an opportunity to end sorrow. But, if one maintains, O monks, that what a man reaps is the result of (some of) his deeds, in that case striving for holiness is possible and also the ending of sorrow" (AN).

The reproductivity of *kamma* leads us necessarily to the problem of rebirth. A problem indeed, for if there is *kamma* there must be rebirth and yet there is none to be reborn according to the teaching of *anattā*. It is again the misconception of self-entity that poses the problem; and it is the process of actuality that solves it. The mere asking of the question, "What is reborn?" is based on the ignorance of the self-less process of *kamma*. *Kamma* is not an entity that moves from life to life, as a visitor goes from house to house; but *kamma* is life itself, in so far as life is the product (*vipāka*) of *kamma*. In each step we make now in full-grown age lie also the feeble attempts of our babyhood. As actions they were a process that ceased with the act, but that process set further processes working, actual processes.

The present actuality, which expresses itself as the result of all the preceding processes, carries in its very action all the efforts that went into the making of the previous actions. This continuity without identity—like a flame arises ever new, being fed by ever-new fuel, and yet depends in its very existence upon its continued burning—this continuity of the process is *kamma*, and this lack of identity is *anattā*.

Kamma thus is not an entity; but a process, an action, energy, in-force, i.e., a force not derived from some external agency, but from its intrinsic nature. Now that in-force which constitutes the process of action, which makes action act, that is craving—like the process of combustion makes the flame burn and consume everything that is combustible, like the mere exposure to the atmosphere sets a process of oxidization going in certain metals.

Now a flame is not "born" from wood or coal or straw, for those materials can lie side by side for hundreds of years without being burnt. They are merely the opportunity given to maintain a flame. A flame originates not in fuel but in friction and can thus arise even in materials that are not combustible, as, e.g., flint and steel. Fuel only proffers an opportunity to the process to continue.

The application to the process of *kamma* will be clear. The actual origin of life is not the sexual act of a male and a female; they only provide the opportunity for a terminating life-*kamma* to take a new lease. As a wick, though dipped and drenched in oil, will not give light unless a flame is applied to it—like visible objects, though coming into focus will not be seen by the eye, if there is no consciousness—so also "it is by the conjunction of three things that conception comes about. If there be the coition of the parents and it is the mother's proper period, but if there is not the necessity of generation, then no conception takes place" (MN 38).

Now, this necessity of generation or rather re-generation is in Oriental fashion poetically described as a heavenly musician presiding over child conception (*gandhabbo*). It is clear, of course, that here is meant that karmic energy, which in its natural tendency of craving seeks to lay hold of new matter as sustenance in its process of action, of life.

A flame which was burning on the wax of a candle may continue to burn on the oil of a lamp, on the cloth of the curtains, on the furniture of the room, on the woodwork of the whole house. This does not mean that wax has become in succession oil, cloth, wood; for these were only the fuel which kept the flame alive; not so much as actively feeding the flame, but as being grasped by the flame passively.

An electric current may produce light in an electric bulb, or music in a radio set, or motion in an electric fan, or heat in a stove. But, once more, this does not mean that light has become in succession music, motion and heat; for the bulb, the radio set, the fan, the stove, were only the means through which the electric current could express itself.

In a similar way the different modes of life, as well as the constant modifications in life, are only different means of expression of *kamma*. Thus in the ultimate sense one ought not to say that Buddhism teaches evolution in the sense of Darwinism, though Darwin was probably right when he taught the Origin of Species. He taught evolution in the biological, physiological sense, i.e., he traced the originating series of the matter through which life expresses itself, as one might trace the origin of a candle to the wax manufactured by the bees without explaining thereby how the candle became a light. Like fire cannot be traced by following the series of fuel dependent on which the process of combustion continued uninterrupted, so the genealogy of man is not shown by tracing the evolution of the body in the series of vertebrates, even though that probably is correct. It is *kamma* as a process of craving which gives the "impulse," the "*élan vital*," as Bergson calls it. In this process, however, it is not the mind and matter which are involved; their evolution belongs to a different type. In this process it is the evolution of *kamma* that causes rebirth (cf. *Milinda Pañhā*, 11.2- 6), and as an evolution the different phases of expression of that *kamma*, be it even in different lives, bear the common responsibility.

This process of kammic evolution is not necessarily progress. Progress can only be considered from a fixed standpoint outside the process, but such a standpoint there is not. Process of evolution, however, could be retrogression as well as progress, because it is mere change or growth; and even degeneration, deterioration, is still a process of growth. Even in the physical sense the decay of one means the growth of another.

The frequently repeated question whether it is possible for a man to be born as an animal is really incorrect from a Buddhist point of view; for this question implies the existence of a human entity to be changed into an animal entity in its following existence.

It is craving, as the inherent force of kammic action, that tends to express, to perpetuate, to reproduce. Without this tendency action would not be *kamma*, would not be craving. But beastly actions of the passions will naturally tend to produce beastly effects, and then the process will be evolution of retrogression. Virtuous actions and self-control will naturally tend to produce holy effects, and then the process will be evolution of progress. Actions of selflessness, of pure unselfishness, will have no tendency to reproduce and hence will not further express themselves in effects.

When a being is born, it is neither created, nor merely propagated by its parents, but it is a product of action in the past. The action (*kamma*) as volition (*cetanā*) has constituted certain tendencies (*saṅkhāra*), inclinations and repulsions, likes and dislikes, a character which, owing to the lust for life (*bhavataṇhā*), will seek to express itself again; and that is the evolution of rebirth (*bhava-paccayā jāti*).

Rebirth will take place where those kammic tendencies will find the most agreeable surroundings to express themselves, the most suitable soil to take root again, the most kindred atmosphere to produce new fruits. This might be called the sympathy of kammic forces. If it thus happens that a mother's womb, having just received the sperm, is physically and kammically well disposed, a conception might take place, finally resulting in the birth of a child, having some or many of the characteristics of its parents, not because it has inherited those from them, but owing to the sympathy and attraction of similar kammic tendencies. Like the lightning from a thundercloud will never enter into the water of a deep well, but will always seek the metal point of the lightning-conductor on the tip of a tower, for there it finds its greatest attraction—so the tendencies of a character will be attracted by, will sympathize with, those tendencies which are nearest in the sense of affinity.

Yet the opposite might happen, when a dying thought contains an element of hate or revenge, for those vices can never be so fully satisfied, as when in near relationship with the disliked object. Then the very antipathy of kammic tendencies might become the reason of attraction, like the positive and negative poles of a magnet.

If at the moment of the sexual act, there is no *kamma* attracted to take rebirth from these particular parents, their act will remain barren.

While the theory of heredity does not explain why not all the characteristics of father and mother are inherited, the Buddhist explanation is thus: that the child does not inherit from father and mother, who only provided the opportunity, but that it brings its own inheritance, namely, *kamma*, with it at the time of conception. It is this third factor, *kamma*, which besides the sperm and the ovum decides the conception at rebirth. *Kamma* thus is the real "natural selection" which struggles on for existence, resulting not in the survival of the fittest, but of the greatest craving, which will reproduce itself for good or for bad, till insight will deprive action of that reproductive force, leading it on to no-more rebirth.

When thus all action will have been stilled, no further craving can disturb the peace, where the wheel of rebirth can no longer revolve, the peace of perfect freedom from lust, hate and delusion, the Deliverance of Nibbāna.

Dependent Origination

"Five causes were there in the past,
And now a five-fold fruit.
Five causes in this present life,
A five-fold fruit to come."

When speaking of origination, one can approach the subject from two different viewpoints. One is the view of those who believe in a supernatural cause and thus maintain an ultimate beginning or creation. To them the Buddha repeatedly declared that an absolute first beginning of existence is something unthinkable, and that all such like speculations may lead to imbecility (AN 4:77). We shall revert to this view after having explained the Buddha's doctrine of origination.

His doctrine is not fruitless speculation, but is based on actuality. Hence it will be understood best, when as starting point is taken not some imaginary time in the untraceable past, called "In the beginning ..." but an actual fact of the present, which is open to investigation and experiment.

The fact of suffering and the fact that *all* is suffering, because all is impermanent, is indeed the actual basis from which one can start the reconstruction pointing towards origination; it is also the basis from which the work of deliverance can be started.

Unless the fact of suffering is understood as universal, as explained on a previous occasion, it is impossible to find out its origin, impossible to find deliverance therefrom. Here is no revelation needed, and hence the supernatural signifies nothing; here mere argument avails nothing, for mere words cannot solve an actual problem. And thus we start not with the beginning, but with the actual, experimental fact that life is sorrow-fraught.

Now it is clear that this sorrow and disappointment, due to the impermanence of all things, is only possible where there is conscious life to perceive the same. Thus we have the well-known formula, *jāti-paccayā jarā-maraṇaṃ*: dependent on birth is old age, death and all kinds of woe. As death should be understood in the sense of dissolution in the physical as well as in the psychical sense, so birth should be understood in the sense of conception, physical and mental. Thus rebirth and death do not occur only once at the beginning and the end of a lifetime respectively, but at every new thought-moment, so that the saying, "*quotidie morior*": I die daily (1 Cor. 15:31), receives an unexpectedly new meaning in the Buddhist sense. It is the wrong view of seeing death only at the end of a lifetime which produces that misconception of a self, transmigrating from life to life.

Death is not caused by birth, neither is sorrow, but both are dependent in their arising on the fact of birth. Thus birth is the *conditio sine qua non,* the *upanissaya paccayā*, the condition of sufficing efficiency. It is the natural disposition (*pakatūpanissayā*) of any birth to give rise to sorrow; not the cause thereof, but the necessary circumstance under which that relation obtains, an indispensable, antecedent phenomenon. The characteristics of decline (*jaratā*) and impermanence (*aniccatā*) are natural to all matter. They are not produced by any principle at all, i.e., not by *kamma*, mind, season or nutriment (*lakkhaṇāni na jāyanti kehici ti pakāsitaṃ*).

Where suffering is dependent on birth by which it is conditioned, birth itself is caused by *kamma.*

"Dependent on the *kamma*-process of becoming is rebirth" (*bhava-paccayā jāti*). It is the active *kamma*-process that produces the passive rebirth-process (*uppatti-bhava*), where the reaction has to work out, where the result (*vipāka*) has to be outlived. It is the will to live that makes one live again. It is this lust for life that conditions the kind of life to come. No other doctrine can explain the differences that appear, though outward conditions may be absolutely the same. This process of becoming is volition transmuted into action with skilful or unskilful consequences. As soon as the opportunity is favourable it will reproduce itself, express itself, according to the nature of the means of expression at its disposal. Thus it is that the process of *kamma* is the process of becoming and the cause of rebirth.

The differences which can be observed even where external conditions of parents, blood and food are equal, as in the case of twins, cannot be without a cause, cannot be mechanical products, for they do not always happen to all. As in the subjective continuity of those beings no other reason can be found, the process of becoming must be due to *kamma.*

It is true that there are many who wish to give this doubtful honour to some supernatural intervention. But this explanation, instead of solving the problem inside the process, induces a mysterious factor from outside, thus making the problem even more complicated and unsolvable indeed. It is no good trying to explain a mystery by one still more intricate. Moreover, he who claims the honour for the good, ought to take also the blame for the evil.

It is the *kamma*-process that leads to rebirth, as a flame burns on through its inner nature in a process of combustion. And like a flame will always lay hold of fresh material so long as that is available, so *kamma* will lay hold of new material to express its process of craving. For *kamma* is essentially volition.

Dependent on clinging arises the *kamma*-process (*upādāna-paccayā bhavo*).

From the different kinds of clinging it can be understood how subtle is its working and how difficult it must be to escape its meshes. There is the grosser clinging to sensuous pleasures (*kāmūpādāna*). Though few are able to free themselves entirely from this snare, it is not so difficult to be at least aware of the danger. All spiritual men have given their warnings—all have spoken in praise of control over the senses.

But not only the body with its natural passions must be tamed; the mind which guides the activities of the other senses ought to be controlled, its wild activities and fancies checked. A forcible repression of the bodily senses only will naturally result in a reaction that might be dangerous from a mental point of view. Suppressed passionate tendencies have often led to serious hallucinations; and if that suppression is done with a supernatural motive, it always leads to fanaticism, where sometimes blood-thirsty hate is taken for love of truth.

The clinging to erroneous opinions (*diṭṭhupādāna*) is, therefore, much more dangerous, because where error is seen as the truth, all further consequences will be seen in the wrong light even though their deduction be correct—like a sum cannot be worked out properly, even if the method be correct, if there was an initial mistake in the thesis. One of the most common erroneous opinions is the one that sees motion everywhere and nothing moved without a cause, and yet maintains that there can be a mover who moves all but not himself.

The clinging to mere ritual (*sīlabbatupādāna*) is the superstition, when, e.g., through outward washing inner purity is sought. Similar actions can be classed as spiritual bribery and only betray a lack of moral courage and sense of responsibility. It is not only an overvaluation of means to a certain end, but reliance upon inappropriate actions which are, therefore, not means at all.

The clinging to the belief in a self (*attavādupādāna*) is the most subtle of all and hence the most difficult to overcome. It is this fetter of self-illusion (*sakkāya-diṭṭhi*) in all its twenty modes which prevents one even from entering the Path to holiness (*sotāpanna*). It is this root of selfishness which underlies all growth of *kamma* and of rebirth. It is the heat of the fire that keeps the water boiling and makes ever new steam develop.

But this clinging could not arise if there were not craving first. Through craving is conditioned clinging (*taṇhā-paccayā upādānaṃ*). It is craving for sense-pleasures (*kāma-taṇhā*) that leads to sensuous clinging. It is craving for eternal existence (*bhava-taṇhā*) which gives rise to clinging to the belief in a self (*attavādupādāna*). It is craving for annihilation (*vibhava-taṇhā*) which is the origin of clinging to erroneous opinions (*diṭṭhupādāna*). By not realizing the necessity of effects arising from causes, the possibility of further effects will be overlooked and thus rebirth denied. Craving for annihilation might also lead one to employ inappropriate means to nullify kammic reactions by superstitious practices (*sīlabbatupādāna*).

Craving is the real turning point, the crank that sets the wheel of rebirth, the machinery of life and death working. Craving imparts selfishness, that is, the "I"-concept, to mere sensation, thus fertilizing the seeds produced by previous action. Here with craving, the problem of rebirth is given anew, and with the cessation of craving this problem is solved. In the process of craving, *kamma* is conceived which in due time will grow out into rebirth and death—like from friction the spark is born which will grow out into a conflagration. With this process of grasping is given the explanation of individuality, for life is a process of grasping.

If craving is dissolved, the whole world becomes a mere play of the senses, where the self is no longer an actor. Where the self does not act there is no *kamma* and no more rebirth, so that with the ending of craving the turning of the wheel of *saṃsāra* will have come to a stop.

This, however, does not explain the beginning, the origination of craving. Craving, clinging, desire, volition, will, is not a force which is stored up to be discharged at any moment, but it arises anew over and over again; and in its arising lies the meaning of this whole play of world-events. For apart from this "I" the world has no meaning. The "I" is a reaction; and without this reaction how can action be known? This reaction is sensation, and on this sensation is dependent craving (*vedanā-paccayā taṇhā*).

Here again, sensation or feeling is not the cause of craving, but merely a condition, for without sensation no craving can arise, and yet not all sensation needs to produce craving. Here alone a break is possible; here alone in the long chain of conditioned reactions it is possible to come to a stop. If all feeling would result in craving with all its evil consequences, the attainment of Arahatship and Nibbāna would be impossible. Like a seed can grow up into a plant under favourable circumstances and yet those circumstances, however necessary, are not the cause of the plant, but mere conditions to its growth—so sensation *can* develop into craving, if the conditions thereto are favourable. The favourable condition to the arising of craving is ignorance, for if knowledge of the real nature of things were present, craving would be impossible. It is thus to ignorance (*avijjā*) that we shall have to trace the origin of craving.

Feeling or sensation in any of its three modes of pleasure, pain or indifference, in so far as it is a *kamma*-resultant, is the condition without which no craving can arise (*vedanā-paccayā taṇhā*). Thus pleasurable feeling might give rise to craving for more; painful feeling to craving for freedom therefrom; and indifferent feeling to craving for its tranquil sensation. Feeling, however, cannot arise without contact (*phassa*); sensation cannot arise without the senses (*saḷāyatana*). Here it is clearly seen that the causal chain of dependent origination (*paṭicca samuppāda*) should not be understood as a pure succession of cause and effect; it is the growth, the development, the evolution process where the successive stage is contained in germ-form, as it were, in the preceding one, requiring only the proper conditions to sprout forth. Thus in the six senses of mind and body are contained the possibilities of contact and sensation. Similarly in consciousness (*viññāṇa*) are contained the other three mental groups of sensation, perception and mental formations (*vedanā*, *saññā, saṅkhāra*). Thus it is said that through consciousness are conditioned corporeality and mentality (*viññāṇa-paccayā nāma-rūpa*) and that dependent on the six senses of body and mind arise contact and sensation (*saḷāyatana-paccayā phasso*). Consciousness and its mental concomitants, hence also sense impression or contact and feeling or sensation, are all simultaneously arising and hence related in the sense of co-existence (*saha jāta-paccaya*), as a candle which is burning, burns together with its heat and light. But they are also mutually supporting one another (*aññamañña-nissaya paccayā*), like "when three sticks are set upright leaning against one another at their upper ends, each of them depends on, and is depended on by, the other two ... if one of them falls, all will fall at the same time" (Ledi Sayādaw).

Consciousness itself, however, is a product of *kamma*-formations in the past (*saṅkhāra-paccayā viññāṇaṃ*). As the *kamma*-process in the present (*kamma-bhava*) will produce birth and its consequences, so the *kamma*-formations of the past (*saṅkhāra*) have produced this present conscious life. Like the *kamma*-process in the present finds its origin in craving and clinging, so the *kamma* of the past was formed in ignorance (*avijjā-paccayā saṅkhārā*). Craving and ignorance are synonymous. Craving is ignorance, for in ignorance we crave for things impermanent, sorrow-fraught and substanceless.

Further back than ignorance we cannot go, for if there would have been a time when there was no ignorance, there ought to have been knowledge supreme. But to say that knowledge supreme has produced ignorance is as nonsensical as to say that perfection could produce imperfection, that goodness could produce evil. Ignorance thus stands as the sufficient reason for life, when life is seen as a process of grasping.

Is ignorance then the ultimate beginning of everything? This question so frequently put is ignorance manifest.

To speak of a beginning where there is no entity is a sheer impossibility. A process can *have* no beginning, but *is* beginning constantly; can have no end, but is ceasing constantly. Not to understand this is ignorance; and dependent on ignorance arise the *kamma*-formations, which through processes of conscious grasping lead to rebirth, which is sorrow-fraught.

It is in ignorance that the "I"-concept is formed; it is in craving that the "I"-concept is maintained. Ignorance creates a delusion, and craving clings to it. And thus comes about this whole play of world-events which turns round the "self" like a wheel round its axle. But as, when the axle is broken the wheel will not turn anymore, so, when the delusion of self is destroyed, when insight has destroyed ignorance, no further craving can arise, no further *kamma* can be formed, the wheel of *saṃsāra* will no more turn, the process of becoming and rebirth will have come to a stop.

Where ignorance thus gives rise to craving, the freedom from craving can only be obtained through the overcoming of ignorance in the insight into the real nature of things. Ignorance also is a kind of understanding—it is *mis*-understanding; it is cognition with craving and thus it leads to formation, i.e., *kamma*. But cognition without craving, that is *right* understanding which does not lead to further formation of *kamma*.

This understanding is not to be obtained by mere reasoning. Through purity of virtue, through renunciation and mind-control, insight will grow—insight into the real nature of things. When things are seen as void of self and impermanent, they will be understood as sorrow-fraught and the First Noble Truth will have been realized. When it is further seen that all our disappointment arises from our craving for things void and impermanent, then craving will become an impossibility. If there is no more craving, there will be no more *kamma*-process of becoming, resulting in rebirth. Thus while ignorance stands as the origin of all this suffering through grasping, insight alone offers the deliverance therefrom.

Where a beginning as ultimate origin cannot be pointed out, just because there are no entities but mere processes rolling on—because nothing has a beginning but is only a phase in the process of evolution which is always beginning—yet this process can come to a stop simply by no more beginning, by no more becoming.

"Let past be past, no future longings house:
The past is dead, the morrow not yet born.
Whoso with insight scans his heart today,
Let him ensure eternal changelessness!"

(*Bhaddekaratta Sutta*, MN 131)

This goal cannot be attained by striving, for striving under any form keeps the process moving. But the truth has to be lived so that it may grow naturally, till the light of insight will have dispelled all shadows of ignorance, and the deliverance from all craving, which is the bliss beyond all feeling, will have surmounted all happiness and sorrow in the cessation of becoming, Nibbāna.

Nibbāna

Sorrow is found in all three worlds,
Its origin by craving wrought,
Its ceasing is Nibbāna called,
The path thereto transcendent thought.

(*Abhidhammatthasaṅgaha* 509)

Once more we must make the universal fact of suffering the starting point of our quest. And if this time our goal is the highest, the best, the final attainment of Nibbāna, even that goal ought to be understood in the light of the truth or suffering. For Nibbāna is the deliverance from all sorrow.

This certainly is not a subject for speculations. As sorrow must be understood and experienced, so the Deliverance therefrom must both be understood and experienced. And only he who has experienced will understand. But that understanding cannot benefit others except in the way of encouragement to follow up along the same path, so that we too may learn and discern, understand and experience "each one for himself" (*paccattaṃ*).

Vānasaṅkhātāya taṇhāya nikkhantattā nibbānan'ti vuccati.

> As a departure from that kind of craving, which is lust, it is called Nibbāna.

(*Abhidhammatthasaṅgaha* 458)

Even if Nibbāna, objectively considered, is viewed as the absolute truth, the ultimate reality, the highest perfection, the further shore, the final goal, and bliss supreme—yet it must never be overlooked that this objectivity is entirely due to our subjective viewpoint. Even if Nibbāna is often described in terms of positive happiness like peace, bliss, calm, permanence, freedom, deliverance—this is only so through the departure of all that had the nature of a fetter to rebirth and sorrow.

Certainly Nibbāna is the highest bliss (*paramaṃ sukhaṃ*). But if this bliss be understood as a blissful experience, a happy feeling or sensation, Nibbāna would be subject to impermanence and sorrow, because all feelings, perceptions, mental formations and concepts are impermanent and therefore sorrow-fraught.

Happiness which can be experienced is, therefore, not the highest bliss, because it bears within itself the germ of dissolution. The highest bliss, therefore, must be beyond the experience of the senses. "It is just because there is no sense-experience that Nibbāna is happiness," said the Venerable Sāriputta.

Thus only by holding fast to the negative aspect of Nibbāna will it be possible to approach the subject intelligently. Yet that is not the real approach. This should be done not by understanding but by realizing.

For the sake, however, of encouragement in the quest for truth, we have also the means of an intellectual approach which has no further meaning and importance, though, than that of a map to a traveller in an unknown land. There, like here, all names are new and strange, but can be identified at each stage of progress till the goal is reached. From the outset we must be prepared, however, to leave behind our own mode of thinking, like the traveller his home. And though travelling on the map only and by reading books can be highly interesting, and can be done in an easy chair at home, yet it cannot be compared with the actual journey, even if that would involve much fatigue and discomfort. What then shall we say about the actual attainment?

But here already we have to leave alone our comparison, and at once the language becomes unfamiliar, for "though there is a road, there is no traveller" (*maggamatthi, gāmako na vijjati*).

That Nibbāna *is*, is beyond doubt; for where there is the thesis of a process, there must be also the anti-thesis of no-more-proceeding. Thus with the thesis of the process of life as suffering is given also the anti-thesis of the deliverance from suffering through the ending of the process of becoming—and with this we have the clearest definition of Nibbāna: cessation of becoming, *Bhavanirodho nibbānaṃ* (S II 117).

Where becoming stands for the arising of sensations and conceptions, for rebirth and its consequences of woe and death, for impermanence and sorrow, for the arising of fear and craving, for the growth of the roots of all evil, of greed, hate and delusion, for the tightening of material and spiritual bonds—there the cessation of becoming will naturally be viewed as bliss supreme. But this bliss of the cessation of becoming can only be understood when becoming itself is understood as suffering.

But because becoming is thought of as desirable—notwithstanding "birth, old age, sickness and death are like cowherds with staves in their hands, which drive beings on, and cut life short as with an axe" (Dhp Com. 135)—because there are few or none that desire absence of rebirth, cessation of becoming is not understood as bliss. In the delusion of self it is seen as annihilation; and annihilation it is—namely, of the delusion of self.

But like a man given over to the excessive use of drugs will always take more, preferring to dream on rather than to face actuality, so the world clings to the delusion of self and considers deliverance therefrom as undesirable. In the quest for truth, however, satisfaction and beauty come last. Both being entirely subjective, they arise and disappear with the idea of self. Self is the shadow made by our own action, moving along with it, inseparable. As the shadow is longest when the sun stands lowest, to become smaller while the sun rises higher, so the delusion of self is greatest when the light of insight is lowest; but with the increase of insight the delusion will decrease. It is this growth of insight that will finally lead to the deliverance from all delusion.

As always in Buddhism, so here in the development of insight also, the starting point is actuality. Thus the first insight required will be insight into the real nature of conditioned things (*sammasana-ñāṇa*) as having the three characteristics of impermanence, suffering and soullessness. They have to be seen as one, for who perceives sorrow but not the transience thereof has nothing but the pain without the hope of deliverance. But as soon as the unreality of life is understood, also the unreality of suffering will be seen.

From this understanding of unreality, insight in the nature of all things as processes (*udayabbaya-ñāṇa*) will ripen. This does not merely mean the observation that things grow and decay, but the understanding that there is nothing but a process of becoming.

The understanding of the process of becoming will naturally lead to the next step, which is insight that becoming is ceasing (*bhaṅga-ñāṇa*). Though this step should follow quite logically, yet it is a difficult one for many who in the very fact of becoming find all their delight. But if becoming and ceasing are seen as two aspects of one process, then insight into what is to be feared (*bhaya-ñāṇa*) will arise naturally. Fear should lead to understanding of the danger (*ādīnava-ñāṇa*) inherent in clinging to mere processes of cessation, and of the reasons to be disgusted with such an empty show (*nibbidā-ñāṇa*).

A desire to be set free and the knowledge thereof (*muñcitu-kamyatā-ñāṇa*) will grow out into re-contemplation (*paṭisaṅkhāra-ñāṇa*), that is, contemplation of the same three characteristics of transience, suffering and soullessness, but with the increased insight as seen from a higher plane.

Insight of indifference to the activities of this life (*saṅkhāru-pekkhā-ñāṇa*) will be a natural consequence of this disgust and deeper understanding, where even-mindedness is due, not to lack of interest, but to lack of self-interest.

The climax of discernment finally is reached with the insight of adaptation (*anuloma-ñāṇa*), which is the gateway to emancipation (*vimokkhamukha*), where the mind is qualified for the Path of holiness.

No morbid asceticism can be the way leading to emancipation, but rather the well-being of a concentrated mind without worry, without agitation, without preoccupation, without craving or clinging to either good or bad. Not even striving in the good sense can procure one this blessed state. For striving is desire; and desire can only arise for something to be attached to. How can there be attachment for what is entirely beyond sensation and mental conception? There can be no desire for Nibbāna, and the attainment of Deliverance is not dependent upon striving.[1] Nibbāna is non-conditioned (*asaṅkhata*), non-created, non-caused, non-made (*akata*). And what is non-composed is not decomposable, is permanent (*dhuva*) and indestructible (*akkhara*).

Like darkness cannot be made, but the light which prevents darkness can be extinguished, so Nibbāna cannot be made, but the passions which prevent it can be eradicated. The three roots of all evil inclinations are greed (*lobha*), hate (*dosa*) and delusion (*moha*). Greed and hate are opposed in character, for greed is desire to get more and hate is desire to get rid of. Thus, though opposed, they are only two forms of desire. And desire is always combined

1. Striving, in the sense of the Fourfold Right Effort, guided by insight and not desire, is however an indispensable part of the Noble Eightfold Path. See also *Bodhi Leaves* No. B. 28, "Escapism and Escape" (Editor, *The Wheel*).

with delusion. We desire for things just because we do not know them, just because we do not realize their impermanent, woeful, soulless nature. We try to grasp the void, because delusion has created a phantom, which like the rainbow finds only existence in ourselves. Trying to grasp that spectre, the rainbow, the horizon, must bring about disillusion, because they have no real existence, but change with the position of the onlooker.

To realize this is to give up craving for them, by which all suffering also will come to an end. And that is Nibbāna!

In the depth of our hearts we feel that bliss finally depends upon rest, upon changelessness. Even the tendency of the senses to attachment is nothing but the longing after rest in the midst of restlessness. Thus even craving is but an attempt to come to this natural equilibrium. That craving does not succeed in reaching the goal is again due to ignorance. What good can be expected from a thought that was born from a misconception? If the goal is misunderstood, no striving can correct that initial mistake. On the contrary, the greater effort employed, the greater also the distance separating in the end.

If peace is sought for, this cannot be obtained by waging war. The only war that can put a stop to all war is the war against self. A war fought against others is a war of selfishness and can never lead to true peace. Like war and peace receive a different meaning dependent on the standpoint of the observer, so life and no-more-becoming obtain their respective values dependent on the point from which they are surveyed. From the worldling's standpoint, which is one of craving, life is real, because life is craving; and then from that same standpoint no-more-becoming is seen as unreal, empty, annihilation. But from a viewpoint beyond the world (*lokuttara*), from where the world is viewed as impermanent, sorrow-fraught and soulless, any craving is seen as a vain attempt—and life itself, which is but craving, is seen as empty and unreal, while no-more-becoming is considered as perfect deliverance and highest bliss.

Thus, though the attainment of Nibbāna can rightly be said to be the absolute content—for craving or desire under any form has become impossible—yet it cannot be hankered after (*appaṇihita*). But when all the fetters have been removed, fetters which arose and were maintained in ignorance, fetters which will disappear with ignorance, when that which cannot be hankered after can be realized. "Hard is the infinite to see, truth is no easy thing to see; craving is pierced by him who knows, for him who sees nothing remains" (Udāna 8.2).

But is Nibbāna then total annihilation?

Even this question is put in ignorance, for there is nothing to be annihilated. Only that which is, can be destroyed. But that which constantly arises, and in arising is nothing but a process of change, and in changing also constantly ceases, that cannot be said to be destroyed; it merely does not arise again. Now it should be well understood that, like arising is a process, similarly cessation is a process, so that even when the process of arising does not occur again, the process of cessation might not have come to a stop yet. Hence we obtain a double aspect of Nibbāna.

The first one, the coming to a stop of the process of arising, is called "*sa-upādisesa-nibbāna*," i.e., Nibbāna with the remnant of the aggregates of craving. Life being conditioned by craving, the aggregates of life, viz. body and mind, are rightly called the aggregates of craving.

As soon as the process of the arising of craving has come to a stop, the grasping of the aggregates that form an individual will cease also. When the lust for life has ceased, no rebirth will take place further, and the highest state—that of an Arahat—is attained. But when the lust for life has ceased, life itself will not simultaneously disappear. As the heat in an oven, which is produced by fire, will remain for some time even though the fire be extinct, so the result of craving which produced rebirth might remain for some time, even though the fire of the passions be extinct. Thus the acts of thought of an Arahat are neither moral nor immoral. His apperception is ineffective. Though he acts, his actions are not impelled by craving and hence they do not constitute *kamma*, either good or bad; they consist merely in the function (*kiriyā-javana*) and are free from tendencies, likes or dislikes (*anusayā*). But where there arises no new *kamma,* there no further *vipāka* can come about.

When, therefore, the result of previous *kamma* is exhausted, even the remnant of the aggregates of clinging will be broken up, and this is called *an-upādisesa-nibbāna* or *parinibbāna*.

While Nibbāna is single in its nature, yet for the purpose of logical treatment it is thus considered as twofold. By using the two kinds of this logical distinction indiscriminately, endless confusion is caused. When thus Nibbāna is said to be a mental state, this applies only to the state of an Arahat, who has overcome all the mental defilements (*kilesa*) and has broken all the fetters (*saṃyojana*) which bind to rebirth.

Like freedom is only a negative concept, being the absence of restrictions, thus the freedom (*mokkha*) of Nibbāna can only be explained as the absence of defilements and mental fetters. But as those defilements are exactly the roots of all evil, the cause of all suffering, Nibbāna can be called the deliverance from sorrow.

Where Nibbāna cannot be aimed at as a positive goal, for "not by striving can world's end be reached" (*gamanena na pattabbo lokass' anto kudācanaṃ,* AN 4), striving becomes possible in the overcoming of the hindrances and obstacles. Thus Nibbāna remains unconditioned (*asaṅkhata*) and uncreated (*akata*), not to be produced by cumulative virtue, not by purification of a soul, or by cleansing of a soul, or by cleansing of self. There is no "ego" to be made free from selfishness in order to obtain purity, but there is an "ego" to be got rid of, an "ego" misconceived by ignorance and born of craving.

When that "ego" is understood as a delusion, the first fetter (*sakkāya-diṭṭhi*) is broken and the stream which leads to Nibbāna is entered (*sotāpatti*). Like, while plunging into the water of a river, the land and the attractions thereof must be left behind, so when entering the stream of holiness, together with the delusion of self, will also disappear all doubts and attachment to ritualistic performances. But in the stream itself further hindrances might occur, and they too have to be overcome. Antipathy (*vyāpāda*) and sense-pleasures (*kāmacchanda*) might retard the progress of the stream-winner, still causing rebirth, though not in woeful states. Only when even the last five obstacles will have been passed, which are desire for rebirth in form or formless spheres, (*rūparāga, arūparāga*), conceit (*māna*) which is the final and most subtle stronghold of the dying "self," agitation (*uddhacca*) and ignorance (*avijjā*), the stream will lose itself in the ocean and the freedom of Nibbāna be attained. As the stream is still hemmed in on both sides by the river banks, so the Path to Nibbāna is beset with difficulties.

But it is exactly in the overcoming of those difficulties that the freedom of Nibbāna can be realized. Once more, Nibbāna cannot be aimed at, desired or longed for, just because it is non-conditioned and does not arise dependent on conditions. But one can strive for the extinction of craving, for the abolition of the slavery of an imaginary self, for the overcoming of ignorance. The factors to this enlightenment (*satta sambojjhaṅga*) include the perseverance of mindfulness (*sati*), the open-mindedness of investigation (*dhammavicaya*) with the steadiness of abiding energy (*viriya*), the enthusiasm of spiritual joy (*pīti*) together with the sobriety of tranquillity of mind (*passaddhi*), the peacefulness of concentration (*samādhi*) with the harmony of equanimity (*upekkhā*).

Renunciation, not as mortification, but as a natural result of insight through which craving and clinging become impossible, is the way by which deliverance from the passions can be attained. Like a lamp must give up its oil so that its light may shine—similarly renunciation is an indispensable factor to enlightenment: renunciation not only of the world but also of the self, "like the wind the leaves from a tree" (Theragātha 2). It is only in perfect renunciation that perfect freedom can be found. It is the will-to-live which leads to rebirth; it is thus the will-to-live that must be conquered, so that Nibbāna may be attained.

This lust for life cannot be cut short by violence. An act of violence against oneself may be caused by disgust with life, yet it remains lust for better life. The will-to-live cannot be conquered by will for no-more-life, but by understanding that there is no self to live. The delusion of the craving for existence can be expelled by the realization of non-self. Then not only the will, will be dissolved, but even the possibility of willing.

When thus the insight of non-self (*anattā*) will have taken the place of delusion (*moha*) and ignorance (*avijjā*)—when being will be viewed as a mere process of becoming, and becoming as ceasing—then the spell which kept us bound so long will be broken, the dream state of hallucination will vanish and reality will be realized. This reality is not the "eternalization" of a self or soul, but the escape therefrom. Therefore Nibbāna is not a deliverance of the self, not a salvation of the soul, but the deliverance from the self, the salvation from the soul, i.e., from the misconceived "I."

Once this deliverance is attained, no more hallucination can occur, because the source which produced this misconception, namely, craving, selfishness, is dried up.

And with this the last word has been said; for, where craving has ceased, the process of becoming, which is grasping, has ceased also. Where there is no more becoming, there is no more rebirth and all its consequences of sorrow, decay and death. And thus Nibbāna is the only Deliverance, the only Freedom, surpassing all understanding, above all emotion, beyond all striving, unconditioned, uncreated, indestructible, whereto all may attain through the overcoming of greed, hate and delusion, through insight and realization in the Deliverance from self.

In soundless depth of breathless thought,
A silent music plays;
While all the universe around
In never-ending waves
Unknowingly, unwillingly,
For that same silence craves.
All men and beasts and things alike,
For independence strive;
For freedom from all wants and needs
Which cause their restless drive.
Thus every deed contains the seed
Through which all will arrive
At even-balanced, cravingless,
Birthless and deathless life.

The Message of the Saints

Thera-Therī-Gāthās

by

V. F. Gunaratna

WHEEL PUBLICATION NO. 135

The Message of the Saints

The field of the Tipiṭaka[1] literature is wide and varied. On the one hand, there are the subtle expositions of the Abhidhamma Piṭaka and the profound discourses of the Sutta Piṭaka, which call for serious thinking and study, while, on the other hand, there are the simple Jātaka tales so fascinating to the young and old alike. Between these two extremes there is a class of Buddhist literature which is lofty in theme but easy to comprehend, which uplifts the mind but does not tax it. To this category belong the inspired verses of those saints—the Theras and Therīs—who were mostly contemporaries of the Buddha. It is these inspired verses that are collectively known as the "Thera-Therī-Gāthās" and they form part of the Khuddaka Nikāya of the Sutta Piṭaka.

The message of the Saints contained in the Thera-Therī-Gāthās[2] does not appear to have fully reached the Buddhist world of today. These exquisite poems are not sufficiently widely known among the Buddhist public; much less widely have they been read and appreciated. It is a pity that their wonderfully inspiring influence is not much felt today. But the fortunate few who have devoted their time to a regular study of these stanzas have never failed to be inspired by the uplifting spirit which continually radiates from them.

Nowhere in the whole of the Buddhist Pali literature do we find such a concentration of poetic beauty and loftiness of thought as in these 337 Thera-Therī-Gāthās.[3] Really, one must know Pali to enjoy to the full the beauty of these verses. Fortunately, however, for those who cannot enjoy the poems in the original, the Pali Text Society has published translations[4]—thanks to the able translator

---

1. Tipiṭaka (lit.: the Three Baskets) is the name of the Buddhist canonical scriptures.
2. Thera: Elder Monk of the Buddhist Monastic Order. Therī: Elder Nun. Gāthā: stanzas.
3. There are 264 gāthās uttered by the Theras and 73 by the Therīs.
4. Published under the titles *Psalms of the Brethren* and *Psalms of the Sisters*. Our thanks are due to the Pali Text Society, London, for kind permission to quote here extensively from these two volumes.

Mrs. Rhys Davids—which have successfully captured and retained much of the spirit and charm of the original gāthās. As it is proposed to give the reader an opportunity of enjoying some of these translated verses, I must acknowledge my indebtedness both to the Pali Text Society and to Mrs. Rhys Davids.

The Background of the Gāthās

These delightfully refreshing verses reflect the religious emotions and inspirations of certain pious men and women of Buddha's time who entered the Order and followed his teachings with genuine devotion. At some time mostly in their youth, the call came to them to forsake the lay life and to take to the life of a homeless monk. This they did in a deeply rooted confidence and persevering diligently they attained Arahantship, Holiness, the final deliverance from the bondage of passions and the shackles of rebirth. Some of these verses reflect their ardent determination to reach their spiritual goal. Some record the struggle within them between the forces of good and evil and finally recall in triumphant mood the victory of good over evil, and their consequent entry into the glorious state of Sainthood. Often it is some trivial circumstance, some trifling incident in life, that gave the initial impetus to the spiritual activity and upliftment of these monks and nuns. Some would record their passionate yearning for the solitary life and their love of forest life with its solitude and the natural beauties and the opportunity it afforded them for quiet meditation. The charms of solitude and the beauties of forest life they have sung in matchless and mellifluous language. The exquisite calm begotten of the disciplined life, the contempt of the grosser pleasures of life which drag the victim down into a whirlpool of never, ending desires have so deeply influenced some of them that these thoughts have become the themes of some of these fascinating poems. Whatever may be the theme, these Gāthās are said to have been uttered by these saints immediately after their attainment of Arahantship as an open acknowledgement[5] of the cause which led to their final enlightenment. They depict, whether subjectively or objectively, some aspect or other of the struggle of

5. This acknowledgement is referred to in the Commentary as *aññā*.

the human mind in its attempt to escape from the slavery of desire, and the consequent beauty of thought combined with beauty of expression make these extremely delightful reading. Sometimes a rebuke uttered by the Buddha or by someone else not only helps a Thera to rid himself of the particular fault which provoked the rebuke but it also urges him most powerfully to progress along the spiritual path leading to the state of Arahantship, sometimes after a very short time. These poems do not contain sufficient data about the monks and nuns who composed them, nor is even the identity of some of them known. Much light, however, is thrown by an ancient Commentary entitled *Paramattha Dīpanī* written by one Bhikkhu Dhammapāla of Kañcipūra (Madras Presidency). This Commentary supplies the background to the incidents mentioned in these Gāthās without which some of them are unintelligible. The Theras in question were laymen who came from various levels of social life to join the Order. There were Brahmins, powerful princes and rich merchants who abandoned the luxurious life of ease and indolence, and donned the saffron-coloured robe for a life of solitude and meditation. There were also cultivators, craftsmen, fishermen, actors, elephant-trainers and labourers. To whatsoever rank or station in life these Theras belonged, there is one common feature which linked one with the other and each with all, namely, their wonderful religious ardour to which they have given expression through these inspired verses.

The Gāthās as a Source of Inspiration

These poems are not only inspired they are also inspiring. To those who wish to increase their *saddhā* (confidence) one can strongly commend the thoughtful reading of these verses over and over again. To any one who is struggling to lead the spiritual life and badly needs encouragement, to any one who has fallen from his high ideal and is lacking the necessary strength of mind to start over again, to any one who is making slow progress on the spiritual path and is in great need of the correct impetus to spur him on to quicker progress, I can think of no other more powerful source of strength than the reading and re-reading of the Thera-Therī-Gāthās. They are so consoling, and so uplifting. They are also so human and so true to life. Herein lies the message of these ancient verses to us. The way of spiritual progress lies in the study and practice of the Dhamma and a contemplation of it followed by intense meditation. But, bare study or bare contemplation is sometimes difficult and dry, and is barren of results. Some extra impetus or motivation is necessary, some extra aid is required, to urge the flagging mind. When the spirit droops, when the struggle is weak, or the struggle is abandoned, what better enlivening process is there to flood our hearts with high hopes and aspirations and to galvanize us to activity once again than quietly listening to how similar situations have been successfully dealt with by these Theras and Therīs of old? The stanzas of these earnest devotees show how they have reacted to set-backs and draw-backs in life similar to those with which we are afflicted, how they too have suffered within their own minds the same conflicts as we have between the forces of good and evil how, despite the powerful urges of evil, they have kept their steadfast gaze on their goal and how their ardent and persistent longing for the goal stood them in good stead, and ultimately helped them to emerge triumphant and obtain the glory and peace of the liberated mind. Situations such as these constitute the inspiring contents of the Thera-Therī-Gāthās, and let us now examine some of them.

Inspiration from a Fall

It was mentioned earlier that some slight incident in life has very often been the starting point of the spiritual activity and uplifting of many of these monks and nuns. Let us now take the case of Bhagu Thera. He was by nature slow and sluggish and was very often found to be in a drowsy condition. One day he left his cell in order to discipline himself and rid himself of this tendency. While he was walking up the flight of steps of a terrace, he fell down. Now, this fall made a deep impression on his mind and set him thinking. We know the story of how when an apple fell Newton began to think, and the discovery of the law of gravitation was the result. This Thera fell. He too began to think, but on far different lines. He began to ponder on the impermanence of all things. Nothing stands for ever. Everything must some day fall. All is *dukkha,* liable to suffering. Bhagu Thera thus made this fall of himself the subject of his meditation, and developing insight, very soon attained Arahantship. Soon thereafter the Buddha came to see him and asked him, "How now, Bhikkhu, do you continue in earnest?" He answered in the following delightful stanzas:

> "Overcome by drowsiness I left my cell for exercise,
> Climbed the terrace-steps and fell thereby, all drowsy,
> To the earth chafing my limbs.
> Once more I stood up. And while I went up and down,
> Within I was all alert, composed, intent.
> There arose in me the deeper thought,
> Attention to the fact and to the cause.[6]
> The misery of it all was manifest.
> Distaste, indifference possessed the mind.
> And so my heart was set at liberty.
> O see, the seemly order of the norm!
> The threefold wisdom have I made my own
> And all the Buddha bids me do is done."

Inspiration from Seeing the Fall and Rise of a Bull

There is another instance of a fall which became the start of thoughts leading up immediately to Arahantship. Here it was not merely a fall that constituted the incident. It was both a fall and a rise. It was the fall and rise of a bull. The Thera concerned was known as Rāmantyavihārin. He was the son of a prominent citizen of Rājagaha. He lived an idle and gay life, but suddenly the call came to him. He heard a sermon of the Buddha, renounced the world and entered the Order. Nevertheless, the comfortable life he had earlier lived still had its attractions for him, so that, though a Bhikkhu, he had made for himself a well-polished room with ample furniture and saw to it that he was well equipped with food and drink. Hence it was that he was known Rāmantyavihārin, which means "dweller in a pleasant lodge." Despite these comforts

6. The original Pali expression represented by this line is "*yoniso manasikāra,*" i.e., the habit of systematized attention which has been highly commended by the Buddha—a way of looking down to the origin and foundation of things as they occur to the mind, as opposed to "*ayoniso manasikāra*" or superficiality in thinking.

he yearned for the greater freedom of the layman's life and, refusing the alms that were offered to him, decided to roam the country. One day as he was seated beneath a tree he saw several carts passing along the road. He noticed one weary bull stumbling at a rough place on the road and falling down. The carter released the bull from the yoke and gave it food and drink. Soon the fatigue was over, the bull arose, it was harnessed again, and again it began to draw the cart. This sight of the bull falling and subsequently rising again made a deep impression in the mind of this pleasure-loving Thera who had fallen off the correct path of a Bhikkhu. Thought he to himself: "Even as this bull having stumbled and fallen has risen again and is drawing his cart again, so it behoves me who have fallen from the high position of a noble recluse, to rise up again and relive the noble life." He began to meditate on this incident and soon attained Arahantship. This Thera's short but beautiful stanza runs as follows:

> "Even though he trip and fall, the mettled brute
> Of noble breed will steadfast stand once more.
> So look on me as one who having learned
> Of Him, the All-Enlightened One, have gained
> True insight, am became of noble breed
> And of the very Buddha a disciple true."

Inspiration from Elephant-Training

Let us now consider the case of Hatthārohaputta Thera, where also a trifling incident led to great results. This Thera belonged to a family of elephant trainers. In his youth he developed a proficiency in training elephants and used to train them very often. One day, as he was training an elephant by the riverside and observing how effectively the savage tendencies of the animal gave way to the influence of his skilful training and also considering what power the presence of the trainer's hook wielded over the animal, he began to think—"Of what avail to me is this elephant-training. Is it not far better for one to train and tame himself?" So thinking he visited the Buddha, heard him preach and entered the Order. He meditated on this incident and ultimately attained Arahantship. His Gāthā too is short but beautiful:

"Once roamed this heart afield, a wanderer
Wherever will or whim or pleasure led,
Today that heart I'll hold in thorough check
As trainer's hook the savage elephant."

An almost similar incident regarding the taming of an elephant has been the cause of the spiritual upliftment of a nun. This will be dealt with later in the section dealing with the verses of the Therīs.

Inspiration from Ridicule

Let us now consider how a trifling incident of an amusing nature led to great results. This was the experience of Lakuṇṭaka Bhaddiya Thera. He possessed an extremely beautiful voice. He was deemed to have the sweetest voice among the disciples of the Buddha, but his physical form was not at all presentable. He was extremely short and for that reason he was called Lakuṇṭaka, which means a dwarf. One day in Sāvatthī a woman was driving a chariot. When she happened to pass this Thera, she laughed exhibiting her teeth. This Thera made that sight of her teeth the object of his meditation and soon arrived at the state of Anāgāmi, the Non-returner. Later he practised mindfulness as regards the body (*kāyānupassanā*) and attained Arahantship. Thereafter he used to repeat these charming verses:

"Beyond the gardens of Ambataka
In woodland wild, craving and craving's root
Withdrawn, and rapt in deepest reverie
There happy sits fortunate Bhaddiya.
And some are charmed by cymbals, lutes and drums
And I in leafy shadow of my trees
Do dwell entranced by the Buddha's Rule.
Let but the Buddha grant one boon to me
And if that boon were mine, I'd choose for all
Perpetual study in control of self.
They who decry me for my shape, and they
Who listen spell-bound to my voice, such folk
In toils of lust and impulse know me not.
The fool hemmed in on every side knows not

The inner life, nor sees the things without
And by a voice forsooth is led away.
And of the inner life he knows not
Yet can discern the things that are without
Watching alone the outer fruits that come
He also by a voice is led away.
He who both understands the inner life
And does discern the things that are without
Clear visioned, by no voice is led away."

(An almost similar incident appears in the *Visuddhimagga.*)

Inspiration from Bitter Criticism

It is interesting to trace the circumstances which led to the Arahantship of Ānanda Thera, the famous disciple of the Buddha who for many years attended on him. It is well-known that Ānanda Thera, being preoccupied with his ministrations to the Buddha neglected his own spiritual development so much that when the Buddha passed away all his disciples were Arahants except Ānanda Thera. Shortly after the Buddha's demise, a monk known as Vajjiputta Thera, who acquired the six-fold supernormal powers, found Ānanda Thera preaching to a large congregation. Vajjiputta Thera, no doubt from the best of motives, criticized Ānanda Thera bitterly, pointing out that he had forgotten his main duty and was still preoccupied with other work. This is how Vajjiputta Thera addressed Ānanda Thera:

"Come and plunge in leafy lair of trees,[7]
Suffer Nibbāna in your heart to sink.
Study and dally not, Gotamid,
What does this fingle-fangle mean to you."

Ānanda Thera was greatly agitated on hearing this bit of sharp criticism. It struck him hard. It also gave birth to a keen resolve to abandon everything else and devote the rest of his time for the one purpose for which he entered the Order, viz. to realize perfect

7. The original of this line is *rukkhamūla-gahanaṃ pasakkiya.*" This is a bidding to betake to the forest (literally, to the foot of a tree) away from the maddening crowd.

Sainthood. He keenly realized the mistake of not having striven for Arahantship so far. What now behoved him, he felt, was not to be preaching to others but to further his own inner development, which he had neglected. Feeling keen remorse he spent that night in intense meditation, walking up and down. Then, as he entered his room, he obtained insight and in the very act of lying down on his couch he attained Arahantship. Ānanda Thera's wonderful devotion and loyalty to his Master is exceptional. There is no greater example in the whole world of a disciple's loyalty to his Master. Even as he lay dying on his death-bed this is what Ānanda Thera uttered:

"The Master has my fealty and love
And all the Buddha's ordinance is done.
Low have I laid the heavy load I bore,
Cause for rebirth is found in me no more."

Inspiration from Rebuke

The reaction that rebuke or reproach causes varies with the individual. To those whose minds are not pliable, who are obstinate, headstrong and insolent, rebuke or reproach can have no salutary effect. It will only make them more stubborn. But in the case of those whose general disposition is one of benevolence and kindness, whose general tendencies are towards good and not evil, a little rebuke can sometimes have the effect of arousing in them such a degree of self-examination and repentance that these thoughts may induce a high resolve to shed their faults and weaknesses whatever they are which have thus been brought to light.

Just such was the case of an Elder known is Vaddha Thera. His mother, a pious lady of the city of Bhārukaccha, had renounced the lay life and had entered the order of Bhikkhunīs or Nuns and subsequently realized Arahantship. Later her son entered the Order and earned a name for himself as an eloquent preacher. One day a desire arose in him to see his mother and he desired to see her alone. He therefore removed his outer robe and went unnoticed to the quarters of the Bhikkhunīs. His mother seeing him come alone and without his outer robe rebuked him severely. This rebuke worked heavily on his mind. He forthwith returned to his monastery, sat himself down in the day-room and, meditating, attained Arahantship.

In his stanzas he freely acknowledged his attainment as being solely due to his mother's rebuke. He refers to this rebuke by the Pali word "*patoda,*" which means a goad or spur. He starts by calling her "*matī*" or mother, but as the inspired verses proceed, she is referred to as "*bhaginī,*" or sister, in the sense that the entire Order of the Bhikkhunīs (of which she was a member) are regarded as sisters from the point of view of the Order of the Bhikkhus (of which he was a member).

As one reads these lines of inspiration one feels how intensely and completely this Bhikkhu must have been influenced by the maternal rebuke. Let us now listen to his gāthās:

"Oh! Well in sooth my mother used the goad.
I marked her word, and by my parent taught
I stirred up effort, put forth all my strength
And won the goal, the Enlightenment Supreme.
Arahant am I, meet for men's offerings,
Thrice wise, the ambrosial vision I beheld.
Conquered is Namuci[8] and all his host
And now I dwell henceforth sane and immune.
Yeah, the intoxicants that once were there
Within, without me are extracted clean.
Nothing does remain nor may they reappear.
Lo! Wise and ripe in grace the Sister was
Who spoke this word of pregnant good to me.
For you now even as for me
No jungle of the mind does bar the way,
A final barrier is made to Ill.
Last mortal frame is this, to which belongs
The way world without end of birth and death
Nor ever comes more rebirth (for you)."

8. Namuci is another name for Māra.

Inspiration from Being Called a Pig

Let us now consider a case where a very bad rebuke had its most salutary effect, that is, the case of Dasaka Thera. He was the son of a slave of Anāthapiṇḍika, the great philanthropist. Later he was given the post of Gate-keeper of Jetavanārāma by Anāthapiṇḍika. After some time, on account of his good conduct, he was released from slavery. Though he was freed he preferred to spend the rest of his life as a Bhikkhu and therefore entered the Order. Strangely, however, from the time he became a Bhikkhu, perhaps due to the sudden cessation of arduous labour, he ceased to be energetic. He became more and more slothful and indolent and began to sleep long after each mid-day meal. When the Buddha was delivering a sermon he would get behind the congregation so that he may remain unnoticed and there he was found snoring away. The Buddha noticing this rebuked him by a verse comparing him to a "*maha varāha*," i.e., a huge pig. This rebuke greatly agitated the Thera's mind and constantly recalling the verse uttered by the Buddha developed insight and realized Arahantship. The verse with which the Buddha rebuked him became his personal verse in the sense that he used to repeat it every now and then, pondering on its meaning, which urged him on to the spiritual heights which he thereby reached. In his own words this *gāthā* acted as a "*paṭoda*" or goad to him. The Gāthā runs as follows:

> "Who waxes slothful and in diet gross,
> Given to sleep and rolling as he lies,
> Like a great hog with provender replete,
> The dolt comes back again and again to birth."

Inspiration from Punishment

There is a kind of pride with which some people are afflicted, which is akin to pride of birth. It is the pride of membership of some institution or body. Are we not reminded of such persons when we find the Thera Channa with egoistic pride speaking of "our Buddha" and "our Doctrine?"[9] This Thera could not rid himself of

9. Channa was born in King Sudddhodana's palace as the son of a maid-servant. This moat probably accounts for his desire to identify himself with the Sakyas by saying, "our Buddha" and "our Doctrine."

this weakness. On account of his pride and his obstinacy, a penalty in the nature of a social ostracism (*brahma daṇḍa*) imposed on him by the Buddha was carried out after his demise. In suffering this penalty Channa Thera learned to eliminate his weakness and soon after attained Arahantship, which he triumphantly proclaimed in the following Gāthās:

> "I heard the Truth which the Great One had taught
> And felt its mighty virtues, known by Him
> Who all things with supernatural insight knew.
> The Path for winning things ambrosial I found.
> Past-Master he in sooth to guide into the way of blest security."

Inspiration from a Curse

An ox belonging to a caravan-leader called Godatta once fell on the road while it was drawing a cart. It was not possible to raise the ox, although it was beaten severely by Godatta. Then, it is said, the ox assumed a human voice and uttered a curse on Godatta. This curse had the effect of impressing deeply on Godatta's mind the real purpose of life. He gave away all his property and, having entered the Order, attained Arahantship. Among the verses he uttered this is one:

> "Even as the mettled brute of noble breed
> Yoked to his load, drawing his load along
> Though worn by burden past his powers (unfair)
> Breaks not away, revolting from his bonds,
> So they in whom, as water in the sea,
> Wisdom abounds, despise not other men.
> This among creatures is the Ariyan rule."

Inspiration from a Dream

There is an interesting case of how great remorse suffered in a dream led to meditation and to the realization of Arahantship. The Thera who so became an Arahant was known as Usabha Thera. He had neglected all his religious duties but was not concerned at all about this neglect. One day he dreamt that he had shaved his head and had donned a crimson-coloured robe and was going on elephant-back to the town for alms. This had attracted the attention of the people, who had gathered in large numbers. Seeing the people, he felt ashamed and forthwith dismounted from the animal. He knew his own unworthiness. Usabha Thera then awoke from his dream. He felt great remorse, and, taking earnestly to meditation, attained Arahantship. His dream had acted upon him as his goad. These are the two verses he uttered:

"A cloak the hue of purple mango-buds
Draping about my shoulder, I bestrode
The back of elephant, and so to seek
Mine alms into the village street I rode.
Down from his back in very shame I slid
When lo! I woke and anguish seized me.
This arrogant self was then made meek and mild,
Purged were the poisons that my mind defiled."

Inspiration from Temptation

There was a Thera known as Sundara Samuddha Thera who was extremely handsome. As a young man the call came to him and he entered the Order. His mother, however, was unhappy in the thought that her son was not married, and when she saw other young men going about with their wives all dressed in the best of clothes and enjoying themselves at festivals, she thought of her lonely son and wept. Noticing this, a young woman of questionable character approached her and offered to entice her son back to the layman's life. The weak-minded mother not only approved the idea but also gave her many gifts. Clad in gay attire she approached the Thera but all her seductive arts failed to win over the Thera. On the contrary, the vile woman's importunities made the Thera all the more determined to pursue his goal and he resolved then and there to exert himself to the utmost in his meditations. Standing where he was he acquired the six-fold supernormal power (*abhiññā*), culminating in Arahantship. His verses reflect his high resolve:

"Adorned and clad to make a gallant show,
Crowned with a wreath and decked with many gems,
Her feet made red with lac, with slippers alight,

A woman of the town accosted me!
'So young, so fair and you have left the world!
Stay here within my rule and ordinance.
Take your fill of human pleasures.
See, I will give you all the means thereto.
It is the truth that I am telling you
Or if you doubt, I'll bring you fire[10] and swear:
When you and I are old, both of us
Will take our staff to lean upon, and so
We both will leave the world and win both ways.'
Seeing that public woman making plea
And professing obeisance gaily decked
In brave array like snare of Māra laid,
There arose in me the deeper view:
Attention to the fact and to the cause.
The misery of it all was manifest.
Distaste, indifference the mind possessed
And so my heart was set at liberty.
Oh! See the seemly order of the norm.
The three-fold wisdom[11] have I made my own
And all the Buddha bids us do is done."

Inspiration from Nature

In all ages and climes the desire for the meditative life often goes hand in hand with the desire for the forest life and the desire to be in communion with nature. Therefore it is not surprising to find several Theras in the Buddha's time exhibiting a great fondness for the forest life with its solitude and its natural beauties, affording, as they do, an opportunity for quiet meditation.

10. This perhaps refers to the ordeal by fire to test one's truthfulness as mentioned in the Laws of Manu.

11. This refers to the three special types of knowledge, viz. knowledge of past lives, knowledge of death and rebirth of beings, and knowledge of the extinction of the taints (*asavas*).

The Inspiration of Usabha Thera

There was once a monk known as Usabha Thera. After he received the higher ordination he resided in the cave of a forest at the foot of a mountain. The rainy season had come. Everywhere the woods were fresh and green. The trees and creepers and bushes were shining with a fresh foliage of healthy green. Now Usabha Thera was thrilled with the charms that nature has thus showered on the forest after the rains. Coming out of his cave one day, and possessing, as he did, the *arañña-saññā*, or forest-sense, he appreciated the loveliness and luxuriant growth of the forest. He began to ponder seriously on the fulfilment of growth that had taken place in all the vegetation of the forest. "These trees and creepers and bushes," he thought, "are unconscious and yet by the season's fulfilment they have won growth. Why should not I, who am conscious and have attained a suitable season, myself win growth by the development of good qualities?" Thinking thus he uttered these delightful stanzas and meditating realized Arahantship:

> "The trees on high by towering cloud refreshed
> With the new rain break forth in verdant growth.
> To Usabha who for detachment longs,
> And has the forest-sense of things,
> Does come (from this responsive spring) abundant good."

The Inspiration of Vana Vaccha Thera

Let us now proceed to the case of Vana Vaccha Thera, who was also thrilled with the charm of forest life. He was a Brahmin of the Vaccha clan and a native of Kapilavatthu. He was born in the forest and because he was so passionately fond of it he was called Vana Vaccha which means "Forest-Vaccha." Later he entered the Order and went back to the forest and remained there meditating until he realized Arahantship. On being once asked by his fellow monks what comfort he gained from the forest, the verse by which he answered shows his great love of nature:

> "Crags with the hue of heaven's blue clouds
> Where lies embosomed many a shining tarn
> Of crystal-clear, cool waters, and whose slopes

The 'herds of Indra' cover and bedeck;
Those are the braes wherein my soul delights."

The Inspiration of Another Vana Vaccha Thera

There was another Vana Vaccha Thera, son of a wealthy Brahmin of Rājagaha. He too entered the Order and having attained Arahantship decided to remain in the forest in complete detachment. Once, out of compassion for his kinsmen of Rājagaha, he emerged from the forest and lived among them for some time preaching the Dhamma to them. When he decided to return to the forest they implored him to live in the Vihara close by, saying that they will wait upon him. He explained to them that he preferred to live in the forest and this he did by uttering a verse which reveals his ardent love of forest-life:

"Crags where clear waters lie, a rocky world
Haunted by black-faced apes and timid deer
Where, beneath bright blossoms, run the silver-streams
Those are the highlands of my heart's delight."

The Inspiration of Kassapa Mahā Thera

A similar delightful expression of the love of forest life is found in the verses of Kassapa Mahā Thera. This is the Thera who practised the thirteen *dhutaṅgas* or austerities and soon realized Arahantship. When he was asked why at his time of life he preferred to live in the forest rather than in a monastery, this was his beautiful answer:

"Those upland glades delightful to the soul
Where the Kareri spreads its wildering wreaths.
Where sound the trumpet-calls of elephants,
Those are the braes wherein my soul delights.
Fair uplands rain-refreshed and resonant,
With crested creatures' cries antiphonal,
Lone heights where silent Rishis oft resort,
Those are the braes wherein my soul delights.
Here is enough for me who fain would seek
The highest good, a brother filled with zeal.
Here is enough for me who fain would seek
A happy ease, a brother filled with zeal.

Here is enough for me who give myself
To studious toil, so am I filled with zeal."

This same Kassapa Mahā Thera was once asked how he was able at his time of life to climb the hills day after day. To this question he replied in the following forceful stanzas:

"Where some do perish as they climb the rocks,
Heir of the Buddha, mindful, self-possessed,
By forces of the spirit fortified,
Does Kassapa ascend the mountain brow.
Returning from the daily round for alms,
Kassapa mounts some craggy point and sits
In meditation rapt, nor clutching aught,
For far from him has he put fear and dread.
Returning from the daily round for alms
Kassapa mounts some craggy point and sits
In meditation rapt, nor clutching aught,
For he among those that burn is cool and still.
Returning from the daily round for alms,
Kassapa mounts some craggy point and sits
In meditation rapt, nor clutching aught,
His task is done; he is sane, immune."

The Inspiration of Cittaka Thera

Cittaka Thera was the son of a wealthy Brahmin of Rājagaha. He heard the Buddha preaching at the Bamboo Grove. Filled with faith he renounced the layman's life and entered the Order. Very soon he realized Arahantship, whereupon he decided to visit the Buddha and pay his respects to him. He was then asked by the other brethren whether he was able to meditate strenuously while living in the forest. Evidently some of the questioners must have thought that the quiet of the forest life predisposes one to indolence and sleep. See, however, the answer given by Cittaka Thera in this vigorous and inspiring stanza:

"Peacocks of sapphire neck and comely crest,
Calling, calling in Karanviya woods
By cool and humid winds made musical.
They wake the thinker from his noonday sleep."

The Inspiration of Vimala Thera

Another Thera of Rājagaha born of a wealthy family was Vimala Thera. Seeing the Buddha one day, he too was filled with faith and betook himself to a mountain cave in Kosala for meditation. One day while he was dwelling in his mountain cave where the heat was oppressive, large rain clouds gathered in the sky and soon there was a severe downpour of rain. Thereafter it was nice and cool. The rains had removed all sense of heat and oppression. The earth was cool and the winds blew. So the Thera was able to persevere in his meditations with eagerness until Arahantship was soon realized. Enraptured and overjoyed he expressed his accomplishment in the following delightful stanza:

> "The burdened earth is sprinkled by the rain,
> The winds blow cool, the lightnings roam on high,
> Eased and allayed the obsessions of the mind,
> And in my heart, the spirit's mastery."

The Aspirations of Tālapuṭa Thera

Nowhere do we find the religious aspirations of devotees so well expressed as in the Thera-Therī Gāthās, and foremost among such expressions are those of Tālapuṭa Thera. This Thera in lay life was a well-known actor who had been giving very successful performances in various parts of India. Once, when he was performing at Rājagaha, the thought came to him to visit the Buddha. Having done so he enquired from the Buddha whether it is true that actors on the stage after death are reborn among certain devas. Thrice the question was asked and thrice the Buddha said "Don't ask this question from me." However, on being asked the fourth time, the Buddha replied that those who induce sensual thoughts in others and cause them to lose earnestness are reborn in hell. On receiving this reply the talented actor wept, for he had been deceived by older actors, who had told him that an actor is reborn in happy states. He then listened to the Buddha's teaching and, full of faith joined the Order. Having realized Arahantship he uttered several gāthās which bespeak his ardent aspirations to attain Arahantship. Here are some of them:

"When shall I come to dwell in mountain caves
Now here, now there, unmated (with desire),
And with the vision gained into impermanence
Of all that into being does become.
Yea, this for me, even this, when shall it come to be.
O! when shall I, who wear the patchwork cloak,
Be a true saint of yellow robe,
Without a thought of what is 'mine'
And from all cravings purified,
With lust and hate, yea and illusions slain,
So to the wild woods gone, in bliss abide?
O! when shall I, who see and know that this
My person, nest of dying and disease,
Oppressed by age and death,
Is all impermanent,
Dwell free from fear, lonely within the woods—
Yea, when shall these things be?
O! when shall I abide (unmoved)
Because of speech abusive, not downcast,
Nor when again my praise be sung
Be filled with complacency
When comes this for me?"[12]

The Therī Gāthās—Their Nature

The Nuns of the time of the Buddha, like the Monks, were renowned for their devotion and piety. As in the case of some of the Theras a trifling incident in life, a trivial circumstance, often became the starting point of their spiritual effort which culminated in Arahantship, and they too, like the Theras, triumphantly proclaimed their achievement in inspired verses. These verses reflect their religious emotions and aspirations. Most of these nuns too had joined the Order in their youth and sometimes within a short time realized Arahantship. As in Thera Gāthās there is reflected in these Therī Gāthās the struggle between the forces of

12. To an actor on the stage it needs much effort to be indifferent to praise and blame.

good and evil and the indomitable resolve to surmount evil and reach the goal. Hence their appeal to us.

We miss however the poetic excellence that characterizes most of the verses of the Theras. We also miss that impassioned longing for solitude and that ardent love of nature and forest-life so beautifully expressed in the Thera Gāthās. Nor do we find in the Therī Gāthās much of that hortatory element which features largely in some of the Thera Gāthās. In language, in sentiment and in outlook there are differences between the verses of the Theras and those of the Therīs. This may be traced to the circumstance that in the homes of the early Buddhist era the role of the woman was so different from the role of the man. There is also the added circumstance that Buddhist nuns (*Bhikkhunī*) were not allowed by their Code of Discipline to live alone in secluded places. There are however these two very noticeable features common to both types of Gāthās, namely, the reflection of great piety and the manifestation of an unflinching determination to reach the goal.

Inspiration from a Burnt-up Curry

A daughter of a nobleman of Vesāli was greatly interested in the practice of the Dhamma and became a lay-disciple of the Buddha. Later she desired to renounce the lay life and become a Nun, but her husband would not hear of this. So she continued performing her household duties reflecting all the while on the Virtues of the Dhamma. One day in her kitchen a curry of herbs was being cooked when suddenly the flames rose high and burnt up all the herbs with a crackling noise. She was watching this. It made a deep impression in her mind. She made this sight the basis of her meditation on the impermanence of things and reached the state of Anāgāmi (Non-returner). Thereafter she gave up wearing jewels and ornaments. On being asked by her husband the reason for this, she explained that she found it difficult to lead the lay life. Her husband consenting, she was ordained by Mahā Pajāpati to whom he took her. Her name as a Nun is not known. Shortly thereafter she attained Arahantship. Later when she was brought before the Buddha, the latter with the object of encouraging her referred to the cause which led to her enlightenment in a Gāthā which thereafter she used to repeat in sheer joy:

"Sleep softly, little sturdy,[13] take your rest
At ease, wrapt in the robe thyself hast made.
Stilled are the passions that would rage within,
Withered as pot herbs in the oven dried."

Inspiration from a Fall

A fall while walking led to results similar to the case of Bhagu Thera, mentioned earlier. In the present case one Dhammā Therī, having gone out for alms one day, was returning to the nunnery when she tripped and fell. She took this as the basis for her meditation and attained Arahantship. Thereupon she repeated this stanza in triumphant mood:

"Far had I wandered for my daily food,
Weary with shaking limbs I reached my rest.
Leaning upon my staff when even there
I fell to earth—lo! all the misery
Besetting this poor mortal frame lay bare
to inward vision.
Prone the body lay.
The heart of me rose up in liberty."

Inspiration from an Elephant's Obedience

Similar to the case of Hatthārohaputta, which had been dealt with earlier, is the case of Dantikā Therī, who was also deeply impressed by the very docile attitude of a well-trained elephant. Returning from a mid-day rest on a hill she saw an elephant meekly raising his foot at the mere bidding of the trainer. She began to ponder deeply. She thought that if training can exert so much influence on a powerful animal, how much more can be achieved if the trainer trains himself. She then began to train her mind in meditation and thereafter attained Arahantship. Then, in a mood of sheer joy, she broke forth in the following inspired verses:

---

13. On account of her sturdy build she was called Sturdy by the people of her area.

"Coming from noonday rest in Vulture's Peak
I saw an elephant, his bath performed, forth from the river issue.
And a man taking his goad bade the great creature stretch his foot.
'Give me your foot'—The elephant obeyed and to his neck the trainer sprang.
I saw the untamed tamed, I saw him bent to Master's will.
And marking inwardly I passed into the forest depths
In faith—I trained and ordered all my mind."

Inspiration from Watching Water Sinking into the Ground

The Paṭācārā Therī in her lay life suffered many bereavements within a very short space of time. She lost her husband and both her children. She also lost her parents and her brother. Consoled in her great grief by the Buddha's admonitions she reached the state of a Non-returner (*Anāgāmi*). One day she was washing her feet with a bowl of water. As she poured that water onto her feet, some of the water trickled some distance away from her feet and sank into the ground. She poured more water. This went further away from her feet and similarly disappeared. She then poured water for a third time. This went furthest away from her feet and similarly disappeared. This incident made a deep impression in her mind. She began to ponder: "Yes, such also is the disappearance of life. Some live a short while and disappear from earth. Others live longer and disappear in middle age. Yet others live to a ripe old age and then disappear. All must sooner or later disappear from this world." She made this incident the basis of her meditation on impermanence. Soon she attained Arahantship and these are the stanzas she uttered:

"One day bathing my feet, I sit and watch
The water as it trickles down the slope.
Thereby I set my heart in steadfastness
As one doth train a horse of noble breed.
Then going to my cell, I take my lamp
And seated on my couch I watch the flame.

Grasping the pin,
I pull the wick right down
Into the oil.
Lo! The Nibbāna of the little lamp!
Emancipation dawns.
My heart is free!"

Inspiration from Bodily Decay

Ambapālī Therī in her lay life was the notorious young woman who lived a life of voluptuous ease. Possessed of great beauty she was sought after by many young nobles of the country. Despite her life of giddy pleasures, the thought came to her one day to build a monastery for the Buddha and his Order. Later, happening to listen to the preaching of the Dhamma by her own son, the Vimala Kondañña Thera, she turned a new leaf. She was now growing old and, observing the devastating changes wrought in her own body by advancing age, began to meditate on impermanence, uttering several verses of great pathos of which only a few are quoted here:

"Glossy and black as the down of the bee my curls once clustered;
They with the waste of years are like unto hempen or bark cloth.
Such and not otherwise runs the rune—the word of the Truth-speaker.
Dense as a grove well planted, and comely with comb, pin and parting;
All with the waste of the years dishevelled the fair plaits and fallen.
Such and not otherwise runs the rune—the word of the Truth-speaker.
Sweet was my voice as the bell of the cuckoo through woodlands flitting;
Now with the waste of years broken the music and halting.
Such and not otherwise runs the rune—the word of the Truth-speaker.
Such has this body been.
Now age-weary and weak and unsightly, home of manifold ills;

Old house whence the mortar is dropping.
Such and not otherwise runs the rune—the word of the Truth-speaker."

Gāthās in Admiration of Recluses

The Rohiṇī Therī from her young days had a great admiration for pious recluses, an admiration which never could be understood or appreciated by her father, who regarded them as an idle crowd doing nothing useful. The father would many a time ask this one question—"*Kena te samaṇā piyā?* Why are recluses dear to you?" The delightful stanzas which she uttered by way of reply, she would often recall after attaining Arahantship. Here are some of them:

"For many a day, dear father, have you asked about recluses.
Now will I proclaim their virtues and their wisdom and their work.
Full fain of work are they, no sluggard crew.
The noblest work they do; they drive out lust and hate.
Hence are recluses dear to me.
And when along the village street they go,
At naught they turn to look; incurious they walk.
Hence are recluses dear to me.
They clutch no coin; no gold their hand does take nor silver.
For their needs sufficient yields the day.
Hence are recluses dear to me."

Conclusion

Apart from the poetic excellence of these stanzas, apart from the sublime emotions they engender, and the note of triumphant joy that resounds within them, these stanzas, one and all, can never fail to exert a powerful influence for good on those who read them. That the struggle experienced within oneself between the forces of good and evil can ultimately end in a victory for the good and that when the struggle is over and the mind is freed from the defilements of greed, hatred and delusion the resultant position is one of calm, peace and happiness, is the unmistakable message of these inspired Gāthās. Indeed this message must be most inspiring when we find that these stanzas forcibly direct the reader's mind to the great fact that any little event in life, any incident howsoever trifling, if it is made the object of deep contemplation can uplift the mind to the highest levels of realization. There is thus in these Thera-Therī-Gāthās a definite and powerful message of hope to those who feel that evil is insurmountable, especially in a highly materialistic age as the present when moral values are discounted and worldly considerations reign supreme.

May the Thera-Therī-Gāthās shed their holy influence on the reader and inspire him to take up the struggle against evil with renewed confidence and redoubled vigour and may he someday reach the goal.

The Problem of Sin

as reviewed by a Buddhist

by

P. M. Rao

WHEEL PUBLICATION NO. 136

The Problem of Sin

This essay is an attempt to try to understand the meaning of the verse from the Dhammapada:

> "Abstaining from all sin, cultivating only the good, and the purifying of one's heart, this is the teaching of the Buddhas."[1]

The problem of sin seems to have dogged the human race practically from its infancy. Though the word "sin" has meant different things to different people in different parts of the world and at different times, the mythologies and religions of the world have assigned an important place to the solution of this problem. Buddhists as well as Hindus believe that sin is the result of ignorance and the destruction of the latter is their common aim. Christians, on the other hand, believe that no amount of knowledge, no amount of human effort can make an end of sin; it is something deep and intrinsic and only the grace of God through Christ can wipe it out. The humanist, with religious zeal, regards all antisocial acts as sin. The Marxist looks upon "deviationism" with the horror an Inquisitor might have felt towards heresy. The newer ideologies have only redefined the concept of sin without succeeding in eradicating the sense of sin.

Indeed the problem of sin is essentially the problem of the sense of sin. The latter is entirely independent of the theories of sin. The Hindu, the Buddhist, the humanist and the rank materialist all suffer from the sense of sin as much as the Jew or the Christian. Were it not so, a change of religion or the profession of a new creed could have rid humanity of this problem. But the very existence of the neuroses—disorders of the psyche in the absence of organic disease—forcibly brings to our notice the omnipresence of the sense of sin, or of the sense of guilt as it is usually called by psychoanalysts. It is one of the chief factors encountered by the analyst in the resistance offered by the patient towards the regaining of mental health.[2]

---

1. Dhammapada 183.
2. *An Outline of Psycho-analysis* by Sigmund Freud, Hogarth Press, p. 45.

But there are many people around us who do not appear to have any sense of sin at all. Does this mean that they do not possess it, or have they managed to solve the problem? It is a psychological fact that, as is the case with the neurotics, it may not be consciously felt as a sense of sin at all; instead it may manifest itself as a vague feeling of dissatisfaction, or of loneliness or boredom, from which the "normal" person tries to escape by throwing himself into work, or social activity, or enjoyment of the senses, or by daydreaming, or, as a last resort, by taking refuge in sleep. Thus the normal man's method of solving the problem is to ignore it. But to camouflage it or to ignore it is not to solve it.

We shall now try to distinguish the sense of sin from allied notions such as the sense of shame or the sense of guilt. The sense of shame has to do with recollections of antisocial behaviour without ethical overtones; and the sense of guilt has to do with the actual breaking, or with a feeling of responsibility for the breaking, of the moral laws recognised by the individual as a member of the society in which he lives. Both these feelings are based on overt acts and therefore directly related to actuality. The sense of sin is essentially different from both of these because it may not be related to actuality; it also does not depend on the beliefs held by the individual or by the society to which he belongs, and it may exist without its existence being recognised as such by the person who has it, as we have already pointed out. Its manifestation may be an intense feeling of loneliness in the midst of society, an intense dissatisfaction in the midst of plenty and a vague restlessness when you ought to be at peace; and its effect on the person may be to drive him into activity or to take refuge in daydreaming or, at the other extreme, to neurosis, insanity, crime or suicide.

No wonder that so elusive a feeling, so varied in its manifestations should have engaged the attention of the priests and medical men through the ages. There is evidence to show that, 1500 years ago, Amerindian tribes inhabiting present-day Latin America suffered from the same sort of neuroses and psychoses as modern man: the affective, schizophrenic, obsessive-compulsive and psychopathic. If it is accepted that a feeling of guilt is an important factor underlying most, if not all, of these afflictions, then an enquiry into its origins becomes interesting.

The first condition for the arising of the sense of sin is that peculiar function of the mind known as the conscience. It approves of some of our actions and condemns some others. A common view is that it is something given to us by a higher power to guide us, and that we can never go wrong if we follow its dictates. But it is not quite convincing to us at all times. The conscience sometimes condemns us for a passing thought, not only for completed acts. In our practical lives we would think it unjust to condemn a person for thinking murderous thoughts and we would consider anyone who supports such "thought control" as unrealistic and dictatorial. The conscience is essentially unrealistic and dictatorial; and the more dictatorial and unrealistic it is the greater will be the sense of sin.

The second condition for the arising of the sense of sin is a deep inner urge to take pleasure and delight in, and, above all, to approve of, the very thought or deed that the conscience condemns. This coexistence of condemnation and approval is what gives the sense of sin that peculiar intensity.

We can illustrate the hollowness of the claims of the conscience to guide us and also its irrationality by means of an example. You see a half-starved bullock trying to pull a heavily laden cart and the driver twisting its tail and whipping it mercilessly. Suddenly your anger flames forth, and, if you are impulsive, you pull the whip out of the hand of the driver and whip him as mercilessly as he had whipped the bullock. Doing this gives you a strange satisfaction and you explain to yourself that your action was motivated by righteous indignation. But if you analyse your action dispassionately you will notice that you derived as much pleasure in whipping the driver as the driver did in whipping the bullock. If you carry out the analysis still further, you discover that you found as much pleasure in the pain of the bullock as the driver himself and you felt an inner urge, demanding immediate satisfaction, to emulate the driver. Your action in whipping the driver was a clever move on your part to satisfy your inner urge as well as the conscience at the same time.

This example not only demonstrates the fallibility and irrationality of the conscience but also brings out one of the most important aspects of the sense of sin—its ability to masquerade as virtue. They used to say of the self-righteous Puritans that they condemned men not so much for their sins as for the pleasure these men got from the sinning; what must have made their condemnation so virulent was the fact that in the depths of their hearts they approved of the very sins they condemned. If you are a professed saint and you have been ill-used by your enemies, you are constrained by your profession from retaliating; but the desire to retaliate persists and the conscience is aware of it. So one recourse is to seeing visions, such as those described in Revelation 6–9 & 10 of the Holy Bible in which martyr-saints, who, when on earth, had long-suffering as the badge of their sainthood, actually plead with God to avenge their blood. Thus saint as well as sinner has been dogged by this sense of sin and has felt the need to assuage it.

Now let us turn to the various methods employed through the ages for tackling this problem of the sense of sin. The earliest attempts known in India were those of the Vedic Aryans. At that time Varuṇa was worshipped as the supreme deity and as Dr. Radhakrishnan remarks: "In almost all the hymns to Varuṇa we find prayers for the forgiveness of sin, filled with confessions of guilt and repentance, which show that the Aryan poets had a sense of the burden of sin and prayer."[3] Later, with the rise in importance of Brahmaṇaspati, sacrifices became more common until, at the time of the Buddha, blood sacrifices had become of supreme importance. But, apparently, all these methods, running the gamut from simple prayers through elaborate ritualism to blood sacrifices turned out to be only temporary palliatives for the sense of sin. People began to look out for new solutions to the old problem.

The Upanishads, while maintaining an attitude of reverence for the Vedas, made direct mystical experience the basis for their philosophy, which linked the identity of the individual self with the Universal Self. This view, especially in its Advaita form, has had great influence on thinkers in India as well as in the West. But if the individual self is in fact identical with the Universal Self, you cannot escape the inevitable corollary that all morality is refuted and that our moral sense is based on an illusion.

Many have been the arguments brought in support of the Vedantic view of consciousness, but the aim here is not to discuss that view—rather it is to investigate consciousness at a level where

3. *Indian Philosophy*, by Dr. S. Radhakrishnan, pp. 77–78.

distinctions between good and evil are no longer perceived. Our focus is not the transcending of good and evil but the transcending of the distinction between good and evil.

Of special interest to us here are the six other systems of philosophy that existed at the time of the Buddha. In the Sutta Piṭaka they are described one after another as if the Buddha was only interested in presenting to us a catalogue of the non-brahmanical systems of his time. But if we look at them more carefully we can discern a common thread running through all of them, namely, attempts to present solutions to the problem of sin. We shall, therefore, try to probe into the motives that might have inspired the six philosophers to propound their theories and methods.

Pūraṇa Kassapa seems to have realised the part played by the conscience in building up the sense of sin and also the belief that went with it, namely, that good actions have good results and evil actions have evil results. So he sought to undermine this belief and hence to cut out the root-cause of the sense of sin by teaching that if anyone kills, steals, commits adultery or speaks falsehood, no sin is committed, and, similarly, that if one practises good deeds through charity, love and compassion, no merit is acquired.

Makkhali Gosāla realised the importance of another aspect of the sense of sin: the word "sin" is significant only if a sense of responsibility for one's actions goes with it. He believed that if men could be taught that it is foolish to believe in personal responsibility for actions for the simple reason that we are only toys in the hands of fate then the problem of sin is solved. His teaching is called *saṃsārasuddhi* or purification through the round of rebirths. According to this, everyone, the sage as well as the fool, the saint as well as the sinner, goes through a definite number of rebirths, at the end of which all, without exception, will attain to the end of the miseries of life. Accordingly, you could behave as you pleased, telling yourself, "It was all predestined."

Ajita Kesakambali took his stand on pure materialism. He felt that it was a stupid notion that living beings had a special status different from that of inorganic matter. He taught that organic as well as inorganic things were made of the four elements, and when one thinks one has killed a living being, or committed adultery, all that has happened is that one group of four elements has reacted against another group of four elements. All this fuss about sin was really a fuss about nothing.

Pakudha Kaccāyana worked out another ingenious scheme to explain away the sense of sin. He taught that every living being was composed of seven elements: the usual four elements and, in addition, ease, disease and the life-principle. The specialty of this scheme lies in the view that not only is each element eternal but that each of them is completely independent of the others and can never act against the others. Thus when you think that you are killing someone you are really causing no harm to anyone at all, for how can you cause any change in eternal unchanging elements?

Sañjaya Belaṭṭhiputta is described in the Suttas as dull-witted and an "Eel-wriggler." His was a system of complete scepticism. He noted that it is a fact that a human being is not content, like the lower animals, to merely react to his environment; he needs a set of beliefs on which to base his world view as well as the norms needed as guides to action. While, on the one hand, this has raised him far above the other animals, on the other, it has given him that sense of sin which appears to act as a drag on his progress. Hence Sañjaya taught his followers to be sceptical with regard to every kind of belief, hoping thereby to destroy the foundation of the sense of sin.

The above five systems thus taught a change in beliefs as a solution to the problem of sin. But, as has already been pointed out at the beginning of this essay, a mere change in beliefs is utterly inadequate as a solution. The Nigaṇṭhas (whose successors are the present-day Jains) realised this and therefore taught that we can make an end of sin through self-discipline. It required of its votaries high ethical ideals and strict and rigorous self-discipline. The Buddha pointed out that such a system is workable only if we knew definitely that we had committed sins in our past lives, that we knew the exact amount of sin we had committed, exactly how much sin has been worn out by discipline and how much is still left over. That criteria for these were never worked out by the Jains is shown by the fact that to this day they expect their saints to fast to death carrying the burden of the sense of sin to the grave.

It might be considered an oversimplification to treat all philosophical systems, as we have done, as if they were expressly invented for the purpose of removing the sense of sin. It is also a fact that one follows a religion as a matter of tradition, or that one accepts a new philosophy because it provides practically workable solutions to social and political problems, or perhaps because it appeals to one's aesthetic sense or to one's reason. But even after accepting all this, if one gets a deeper and more abiding satisfaction at all from one's religion or philosophy it will be if, in addition, it provides a solution to the problem of sin. Take the case of a person suffering from a dire disease and a Christian faith healer comes along and miraculously cures him. He gives up his former religion and embraces Christianity out of faith. He is happier than before in his new religion and if it happens that his former religion had insisted, as in Buddhism, that one cannot escape from the results of one's actions, then a fresh cause for a deeper satisfaction for him, in his new religion, will be the teaching about grace and forgiveness of sins. Thus any philosophy of a general type which includes a world view is sure to have an aspect dealing with the problem of sin.

We shall now briefly look at the problem of sin in the West. The result of the impact of Christianity was to intensify the sense of sin. It has already been shown that the conscience tends to identify the thought with the deed. This tendency was endorsed and intensified by Jesus in his Sermon on the Mount: "But I say unto you, that whosoever looketh on a woman to lust after her hath committed adultery with her already in his heart. And if thy right eye offend thee, pluck it out, and cast it from thee: for it is profitable for thee that one of thy members should perish, and not thy whole body should be cast into hell." This intensification of the sense of sin together with the perverse satisfaction that the conscience gets when anybody at all is punished for wickedness led to witch-hunting and the horrors of the Inquisition. The laity could, temporarily at least, alleviate their sense of sin by the enjoyment of the "holy" satisfaction of watching the tortures of the condemned. The monks, who could not take part in the actual tortures, turned instead against themselves and practised flagellation and other forms of self-torture.

With the rise of scientific materialism, however, these methods of satisfying the conscience became outdated. The primitive pleasure that was derived by regarding the mentally afflicted as wicked had to give place to compassion for them. From this arose a greater awareness of mental afflictions—from the mildest neuroses to insanity and even to crime—as curable diseases. The struggle in men's hearts between what they wished to do and what they felt they ought not to do came up again, but now from the point of view of mental health. The psychotherapists have had to develop theories and devise methods for the treatment of the neuroses and other forms of mental ill-health. As many of the neuroses are directly traceable to what we have described as the sense of sin, it would be instructive to see what modern scientific theories have to say about the problem. We shall look into the theories of Freud as a typical case and try to see to what extent they succeeded and to what extent they failed in their objective.

According to Freud, the human personality may be divided into three provinces—the Id, the Ego and the Super Ego. The Id, whose field of activity is entirely in the unconscious, contains everything that is present at birth, that is fixed in the constitution and, above all, includes the instincts—which are basically two: Eros (the unifying instinct) and the Death instinct (or the destructive instinct). The Id works on the pleasure principle and always desires instinctual satisfaction whenever an internal tension is felt. The Id is never in direct contact with reality. Mediating between it and the external world is the Ego, which works on the reality principle. It decides whether the demands of the Id are to be satisfied at all or postponed according to the necessities of self-preservation in the real world.

The most important aspect of the personality for our purpose here is the Super Ego: it forms when the child is about five years old and takes the place of the parents and later of the teachers and other influential persons in society; but the Super Ego is much stricter and harsher in its judgments than the real parents or teachers and is ready to punish the Ego not only for actual acts but also for its thoughts and its unexecuted intentions. This shows that the Super Ego, like the Id, is not in direct contact with reality. The Ego has to try to steer a course between the demands of the Id, the threats of the Super Ego and the necessities of the real world. In normal people, if the Ego decides to disagree with the Id or the Super Ego, it takes advantage of the fact that both of them are not in direct contact with reality—it tries to placate the former by offering it substitute objects in place of the ones demanded by it and the latter by the method of rationalisation. The example of the bullock cart driver illustrates both: the punishment meted out to the driver satisfies the aggressiveness of the Id as well as the moral indignation of the Super Ego.

When the Ego is weak or the Super Ego cruel and harsh, mental and psychosomatic diseases make their appearance; this is where the psychotherapist steps in and uses his methods to turn the patient into a normal person. A normal person is supposed to be one who is well-adjusted to society—but if the sole aim of each member of a society were to be well-adjusted to it, society would stagnate. Great men could alter society for the better precisely because they were not adjusted to it. Besides, society is not monolithic; it contains many strata and each stratum has its own norms of morality and behaviour. So if any society wishes to maintain its stability, it cannot afford to be more moral or less moral than necessary for its stability. If those in charge of the sanctions behind society insist on a higher standard of morality, vice goes underground and leads to corrupt practices—as an example we may take the failure of prohibition in the USA and elsewhere. On the other hand, if the standard of morality is lowered, as for instance in persons in politics or public life, it can only lead to disruption of society, rebellion and chaos.

The attitude of society towards moral standards has, therefore, always remained flexible. Take the case of the institutions of marriage and prostitution. When a high standard of morality was expected within the marital relationship, prostitution was not only countenanced but encouraged. But a lowering of the intra-marital standards of morality has gone hand in hand with a discouragement of the institution of prostitution. Becoming adjusted to this society is essentially the same as coming to terms with our lower self. The modern solution to the problem is, therefore, the same as that of the five materialist philosophers at the time of the Buddha: sex relations are to be freer and the aggressive instincts are either to be channelled into the field of sport or to be used to work up hysteria against an enemy. A natural consequence of this attitude has been to regard attempts at overcoming the passions as signs of mental disease.

A reflection of this modern trend can be seen in the fields of literature and education. In James Hilton's *Lost Horizon* a simple method for attaining sainthood as practised in the earthly paradise at Shangri-La is described. With the help of a powerful herb the span of life is extended to more than three hundred years, and the aspirant to sainthood, after a century or more of self-indulgence in all the passions, finds the passions dropping off by themselves—he becomes a saint by virtue of being too old to have any passions and of being too young yet to die. Similarly, in the story *Siddhartha* by the German Nobel Laureate Hermann Hesse, a young man falls in love with a beautiful courtesan and then makes his love for her the basis for the highest spiritual attainment.

This general movement towards a slackening of the barriers against free indulgence of the passions has been helped by the studies of the anthropologists. In the schoolroom and the college campus, boys and girls have been encouraged to discuss sex freely; learned lecturers have taught them to appreciate the fact that among the Melanesians the elders trained their children in the art of self-abuse, and that in Samoa bedrooms have no walls. Thus the solution seems to be to make the Super Ego less harsh by making freer sex acceptable to society. But how far has this method succeeded?

The direct result of the labours of the scientifically minded social reformers appears to have been the rise of the "beat" generation. The chief articles of faith of these angry young men are an insistence on free sex experience and the enjoyment of tabloid mysticism provided by LSD and marijuana. The latest to join them are the micro-boppers, children between the ages of eight and twelve, all boasting of their sex experiences. This close association between free sex and the marijuana pipe dreams should remind psychoanalysts of what they must have often encountered in their professional practice: when the Ego is hard-pressed by an intolerant Super Ego, the former may choose one of two ways of escape—it may overthrow the Super Ego, as in mania or hypomania, or it may withdraw from reality and thus create an inner world where a Super Ego is unnecessary, as in schizophrenia. The behaviour of the "beat" generation should strongly remind them of the schizophrenics. The culmination of the reform movement seems to have been reached now when it becomes difficult to distinguish between those within the mental institutions and those outside them.

Thus we have shown that the deep sense of evil in our hearts cannot be removed by prayers and incantations, or by sacrifices, or by the grace of a deity, or by changing one's beliefs, or by self-discipline, or by adjusting to society, or by changing the social norms. The final verdict of Freud on this problem was: "It seems as though the activity of the other agencies of the mind is able only to modify the pleasure principle but not to nullify it; and it remains a question of the greatest theoretical importance, and one that has not yet been answered, when and how it is ever possible for the pleasure principle to be overcome. The consideration that the pleasure principle requires a reduction, or perhaps ultimately the extinction, of the tension of the instinctual needs [that is, a state of Nirvana] leads to problems that are still unexamined in the relations between the pleasure principle and the two primal forces, Eros and the death instinct."[4]

Is the prospect so bleak? Can no way be found? We can come to a definite conclusion only after a study of what Buddhism has to say in the matter. In Buddhism it is the Way and actual practice that are all-important; the psychological notions with which we shall begin only serve to help us appreciate the validity of the methods.

According to Buddhism, the personality of a human being at any moment is the sum total of all the instincts and tendencies that he was born with and of what he has made of himself up to that moment. At the same time it is taught that consciousness (*citta*) is essentially pure and bright and it is only due to adventitious circumstances that it becomes impure; and these adventitious circumstances are our actions, which are guided by what are known as the *hetus* or root-causes. The morally good roots are *alobha* (greedlessness), *adosa* (hatelessness), and *amoha* (non-delusion). The morally bad roots are *lobha* (greed), *dosa* (hatred), and *moha* (delusion).

But to assess the validity of the method taught by the Buddha for tackling the problem of sin we must first understand how we came by our instincts and tendencies at birth. The type of consciousness at birth is called the *vipāka* (resultant) consciousness and is the result of our actions in the previous life. This important matter is better explained by Ven. J. Kashyap:[5]

4. Freud, op. cit., p. 68.

5. Taken from *The Abhidhamma Philosophy* by Ven. J. Kashyap, Vol. I, p. 7.

"The bad *hetus* ... are the animal qualities in man. They come as fits of instinctive impulses. Under their influence, they make a man lose his self-consciousness and reasoning faculty.

"The *vipāka* (resultant) of immoral consciousness, therefore, is a very dull and feeble consciousness, eminently instinctive. It must be *ahetuka* (without root-causes), for it is too feeble to be rooted in the *hetus*.

"The *vipāka* of a moral consciousness, with weak *hetus*, is also a feeble consciousness, and therefore *ahetuka*.

"The good *hetus—alobha*, *adosa*, *amoha*—on the other hand, are the higher rational qualities in a man. One who develops these in himself is able to overcome his instinctive side, and make his consciousness more moral and rational.

"The *vipāka* of strong moral consciousness, therefore, is a consciousness as strong and good as the types of moral consciousness themselves, accompanied by the *hetus* (*sahetuka*). It is *sahetuka* strong enough to be rooted in the *hetus*."

From the above analysis it becomes clear that the *vipāka* of strong immoral consciousness is a feeble, non-rational, instinctive type of consciousness, whereas the *vipāka* of a strong moral consciousness is strong enough to be rooted in the *hetus*. Thus according to the explanation offered by Buddhism, the consciousness of animals, and of some human beings like those who are born idiots, are all too feeble to be rooted in the *hetus*. The reason is that the former are the *vipāka* of strong immoral consciousness and the latter of feeble moral consciousness—hence both of them are morally neutral.

If we accept the above analysis as convincing, we can try to imagine how the human consciousness might have developed during evolution, although Buddhism, interested as it is in spiritual evolution in the vertical direction, has nothing to say about biological evolution in the horizontal direction. Perhaps in primitive human society the consciousness was mainly instinctive and therefore not rooted in the *hetus*. These children of Nature might have loved and fought and mated and died essentially like the lower animals; but their consciousness was human and therefore we might be able to imagine what sort of world they saw around them. It must have been a world of pure experience, of wonder and awe and terror, of strong but short lived loves and hatreds and yet devoid of notions of good and evil. It must have been a world of concrete things, alive and tangible: a non-rational world withal, yet man must have felt completely at home in such a world enjoying not only its pleasures but also its pains. Indeed there must have been moments in his life when he felt a one-ness with the whole universe and with all the living things in it. Perhaps it is this world, which Aldous Huxley described as "a blissful sub-rational eternity on the hither side of good and evil,"[6] that we perceive in our mystic moments when we are temporarily dissociated from the rational parts of our natures. This also probably explains why the mystic experience is so much more delectable and appears more real than the world of actuality.

But fully developed man is essentially a rational creature. While our instinctive nature recognises only experience, our rational nature is dissatisfied with it and wants to take an objective view of things. This is what we mean by "being aware of things." This objectivity extends even to his subjective world—when he uses this faculty, he is said to have "self- awareness." As pointed out by Ven. J. Kashyap, as our instinctive impulses rooted in the bad *hetus* come up, they oppose our self-awareness and rational faculty and try to swamp them. It is our rational faculty that opposes and tries to curb the instinctual drives. Thus the specific teaching of Buddhism is that, apart from our rational faculty, there is no separate entity equivalent to our everyday notion of a conscience. It is of this rational faculty that the Buddha spoke when he taught:

> "There is no secrecy in this world when one has committed sin. For, your own self, O man, knows what is truth and what is falsity!"[7]

The objective aspect of the rational faculty (perhaps by reason of its objectivity) creates in us a strange dissatisfaction with the world. All its loves and hates and fears which appear to us to be so essential and to form the very core of our being are seen to be insubstantial and non-essential in our truly rational moments. But our thirst for life is so great that, in our ignorance, we misunderstand this dissatisfaction. Instead of realising that this

---

6. *Perennial Philosophy*, 1961, p. 175.

7. AN 3:4.

feeling of dissatisfaction is the result of an insight into truth, we turn our rational faculty to attempting to drown the feeling. This always takes the form of some kind of activity of the body or of the mind or of both. In our wrong-headedness (*ayoniso manasikāra*), we ask (if we are metaphysically inclined): "Was I in ages past? Was I not in ages past? What was I then? How was I then? From what did I pass to what?"—and similarly "he questions about the future and the present and comes to the conclusion that he has a self, or that he has no self, or that his self is eternal," etc. (MN 2).

This inability to be alone with oneself is a sure indication of our escapist tendency. If a man goes to sleep because he is bored and not because his body or mind is in need of rest—he is an escapist. If a man throws himself into work or social activity or sense-enjoyment because he cannot do without them—he is an escapist. If a man practises austerities and tortures himself ceaselessly—he is an escapist. If a man has been successful in his worldly life, and though he has everything that he wants he suffers from an intolerable boredom and frequents the parlours of the psychiatrists—he is an escapist.

All these are the results of misapplication of our rational faculty. If we were to apply it properly (*yoniso manasikāra*) we would arrive at two of the truths about the unsatisfactoriness of the world, namely: 1. the world of experience cannot give us true and lasting satisfaction; and 2. the dissatisfaction is due to the fact that, in spite of frustrations, we continue to expect this world to give us satisfaction—in other words, our frustrated desires are the cause of our dissatisfaction. If it happens that one is also a follower of the Buddha, one learns two more truths: that there is such a thing as putting an end to this dissatisfaction; and that there is a way to its attainment. These are the only supreme truths in the world; the other truths about which religious people dispute and quarrel are the offspring of their imaginations.

If we now apply our rational faculty to the subjective sphere, we arrive at a slightly different set of results. The average unregenerate person in his spontaneous moments feels the urge to go after and take whatever he wants, to attack or sometimes even to kill any person who comes in the way of the satisfaction of his desires, to satisfy his sexual appetite whenever it arises. But when he turns his rational faculty on to these urges, he sees himself in relation to other living beings and realises that these urges are for self-satisfaction at the expense of others, and so he feels a strange dissatisfaction with them. On the other hand, refraining from lustful actions, refraining from taking what is not given, refraining from onslaught on creatures, and refraining from untruth gives him a strange satisfaction (*avippaṭisāra*, or absence of regret or remorse). But still he allows his desires to rule over him; and instead he turns to society and its sanctions to regulate them. He gets society to approve of murder so long as it is done for the good of the tribe to which he belongs and is practised on those who do not belong to it. He gets society to recognise the institution of marriage to regulate sexual relations, and to institute rules for the recognition of the ownership of property. Many other social institutions follow.

As soon as society takes over the functions that rightly belong to the individual's rational faculty, the foundation is laid for what we call conscience—the Freudian Super Ego. Parents and teachers are no longer true guides but are only representatives of society. Conscience, like society, is an attempt at a compromise between the truth as revealed by our rational faculty and the need to satisfy our urges. Hence the conscience is neither rational like our rational faculty nor non-rational like our instincts, but irrational. Besides, it arrogates to itself the punitive functions of society and makes life miserable for the individual. It is of this conscience of ours that the Blessed One speaks when he tells us:

> "They who feel shame where is no cause for shame and they who feel no shame when they ought to be ashamed—both enter the downward path following false views.
>
> "They who fear when there is no cause for fear and they who do not fear when they ought to fear—both enter the downward path following false views.
>
> "They who discern evil where there is no evil and they who see no evil in what is evil—both enter the downward path following false views." (Dhp 316–18)

It is this irrational conscience of ours that is unable to distinguish between thought and action. The rational way of looking at this relation between thought and action can be seen from the very first two verses of the Dhammapada:

> "(The mental) natures are the result of what we have thought, are chieftained by our thoughts, are made up of our thoughts. If a man speaks or acts with an evil thought, sorrow follows him (as a consequence) even as the wheel follows the foot of the drawer [i.e., the ox which draws the cart].
>
> "(The mental) natures are the result of what we have thought, are chieftained by our thoughts, are made up of our thoughts. If a man speaks or acts with a pure thought, happiness follows him (in consequence) like a shadow that never leaves him."

The following points are to be noted from a study of the verses above:

1. What we are at any moment can be judged from the thoughts that are passing through our minds at that moment as well as by all the thoughts we have thought before that moment and thus permitted to modify and mould our characters.
2. A good or evil result follows when an action initiated by a good or evil thought is completed.

The Abhidhamma explains the evils of killing and of sexual misconduct as:[8]

> "The following five conditions are necessary to complete the evil of killing: (i) a living being, (ii) knowledge that it is a living being, (iii) intention of killing, (iv) effort to kill, and (v) consequent death.
>
> "Four conditions are necessary to complete the evil of sexual misconduct: namely, (i) the thought to enjoy, (ii) consequent effort, (iii) means to gratify, and (iv) gratification."[9]

We can compare this broadly realistic attitude with the teaching of Jesus already quoted that "whosoever looks on a woman to lust after her has already committed adultery with her in his heart."

---

8. From *The Buddha and His Teachings*, by Ven. Narada Thera, pp. 373– 374.
9. Buddhism certainly recognises purely mental acts, but it does not make the mistake of equating, say, a passing thought of ill-will (e.g., rising anger immediately restrained [cf. Dhp 222]), a constant dwelling on thoughts of ill-will not leading to overt action (*vyāpāda*), and a murder deliberately planned and executed.

Though it is doubtful whether, in practice, any priest was actually unfrocked for thinking adulterous thoughts, this teaching has undoubtedly given the Christian a harsh and intolerant conscience.

A further consequence of the rational attitude Buddhism has towards sin is that sin is not considered as something wicked and intrinsic, but as something that has arisen in consequence of a misapplication of our rational faculty. In other words, it is something born of ignorance, a foolish act (*akusala*), and the sinner is a fool (*bāla*).

From this account of the Buddhist explanation of the arising of sin, are we in a better position to solve the problem of the eradication of the sense of sin? Is it enough if we listen to the voice of our rational faculty, lead blameless lives and train our minds to think only good thoughts? Training ourselves to think good thoughts certainly produces in our minds a deep satisfaction and an atmosphere of peace and joy; but, as has already been pointed out, the inner core of our being is made up of our instinctive urges and is entirely non-rational. No amount of rational thinking and the doing of good deeds can in any way modify or even affect our inner core. It is like arguing with an idiot or an insane person. It is for this reason that the Blessed One scoffed at the Nigaṇṭhas for believing in the perfectionist doctrine that by austerities and discipline we can make an end of evil (MN 101). Can it be done by attaining the *jhānas*? There is the belief, held even today, that in a *jhānic* state one is "in tune with the Infinite." But the Blessed One pointed out, as in the *Sallekha Sutta*, that the *jhānas* and *āruppas* are only easeful and peaceful states. The Buddhist analysis, up to this point, appears to support the Freudian thesis that the pleasure principle of the Id can only be modified but not nullified.

But the Buddha has shown the world a way of nullifying the pleasure principle. To understand this better, let us consider how even ordinary people are sometimes able to give up powerful habits without putting up a struggle. Take the case of a young man of good family, well-educated and of excellent manners—but fond of the cruel sport of hunting animals for pleasure. All attempts to persuade him to give it up had proved fruitless. His appeal to materialistic theories in support of his actions showed that there was in him a cruel streak that would not be denied satisfaction. One day he went with his gun to hunt as usual, carefully stalked a deer and shot it down. He saw it fall and went forward to take possession of the kill. But when he came closer he saw that the buckshot had ripped open the side of the deer and a dead foetus was hanging out. The deer was still alive but did not make the usual struggle to escape. Instead, it lifted up its head and looked at its enemy; in that look the young man saw not a hint of terror but a look of indescribable sorrow and almost of pity. Then the deer dropped back dead. The young man threw down his gun and went home in a high fever. He was confined to bed for a month. On full recovery it was discovered that not a hint of that cruel streak that was formerly in him was in evidence. What caused this sudden transformation of character? To explain it in terms of conditioned reflexes or as the result of a sudden alteration in the centre of emotional excitement, as William James would put it, is to appeal to dogma on insufficient grounds.

Soviet Russia swore by the method of conditioned reflexes for the cure of the neuroses, but, if recent newspaper reports are to be believed, attempts are being made to introduce Freudian methods. In the USA, where there were no restrictions on the methods employed, a conference of psychotherapists condemned the attitude of the psychiatrists in trying to treat the neuroses as if they were diseases and recommended persons of the stature of gurus to help the afflicted. All this goes to show that no infallible and completely convincing theory of the neuroses has yet been worked out. Without being dogmatic, therefore, we shall have a look at the important aspects of the above case of a permanent change of character.

First, it was an intense experience. Secondly, the experience was coupled with the realisation of a truth, namely, that there is no essential difference between the killing of a human being and the killing of an animal. And, thirdly, the urge to kill had been completely wiped out, a feat that no amount of conscious struggle could have accomplished.

This qualitative and permanent transformation of character we shall refer to as "transcendence"—provided the quality affected by the transformation is an inborn one and not one acquired in this life. It has already been pointed out that our inborn tendencies belong to the sphere of the non-rational and that they can understand and be at home with experience and experience alone.

This is the reason why a realisation of the truth alone is unable to affect our inner core. Experience alone is equally powerless, since, to our inner core, one experience is as good as any other—it enjoys them all. It is only when that peculiar combination of truth and experience that we can call "experiencing of truth" takes place that our inner core is transformed and transcendence takes place.

The path taught by the Buddha included the way of transcendence. A clear distinction has been drawn in the teaching between the mundane (ordinary) and supramundane (transcendent) aspects of the path—the former for the overcoming of evil moral habits acquired in this life and the latter for the transcending of the innate tendencies. The supramundane path is attainable only by the method of transcendence, and that too, only when the truth experienced is the Truth of Suffering. In the mundane path, certain traits of character which depend on our innate tendencies may be transformed by this "ordinary" method—but the process is not irreversible if the truth experienced is not the sole ultimate truth, namely, the Fourfold Truth of Suffering. Irrational fears, for instance, do not yield to rational thought: it is useless telling ourselves that these fears are groundless. The Bodhisatta's conquest of irrational fears is thus described in the *Bhaya-bherava Sutta*:

> "I would seek out haunted shrines in woodland or forest or under tutelary trees and there abide in those awesome and grisly scenes—perchance there to discover fear and dread ... As I abode there, either an animal passed along, or a peacock knocked off a branch, or the wind rustled the fallen leaves, so that I thought this must surely be fear and dread coming. Thought I: 'Wherefore am I doing nothing but await the coming of fear and dread? Come as they may, I, just as they find me, will even so overcome them without changing my posture for them.'
>
> "I was pacing to and fro when fear and dread came upon me; I continued to pace to and fro till I had overcome them, neither standing still nor lying down." (MN 4)

Here it is important to note that the Bodhisatta did not change his posture; to have changed it would have meant effort and struggle against the oncoming fear. Without struggling, without opposing, the experience of fear was transformed into experience of the truth that there was nothing to be afraid of, that the noise that set off the dread was only due to the rustle of leaves in the wind or due to a twig being broken off by a peacock. With this realisation the Bodhisatta was able to transcend his irrational fears.

When we grow from childhood through adolescence into manhood, many changes take place. We give up playing with the toys of childhood; we also cease feeling some of those childish fears that appeared to be so overwhelming when we were children. If we could but remember them, there must have been moments in our adolescence (a period when we become aware of new and unfamiliar emotions), when we realised the silliness of playing with toys and the stupidity of allowing ourselves to be overwhelmed by those childish fears. We may think that a real transcendence has taken place, but the hallmark of transcendence is that, normally, there is no reversibility of the process. We have to make this qualified statement because, according to Buddhism, only transformations based on the Fourfold Truth of Suffering are absolutely irreversible, while those based on mundane truths are sometimes reversible: it is a well-known fact that during hypnotic trance, regression to earlier states is possible.

Psychoanalysts are aware that many of the neuroses arise out of the inability to transcend certain childish attitudes, and the analyst attempts to make the patient realise this fact. But very often, a mere realisation, in the sense of a purely intellectual acceptance of the truth, does not effect the cure. It must come not as a realisation but as a revelation, a flash—the truth, in other words, must be experienced. But the psychoanalyst stops as soon as the patient is transformed from an immature adult into a mature one without realising that an adult, with his hates and lusts and above all with that sense of sin, is still a child.

Transcendence is not a contradiction or suppression of an existent state but is the attainment of a new dimension which cannot be explained in terms of the conditions within that state. A study of the characteristics of transcendence reveals some remarkable facts. A few years ago we would have found it easy to declare in what sense man transcended the machine. But since the growth of cybernetic science and the construction of life-imitating machines, even scientists, in fact scientists more than others, have insisted that there is no clear-cut line dividing man from the machine, that both are equally pseudo-purposive.

The Buddha was critical of such deterministic views. He said: "To those who fall back on something done previously as the essential reason, there comes to be no desire or exertion connected with the idea that this is to be done or this is not to be done" (AN 3:7). He wished to point out that sectarians who held this deterministic view of actions and their results thought that thereby they could shut their eyes to the need to have to make choices in this world.

In man, the inevitable result of self-awareness is that we see ourselves in relation to the rest of the universe. The first result of this is the realisation that we are bound; to be aware that one is bound is to realise the existence of an infinite number of problems to be solved; to realise the existence of problems is to engage in effort to solve them—this is to engage in a truly purposeful activity of solving the problems. The machine, on the other hand, has no self-awareness, has no realisation that it is bound and therefore has no problems, though it may be able to solve them faster than man. The machine solves the problems provided by man with the help of the pseudo-purposive machinery built into it by man. Was it not Engels who pointed out that "to know one is bound is to be free"? It is because of his self-awareness that man is an economic animal, an ethical animal, a political animal, an animal aware of the meaning of history and an animal capable of creating newer and ever newer sciences.

With the insight we have gained into transcendence, we can say that to realise that we are bound is to transcend the mere machine, to recognise the existence of the problem of sin is to transcend the mere animal, to experience the Truth of Suffering (i.e., of the unsatisfactoriness of the world of experience) is to transcend mere man.

Thus the solution to the problem of sin is its transcendence. The supreme importance of direct experience in Buddhism is to be seen from the preponderance of the many words in it related to the word *passati* or "to see." Direct experience is always described as a "seeing," perhaps because visual experience is the highest form of direct sense-experience and perhaps also because most of our knowledge of the world is acquired through it. The Buddha himself is called *samanta-cakkhu* (all-seeing), the Dhamma is *ehi-*

passika (come and see), the first flash of insight into the truth is called *dhamma-cakkhu* (the eye of truth), the contemplation on the impermanence, unsatisfactoriness and not-self-ness of worldly things is described as *anupassanā* (observing), spiritual insight is called *vipassanā* (seeing clearly) and the final act directly leading to Arahantship is *jānāti passati* (to know and to see):

> "He realises as absolute truth: 'This is suffering, this is the arising of suffering, this is the cessation of suffering and this is the Way to the cessation of suffering.' He realises as absolute truth: 'These are the *āsavas*, this is the arising of the *āsavas*, this is the cessation of the *āsavas* and this is the Way to the cessation of the *āsavas*.' From knowing and seeing thus, his mind is freed from the *āsava* of sense-desires, from the *āsava* of love of continued existence, from the *āsava* of ignorance—and from being freed arises the knowledge that he is free." (DN 2)

The purpose of this knowing and seeing, of "the experiencing of truth" as we have called it, is to transcend the latent tendencies known in the Pāli language as *anusayas*, which form the non-rational inner core of our being. The various expedients we think up in order to escape from facing the Truth of Suffering have their origin in these *anusayas*: our love for metaphysical theories from *diṭṭhānusaya*, love for scepticism from *vicikicchānusaya*, the desire for sense-enjoyment from *kāmarāgā-nusaya*, taking delight in hurting others from *paṭighānusayā*, pride and self-righteousness from *mānānusaya*, all activities undertaken for sheer love and attachment for continued existence from *bhavarāgānusaya*, and all the other activities that we undertake through ignorance and confused thinking from *avijjānusaya*.

The way of transcendence is known in the scriptures as *lokuttara magga* (Supramundane Path) and its purpose is only to transcend the *anusayas*. Transcending all the *anusayas* may not be possible at one time and hence four stages of transcendence have been described in the Dhamma. The first two *anusayas* are transcended by the Sotāpanna, the next two are attenuated by the Sakadāgāmī and transcended by the Anāgāmi, and the last three are transcended by the Arahat.

To know how transcendence takes place in theory is not enough. There are certain dangers and difficulties inherent in the practical application of the method described below. This can be illustrated from the examples already quoted of the character transformation of the hunter and the Bodhisatta's victory over irrational fears. In the former, the hunter's friends and relatives had constantly been telling him of the wickedness of his ways and this was probably at the back of his mind when he had the experience. Similarly, when the Bodhisatta exposed himself deliberately to the fears in the lonesome forest he was already intellectually convinced of the irrational basis of his fears. Both had the right mental atmosphere at the moment of experience; if the wrong mental atmosphere had been present the results might have been different. Even if one has the right mental atmosphere it might not always be possible to arrange for an experience of the right intensity and at the right moment; or the morbid aspect of the experience might overcome and unbalance the mind.

The Noble Eightfold Path encompasses these contingencies. The very first step is to have the Fourfold Truth of Suffering impressed on the mind; the next step is to remove all those unwholesome tendencies of character that have been acquired by us, in one way or another, throughout our life. The method of this removal is described in the *Sabbāsava Sutta* (MN 2). Those acquired by allowing the mind to dwell upon attractive and repulsive objects are to be removed by self-restraint, those developed through attachment to articles of daily use such as food and clothing are to be removed by using them solely for supporting or protecting the body, those acquired by allowing oneself to be overcome by physical discomforts are to be removed by bearing them with patience, those acquired through evil company are to be removed through shunning it, and those acquired by failure in watching over one's thoughts are to be removed by constant watch over them. This removal of unwholesome tendencies creates in us an atmosphere of deep satisfaction known as *avippaṭisāra* (absence of regret or remorse). This atmosphere is to be deepened by the development of wholesome qualities like loving-kindness, compassion, joy in the happiness of others and equanimity in all circumstances.

If an intense experience is encountered during this stage, there is the possibility of being overcome by the morbid aspect of the situation. In this circumstance, the exercise of watching one's breath calms the mind and helps one to maintain one's equanimity.

Next we come to a step that is specifically Buddhist. This is the development of awareness in all its aspects. We have emphasised that it is in self-awareness that we transcend the mere animal and that it is self-awareness coupled with our rational faculty that makes us realise the Truth of Suffering. Special exercises, therefore, have been worked out for the development of self-awareness in all our daily activities.

These exercises comprise the practice of *vipassanā*—the attempt to experience the Truth of Suffering by means of meditations on the corruptibility of all conditioned things. This can be carried out by the contemplation on the loathsomeness of one's own bodily constituents or, if necessary, by contemplation on the various stages of corruption of a corpse in a cemetery. If, however, one has a special aptitude for what are known as *jhānas* one may develop a subtle state of the mind with which one may attain *yathābhūta ñāṇadassana* (the ability to see things as they are)—with the help of this ability one can see the Truth of Suffering in the ordinary events of life and thus dispense with the need for intensity of experience.

Such, in brief, is the way of transcendence. To close this essay we can do no better than quote from the scriptures and demonstrate two of the most essential points of the Path—1. the proper frame of mind, and 2. the fourfold Truth of Suffering which alone is capable of effecting absolutely irreversible transcendence:

> "And the Exalted One saw Suppabuddha, the leper, sitting in that assembly, and at the sight he thought: 'This one here is of growth to understand Dhamma.' So for the sake of Suppabuddha, the leper, he gave a talk dealing in due order with these topics: on alms-giving, virtue, the heaven world, of the danger, meanness and corruption of sense-desires and the profit of getting free from them.
>
> "And when the Exalted One knew that the heart of Suppabuddha, the leper, was ready, softened, unbiased, elated and believing, then he unfolded those Dhamma teachings which the awakened ones have themselves discovered, namely: suffering, the arising of suffering, the ending of suffering and the way leading to the ending of suffering.
>
> "Then just as a white cloth, free from stain, is ready to receive the dye, even so in Suppabuddha, the leper, as he sat

there in that very seat, arose the pure, stainless Dhamma-sight, the knowledge that whatsoever is of nature to arise, that also is of nature to end."[10]

10. Udāna 5:3, translation by F. L. Woodward.

The Buddhist Wheel Symbol

by

T. B. Karunaratne

WHEEL PUBLICATION NO. 137/138

The Buddhist Wheel Symbol

All ancient religions have in the course of time developed many symbols to express various doctrinal concepts visually. Buddhism does not lag behind in this sphere but in fact has given rise to many new symbols in addition to what it has derived from the common Indian heritage. To these symbols which were adopted from pre-Buddhist India, Buddhism has given new interpretations to suit its own purpose. Of these, the *dhamma-cakka*, the evermoving wheel of law, is the most prominent symbol of the Buddhists.

The Pali commentaries of Sri Lanka refer to a number of wheels recognised by Buddhists. Buddhaghosa mentions *sampatti-cakka*, the wheel of happiness, *lakkhaṇa-cakka*, the wheel symbol on the soles of the Buddha's feet, *rathaṅga-cakka*, the chariot wheel, *iriyāpatha-cakka*, the wheel of movement or postures, *dāna-cakka*, the wheel of liberality, *ratana-cakka*, the ideal wheel of a universal monarch, *dhamma-cakka*, the wheel of law of the Buddha, and *urasi-cakka*, the wheel of torture.[1] To this list Gurulugomi[2] adds *praharaṇa-cakka*, the discus, *asani-cakka*, the wheel of thunderbolt, *dāru-cakka*, the wheelright's wooden wheel, and *saṃsāra-cakka*, the wheel of life. The last mentioned wheel is also known as *bhava-cakka*, the Wheel of Becoming. In our discussion on the iconography of the wheel, universally accepted as the distinctive symbol of Buddhists from very early times, we are concerned mainly with the *ratana-cakka*, the *dhamma-cakka*, the *lakkhaṇa-cakka* and the *saṃsāra-cakka* or the *bhava-cakka*.

The *ratana-*, *dhamma-*, and *lakkhaṇa-cakkas* in their unadorned forms are identical, and are represented in art in the likeness of a chariot wheel (*rathaṅga-cakka*), whereas in their elaborate or perfect forms (*sabbākāraparipūraṃ*) the *ratana-cakka* and the *dhamma-cakka* assume the same form while the *lakkhaṇa-cakka* differs from the former in detail. The *saṃsāra-* or *bhava-cakka*, differing in form as well as in significance, is a later development (see Chapter IV).

1. *Papañcasūdani*, Part 2, p. 27 ff. (P.T.S.).
2. *Dharmapradīpikāva*, ed. by W. Soratha Thera, p. 186.

I. The Ratana-Cakka

The *ratana-cakka*, the ideal wheel, is described as the divine wheel that appears to one who is destined to be a *cakkavatti-rājā*, a universal monarch. In this connection it must be mentioned that the Buddha is considered the spiritual counterpart of a universal monarch. A universal monarch is the ideal layman (*āgārika-ratana*). He is the highest among those who enjoy worldly pleasures (*kāmabhogīnaṃ aggo*). On the other hand, the Buddha is the ideal recluse (*anāgārika-ratana*), the highest among those who have removed the covering of defilements (*vivaṭṭacchadanānaṃ aggo*). Both the Buddha and the universal monarch are possessed of the *mahāpurisa-lakkhaṇa*, the auspicious marks of a Great Being. It is said that a person born with such marks is destined to either be a universal monarch or a Buddha, an Enlightened One, depending on the course of life each one prefers to pursue. A universal monarch is blessed with the seven unique possessions (*satta-ratana*), namely, the ideal wheel (*cakka-ratana*), the ideal elephant (*hatthi-ratana*), the ideal horse (*assa-ratana*), the ideal gem (*maṇi-ratana*), the ideal wife (*itthi-ratana*), the ideal householder (*gahapati-ratana*), and the ideal counsellor (*parināyaka-ratana*).[3] Of these, the ideal wheel is the most important, because the appearance of this is the first indication that the king has become a universal monarch.

It is stated that a king having perfected the ten virtues of a universal monarch observes the eight precepts on a full-moon day and then retires to the topmost floor of his mansion, when the divine wheel rises from the eastern ocean and comes through the sky like a second full moon. It circumambulates the mansion where the monarch awaits its arrival, and appears close to the window within his sight. When the monarch sees it, he pays it due homage and sprinkles water over it from a golden vessel and wishes it to go forth. On the command of the monarch, the great wheel starts on its mission and the conquest of the world begins. From the time the *cakka-ratana* appears, the monarch concerned is entitled to the designation *rāja cakkavatti*—the sovereign mover of the wheel—and along with his retinue he follows it through the sky.

3. *Dīgha Nikāya*, Vol. II, p. 172 (P.T.S.).

Wherever the wheel goes the kings of those regions pay homage to the wheel and accept the suzerainty of the universal monarch. Just as a universal monarch causes the ideal wheel to turn, the Buddha too sets the wheel of law (*dhamma-cakka*) in motion.

The *Mahā Sudassana Suttanta* of the *Dīgha Nikāya* describes the ideal wheel of a universal monarch as having a nave (*nābhi*), a thousand spokes (*sahassārāni*), and a felly (*nemi*).[4] When the sculptors represented the wheel symbol on the Asokan capitals they seemed to have followed the description as given in *Dīgha Nikāya* (Pl. II, Fig. 2). This impression of the wheel set the pattern for later sculptors who elaborated on it (Pl. II, Figs. 3, 4, and 5).

The elaborate or perfect form of *cakka-ratana* which is identical with the *dhamma-cakka* is depicted in art with certain details that are normally not found in ordinary forms of the wheel symbol.[5] The component parts of an ordinary *cakka* are the nave, the spokes, the felly, and *nemi maṇi*, the bubble-like features adhering to the rim, in between the spokes. On the other hand, at Sāñchī, Bārhut, and Amarāvatī there are representations of the perfect form of *ratana-cakka* displaying certain features, of which the most characteristic are the adornments round the felly of the wheel, which, to my knowledge, no one has so far interpreted satisfactorily. In this respect Pāli and Sinhalese literary works of Sri Lanka give a vivid description of the perfect form of the *ratana-cakka* explaining what these features are and what they signify. For example, in *Sumaṅgalavilāsinī*, Buddhaghosa (5th century ACE) describes the perfect form of the *ratana-cakka* thus:

"As this wheel is possessed of divine qualities it is described as '*dibbaṃ*'; as it has thousand spokes it is said to be *sahassāraṃ*; as it has a nave and a felly it is said to be '*sanābhikaṃ, sanemikaṃ*,' as it is perfect in every respect it is described as '*sabbākāra-paripūraṃ*.'"

The nave, by reason of which the *cakka-ratana* is described as having a nave, is made entirely of sapphire. In the centre of the nave there is a hole lined with silver, and in it indentation clean and shining, which appears like the teeth of a smiling face. The outer rim of the nave is made of silver and it has the resemblance

4. Ibid., p. 172.

5. Sir John Marshall and A. Foucher, *The Monuments of Sāñchī*, Vol. 3, Plate LXXIV, Fig 3 a.

of a full moon with a hole in its centre. Around the hole of the nave decorative lines are shown clearly. Thus the nave of this *cakka-ratana* is perfect in every respect.

The spokes, by reason of which the *cakka-ratana* is described as having a thousand spokes, are all made of seven kinds of precious jewels. They shine like the rays of the sun. The knobs and the decorative line work are well marked on them. Thus the spokes of the *cakka-ratana* are perfect in every respect.

The felly, by reason of which the *cakka-ratana* is described as having a felly, is made of pure and polished, deep-red coral. The circular lines demarcating the joints of the felly shine like a strip of pure *jambunadi* gold, reddish in hue. Thus the felly of the *cakka-ratana* is perfect in every respect.

Around the felly of the *cakka-ratana* there are one hundred coral shafts—one shaft in-between every set of ten spokes. These coral shafts are hollow inside and have holes on the surface as in flutes. When the wind blows, these shafts produce notes as sweet as the music of the five musical instruments played upon by a talented musician. These melodious notes are lovely, enticing, desirable, and intoxicating. Surmounting these shafts are white umbrellas (*chatta*), and on either side of these there are two spears (*satti*) to which garlands are fastened. Thus surrounding the felly of the *cakka-ratana*, there are one hundred white umbrellas and two hundred spears supporting garlands. Inside the two holes on either side of the hub of the *cakka-ratana* there are two faces of lions, from the mouths of which issue forth a pair of pearl garlands as thick as the trunks of two mature palm trees, and which are resplendent like the rays of the moon, surpassing in beauty the heavenly river. At the end of these pearl garlands there are two tussels woven of red fluff, resembling the early morning sun. When the *cakka-ratana* together with these two garlands goes forth revolving in the sky it appears as if three wheels are revolving together. Thus is the ideal wheel perfect in every respect."[6]

It must be mentioned that one of the key words in the text quoted above has been rendered incorrectly in the Pāli Text Society (P.T.S.) edition of *Sumaṅgalavilāsinī* as well as in

6. *Sumaṅgalavilāsinī*, Part 2, p. 617 ff. (P.T.S.) (Commentary to the *Mahāpadāna Sutta*).

Mahābodhivaṃsa. Describing the features that adorn the felly of the wheel, the P.T.S. texts run as follows: "*Tassa kho pana pavāla daṇḍassa uparisetacchattaṃ ubhosu passesu samosarita-kusuma-dāmānāṃ dve pantiyo ti; evaṃ samosarita-kusuma-dāma-panti satadvaya-parivāra-setacchatta-dhārana-pavāla-daṇḍa-satena...*"[7]

According to this reading, attending on the white umbrella there are rows (*panti*) of garlands, and altogether there are two hundred such rows. Evidently this conveys a wrong idea. Here the correct reading as found in Siamese and Burmese script editions of the particular texts is as follows: "*Tassa kho pana pavāla-daṇḍassa upari-setacchattaṃ ubhosu passesu samosarita-kusumadāma dve sattiyo ti; evaṃ samosarita-kusuma-dāma-satti-satadvaya-parivāra setacchatta-dhārana-pavāla-daṇḍa-satena...*"[8] "*Kusumadāma-satti,*" meaning a spear bearing garlands, as found in the latter editions, is correct for it conveys the correct sense. Moreover, the Sinhalese translation of *Mahābodhivaṃsa* known as the *Sīhala Bodhivaṃsaya* (13th century A.C.), translates the corresponding passage thus: "*E pabalu daṇḍu mattehi dhavalcchatrayakä dälayehi elvana lada maldam äti aḍayaṭi dekekä dekekäyi mese elvana lada maldam äti aḍayaṭi desiyakin pririvarana lada dhavalacchatra siyayak darannāvu ...*"[9] As evidenced by the above passage, the *Sinhala Bodhivaṃsaya* is clear on this point and renders the Pāli word "*satti*" as "*aḍayaṭi*" (Sk. *ardha-yasti*) meaning a short spear. The author of the Pāli *Mahābodhivaṃsa* has incorporated in his work the passage directly from *Sumaṅgalavilāsinī* itself. The reading "*kusumadāma-panti*" may have been a scribe's error which the editors of the P.T.S. texts have accepted as the correct form.[10] Moreover, as the ensuing pages will show, the iconographical features of the wheel symbols also prove the correctness of the Siamese and Burmese script editions of *Sumaṅgalavilāsinī* and Pāli *Mahābodhivaṃsa*.

---

7. *Mahābodhivaṃsa* (P.T.S), edited by S. Arthur Strong, p. 68.

8. *Mahābodhivaṃsa*, Sinhalese script edition by the Venerable P. Sārānanda Thero, 1898, p. 206.

9. *Sīhala Bodhivaṃsaya*, edited by the Venerable Baddegama Dhammaratana Thera, pp. 204–205.

10. *Mahābodhivaṃsa* (P.T.S.), p. 67 ff. In a footnote "*satti*" is given as a variant reading.

The description of the *cakka-ratana* in *Sumaṅgalavilāsinī* as well as in the Pāli *Mahābodhivaṃsa* and its Sinhalese version clearly indicate that a perfect form of the *cakka-ratana* (in this case *dhamma-cakka* is also implied) has one hundred white umbrellas attended by two hundred spears bearing garlands right round its felly. Now let us focus our attention on some of the actual representations of the wheel and other relevant decorative elements depicted in the earliest specimens of Buddhist art, which have a bearing on our discussion. Some of the elaborate wheel symbols from Sānchi, Bārhut and Amarāvati display certain decorative elements such as *nandipāda* or *triratana* symbols and semicircular features in alternating positions right round the felly of the wheel (Pl. II, Figs. 3, 4 and 5).

At the outset it must be mentioned that nowhere in Indian or Sinhalese art has the umbrella (*chatta*) and spear (*satti*) been depicted in association with the wheel symbol exactly as described in the texts quoted above. But there are instances where this motif in separate form—i.e. umbrella attended by two spears (*satti*) bearing garlands or flags is depicted. Bas reliefs from Sāñchī and Sri Lanka show stūpas surmounted by umbrellas attended by spears as described (Pl. III, Figs. 8 and 9). Sāñchī has reliefs where processions, etc., are depicted showing people carrying spears to which garlands are fastened exactly as described in *Sumaṅgalavilāsinī* and other texts (Pl. III, Fig. 11). Spears in all these instances invariably terminate in the triple-pronged (*triśūla*) form commonly referred to as *nandipāda* or *triratana*. However, it must be mentioned that "*satti*" can mean a spear with a single blade (*śūla*) as well. In this connection umbrellas displaying two garlands hanging from either end of the canopy are also important (Pl. III, Fig. 12 b). This form of the umbrellas can be interpreted as another mode of representing the umbrella and spear motif. It is significant that such umbrellas are depicted as surmounting the wheel symbol at Sāñchī and elsewhere (Pl. VI, Fig. 19). Bearing these facts in mind when we trace the evolution of the decorative motifs edging the felly of the wheel symbols under discussion, we can clearly see the connection between the literary tradition in Sri Lanka and the earliest specimens of Buddhist art of India.

In depicting an umbrella on the felly of a wheel, it has in course of time degenerated in form, as usual in art. The umbrella even in its most elaborate form has been already highly stylized when depicted in early sculpture at Sāñchī and Bārhut (Pl. III, Fig. 12 a and b). It is usually flat and wheel-like in shape and clearly shows the spokes that support the ribs of the umbrella. Two garlands are shown as hanging from either side. Pl. III, Fig. 12 c, shows an umbrella from a coin, where the garlands have apparently merged with the umbrella proper, thus giving it the resemblance of an arrowhead. The spokes and the shaft too have lost their distinctive features and have become a support of the canopy tapering downwards. Pl. III, Fig. 12 d shows that the height of the shaft has been further diminished and the umbrella is reduced to a mere semicircle. All that remains of the spokes and the shaft of the umbrella are the two arches within the semicircle. Pl. III, Fig. 12 e shows a further development where the umbrella has lost all its significance and has been depicted as a leaf motif. Pl. III, Fig. 12 f is a similar conventionalised umbrella from a Tibetan *dharma-cakra*. Here the shaft and the spokes are represented by three short lines radiating from the centre. Pl. III, Fig. 12 g shows a modern adaptation of the same. It has lost all vestiges of an umbrella and is merely a semicircle.

Just as the umbrella in this position gradually diminished in height and ultimately lost all vestiges of the shaft leaving a semicircular bubble or a leaf ornament to represent the *chatra* (umbrella), it can be explained that the spear which originally bore garlands also lost both the garlands and the shaft, leaving the characteristic symbol *satti*, single *śūla* or *triśūla* (*nandipāda* or *triratana*) to represent the spear (Pl. III, Fig. 12 a, b, c, d, and e).

This brief introduction explaining the conjectural evolution of the umbrella and spear motif will be of assistance in understanding how the elaborate umbrellas and spears, the latter bearing garlands, around the felly of the *ratana-cakka* gradually lost their original forms and were reduced to more or less geometric patterns. Thus we see that the bubble and the triangle (*śūla*) or three-pronged spear (*triśūla*) pattern edging the felly of the wheel is in fact the conventionalised umbrella and spear motif described in *Sumaṅgalavilāsinī*. Hence these symbols can be described as perfect forms of the *ratana-cakka*, here used to represent the *dhamma-cakka*, the Wheel of the Law. F. C. Maisey, A. Foucher, Sir John Marshall, and other reputed scholars have identified these features as umbrellas and *nandipādas*.[11] But as I have pointed out, it is in the light of *Sumaṅgalavilāsinī* and other literary works preserved in Sri Lanka that their exact nature and the significance can be satisfactorily interpreted.

The following examples of wheel symbols, each bearing a circle of highly stylised umbrellas and spears edging the felly of the wheel, clearly show various ways in which the elaborate or perfect forms of the wheel have been depicted in art. A. Foucher in *The Beginnings of Buddhist Art* has cited a number of wheel symbols from ancient Indian coins of which one shows knob-like external features right round the felly (Pl. IV, Fig. 14).[12] He identifies these features as umbrellas. Here the umbrella being the more prominent symbol stands alone unaccompanied by spears. Pl. II, Fig. 6 shows a Tibetan *dharma-cakra* where the umbrellas have been reduced to semicircular features with three short lines radiating from the centre, reminiscent of the ribs and the shaft of the umbrella.

The recent adaptations of this type of *dharma-cakras* have done away with this last vestige and have retained only the semicircle, which is more or less like the knob-shaped end of the spokes projecting through the felly of the wheel (Pl. II, Fig. 7). In spite of the fact that these semicircular features bear no resemblance to umbrellas, there is no doubt that they are derived from the original *chatra* symbols. However, any further distortion, for example, the elongation of the *chatra* symbol to look more like a rod, is undesirable as it will definitely interfere with the significance of the wheel as a symbol.

Pl. II, Fig. 4 shows a wheel from Sāñchī displaying *chatta* (umbrella) symbols alternating with *nandipādas* or the so-called *triratana* symbols. Here the *nandipāda* occupies exactly the same position in which, according to the *Sumaṅgalavilāsinī* account of the *ratana-cakka*, spears (*satti*) bearing garlands are to be depicted. In some wheels, instead of a *nandipāda*, a triangular member is shown (Pl. II, Fig. 3). Just as *nandipāda* stands for a spear (*satti*) terminating in a three-pronged member (*triśūla*), the triangular feature too stands for a spear terminating in a single *śūla*. In short,

11. Sir J. Marshall and A. Foucher, *The Monuments of Sāñchī*, Vol. I, p. 189.
12. A. Foucher, *The Beginnings of Buddhist Art*, Plate I.

the spear (*satti*) is represented by either a *śūla* or *triśūla*. It appears that Buddhists referred to *nandipāda* or *triratana* by the term *satti* (Sk. *śakti*). Sir John Marshall maintains that the detail of umbrellas edging the felly was directly copied from the original wheel from Sārnāth.[13] Sir Arthur Cunningham, too, in his conjectural reconstruction of the wheel that once crowned the arch (*toraṇa*) of the Bārhut stūpa, depicts it incorrectly as a bubble in between the umbrellas.[14] Evidently both these scholars have treated it as a meaningless piece of decoration. According to the texts cited in this connection, the number of spears should be twice the number of umbrellas. To be exact, there should be one hundred umbrellas and two hundred spears (*satti*) bearing garlands. But unlike in a literary description, in art if two spears are depicted side by side it would interfere with the artistic rendering of the design. Hence on aesthetic grounds, it is permissible to depict one spear in place of two mentioned in the texts. Thus these wheels with an edging of umbrellas and spears on the felly actually represent the perfect form of the Wheel (*sabbākāra-paripūra-ratana-cakka*) of the universal monarch. At Sāñchī, Bārhut, and Amarāvati they are used to represent the *dhamma-cakka*.

In later representations of wheels both the pattern and the emphasis on the symbols show a marked change. In the examples mentioned earlier, the spear (*satti*), whether as single-pointed (*śūla*) or three pronged (*triśūla* or *nandipāda*) weapon, is represented on a smaller scale when compared with the umbrella, to show that it occupies a subordinate position. On the other hand there are wheels especially from Amarāvati displaying *satti* symbols very prominently, whereas the umbrella has been reduced to a very insignificant and stylised semicircular feature cramped between the former symbols (Pl. II, Fig. 5). In another wheel the umbrella has been totally converted into a leaf pattern, which clearly shows that by the 2nd century CE some sculptors in India had already forgotten the original significance of these features. By this time it appears that the spear (*satti*) as a symbol has grown in importance and even superseded the umbrella. Just as there are wheels with an edging of umbrellas around the felly, there are also wheels which

13. Sir John Marshall and A. Foucher, *The Monuments of Sāñchī*, Vol. I, p. 109.
14. Sir Arthur Cunningham, *The Stūpa of Bārhut*, Plate XVII.

display spearheads (*satti*) in place of umbrellas (Pl. IV, Fig. 16). *Satti* (spearhead) has been used here in its truly symbolic form.

The umbrella and the spearhead, in alternating positions around a circle, are found in the earliest specimens of Indian art, as is proved by the impressions on ancient coins where this feature is very clearly represented (Pl. IV, Fig. 15).[15] Here the umbrella and the spearhead (*satti, triśūla, nandipāda*), although highly conventionalised, are prominently shown while the wheel, a mere disc without spokes, is comparatively very insignificant. Nevertheless the transition from this form to the more elaborate form of the *dhamma-cakka* is not difficult to trace.

It is well known that the umbrella is a symbol of sovereignty. Thus in the *ratana-cakka* of a universal monarch it signifies his sovereignty. Spears (*satti*) bearing garlands stand in attendance (*parivāra*) on an umbrella emphasising its importance as a symbol. In this respect it must be mentioned that *satti* (Sk. *śakti*) also signifies regal splendour and power. It is said that a universal monarch with the assistance of his *ratana-cakka* conquers the universe (*ajitaṃ jināti*),[16] thus bringing into subjugation other monarchs. The circle of umbrellas attended by *sattis* (spearheads) edging the felly of the wheel symbols, just described, signifies this subjugation of the universe by the universal monarch. Here, the number hundred as mentioned in *Sumaṅgalavilāsinī* is important, for ancient writers usually refer to a hundred kings ruling India. The hundred kings here symbolizzed by a hundred umbrellas generally stand for all the kings of the universe. When Buddhists adopted the umbrella symbol they took for granted the symbolism it originally possessed and added something more—a specific Buddhist significance. Buddhists generally recognise three kinds of umbrellas, namely, the human (*mānusī*), divine (*dibba*), and spiritual emancipation (*vimutti*). Thus the umbrella depicted in association with *dhamma-cakka* actually signifies *vimutti-chatta*. The umbrella and the spearhead (*satti*) motif on the felly of the *dhamma-cakka* signifies that the Buddha as *saddharma-cakravarti*, the universal monarch of the Norm, has conquered the world and established a spiritual overlordship over the world. In brief, the perfect form of the

15. A. Foucher, *The Beginnings of Buddhist Art*, Plate I.
16. *Papañcasūdani*, Part III, p. 365 (P.T.S.).

Wheel (*ratana-cakka*) signifies the universal monarch's sovereignty over the Universe, and the Buddhists adopted the same form of the wheel to signify the Wheel of the Law of the Buddha. Although the wheel symbols discussed in the previous pages conform to the description of the ideal wheel of a universal monarch, in art they have been used to depict the *dhamma-cakka*.

The above discussion on the iconographical features of the wheel symbol, I suppose, proves that it is quite in conformity with the tradition to depict umbrellas and spearheads (*satti*) on the felly of the *dhamma-cakka*, although in Sri Lanka this type of wheel has not been discovered so far. The modern designs of the wheel symbol with a trace of encircling umbrellas are recent adaptations most probably based on Tibetan *dharma-cakras*.

Apparently those who designed them were unaware of the significance of the knob-like projections which are really the highly stylised umbrella symbols edging the fellies of the wheels. Next, the question arises whether it interferes with the idea of motion (*pravartana*) of the wheel to depict the umbrellas and spearheads (*satti*) on the felly of the wheel. Although the wheel symbol has been created after the cart wheel (*rathaṅga-cakka*), according to the texts it is supposed to go revolving through the sky. Buddhaghosa describes this in detail thus:[17] "This *cakka-ratana* proceeds through the sky, not very high but just above the summit of trees, so that those who accompany the *cakka-ratana* (through the sky) are able to enjoy the fruits, flowers and tender leaves of the trees, at their pleasure. Also the *cakka-ratana* moves at a height that is neither too high nor too low so that people on earth are able to point out and say, 'That is the king; that is his deputy and that is his commander in chief!'" Both the writers who described the *cakka-ratana* in literature and the artists who depicted it in art considered it as a wheel that is supposed to move through the sky, and the umbrellas and the spears (*satti*) bearing garlands that adorn the felly were not considered an impediment to its revolving movement (*pravartana*).

The felly of an ideal wheel is also described as studded with gems (*nemi maṇi*).[18] Elsewhere, they are referred to as *maṇika*, meaning

17. *Sumaṅgalavilāsinī* (P.T.S.) Part II, p. 617 ff.
18. *Sumaṅgalavilāsinī* (P.T.S.), Vol. 2, p. 447.

a bowl-shaped gem. On the Asokan wheels these are represented as bubble-shaped ornaments attached to the inner side of the rim of the wheel, in between the spokes. *Samantakūtavaṇṇanā* refers to spokes adorned with pot-shaped and bubble-shaped ornaments (*ghaṭika-maṇikāvalīhi susanṭhitā*).[19] In Indian architecture, sometimes pillars are depicted as springing from or terminating in vases (*pūrṇa-ghaṭa*), symbolic of abundance. Here it is implied that the spokes of a wheel symbol are depicted as pillars which terminate in pot ornaments.

In describing the perfect form of the *cakka-ratana*, *Sumaṅgalavilāsinī* states that in addition to other features the holes in the nave of the wheel have two lion faces from the mouths of which issue forth two pearl garlands.[20] The lion face in this position has been actually depicted in an arch surmounting a *stūpa*. The indentation on the inner side of the rim of the arch around the lion face is clearly represented (Pl. IV, Fig. 17).

Dhamma-cakkas which display garlands hanging from the wheel are also met with. Pl. VI, Fig. 19 shows a *dhamma-cakka* shrine in which the garlands hanging from the nave are prominently displayed. Another *dhamma-cakka* from Sāñchī shows that garlands form an important feature in the scheme of decorations (Pl. V, Fig. 18). Four garlands are shown as hanging from two pegs (*nāga-danta*) above the *dhamma-cakka* and two others from the stems of two lotus buds acting as pegs. The wheel is depicted as surmounted on a seat of three lions and from the mouths of two of the flanking lions a pair of garlands issue forth, thus bringing to one's mind the description in *Sumaṅgalavilāsinī*, which says that two pearl garlands issue from the mouths of two lion heads that are set in the holes on either side of the nave of the wheel.

It is said that the nave of the *cakka-ratana* is constructed of sapphire (*indra-nīla-māṇikya*). The *Dīgha Nikāya* also refers to gems adorning the rim of the wheel. Benjamin Rowland states that the naves of the wheels on Asokan capitals were originally set with gems of various colours.[21] *Sumaṅgalavilāsinī* describes

---

19. *Mahābodhivaṃsa* (P.T.S.), ed. by Arthur Strong, p. 67. Also see *Samantakūṭavaṇṇanā*, edited by the Venerable M. Ñānissara Thera, p. 765.
20. *Sumaṅgalavilāsinī* (P.T.S.), Part. II, p. 618.
21. Sir Benjamin Rowland, *The Art and Architecture of India*, p. 41.

the wheel as constructed of precious jewels, stones, and metals of various colours.[22] It is stated that the hole in the nave of the *cakka-ratana* is lined with silver, the spokes are constructed of seven kinds of precious jewels, and the felly of the wheel is made of red coral. Thus red, blue, white, and yellow are prominently displayed in the scheme of colours employed in the wheel. These colours, which are symbolical in purpose, have been intentionally employed, thus enhancing the magical qualities of the wheel.

Although no single wheel symbol has been depicted exactly as the perfect form of the *cakka-ratana* described in the *Sumaṅgalavilāsinī*, the instances of pearl garlands hanging from the hub of the wheel, garlands issuing from the mouths of lions forming the seat on which the wheel is placed in position, and the front view of the wheel with garlands issuing from either side of the hub, as well as from the lion face that is framed within the dented rim of the nave, are clear indications that the artists of ancient India have depicted various aspects of the perfect form of the *ratana-cakka* conforming to a certain accepted scheme as reflected in literature. This clearly proves that *Sumaṅgalavilāsinī* has preserved a tradition that was well known in India as early as the 1st century C.E. or even earlier.

II. The Dhamma-Cakka

The iconographical features of the wheel described above are that of the ideal wheel (*ratana-cakka*) of the universal monarch. Nevertheless the representations of the perfect forms of the wheel symbol in Buddhist art that conform to the description of the *ratana-cakka* actually depict the *dhamma-cakka*, the Wheel of Law of the Buddha. Nowhere in Indian art has the perfect form of the *ratana-cakka* (i.e., that of the universal monarch) been depicted, although a number of bas-reliefs showing the universal monarch with his seven Ideal Possessions (*satta ratana*) are found in India as well as in Sri Lanka. In these illustrations the wheel symbol is depicted in its unadorned form.[23]

22. *Sumaṅgalavilāsinī* (P.T.S.), Part II, p. 618.
23. Heinrich Zimmer, *Art of Indian Asia*, Vol. 2, Pl. 37.

The earliest Buddhist monuments that have the *dhamma-cakka* symbols are the Asokan pillars. Of these the most important one is from Sārnāth, the fragments of which are preserved in an archaeological museum. However, a bas-relief from Sāñchī shows exactly how this Asokan pillar would have looked (Pl. V, Fig. 18). The wheel is mounted on a seat of three adorned lions which in turn stand on a circular plinth adorned with four animals, lion, elephant, bull, and horse. In between the animals, four smaller wheels are depicted. The plinth is mounted on a lotus-shaped bell. In later examples, the *dhamma-cakka* is depicted as mounted on a *satti* (*nandipāda*) (Pl. I, Fig. 1) and the lotus-shaped bell assumed the shape of a *pūrṇa-ghaṭa*. This elaborate capital is placed on a tall, slightly tapering pillar. Commenting on the symbolism of the Sārnāth pillar, Dr. Benjamin Rowland says, "The Sārnāth column may be interpreted, therefore, not only as a glorification of the Buddha's preaching symbolised by the crowning wheel, but also through the cosmological implications of the whole pillar as a symbol of the universal extension of the power of the Buddha's Law as typified by the sun that dominates all space and all time, and simultaneously an emblem of the universal extension of Mauryan imperialism through the Dharma. The whole structure is then a translation of age-old Indian and Asiatic cosmology into artistic terms of essentially foreign origin and dedicated, like all Asoka's monuments, to the glory of Buddhism and the royal house."[24]

Although the *dhamma-cakka* was used to depict the doctrine in general, it primarily stood for the first sermon of the Buddha. It is stated that the Buddha delivered the *Dhamma-cakka Pavattana Sutta* to the group of five monks at the Deer Park at Bārānasi. In early art this incident is illustrated by a wheel flanked by a pair of deer. The Buddha as well as the group of five monks was not shown, in conformity with the then prevalent tradition. But later, when the Buddha images came to be used, whenever this incident of the first sermon was depicted, the *dhamma-cakka* with or without the deer was depicted on the seat of the Buddha. In most of the Gupta and Mathurā Buddha images this motif is represented. Later, with the development of "Buddhology," this simple motif developed into a highly complicated form where the

24. Sir Benjamin Rowland, *The Art and Architecture of India*, p. 42.

dhamma-cakka is shown as surmounted on a pillar of which the base is in the world of divine serpents, where the male and female serpents are shown as paying homage to it. Two divine serpents are shown in the act of holding the pillar in position. The wheel is shown in front view with two garlands hanging from either side of the hub. The pillar rises through a cavity in the earth's crust and its upper portion is shown as appearing in the human sphere; two devotees and a pair of deer are seen paying homage to the wheel. Just above the wheel, the Buddha is depicted in heroic dimensions seated on a throne attended by divine beings. Here too the group of five monks is not represented. Two additional *dhamma-cakka*s are seen at the background on either side of the Buddha image.[25]

At Amarāvati, a number of bas-reliefs show elaborately carved *dhamma-cakka*s surmounted on pillars at the foot of which an empty seat is prominently depicted. On the footstool, the footprints of the Buddha are displayed. These pillars in complete form signify the Buddha and are iconographically related to the fiery pillars depicting the Buddha. Human as well as divine beings are shown as paying homage to the monument, which is an elaborately carved pillar on which the *dhamma-cakka* is prominently displayed.[26]

A number of bas-reliefs from Sāñchī and Bārhut show the *dhamma-cakka* in a shrine. In Pl. VI, Fig. 19, the *dhamma-cakka* is placed on a flat seat and a royal umbrella is raised above it. Inside the shrine two men are shown in the attitude of worshipping the wheel, while just outside the shrine pedestrians as well as people on elephants, horses, and chariots are seen circumambulating the shrine. Evidently, they form the fourfold army—namely, the elephants, cavalry, chariots, and the infantry—of the king who is depicted as visiting the shrine in a chariot.

Sir Arthur Cunningham, on inscriptional evidence, describes this bas-relief as illustrating the visit of King Pasenadī Kosala, a contemporary of the Buddha. It is believed that the shrine is an illustration of the *punyasālā* he is supposed to have built for the

25. Heinrich Zimmer, *Art of Indian Asia*, Vol. 2, Pl. 80.
26. Ibid., Vol. 2, Pl. 96.

use of the Buddha.[27] However, this illustration and other similar ones bring to one's mind the description of how the universal monarch, accompanied by the fourfold army and his retinue, followed the *cakka-ratana* on its voyage of conquest.

Although the *dhamma-cakka* primarily symbolised the preaching of the first sermon and thereby the doctrine in its wider sense, it was also used to represent the Buddha himself. It is well known that during the earliest phase of Buddhist art, the Buddha or the Bodhisatta in his last life on earth was never represented in human form but by a symbol such as the Wisdom Tree (*bodhi*), the Wheel of the Law (*dhamma-cakka*), the *stūpa*, or the footprint (*pāduka*). Thus among the representations of the *dhamma-cakka* in art, there are a few that can be interpreted as iconic representations of the Buddha. For instance many of the wheel symbols depicted as placed on a pedestal or housed in a shrine actually represent the Buddha (Pl. VI, Fig. 19). Here the *dhamma-cakka* can be interpreted as *dhamma-kāya* of the *trikāya* doctrine of Mahāyāna Buddhism. Dr. Ānanda Coomaraswamy has pointed out that, although in the Pāli canon the Trikāya doctrine had not yet developed, there are occasional references in the *Dīgha Nikāya* and the *Sutta Nipāta* to the concept of Dhammakāya. In the *Dīgha Nikāya* the Blessed One is spoken of as *dhammakāya* or *brahmakāya*[28] and in the *Saṃyutta Nikāya* the Buddha says "He who sees Dhamma sees me, who sees me sees the Dhamma."[29]

III. The Lakkhaṇa-Cakka

The *lakkhaṇa-cakka* is described as the auspicious mark on the soles of the feet of the Buddha. It is said that Buddha's palms are also marked with the wheel symbol. In its unadorned form the *lakkhaṇa-cakka* is identical with the ordinary form of the *ratana-cakka* and *dhamma-cakka* (Pl. VII, Fig. 20), but in its perfect form it is a highly elaborate symbol, surpassing in detail even the perfect form of the *ratana-cakka* of the universal monarch.

---

27. Sir Arthur Cunningham, *The Stūpa of Bārhut*, p. 110.
28. *Dīgha Nikāya* (P.T.S.), Vol. III, p. 84.
29. *Saṃyutta Nikāya* (P.T.S.), Vol. III, p. 120.

Buddhaghosa describes the *lakkhaṇa-cakka* thus: "*Cakka* means the wheels on the soles of the feet of the Buddha; the spokes and the felly are mentioned in the canonical texts (i.e., Pāli); by *sabbākāraparipūraṃ* these special features are intended; in the centre of the wheel that is in the middle of the sole there is the nave; surrounding the nave there are the circular lines; at the opening of the nave there is the covering sheath; the hole of the nave is seen; also there are the spokes and the circular lines round the spokes; the felly is seen; the bowl-shaped gems on the nave are seen; all these are mentioned in the canonical texts. Further details are not given there; these should be known as follows: attending on the wheel there are the spear (*satti*), *śrīvatsa* (*sirivaccha*), conch (?), (*nandi*), *svastika* (*sovatthi*), ear-rings (*vaṭaṃsaka*), powder box (*vaḍḍhamānaka*), pair of fish (*maccha yugala*), auspicious seat (*bhaddapīṭha*), elephant goad (*aṅkusa*), mansion (*pāsāda*), triumphal arch (*toraṇa*), white umbrella (*setacchatta*), sword (*khagga*), palm-leaf fan (*tālavaṇṭhaka*), cluster of peacock feathers (*mora-hattha*), fly whisk (*vāla-vījanī*), diadem (*uṇhīsa*), cluster of gems (*maṇi-paṭṭha*), garland of flowers (*sumana-dāma*), blue water lilies (*nīluppala*), red water lilies (*rattuppala*), white water lilies (*setuppala*), red lotus (*paduma*), white lotus (*puṇḍarīka*), filled vessel (*puṇṇa ghaṭa*), filled bowl (*puṇṇa pāti*), ocean (*samudda, cakravāṭa*), mountain range (*cakkavāla*), Himalaya forest (*Himavā*), Mount Meru (*Sineru*), moon (*candimā*), sun (*sūriya*), stars (*nakkhatta*), four great continents (*cattāro mahādīpā*), two thousand islands that surround them (*dve parittā dīpā sahassāni*), and the universal monarch together with his retinue (*rājā cakkavatti saseno*); all these are attending on the wheel."[30] In later texts more signs, generally referred to as 108 in number, are added. For example, in addition to those enumerated by Buddhaghosa in *Sumaṅgalavilāsinī*, Gurulugomi in *Dharmapradīpikāva* mentions as auspicious marks, animals such as lions, tigers, bulls as well as mythical creatures like *kinnaras*, *makarās*, *garuḍās*, various kinds of birds and divine beings like gods of the six heavens, Brahmas of the sixteen Brahma worlds.[31]

The perfect form of the *ratana-cakka* has only a few of these auspicious signs such as the umbrella, spear (*satti*), and garlands

30. *Sumaṅgalavilāsinī* (P.T.S.), Part II, p. 445.

31. *Dharmapradīpikāva*, edited by W. Soratha Thera, p. 5.

attending on it whereas this definition of the *lakkhaṇa-cakka* shows that all that is representative of this universe, the auspicious symbols, the earth with its flora and fauna, the universal monarch together with his seven ideal possessions, the heavenly bodies such as the sun, moon, and the stars, and finally the heavens and the Brahma worlds themselves, are depicted as attending on the wheel symbols on the soles of the feet of the Buddha.

The *lakkhaṇa-cakka* is symbolic of the supremacy of the Buddha. Buddhaghosa, in describing the quality of *asādhāraṇa-ratana*—extraordinary gem—with reference to the Buddha, says that between the animate and inanimate objects of value (*ratana*), the animate ones are superior; among the animate the human beings are superior; of human beings men are superior to women for the latter attend on men; men recluses (*anāgārika-ratana*) are superior to laymen because *rājā-cakkavatti*, the highest among laymen (*āgārika-ratana*) pays obeisance to recluses; among various grades of recluses the Buddha is the highest. The *lakkhaṇa-cakka* depicts this supremacy of the Buddha, for, from the inanimate objects of value (*aviññāṇaka-ratana*) to the highest of the divine beings, the Brahmas, are depicted as attending on the *lakkhaṇa-cakka* on the soles of the feet of the Buddha.[32]

In art the *lakkhaṇa-cakka* has been depicted from very early times in association with Foot Prints (*pādukā*) of the Buddha, which have been used to signify the Blessed One. In these the wheel is identical with the ordinary form of the *ratana-cakka* or *dhamma-cakka*. However, in the later phase of Sāñchī and at Amarāvati and Mathurā elaborate forms of the *lakkhaṇa-cakka* are met with. Pl. VII, Fig. 20 shows a *pādukā* marked with the *lakkhaṇa-cakka* attended by a spear (*satti*), a *svastika* (*sovattika*), and an auspicious seat (*bhadra-pīṭha*). One of the most elaborate of the earliest *lakkhaṇa-cakka*s is from Sri Lanka (Pl. VII, Fig. 22). It displays a spear-head (*satti*), an umbrella (*chatta*), a *śrīvatsa* (*sirivaccha*), an auspicious seat (*bhadra-pīṭha*), a conch (*saṅkha*), a cluster of peacock feathers (*mora-hatta*), or a palm-leaf fan (*tālavaṇṭhaka*), standards and banners (*dhaja-patāka*), an elephant goad (*aṅkusa*), a filled vase (*puṇṇa-ghaṭa*), and a pair of fish (*maccha-yugala*) surrounding the wheel, which is in the centre of the sole,

32. *Paramatthajotikā*, p. 216 (Sinhala script edition).

while the *svastika* is repeated on the tips of the five toes. However, the most complete form of the *lakkhaṇa-cakka* is found in the Far Eastern countries such as Siam (Thailand) and Cambodia.[33] An elaborately carved specimen of the Buddha's footprint from Ankor Wat in Cambodia shows practically all the 108 auspicious signs that attend on the *lakkhaṇa-cakka*.

IV. The Bhava-Cakka

In the Ṛgveda the wheel of Sūrya, the sun, has 12 or 5 or 360 spokes, signifying the months, seasons or days of the year respectively.[34] Thus it signifies the year as measured by the sun in its course. When the wheel was first used as a Buddhist symbol, it was not known whether the component parts of the wheel signified any particular aspect of the doctrine. It appears that it originally represented broadly the entire doctrine and particularly the First Sermon, which is really a synopsis of the Teaching. Its thousand spokes referred to in the texts actually depicted the rays of the sun, and the earliest wheel symbols have proportionately a large number of spokes to depict this particular feature. In later wheel symbols the number of spokes is generally reduced, but apparently they do not signify any particular aspect of the doctrine. However, the Tibetan wheel symbols have eight spokes which most probably signify the Eightfold Path (*ariya-aṭṭhaṅgika-magga*), and the modern wheel symbols generally have the same number of spokes.

The Tibetan *bhava-cakka* or *saṃsāra-cakka*, the Wheel of Becoming or Wheel of Life, illustrates a particular aspect of the Dhamma, namely, the doctrine of Dependent Origination (*paṭicca-samuppāda*) and thereby the doctrine of rebirth. The Tibetan version of the Wheel of Life conforms to the description given of it in the *Divyāvadāna*,[35] a Buddhist Sanskrit work of the Sarvāstivāda school. This work describes the origin of the *bhava-cakka* and the manner in which the picture is to be made. The wheel is shown as being in the grip of a three-eyed demon wearing a tiger's skin,

33. J.R.A.S. (C.B.), Vol. XXXI, pp. 384–387. Also see footnote.

34. A.K. Coomaraswamy, *The Elements of Buddhist Iconography*.

35. *Divyāvadāna*, edited by E. B. Cowell and R. A. Neill (1886), p. 300.

who symbolises impermanence (*aniccatā*). The wheel consists of three concentric circles of which the innermost, corresponding to the nave of the wheel, depicts three animals, a bird (dove or cock), a snake and a pig, each catching the tail of the animal in front, symbolising lust, hatred, and delusion respectively. The next circle, which is the largest of the three, corresponding to the area occupied by the spokes of a wheel, is divided into five or six segments in which the destinies (*gati*) of living beings, i.e., the realms of their rebirth, are shown in detail. The last circle, which is the felly of the wheel, is divided into twelve sections depicting the twelve links of Dependent Origination.[36]

Though in Theravāda literature there is no mention of an actual pictorial execution of a "Wheel of Life," yet the concept of comparing Dependent Origination to a wheel is not unknown. In the *Path of Purification* (*Visuddhimagga*), the famous commentator Buddhaghosa Ācariya says:

"It is the beginningless round of rebirths that is called the 'Wheel of the round of rebirths' (*saṃsāracakka*). Ignorance (*avijjā*) is its hub (or nave) because it is its root. Ageing-and-death (*jarā-maraṇa*) is its rim (or felly) because it terminates it. The remaining ten links (of the Dependent Origination) are its spokes (i.e., karma formations [*saṅkhāra*] up to process of becoming [*bhava*])."[37]

In another passage of the same work, the components of the wheel are associated with the twelve links of Dependent Origination in a slightly different way:

"Its hub is made of ignorance and craving for becoming (*bhavataṇhā*); its spokes consist of formations of merit, etc. (*puññādi-abhisaṅkhāra*); its rim is ageing-and-death; it is joined to the chariot of triple existence (*ti-bhava*) by piercing it with the axle made of the origin of cankers (*āsava-samudaya*).[38] This Wheel of the Round of Rebirths has been revolving throughout time that has no beginning."[39]

36. *Marg*, Vol. XVI, No. 4, pp. 19 ff. Plate facing p. 25.

37. *Visuddhimagga* (text ed. P.T.S.), Vol. I, p. 198 (*The Path of Purification*, tr. by Ñāṇamoli, VII.8).

38. See *Majjhima Nikāya*, Sutta 2: "With the arising of cankers there is the arising of Ignorance."

39. *Visuddhi Magga*, Vol. I, p. 198 (Translation: Ch. VII, §7).

Elsewhere in the same work it is said:

"Becoming's Wheel reveals no known beginning;
No maker, no experiencer is there;
Void with a twelvefold voidness, and nowhere
It ever halts; for ever it is spinning."[40]

As it has been rolling on from time immemorial "its times are three, i.e., past, present, and future. The first two (of the twelve) factors as given in the Pāli text, namely ignorance and formations, belong to the past time; the following eight, beginning with consciousness and ending with becoming, belong to the present time; the last two, birth and ageing-and-death, belong to the future time."[41]

V. The Significance of the Wheel

In order to understand the significance of the wheel it must be remembered that it was in some form or other originally connected with the solar disc. In the Ṛgveda, Sūrya is described as a chariot having one wheel.[42] It is this solar symbol conceived as a chariot wheel that later became the weapon of Vishnu, the deified form of Sūrya, the world-conquering divine wheel of the universal monarch and the Wheel of Law of the Buddha. Further, in the Ṛgveda, Mitra (another form of Sūrya) is described as the eye of the world. Thus the sun traversing through space is conceived as the eye that watches and illuminates the entire world.[43] Hence in one sense the wheel (*cakka*) as well as the eye (*cakṣu*; Pāli: *cakkhu*) are synonymous. In this connection it is interesting to note that the realisation of the Truth is very often described as *cakkhuṃ udapādi*—the eye of wisdom dawned. Here the eye is the wisdom (*paṭivedha-ñāṇa*).

In this connection the interpretation of the term "turning of the wheel of Dhamma" in the commentaries of Buddhaghosa is of significance. Here the wheel is conceived as intellect, knowledge,

40. Ibid. Vol. II, p. 576 (Translation: Ch. XVII, § 273).
41. Ibid. Vol. II, p. 578 (Translation: Ch. XVII, § 287).
42. A. A. Macdonell, *The Vedic Mythology*, pp. 31 and 88.
43. Ibid., p. 30.

wisdom, insight (*ñāṇa*) which is twofold—*paṭivedha-ñāṇa*, the wisdom of self-realisation of the Truth, and *desanā-ñāṇa*, the wisdom of proclamation of the Truth—both of which are a prerogative of the Buddha. *Paṭivedha-ñāṇa* is further explained as born of intellect (*paññā bhāvitaṃ*) and bringing the fruit of Holiness (*ariyaphalāvahaṃ*) to oneself. On the other hand, *desanā-ñāṇa*, the wisdom of the proclamation of the Truth, is born of compassion and brings forth the fruit of Holiness in the disciples (*karuṇāphalabhāvitaṃ sāvakānaṃ ariyaphalāvahaṃ*). The former is supermundane (*lokuttara*) and the latter mundane (*lokiya*).[44]

Paṭivedha-ñāṇa is further explained as that which is in the course of being realised (*uppajjamānaṃ*) and that which is realised (*uppannaṃ*).[45] From the time when the Bodhisatta as the hermit Sumedha at the feet of the former Buddha Dīpaṅkara resolved to achieve Perfection, up to the time of realisation of the Path of Arahatship (*arahatta magga*), the *dhamma-cakka* is described as being in the course of realisation. The moment when he finally realised the fruit of Arahatship (*arahatta phala*) at the *Bodhi-maṇḍala*, the *dhamma-cakka* was realised. Similarly, *desanā-ñāṇa* too is twofold. It is described as being proclaimed up to the time Aññākoṇḍañña, one of the group of five monks to whom the Buddha preached the First Sermon, reached the fruit of Arahatship. The moment when he obtained the fruit of Arahatship the *dhamma-cakka* is described as proclaimed (*pavattitaṃ*). Thus the turning of the wheel of law in Buddhism has the sense of realising (*paṭivedha-ñāṇa*) and proclaiming the Truth (*desanā-ñāṇa*).

Now it is clear that the wheel symbol is used to signify the doctrine as well as many other concepts associated with Buddhism. As the ideal wheel of the universal monarch, it assists him to conquer the world by righteous means. It is his symbol of power (*ājñā-cakra*). In Buddhist doctrine it symbolises the doctrine as well as the Buddha as *dhammakāya*. Then it signifies various other concepts such as the cycle of births (*saṃsāra* or *bhava*) in close association with the doctrine of Dependent Origination (*paṭicca-samuppāda*). Thus the wheel symbol came to be accepted as the most appropriate symbol of the Buddhists,

44. *Manorathapurāṇī* (P.T.S.), Vol. I, p. 120.
45. *Papañcasūdanī* (P.T.S.), Vol. 2, p. 26.

both in physical as well as metaphysical spheres. Hence the ancients described the wheel—both in the sense of *ratana-cakka* as well as *dhamma-cakka* as:

> "Rich in ornamentation, incalculable in value,
> Unparalleled, a sight rarely seen,
> Associated solely with supreme beings,
> It's aptly called Ratana, a gem supreme."
>
> *Cittīkataṃ mahagghañca—atulaṃ dullabha dassanaṃ,*
> *Anomasattaparibhogaṃ—Ratanaṃ tena pavuccati.*[46]

46. *Sāratthapakāsinī* (P.T.S.), Vol. 3 p. 152 (Commentary on *Saṃyutta Nikāya*).

Plates

PLATE I

Fig. 1: A perfect form of the Wheel sustained by a *satti* (*nandipāda*), Sāñchī; 1st century C.E.

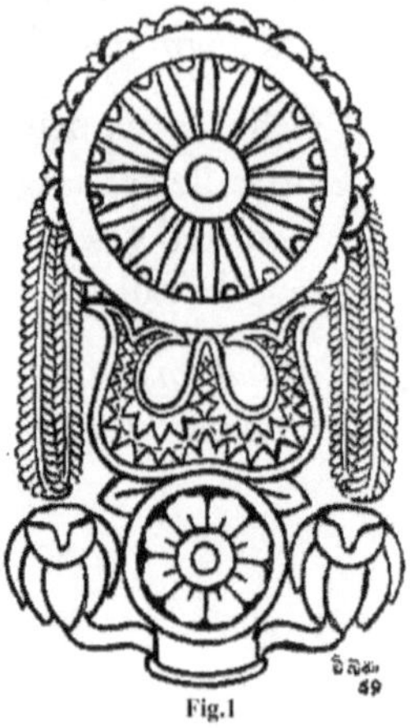

Fig.1

Plate I

PLATE II

Fig. 2: Asoka Wheel, Sārnāth; 3rd century B.C.

Fig. 3: A wheel adorned with *chatta* and *satti* motif, Sāñchī; 1st century A.C.

Fig. 4: Eight-spoked wheel adorned with *chatta* and *satti* motif, Sāñchī; 1st century A.C.

Fig. 5: Wheel adorned with *chatta* and *satti* motif, Amarāvati; 2nd century A.C.

Fig. 6: Tibetan *dharma-cakra*.

Fig. 7: A modern wheel symbol.

Plate II

PLATE III

Fig. 8: Stūpa surmounted with *chatta* and *satti*, the latter bearing flags, Sāñchī; 1st century A.C.

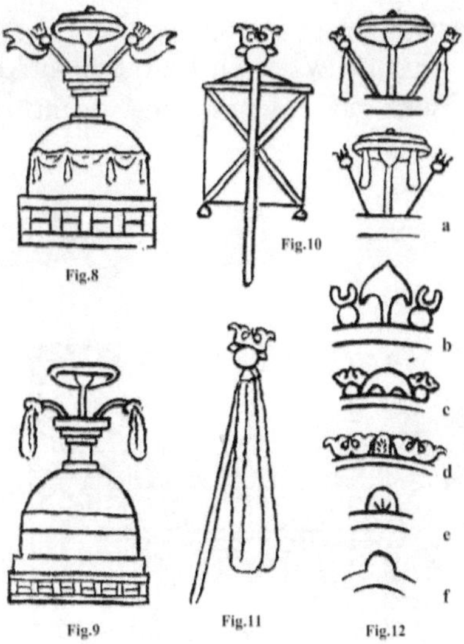

Plate III

PLATE IV

Fig. 13: Solar symbol from a coin; 3rd century B.C.

Fig. 14: Wheel adorned with a circle of *chattas*, from a coin; 3rd century B.C.

Fig. 15: *Chatta* and *satti* motif from a coin; 3rd century B.C.

Fig. 16: Wheel adorned with *satti*; 1st century A.C.

Fig. 17: Lion face within an arch—a detail from a bas-relief, Amarāvati; 2nd century A.C.

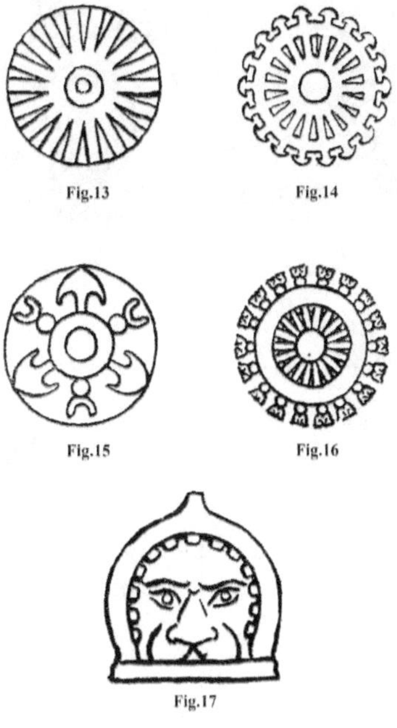

Plate IV

PLATE V

Fig. 18: Wheel on a lion pillar adorned with garlands, Sāñchī; 1st century A.C.

Fig.18

Plate V

Fig.19

Plate VI

PLATE VI

Fig. 19: *Dhamma-cakka* shrine—a bas-relief from Bārhut; 2nd century A.C.

PLATE VII

Fig. 20: Foot Print, Amarāvati; 2nd century A.C.

Fig. 21: Foot Print, Amarāvati; 2nd century A.C.

Fig. 22: Foot Print, Anurādhapura; 2nd century A.C.

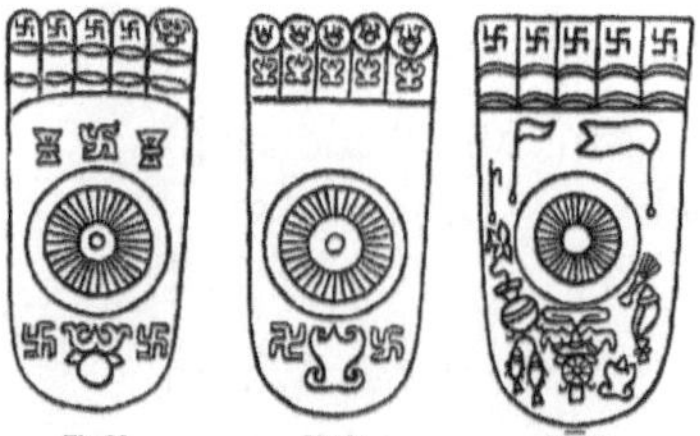

Fig.20 Fig.21 Fig.22

Plate VII

Figure Sources

Figs. 13, 14, and 15 are drawn after Figs. 5, 6, and 13 of Plate I of *The Beginnings of Buddhist Art* by Alfred Foucher.

All illustrations from Sāñchī are drawn from photographs appearing in *The Monuments of Sāñchī* by Sir John Marshall and Alfred Foucher.

For the originals of Figs. 20 and 21 see *Sculpture from Amarāvatī in the British Museum* by Douglas Barrette and The Buddhist Stūpa at Amarāvatī and Jaggeyyapeṭa by J. Burgess.

Fig. 19 is after an illustration from *The Art of Indian Asia* by Heinrich Zimmer.

Fig. 22 is a freehand drawing after a piece of sculpture from the National Museum of Sri Lanka, Colombo.

Prayer and Worship

by

Francis Story

WHEEL PUBLICATION NO. 139

Prayer and Worship

Once when the Buddha was talking to the prominent lay disciple Anāthapiṇḍika, he made the following comment on the uses of prayer:

> There are, O householder, five desirable, pleasant and agreeable things which are rare in the world. What are those five? They are long life, beauty, happiness, fame and (rebirth in) the heavens. But of these five things, O householder, I do not teach that they are to be obtained by prayers[1] or by vows.[2] If one could obtain them by prayers or vows, who would not do it?
>
> For a noble disciple, O householder, who wishes to have long life, it is not befitting that he should pray for long life or take delight in so doing. He should rather follow a path[3] of life that is conducive to longevity. By following such a path he will obtain long life, be it divine or human.
>
> For a noble disciple who wishes to have beauty, happiness, fame and (rebirth in) the heavens, it is not befitting that he should pray for (them) or take delight in so doing. He should rather follow a path of life that is conducive to beauty, happiness, fame and (rebirth in) the heavens. By following such a path he will obtain (rebirth in) the heavens.
>
> Aṅguttara Nikāya, Pañcaka Nipāta (The Fives) No. 43

Among the Teachers of his time the Buddha was known as a *kammavādin*,[4] one who taught the efficacy and importance of actions. In his doctrine and discipline it is not through supplicating unseen powers by traditional religious ceremonies that man obtains benefits he desires; they have to be earned by living the good life in thought, word and deed. This indeed is the basis of Buddhist ethical teaching. The law of moral compensation

---

1. Prayer: *ayacana-hetu.*
2. Vows: *patthana-hetu.*
3. Comy: *dana, sila, bhavana;* liberality, virtue, meditation.
4. Not the *karma-yoga* of the *Bhagavadgita*, which consists in observing religious ritual and caste duties.

and retribution inherent in the causal structure of events is the principle which alone can lift rules of conduct out of the sphere of the purely man-made and arbitrary, and place them on a universal basis. Without that, they are subject everywhere to the exigencies of situation and fashion, and people of intelligence are bound to query their validity. All the various symptoms of present-day moral doubt and disintegration are basically due to the lack of understanding of this principle of moral cause and effect.[5]

The third of the ten fetters to be broken before *sotāpattimagga*, the first stage of deliverance, can be reached is *sīlabbataparāmāsa*, the belief in and clinging to empty ritual. In the time of the Buddha this meant the rituals of the Brahmins, such as tending the sacred fire (mentioned as a useless practice in the Dhammapada), and the vows of extreme asceticism taken by naked recluses of the Nigaṇṭha school, and others who lived like dogs or cows. *Sīlabbataparāmāsa* also embraced offerings and sacrifices to the gods; in fact, all the elaborate formalism of Vedic religion. The Rig Veda, which was old before the Buddha's birth, was a collection of hymns and prayers.

The Buddha, who declared himself "also a knower of the Vedas," was familiar with them and had found them to be useless as aids to Enlightenment. In the text quoted above he even rejects them as a means of obtaining mundane benefits. To understand this position taken by the Buddha it is necessary to examine the nature of prayer and worship in general.

It seems to be a fundamental instinct in human nature to turn to prayer in times of need or perplexity. Prayer is an appeal to a higher power, either for guidance or to intervene in a situation which the individual feels himself unable to ameliorate by any effort of his own. The external power whose benevolence he invokes may be real or imaginary, but whichever it is, cases are cited which seem to show that this kind of prayer is sometimes followed by the desired result. It may be that this was what Voltaire had in mind when he wrote that if God did not exist it would be necessary to invent him.

5. In Buddhism, *kamma* (volitional act, involving choice between wholesome and unwholesome action) and *vipāka* (result of such action, in the present life or a subsequent one).

The aphorism does not at all imply that God does exist, for clearly Voltaire held other views. What it does suggest, rather strongly, is that he recognised the existence of a common need, the wish to believe that there is an invisible power, stronger than those acting within the familiar framework of causality; a power, moreover, that is intelligently interested in human affairs and is willing to mould events to our satisfaction.

How primeval this instinct is can be seen from the earliest records of prehistoric man, which date from a time when prayer, or something like it, was conceived in terms of sympathetic magic. The first evidences of human pictorial art are the drawings of deer and buffaloes transfixed by hunters' arrows, left to us by the early cave dwellers, and they were most likely intended to serve magical purpose. By picturing in anticipation the slaying of these animals, primitive man believed that he could ensure the success of his hunting expeditions. He supposed that by depicting the situation he desired he could bring it about. From this belief, that by willing an event, and giving it concrete and visible form, it could be made an actuality, must have come the idea of prayer. We do not know what strange ceremonies may have accompanied the execution of these cave drawings to give them magical potency, nor whether they did indeed bring results. All we know is that they are there, and from magical usages still to be found in many parts of the world we are able to divine their purpose. They are functional, not decorative, art.

Since we have been led so far back into man's obscure past, it is tempting to speculate that the notion of worship, which is linked with that of prayer, may be present in a crude form at an even lower stage, perhaps among other primates. Tales have been told of travellers seeing apes at the time of the full moon performing something like ritual dances while gazing at the lunar disc, clasping their hands and bending their bodies in an equivalent to the human posture of genuflexion. Such tales are naturally dubious, but there is no really conclusive reason for disbelieving them. The instinct to worship is clearly of such antiquity that it may well be present at this level. The higher apes show so many human characteristics that it would be strange rather than otherwise if this one very universal element were absent from their behaviour when in their natural state. It has not been observed among chimpanzees or orangutans in captivity, so far as I am aware; but it may be that the animals, seeing the inability of their lunar god to release them, lose their faith; or, since all their needs are provided by man, neglect their religious duties.

It would be fruitless to enter here into a discussion regarding the existence of a God or gods able to answer prayer. A more profitable line of inquiry is to ask whether man's thought itself is capable of interfering with the natural progress of events which lie outside his direct control. As I have already remarked, it sometimes seems as though prayers can produce results. But is this really so? It is rather more probable that the cases in which prayer seems to have been "answered" are far outnumbered by those in which it is not, but that it is the cases of seeming success that are noted and recalled, while the fruitless examples are forgotten. When a positive response appears to have been made to the prayer it may be due to chance (that is to say, to other, unknown causes), for among a great number of petitions chance on average will ensure that some prayers must be followed by the result prayed for. It is only where the chances against the occurrence of a particular event that has been prayed for are very much above average, yet the event takes place, that we are justified in looking for another element besides chance in the situation.

And here we cannot but take notice of the peculiar pattern of events to which Carl G. Jung has given the name "acausal synchronicity." This denotes, for want of a better term, the occurrence of a series of apparently chance events, all belonging to the same order of things or having reference to the same object, where no causal connection between one event and the others can be discerned. To give what is perhaps the commonest example of this, one may light upon an interesting item of information which has never come to one's notice before, although it is within the ambit of one's normal interests. Shortly afterwards one finds a reference to the same item in a book, newspaper or magazine; and this reference may be followed by others in quick succession, as though a source connected with that particular subject had been tapped, while it is impossible to trace any connection between the random events which are bringing it to one's attention. The whole series of events is seemingly haphazard, yet it carries a suggestion that each may be a part of some structure of relationships that underlies the causality of the sensible world, or which projects our familiar system of causal relationships into other dimensions where we cannot follow it. What we are observing is the penetration of one level of reality by outcroppings from another. Every event of which we are conscious has a genealogy in time, but it is not at all certain that an event in its totality conforms to its measurable aspect as that is known to us and as it can be stated in terms of temporal sequence. To grasp its organisation we are compelled to think in terms of mutual and coincidental dependence as well as in terms of sequential causality, just as we are when considering *Paṭiccasamuppāda,* the Buddhist doctrine of Dependent Origination.

Seen in this context, the praying for a certain thing to happen, and its subsequent happening, may not be events related to one another in the temporal order with which we are familiar: both events may be dependent upon a substructure which is extra-spatial and extra-temporal, a total event of which we are conscious only in those parts of it which project into our world structure and are spatially and temporally limited. Thus a constellation of unrelated events may enter into our experience without our realising that each event belongs categorically to one total event that lies outside our time-and-space-conditioned awareness. They are outflowings from another level of causality of which we have no sensory information, but which stands in relation to our normal area of awareness much as the world of nuclear physics stands in relation to the Newtonian world. It is becoming more and more evident that time on the subatomic level is not the time that we know. Its freakish behaviour is causing scientists to revise many of their ideas in the attempt to reconcile it with the concept of causality in conventional physics; and this is hardly surprising when they have stumbled upon an order of time which apparently admits of movement in both directions, or, in popular parlance, a time that moves backwards.

But that is perhaps stating the case too crudely. The situation as it stands at the time of writing is that the behaviour of neutrinos and other elementary particles with a lifespan of one billionth of a second in the subatomic world does not adhere rigidly to the parity and time reversal invariance principles, which are fundamental to the principle of causality in physics. It seems also that some particles found in superdense stars can travel faster than light; which gives rise to the inference that signals sent out by these particles travel backwards in time and reach their destination before they are emitted from their source. But it is notoriously unsafe to base any philosophical conjecture on the ever-shifting sands of science.

The universe of concepts is a closed system, and although it may expand into incredible realms, the conceptual mind can travel only around its inner circumference, to reach no final resting place. It is not by journeying to the world's end that the real nature of things can be discerned, but only by making a breakthrough into other levels of consciousness. This has always been axiomatic in Buddhism. All that science can contribute to ultimate knowledge is the negative demonstration of the conditioned and relative nature of the world, which is only the starting point of Buddhism's venture into reality.

A further hint of the paradoxical state of affairs that science appears to have disclosed in the world structure may be found in the numerous cases of well-authenticated precognition. If precognition, as distinct from mere prediction, is a fact, it means that our accepted view that cause must precede effect is not valid in all circumstances. Normally, an event which we perceive takes place before our perception of it, if only by a split second. This agrees nicely with our belief that the event represents cause and our perception of it is its effect. But if an event is actually seen occurring before it takes place, the effect has come about before the cause, and the relationship in sequence between them has been reversed. This points to a state of things in which, using a different mode of apprehension, it could be seen that our willing of an event to occur is not the cause, but could be the result, of its subsequent occurrence. If this is so, belief in the efficacy of prayer founded upon instances in which it seems to have brought results may be due to nothing but a misunderstanding of extra-temporal causality, or what Jung called acausal synchronicity. Altered states of consciousness experienced under special conditions are themselves sufficient proof that the time which is dominated by events and space relationships is by no means the only order of time, nor is our world the only plane on which the mind can function. Consciousness is confined to this sphere just so long as it depends solely upon the sensory contacts possible to the human body for its support. For these, the space-time continuum is the framework necessary to give them definition and meaningfulness. There is more than a symbiotic relationship between space, time and events; they are all aspects of the same conceptual reality that forms the structure of relative or conventional truth, and which Buddhism calls *sammuti-sacca*. All phenomena that we apprehend through the senses are made up of mutually-conditioned factors belonging to the same order of interdependence, and this state of things holds good throughout the material universe. But matter itself is now known to exist in unfamiliar states, in which different orders of causality obtain, so that it is clear that none of these states represents an absolute, rock-bed foundation to the edifice of our cognitive experience.

Many people, among them Balzac, who made much of it in his novels, have held the belief that the human will can be concentrated into a force, quasi-material, which is capable of acting upon the flow of events and of altering its direction. This is an attractive and not altogether impossible idea, but to do justice to it a rather oblique approach is needed. We have seen that modern physics is tending to become somewhat mystical, if by that word is understood the entertaining of concepts that lie outside direct observation. But biology, which claims to hold the key of life, or at least of living organisms, is still firmly entrenched in materialism. Therefore to speak of "science" as though it were a homogeneous system that presents a solid front against everything metaphysical is very deceptive, to say the least. Whether the various scientific disciplines will ever form a unified body is doubtful. Between them there still lies a lot of untrodden ground, and those who are attempting to explore it, the parapsychologists, are not receiving much encouragement. Among parapsychologists, too, many are not interested in physical phenomena. Beyond a few experiments in psychokinesis and some, by amateurs, in trying to promote the growth of plants by prayer, not much has been done to test the potency of thought when it is directed towards influencing external objects without physical contact. The most impressive of such experiments to date have been conducted in Russia. In January 1969 I saw a film, brought from Russia by American parapsychologists, of tests that were carried out on a

Russian woman who it is claimed has the ability to move objects by mental concentration. Some small articles were placed on a stand in front of her, under a glass dome. Pictures were taken from various angles to show that there was no physical contact between the woman and the objects, the stand and the dome. She appeared to be concentrating intensely, moving her body from side to side and forward and backward. The objects under the glass certainly moved, always towards her. It seemed rather unlikely that fraud was involved since the experiments, or at least the exhibiting of the film, had not been approved by the Russian authorities. It had been shown to the American parapsychologists clandestinely, and brought from Russia in secret. It may be presumed that the experiment was scientifically controlled, but one defect in its presentation by motion pictures lay in the fact that there was no means of ensuring that the objects were not of metal or contained metal, and could not be influenced by magnets.

Whether there is any power in prayer to influence events, and if there is, whether it resides in an external agency or is an unknown faculty of the mind, must rest undecided. Rather than trying to settle the issue on the basis of observed facts it is more instructive to examine the rationale of worship. By this I mean the worship of deities for specific ends, for it was this that gave the first impulse to religion and which still provides the chief motivation in theistic worship for the majority of people.

Most prayers are for gain, although today it has become rather unfashionable to admit that self-interest enters into religion at all. The best known prayer in the world makes the appeal, "Give us our daily bread; and forgive us our trespasses...." The point to be noted is that the idea that man should not expect rewards from his religion, and that to do so is in some way unworthy, is only of very recent origin. It has come from the growing tendency to make religion conform to the ideas of humanism, which itself has nothing more to offer as the result of living the good life than the bare satisfaction of doing so. According to the bleak ethics of this school, an honest tradesman whose business is being crushed out of existence by an unscrupulous competitor must be happy in the knowledge that his own moral life is sound. That is the only recompense he will ever get for suffering for his principles. What is to become of the poor man's happiness, in the midst of the ruin brought about by his dishonest competitor, if he ever questions the validity of "natural law," or whether ethics exist in nature at all, is best left to the imagination. If he does, he will feel cheated; for as P. M. Rao has pointed out in a penetrative essay, *The Problem of Sin*,[6] "No amount of rational thinking and the doing of good deeds can in any way modify or even affect our inner core. It is like arguing with an idiot or an insane person." The concept of doing good solely for its own sake and without any belief in an adjustment of the moral balance is an invention of humanism; it can scarcely be found in the original form of any religion. It is assumed, a priori, in religious thought that there are transcendental rewards for living righteously and evil consequences for violating the sacred laws. This element is as strong in Jesus' Sermon on the Mount as it is in any other religious exhortation, as an unbiased reading of it will testify. On one occasion the Buddha suggested, for the sake of sceptics who could not believe in a continuation of life after the dissolution of the body, that to obey the moral law was an end in itself, leading to an untroubled mind and an unblemished reputation in the world; but so far as I am aware this passage is the only one of its kind.[7] In many other texts the Buddha condemns the theory that there are no heavens and no hells, and no consequences of good and bad deeds in an after state, as being beliefs that make the good life almost impossible.

Regarding the Bhikkhu life itself the Buddha said, "A man will not give up an inferior pleasure except with the prospect of gaining one that is superior." By this he meant the surrender of sensual, worldly joys for the higher and more secure happiness to be found in the *jhānas*, and ultimately in Nibbāna.

So it is as well to recognise that most men worship as they trade—for gain of some kind. Their prayer is a respectful attempt to strike a bargain with some deity in which they tender so much faith, or so much self-denial in mild forms of asceticism, in the hope of receiving substantial benefits, here or hereafter. Prayer and fasting, the burning of votive candles and the observance of holy days all belong to this aspect of religion.

---

6. The Wheel No. 136, see above p. 128.
7. The *Kālāma Sutta* (The Wheel No. 8).

In principle there is nothing discreditable in this, but its practice gives rise to some anomalous situations, of which most people today have become aware. For example, when two countries professing the same faith are at war with one another, each will pray to the same God for victory, and ecclesiastics will bless the regiments and weapons of destruction before they go into action. But if God is certain to grant victory to the more righteous of the two powers, to ask him to do so seems superfluous. If both sides are equally in the right (or equally in the wrong, which is more likely) the deity is placed in an awkward quandary, which can be resolved only by giving victory to the side that has pleased him most or displeased him least. Again, it is to be presumed that he would do that in any case, even if it is only a pyrrhic victory. Or is it believed that he can be persuaded to overlook faults if sufficient praise and flattery are lavished upon him, and give the victory to the unworthy? Expressed thus crudely, the theist would doubtless call this a blasphemous idea; but it is hard to find any alternative possibility. In the human mind, of course, the difficulty is readily overcome by the naive tendency of each side to believe that it is in the right. Which again brings us back to square one: for if a nation believes it is in the right, it should also believe that God will automatically grant it the victory.

Again, it is generally held that an omnipotent God, who is benevolently disposed towards his devotees, will ensure that they get whatever is best for them. He may be assumed to have made up his mind as to what he will grant and what he will withhold, and that whatever he decides will be for their greatest advantage. If that is so, a prayer can only be an attempt to make God's decision for him, or to persuade him to change his mind, as though it is the petitioner, not God, who knows best. Even if the prayer is followed by the formula, "Yet not my will but thine, O Lord, be done," the situation is not materially altered. The addition merely transforms the request into a reminder that this is what the devotee would like God to do for him. And if God possesses the attribute of omniscience he must know what is desired before the prayer is uttered. Omniscience also implies that God knows whether the prayer will be granted or not before it is made. Whichever way one looks at it, the idea of praying for some specific end is difficult to justify logically. If prayer is effective in any circumstances it must be because some principle entirely different from that of divine intervention is brought into play.

What has been said applies, of course, only to strictly monotheistic systems. Under a polytheism such as that of ancient Greece or of popular Hinduism, where no god is omnipotent but all have varying degrees of power in relation to one another, or special areas of jurisdiction, praying to any one of them is like applying to a superior in worldly rank, who by exerting himself on one's behalf may be able to accomplish what is required of him, and will do so if one can gain his favour, even if the devotee is morally unworthy or if the granting of the request is not to his best advantage in the long run. For this to be the case it requires gods who have human characteristics, who are limited in power and who are not too exacting in ethics. Precisely such are the gods worshipped in popular Hinduism.

If this point should be challenged, the legendary accounts of the gods in the Purāṇas may be consulted for verification. These bear many similarities to the Graeco-Roman myths. Aside from whether prayer to such gods is effective or not, it can be more reasonably justified than can prayer to a sole, omniscient and omnipotent deity. This is but one of many advantages that polytheism has over monotheism when it is necessary to give a rational account of the belief in supernatural intervention in human affairs.

The concept of one omnipotent God raises many problems besides those connected with prayer. Formerly the difficulties were glossed over by theologians, but for practical purposes every monotheism has had to be in effect a dualism not unlike that of the Manicheans, with a principle of evil opposed to that of good. A system with only one Cause and Mover cannot be made to work.

Though the general purpose of prayer may be the same wherever it is resorted to, the things for which individual men pray have always shown a rich variety. The unspiritual man tends to pray for material profit or victory over his rivals, for success in business or to gain the bubble reputation at the shrine rather than the canon's mouth. The more devoutly inclined pray for higher wisdom, for communion with their God, for forgiveness of their sins or for the welfare of humanity. This higher type of religious impulse is found among some comparatively rare followers of every creed, and the form and content of their prayer is more akin to the Buddhist discursive meditations (on *mettā*, for example) than are the petitions of those who crave material benefits. All the same, behind the prayer there usually lurks a personal wish, the longing for salvation and immortality. And it is in this regard that Buddhism takes an altogether different position.

In Buddhism there can be no question of calling upon a deity for aid so far as ultimate liberation, the attainment of Nibbāna, is concerned, for it is recognised as being something that no external power can bestow. On the lower level, Buddhism is not intent upon the kind of benefits that deities may be assumed to confer. Except insofar as it is the field of moral choice where alone striving for Nibbāna is possible, the life of this world is not the concern of Buddhism in the same way as it is to the creeds which teach the existence of a Creator-God who is thought to be actively interested in the welfare of his creatures and responsible for it. The Buddhist knows that he himself is the sole author of his being, or rather that he is the product of Ignorance conjoined with Craving, and that the Dhamma is not a vehicle for the increase of mundane pleasures and attachments, but a means of gaining release from the suffering they bring. Since the gods themselves are involved in *saṃsāric* conditions, they cannot help. The Noble Eightfold Path is a way that each has to tread by his own effort: "*Appamādena sampādetha*"—"Strive with earnestness," was the Buddha's final exhortation. Neither liberation nor even the courage and determination to strive for it are things that prayer can bring.

And if it is useless to pray to any gods, it is equally so to pray to the Buddha. He is not a creator, preserver or destroyer of the universe; neither is he a dispenser of favours nor a supreme punitive power. The principle of Buddhahood is not attached to an entity. When the Buddha is worshipped it is as a teacher, the greatest Teacher of all beings, and such devotion is a spiritual exercise; the Great Wisdom (*Bodhi*), last personified in the Master, is the true object of veneration.

The *pūjā* offered by Buddhists therefore cannot be called prayer, since it contains none of the elements usually present in the attitude denoted by that word. The Buddha image is a cenotaph, enshrining nothing more than the idea of the Master who once lived, the symbol of his presence—which, all the same, is more immediately felt in the Dhamma he taught and becomes ever more so as it is penetrated with understanding. The outward aspect of *pūjā*, the offering of flowers, lights and incense, is not only a token gesture of homage; it also carries a deep symbolism, which is expressed in the Pali formulas that are recited at the time. The transient beauty of the flowers, so soon to lie withered on the tray, reminds the devotee of the impermanence of all composite things: "Even as these flowers must soon wither, so shall my body lie crumbling in decay."[8]

The candles or lamps recall the Great Teacher whose Bodhi dispels the darkness of Ignorance: "These lights I offer to the Teacher who is the Light of the Three Worlds." The incense symbolises the sweet and cleansing fragrance of the Dhamma which permeates the mind; it also stands for the pleasing odour of good deeds which, like the scent of Tagara blossoms, can be recognised from afar (Dhammapada, vv. 11–12).

For the rest, Buddhist devotion is the mental or vocal recitation of the supreme qualities of Buddha, Dhamma and Sangha, followed by homage to the Buddhas of the past and future (for homage in anticipation is perfectly reasonable), and the recitation of the *Mettā*, *Mahā Maṅgala* and other Suttas, especially any Sutta which is particularly appropriate to the occasion. It is, in short, an act of mental purification and is carried out with that intent alone.

In Buddhism the cult of devotion (*bhakti*) is certainly not absent; but it is restrained, and emotional transports are not encouraged. Particularly this is so on the levels of the highest endeavour. The Buddha rebuked a monk who showed an excessive attachment to his person which was interfering with the monk's progress, and on his deathbed he praised a Bhikkhu who had retired to practise Bhāvanā instead of watching beside him to the end (*Mahāparinibbāna Sutta*).[9]

There is a story of a Christian missionary who found a Chinese priest chanting in a temple. When the Chinese had finished, the missionary asked him: "To whom were you praying?" The

---

8. See "Flower Offering," by Kassapa Thera, in *Devotion in Buddhism*, The Wheel No. 18.

9. *The Last Days of the Buddha*, *The Wheel* No. 67/69.

Chinese looked faintly surprised. "To no one," he replied. "Well, what were you praying for?" the missionary insisted. "Nothing" said the Chinese. The missionary turned away, baffled. As he was leaving the temple, the Chinese added, kindly, "And there was no one praying, you know."

The Chinese in that story understood perfectly the psychology of prayer as an instrument of mental purification. If it were understood in this sense by people who can no longer believe in any god to pray to, they might still be able to contact sources of power within themselves that have become closed to them by reason of their scepticism. Prayer of this kind, which is not really prayer at all, can be an instrument of potency in itself, irrespective of whether it invokes any external agency or not. When it takes the form of an interior dialogue, or approaches abstract contemplation, it has a real therapeutic value that is entirely lacking in prayer for the fulfilment of desires or for supernatural intervention.

To pray for the welfare of others, when the prayer is untainted by thoughts of self, is another action that brings into play the higher mental impulses (*adhicitta*), and one that, whatever invisible power it may seek to invoke, makes for spiritual growth. This kind of prayer, even though it may be the outcome of wrong assumptions, such as the belief that it will be heard by a Heavenly Father or transmitted to him by one of his angelic emissaries, has its own value, a value that cannot be assessed in any way except by reference to the internal experience that accompanies it and leaves its stamp upon the mind. It may be called the first approach to the divine abidings (*brahma-vihāra*) by way of mental purification through *mettā* (loving-kindness) and *karuṇā* (compassion). Such prayer, when it is accompanied by erroneous views, may have in it too much of emotion to achieve *upekkhā* (equanimity or detachment), and may be too narrowly restricted to concern for those who are in a pitiful plight to include *muditā* (joy in the happiness of others), but nevertheless it opens up the heart and prepares it for a more comprehensive understanding of the truths which, thoroughly penetrated, bring wisdom and insight. An example of this may be seen in the case of Kisā Gotamī, whose distracted prayers for the revival of her dead child were the prelude to the dawn of higher knowledge.

In a sense it may be likened to those moral principles found in all religions which, although they are grounded on false views (*diṭṭhi-nissita-sīla*), are good in themselves, and the observance of which is kammically wholesome.

There is another kind of prayer, also, which takes effect, if not in outward circumstances in the individual's subjective experience. It is that which is wrung from a man in the last extreme of anxiety, anguish, perplexity or remorse for a wrong deed that he cannot undo, when he is more concerned for the harm it has caused someone else than he is for any punishment it may bring upon himself. In crises such as these, the spontaneous and irrepressible cry from the heart is an emotional and spiritual catharsis, and it often brings relief from internal tensions that can neither be relaxed nor any longer endured. Remorse in itself is a purely negative emotion and Buddhists do not usually surrender themselves to it, knowing it to be an unwholesome and unprofitable state of mind. If it does arise, it should be translated into beneficial action. The best way of dealing with a situation of this kind, should it occur, is to determine to avoid actions likely to cause it in future, and then to counteract the unwholesome *citta* that has arisen by some deed, or some positive thought, of a wholesome nature. But for those not trained in the Buddhist discipline, prayer is often the only means of finding relief in unbearable situations, and it is not without benefit. If it is a question of some moral problem to solve, the release of tension brought about by praying restores the balanced calm necessary to view the problem in its true light and come to a decision. But in the resort to pray for escape from remorse there lies an insidious danger. It is that the prayer, and the resulting sensation of relief from the burden of guilt, may lead to a belief that the wrong deed has been forgiven and washed out, though not expiated, and that there is no need to take any further action. Unless the penitential prayer is accompanied by a genuine resolve to make whatever restitution may be possible, and to exert oneself to do better in future, the release from anxiety it has brought will be a delusion, and possibly a very harmful one, like putting a soothing dressing on a wound that is turning gangrenous. It is a device for suppressing the guilt feeling instead of removing it altogether. Past unwholesome kamma cannot be undone or blotted out by wishful thinking, but it can be counterbalanced, and in part at least mitigated, by good kamma of the present and future. If the prayer leads to this insight, in however vague a way, and inspires wholesome action, it is good. If not, it is altogether useless. It has given temporary relief without correcting the fault, which will continue to appear, again and again, in recurring situations of a like nature.

Certain Christian sects, taking an extreme view of man's helplessness in the grip of an incurable corruption and of the doctrine that salvation can come only through grace from without, have taught that the devotee must yield himself to the utmost depravity before he can enter into communion with God,[10] in the belief that "the greater the sin, the greater the forgiveness." Heretical though these sects may have been, the germs of their error are to be found in orthodox Christianity itself, from the Old Testament doctrine of Original Sin down to its New Testament corollary of vicarious atonement and the preference Jesus seems to have shown for sinners over the righteous. This has helped to form ambivalent attitudes towards sin and redemption in the Western mind; attitudes which often bring confusion, and consequent anxiety, to problems of moral responsibility. It has also, in an indirect way, been the cause of an exaggerated concern over the actions of others. In recent times this has shown itself in feelings of guilt arising through an acute sense of personal identification with the societal group and its collective acts of the past, extending to cases where the individual had neither taken part in the group activities he condemns, nor even approved of them, and where, consequently, Buddhism would see no personal guilt involved. Since a mistaken sense of guilt is almost as unhealthy a state of mind as one based upon reality, it might be supposed to be also an uncomfortable one; but there is in fact some reason to believe that the Western mind finds feelings of collective guilt easier to support than the sense of an individual rightness which it has been taught to regard as Pharisaic. The current tendency to level off distinctions may also have something to do with this, making it more comfortable to be a sinner in company, or

10. *Histoire du pantheisme populaire au moyen age at au seizieme siecle*, Auguste Jundt.

to imagine oneself one, than to be a good man alone. The idea of the church congregation, the flock, is the spiritual father of "togetherness," and while it may be a good thing in certain respects it has disadvantages in others. One man may be tempted to throw the entire burden of his moral responsibility upon the group, while another, more conscientious, may tend to take the weight of collective guilt onto his own shoulders and become a victim to feelings of personal involvement that are entirely unwarranted. In the circumstances the good but worldly-minded man tries to interfere. He becomes a reformist—that is to say, if he goes far enough, an executioner.[11] The more spiritual retires to solitude and prayer.

The religious background to this state of affairs is further complicated by the fact that there are two streams of thought in Christianity, due to its eclectic origins: one is predeterministic, the other is dynamic and more akin to the *kamma-vāda* of Buddhism, and since the conflict between them has never been satisfactorily resolved it has been left for sectarians to place the emphasis on whichever reading they prefer. Jansenism, with its theory that some are chosen for salvation from the beginning, and Calvinism, with its similarly pre-elective view, are typical examples of the attitudes that must result from belief in an omnipotent and omniscient deity; other churches attempt, with varying degrees of success, to hold a balance between doctrines that are not easy to reconcile. Whether the new "God is dead" theology will eventually remove the difficulties or whether it makes a crack in the fabric which must quickly lead to its collapse remains to be seen. What will most surely be affected by it is the attitude towards prayer, and especially towards prayer that calls upon a personal deity for intervention in mundane affairs. In the absence of such a deity there are, however, some alternative possibilities that are not entirely without support in actual experience. We may glance at them, although it is not practicable to discuss them in detail here.

Elsewhere[12] I have mentioned some evidence which seems to

11. Some of the great criminals of history—the Cromwells, the Robespierres, the Marats—were not the less criminal because they were necessary. But others have been criminals without being necessary.

12. *The Case for Rebirth*, The Wheel No. 12/13.

suggest that intelligences from other planes of being do occasionally intervene in the affairs of the living, and I am far from discounting this possibility. But in those cases that have come to my notice and which appear to me most worthy of credence help seems to have come not from any of the gods recognised by theistic systems but from beings now in one of the lower heavenly states who were formerly connected by ties of relationship or friendship with the person who receives the help. In these cases it seldom, if ever, takes the form of material assistance, but rather that of guidance in times of perplexity, comfort in times of stress and warnings of impending danger. It also seems to come spontaneously rather than in answer to any prayerful demand, unless an unspoken call for help constitutes a prayer. Moreover, it appears to have come in a number of cases when the person concerned was quite unaware that he was in need of help. One such case is that of a European Buddhist monk who affirms that he has several times been saved from a totally unsuspected danger by what he calls his "protecting hand." This sometimes manifested to him as an internal voice, sometimes in the form of physical restraint. On one occasion it took the second form when, running from pursuers in pitch darkness, he was suddenly arrested, as though by an invisible barrier, to find that he had been heading straight for a precipice. Again, the explanation could lie in a psychic faculty of the person concerned, which precognises the peril and alerts the conscious mind to its presence. Relatively few people who have known such experiences, however, are willing to accept this explanation. To them it always appears as though some external agency had been at work, and it would be altogether arbitrary to dismiss their conviction as groundless. Many examples of this type of experience are to be found in the literature of psychical research, and they have not yet been given a satisfactory explanation that rules out the external agency hypothesis. Some of the recorded cases, taken at their face value, point as definitely to some kind of intercommunication between the human world and other planes of existence as do similar accounts given in Buddhist texts. In this connection it is worth noting that the present-day positivist tendency to regard Buddhism as being "only a philosophy" could easily be corrected if its advocates would study the material on this subject to be found in the earliest Buddhist canonical texts, and make an unbiased attempt to interpret it in the light of contemporary research in parapsychology.

We have seen that Buddhist *pūja* has nothing in common with the offerings made to gods who are believed to be mystically present in their images, and that Buddhism is little concerned with the eight worldly conditions,[13] except in relation to the truth of *dukkha*. But Buddhists are human, their lives filled with ordinary preoccupations and anxieties, for themselves and for those dependent upon them. Buddhism, which starts as a very realistic system of ethico-psychology, recognises two forms of aspiration, the worldly and the transcendental, *lokiya* and *lokuttara*. He who wishes to be wholly world-transcending in his aims must of necessity give up mundane attachments. Ultimately there is no avoiding the choice between one and the other. Yet this does not mean that one still remaining in the world rejects the higher life completely. The path of renunciation lies through actions that bear good results (*kusala kamma*) to the abandoning of all result-bearing actions, the good equally with the bad, when Arahatship is reached. And so the ordinary lay Buddhist, just as much as the Christian, Hindu and Muslim, sometimes feels the need of help from a higher source in his everyday affairs.

The Mahāyāna did not have to invent a god for this purpose; it has the Bodhisattvas who, unlike the Buddha, are still benevolently active in saṃsāra. But the very early Buddhists, before the advent of the Mahāyāna, evidently had to be advised against resorting to the gods of the Vedic pantheon for the fulfilment of their wishes. The Buddha was particularly emphatic against Vedic worship when it involved costly and inhumane sacrifices, and when it was mistakenly believed to confer *mokṣa* (deliverance). It was one of the Devas themselves who asked the Buddha what was the highest (most effective) of the propitious observances to bring about happy results. The commentary to the *Maṅgala Sutta* tells us that the propitious observances (*maṅgala*) in dispute were the Brahmanical ceremonies at birth, name-giving, marriage and so on, at different stages of life. The Buddha's reply was that the observance most certain to bring felicity was to live in accordance

13. *Aṭṭha-loka-dhamma:* Gain and loss, honour and dishonour, happiness and misery, praise and blame.

with Dhamma. By this he meant that a man's good *kamma* is his only certain protection from the ills of the world, not the observance of religious ceremonies, smearing one's forehead and that of others with ashes, interpreting good and bad omens and lucky or unlucky hours of the day, and offering food to gods who were unable to eat it, or, if they really were gods, had no need of it. According to Buddhism—and not merely commentarial Buddhism, but the Buddhism of the oldest texts—what the Devas need and welcome is a share of the merit that only human beings can gain, through deeds of charity, compassion and duty towards the Sangha. The right living of a householder is fully set out in the *Sigālovāda Sutta*,[14] where the Buddha resourcefully takes advantage of the erroneous views of the young layman Sigāla to show him the right path to peace of mind and prosperity. The teaching given in the *Sigālovāda Sutta* sets forth in detail the moral code (*sīla*) of a householder, and is the same as that summarised in the quotation at the beginning of this essay. It emphasises man's ability to enrich his own life with meaning and value, without dependence upon supernatural aid.

Yet despite this, the practice of appealing to gods for *lokiya* benefits persists among Buddhists, and to give a clear idea of what is meant by this, some explanation of the two terms *lokiya* and *lokuttara* must be given. Buddhism recognises *lokiya* experience as well as *lokiya* aspiration, and *lokuttara* experience as well as *lokuttara* aspiration. But *lokiya* aspiration and experience bear a wider connotation than does the word "mundane." As a descriptive and defining term *lokiya* relates to all forms of consciousness and of existence within the thirty-one abodes of *saṃsāra*. Even the heavenly states are included in that which is *lokiya*, "worldly" or "mundane." The "world" in Buddhism is not only the sensible world of ordinary consciousness; it is the unseen environment of that world as well, comprising many planes of existence related to consciousness, and one to unconsciousness. As corollary to this, the definition of *lokuttara*, the "supramundane," is narrower; it relates solely to the state outside of conditioned phenomena: that is, Nibbāna. Therefore in Buddhism the desire to be reborn in a heavenly state is just as much a *lokiya* aspiration as would be, for

14. Included in *Everyman's Ethics*, The Wheel No. 14.

example, to wish for promotion in one's job or success in a business venture. There is thus a displacement of values when a comparison is made between the Buddhist terms *lokiya* and *lokuttara,* and what they denote, and the English words used to translate them. In Western thinking, heavenly existence is considered to be supramundane, and the mundane is only life as experienced on this earth, the world known to us through the senses.

It follows, then, that the devas to whom Buddhists sometimes pray in the *devalas* and Hindu *kovils* in Sri Lanka, and the *nats* similarly worshipped in Burma, are worldly powers. Among the thirty-seven *nats* of Burma, some were semi-legendary, semi-historical persons; they are indigenous local deities who have no connection with the Hindu gods. One of them, indeed, was a Muslim in his life on earth, and is still considered to be a follower of that faith. His cult devotees, although themselves Buddhists, abstain from eating pork, just as the Buddhist followers of Hindu gods in Ceylon avoid meat, fish and eggs, the sole object being to keep in the good graces of their patrons. These godlings (*devatā*) are approached with homage and suitable offerings to win their favour exactly as a king's minister or the head of a business corporation might be waited upon, flattered and offered services with the same end in view. This practice, although it is found in all Buddhist countries, with variations, has nothing whatever to do with the Buddha's teaching of the way to bring suffering to an end. It caters for a human weakness which Buddhism in its purest form exhorts man to transcend. Even though the aspiration to be reborn in a heavenly state is a *lokiya* aspiration, the *lokiya* deities are no more capable of granting it to a human being than is his works manager or the chairman of his board of directors.

But there is another way offered by Buddhism to those who have worldly ambitions for wealth, fame and pleasure. This is the forming of a wish accompanied by a good action (*kusala kamma*); it is the "meritorious deed" which, unless it is obstructed by some heavier *kamma* of an unwholesome kind, brings the desired result in the present life, and if delayed, bears fruit in a subsequent one. The wholesome *kamma* linked to the wish reinforces it by rendering the person who makes the wish worthy to have it fulfilled. This makes use of the principle of *kamma* and *vipāka,* and it is effective; but it is not to be used for an evil purpose, such as doing harm to an enemy or gaining unlawful advantages over others. To try to make use of the law of moral causality in such a way would be demeritorious in the last degree, since it could not fail to rebound on its source, the misguided person who had generated the unwholesome intention. One in whom wisdom is developed will never resort to any device for causing harm to an enemy, be it in the natural way or by invoking the aid of inferior deities. So far as protection from injury to himself by an enemy is concerned, he knows that so long as his own *kamma* is good, no hostile power, human or superhuman, can seriously affect him. He may be wounded, as the Buddha was by the stone hurled at him by Devadatta, but eventually more ill will come to the aggressor than to his intended victim.

There can be no doubt that prayer on the higher level, where it approaches meditation, can be instrumental in bringing about alterations in mental attitudes and consequent behaviour; whether it can cause lasting alterations in the structure of personality must depend upon the degree to which its influence penetrates to the unconscious strata. For this to happen, another mode of consciousness must be brought into play, and it is here that prayer, which by its nature is discursive, has to give way to the technique of bare attention or mindfulness (*satipaṭṭhāna*), which rigorously excludes conceptualisation. It is not with this that we are concerned at present, but with prayer as a means of gaining specific ends.

Prayer which is for something is an expression of desire, and desire is only a weaker word, and so less pejorative, for craving. A desire that is strong enough to seek expression in prayer can scarcely fall short of craving, though it may be far from the craving for drink or drugs which has given the word its objectionable colouring. Now, craving (or thirst—*taṇhā*) is the factor which supports and promotes grasping (*upādāna);* that is, attachment to the components of personality. This grasping supports the process of becoming (*bhava,* the life-continuum), and the life process in turn brings about arising (*jāti*), which is both the arising of the successive moments of existence in the psychophysical order that constitutes the ordinary life continuum and the arising of the first consciousness moment in a new series after death; in other words, arising in a new birth. Thus craving is the kingpin of the mechanism, or the *élan vital* which keeps it going.

It is a psychic energy which manifests itself in the will-to-be and the will-to-do and the will-to-possess. In another guise, it is the will-not-to-be, the deathwish, the craving for annihilation (*vibhava-taṇhā*).

Prayer for something that is desired must necessarily be an expression of one or other of these cravings. People have even prayed for oblivion in death. Therefore a prayer of great intensity is a method of concentrating and harnessing craving. And since craving is the base of the life process and an extremely powerful psychic force, prayer of this kind may be effective to some degree. The dynamism inherent in a single-minded wish might indeed act upon the inert factors of a situation much as Balzac supposed it to do.

To express a wish is to bring oneself a step nearer its fulfilment. To concentrate upon it to the exclusion of all extraneous desires is to give it the driving force of the psychic component that sustains life itself.

And that is a dangerous undertaking. Someone once wrote: "Take care what you desire before you are twenty—for you will surely get it." In youth the desires are strongest; they are also the most deeply felt. But how many people, having obtained what they wished for most when they were young, have found that they no longer want it; that their desires have taken a different turn, have fastened themselves onto new objects. How many more have spent themselves in many years of striving and scheming for wealth, voluntarily stripping themselves of all other interests, only to find when at last they possess the riches they craved for in their youth of poverty that they have so robbed and depleted themselves of all capacity for happiness that they cannot enjoy any of the advantages that money brings, and that alone make it desirable. The sad fact is that most men, when they wish, wish for the wrong thing; or, like Midas in the Greek myth, wish for it in the wrong way.

To desire and work for the acquisition of a special skill is more sensible, for at least there is a good chance that it may become woven into the texture of the *saṅkhāras* and manifest anew in subsequent lives. Unlike the self-made millionaire, the man who sets his mind upon becoming a great musician, artist or writer does not have to leave behind him all the fruits of a lifetime's labour when he goes to the grave. No reckless hand will carelessly throw to waste everything he so painfully amassed, after he is gone, and no one else's life will be ruined in the process. On the contrary, he will carry with him into his next life something—and perhaps a great deal—of the art or science that he loved and strove to perfect; and another genius will enrich the world.

But in the final reckoning, any form of desire is prone to cheat him who harbours it. Prayer is a vehicle of desire, and desire is wedded to the deceptive idea of selfhood. The only safe wish is the wish to attain Nibbāna, the wish to strip away all desire and all delusion connected with desire. When that wish is fulfilled there is nothing left to wish for, and the weary round is over. And because prayer, whether it is effective or not, does not tend towards the attrition of desire nor to the uprooting of the delusion of self, it has no importance in the Noble Discipline of the Buddha.

Survival and Karma in Buddhist Perspective

by

K.N. Jayatilleke

M.A. (Cantab), Ph.D (London)

Professor of Philosophy

University of Ceylon

WHEEL PUBLICATION NO. 141/142/143

I. The Buddhist View of Survival

In this talk I will state and examine the Buddhist view of survival. At the same time I wish to stress the fact that apart from briefly examining the intelligibility of the theory I do not propose to consider here its truth (or falsity) in the light of modern evidence, which I shall do in a later talk.

It is necessary to have a clear and authentic formulation of the Buddhist conception of survival as found in the early texts since there seem to be some misconceptions about this. We may briefly state some of these misconceptions.

Misconceptions

According to one view, the Buddha lived in a society in which the doctrine of rebirth was universally (or widely) taken for granted from time immemorial. The Buddha himself saw no reason to question this belief, which he accepted uncritically and dogmatically.

Another such misconception may be stated as follows: The Buddha's doctrine of *anattā* or no-soul was a denial of the existence of an animistic soul which survived the death of the body and transmigrated. Since nothing survived the death of the body, Buddhism is a form of materialism. The Buddha utilised the doctrines of rebirth and *karma* prevailing in this society (so they say) to impart ethical teachings but did not himself believe in these doctrines.

There is yet another misconception. According to this view, the Buddha was not interested in nor held specific views about the question of human survival or life after death. He roundly condemned speculation about the past or future (i.e. about prior lives or future lives) as unprofitable or mistaken. He was only concerned with man's present state of anxiety, suffering and dissatisfaction and the solution for it.

These misconceptions can be cleared only by making a careful study of the authentic early texts of Buddhism. When we do so we find that the Buddha did assert (i) the continuity without identity of individuality due to the operation of causal factors,

(ii) the doctrine of anattā, which denied the existence of a physical, mental, psychophysical or independent entity within or related to the psychophysical aspects of personality, and (iii) that he rejected mere metaphysical speculation about prior or future lives which did not result in the verification of facts about them.

Historical Background

In order to understand the Buddhist view of survival it is desirable to have some knowledge of the views presented by pre-Buddhist thinkers, i.e. prior to the rise of Buddhism since the Buddhist conceptions were often presented in contrast to them.

It is a remarkable fact that in no other age in the history of thought was a solution to the problem of survival sought with such intensity as in this period and nowhere else can we find such a variety of views put forward.

Logically there are four possible points of view that we can adopt with regard to the question of survival. We may say (i) that we survive death in the form of discarnate spirits, i.e. a single afterlife theory, (ii) that we are annihilated with death, i.e. a materialist theory, (iii) that we are unable to discover a satisfactory answer to this question or there is no satisfactory answer, i.e. a sceptical or positivist theory, and (iv) that we come back to subsequent earth-lives or lives on other similar planets, i.e. a rebirth theory.

The Buddhist texts record several variants of each of these four types of theories. Let us take the variants of single afterlife theories or one-life-after-death theories.

Single After-life Theories

There are thirty-two single afterlife theories listed in the *Brahmajāla Sutta*. According to what philosophers or religious teachers who put forward these theories assert, they are broadly classified into theories which posit that the soul after death is (A) conscious (*saññī*), (B) unconscious (*asaññī*), and (C) super-conscious (*nevasaññāsaññī*).

There are sixteen variants of (A) and eight each of (B) and (C). The sixteen variants of (A) are due to:

1. Variations regarding the material form of the soul:
   (i) has a subtle material form
   (ii) has no such form
   (iii) has for some time a subtle material form and then has no such form
   (iv) has no such form but has the power of manifesting one.

2. Variations regarding the duration of the soul:
   (i) comes to an end
   (ii) is eternal
   (iii) changes its state after some time and becomes eternal
   (iv) does not exist in time.

3. Variations regarding the nature and extent of consciousness:
   (i) is conscious of unity
   (ii) is conscious of diversity
   (iii) is of limited consciousness
   (iv) is of unlimited consciousness.

4. Variations regarding the hedonic tone of the experiences
   (i) is extremely happy
   (ii) is extremely unhappy
   (iii) is partly happy and partly unhappy
   (iv) does not experience happiness or unhappiness, i.e. has a neutral hedonic tone.

Only variations 1 (i)–(iv) and 2 (i)–(iv) are considered applicable to those who hold that the soul is (B) unconscious or (C) superconscious after death.

The above classification appears to be a purely logical one, but the fact that many of these theories can be traced to pre-Buddhist literature proves that it is not.

Thus Prajāpati held on the basis of rational and metaphysical speculation that the soul was "conscious and having its own form after death" [1] i.e. A 1 (i). Uddālaka held that the soul was "unconscious and without form" after death—i.e. B 1 (ii). The *Taittirīya Upaniṣad* holds that the soul has a subtle material form for some time after death and then ceases to have such a form—i.e. A 1 (iii). Yājñavalkya has tried to show that the soul is "neither

1. *Chāndogya Upaniṣad*, 8–12.

conscious nor unconscious after death and has no form"—i.e. C 1 (ii). The *Brāhmaṇas* often speak of a "second death" after personal survival—i.e. A 2 (i).

The one-life-after-death theories held by people in the West who subscribe to different forms of theism or spiritualism are also classifiable as permutations and combinations of the above alternatives. Thus the views held by those who subscribe to the belief that the soul survives as a discarnate spirit for all eternity, or those who say that the soul goes to heaven or hell for eternity after death, or those who maintain that the soul sleeps with the body till a day of judgement when its state is changed, or those who believe that the soul goes to purgatory till a day of judgement—all these views are classifiable under the above scheme.

Materialists

In sharp opposition to those who held dualist theories of body-and-soul and claimed that there was only a single life after death were the materialists, who denied a life after death altogether. Seven schools of such materialists are referred to in the *Brahmajāla Sutta* and some of these are independently referred to in the non-Buddhist literature.

The most extreme of them held there is no mind or soul apart from the body which was entirely a hereditary product of one's parents (*mātāpettika-sambhavo*) and the material elements. What we call "mind" are the patterns of movement in our bodies. The modern version of this is called central state materialism,[2] which tries to do away with phenomenal factors such as "experience," "consciousness," etc. According to this theory when we say that a person is happy, it refers not to a mental state but to a physical state which has among its consequences that it causes a person to behave in a characteristically happy way.

Another school held that the mind is an emergent product which has a material basis and its condition is determined by the food we eat. They argued that just as much as when we mix up certain chemicals in certain proportions, there emerges the

2. See J. J. C. Smart, *Philosophy and Scientific Realism*, Routledge & Kegan Paul, London, 1963.

intoxicating power of liquor, even so the material particles of the body and the food we eat go to form the mind, which is an emergent by-product. There were also schools of mystic materialists who by the use of drugs claimed the possibility of achieving expansions of consciousness (called *micchā jhāna*, wrong *jhāna*, in the texts).

All these schools of materialists were characterised by the fact that they did not hold that mind and body were two different entities but were one and the same entity, either denying the reality of mental phenomena altogether or asserting that they were epiphenomena or accompaniments of the state of body.[3]

Sceptics

The dialectical opposition between the dualistic soul-theorists, who asserted the reality of survival, and the monistic materialists, who denied survival, had already resulted prior to Buddhism in the rise of several sceptical schools of thought. The *Kaṭha Upaniṣad* states, "This doubt is there with regard to a man deceased—'he exists' say some; 'he exists not' say others."[4]

The four schools of Sceptics (*amarāvikkhepikā*) in the *Brahmajāla Sutta* adopted scepticism on the basis of various intellectual or pragmatic grounds. Some maintained that in holding the view either that "there is survival" or that "there is no survival" there results an involvement or entanglement (*upādāna*) in a theory and this promotes mental unrest. Others argued that in holding or denying the theory of survival one is led by one's prejudices for (*chanda, rāga*) or against (*dosa, paṭigha*) and that, therefore, truth demands that we do not come to any definite conclusions. Yet others avoided making definite pronouncements for fear of being engaged in debate. Others again like Sañjaya argued that statements about an afterlife, about moral responsibility, or about transcendent existence were not verifiable and therefore it was not possible to discover their truth or falsity.

Among those who held a dualist hypothesis and asserted "the eternity view" (*sassatadiṭṭhi*) were not only the single afterlife

3. For modern versions see, "The Identity Hypothesis: A Critique," in J. R. Smythies, *Brain and Mind*, Routledge & Kegan Paul, London, 1965.

4. *Kaṭha Upaniṣad*, I. 20.

theorists but those who held several variants of rebirth theories as well. It is important to bear in mind the fact that Buddhism was opposed to all these theories, including the rebirth theories that had been propounded. The Buddha did not posit the existence of an unverifiable, unchanging entity to account for his theory of re-becoming and rebirth. Nor did he hold that the process of re-becoming was strictly determined by past karma, by natural causes or by the will of God. Causal factors were operative no doubt but they were not deterministic. Besides, some rebirth theories held that beings could be reborn even as "rice and barley, herbs, beans, sesame plants and trees."[5] The Buddha did not subscribe to such a point of view. In fact it is doubtful whether the Buddha held that there was rebirth at the lowest levels of life. The Buddha later recounts as a mistaken view some of the beliefs of Jainism, which he put to the test prior to his enlightenment. In one place he says, "I used to walk up and down conscientiously extending my compassion even to a drop of water, wishing that the tiny beings in it may not come to harm."[6]

Buddhist Solution

It is in the historical context outlined above that the Buddha appeared on the scene and sought a solution to the riddle of life. It is therefore not correct to say (as many scholars have done) that the Buddha took for granted the belief in rebirth current in society at the time. As is evident from the Buddhist and the non-Buddhist literature, there was a variety of views on the question of survival at the time covering almost every possibility that one can think of.

Besides, the belief was not of very great antiquity. It is absent in the *Vedas*, it is merely hinted at in the *Brāhmaṇas*, and the early *Upaniṣads* present a variety of views, some of which clearly reject rebirth. By the time of the Buddha, the materialists had made such an impact on society that the Buddha classifies the prevalent theories of his time as those of the Eternalists and of

5. *Chāndogya Upaniṣhad*, 5. 13 6.

6. "*Yāva udabindumhi me dayā paccupaṭṭhitā hoti: mā'haṃ khuddake pāṇe visamagate saṅghātaṃ āpādessanti*," MN 12/M I 78.

the Materialists. In addition, scepticism was so rampant that the elite (the *viññū purisā*) did not subscribe to any specific belief. They were no doubt interested in the problem and people like Pāyāsi even performed experiments to test the validity of the belief in survival. One of the experiments carried out was that of weighing the body immediately before and after death. (See DN 23.) Finally, an unquestioning acceptance of the belief in rebirth is hardly consistent with the spirit of the *Kālāma Sutta,* where the Buddha asks people to adopt a critical attitude towards traditional beliefs.

The Buddhist theory of survival has its origin in the Enlightenment of the Buddha and not in any traditional Indian belief. It is said that it was on the night of his Enlightenment that he acquired the capacity to know his prior lives. It was when his mind was composed, clear, cleansed and without blemish, free from adventitious defilements, pliant and flexible, steadfast and unperturbed, that he acquired this capacity to recall hundreds and thousands of prior lives and the prehistory of the universe, going back through the immensely long periods of the expansions and contractions of the oscillating universe. This is, in fact, called the first important item of knowledge, which broke through the veil of ignorance (*ayaṃ paṭhamā vijjā*).

The second important item of knowledge (*dutiyā vijjā*) was obtained by the exercise of the faculty of clairvoyance (*dibba-cakkhu*), with which the Buddha was able to see among other things the survival of beings in various states of existence, the operations of karma, galactic systems, clusters of galactic systems and the vast cosmos.

The Five States of Existence

In the *Mahāsīhanāda Sutta* there is a reference to the five states of existence. They are as follows: (i) the lower worlds (*duggati, vinipāta niraya*), (ii) the animal kingdom (*tiracchāna-yoni*), (iii) the spirit sphere (*pettivisaya*), (iv) human beings (*manussa*), and (v) *devas* or higher spirits.

While the "lower worlds" (*vinipāta*) are also called *niraya* (hells), we must not forget that "hells" (*pātāla*) in the popular sense are denied. It is said that the common man believes that there is a hell or nether world in the bottom of the ocean, but

Buddha says that this belief is false and states that "hell" is a term for painful sensations. Yet elsewhere there is a reference to worlds which the Buddha claims to see in which everything one senses is unpleasant and the thoughts that come to one's mind are disagreeable and foul. In contrast, it is said that there are worlds in which everything one senses or experiences is pleasant. About the existence of devas, the Buddha says when asked the question as to whether they exist, that he knows on good grounds that they exist. When further questioned as to why he used the qualification "on good grounds," he says that it is because it is commonly taken for granted that devas or higher spirits exist (MN 100.42/M II 131).

The five states of existence are graded according to the amount or degree of pain or pleasure experienced in them. According to this description, the human world is one in which one experiences "more pleasant than unpleasant experiences."[7] In the spirit-sphere it is more unpleasant than pleasant. In the animal sphere it is unpleasant since animals are supposed to live in a state of constant fear with strong unsatisfied instinctive desires such as hunger and thirst. In the "lower worlds" it is said to be very unpleasant. In the deva worlds, on the other hand, it is extremely pleasant.[8]

The person who is pictured as faring on in these states of existence is conceived as one who is oppressed by the heat, exhausted, afraid and thirsty. The lower worlds are compared to a pit of coals into which he falls, animal existence is a pit full of excrement, existence in the spirit-sphere is like coming under a tree in a desert without much shade, human life is compared to coming under a large and shady tree, while the deva world is compared to a well-furnished and beautiful palace. In contrast, Nibbāna is said to be analogous to the above person who is oppressed with heat, exhausted and thirsty, reaching a lake where the waters are cool and clear, bathing in it, quenching his thirst and sitting or lying down in an adjoining glade experiencing extreme happiness.[9]

From the descriptions given in the early texts the usual tendency is for a person to survive as a departed spirit or a discarnate

7. "*Sukhabahulā vedanā vediyamānaṃ*," MN 12.40/M I 75.
8. "*Ekanta-sukha-vedanā vediyamānaṃ*," ibid.
9. Ibid.

spirit in the spirit-sphere and come back to an earth-life since the normal character of human beings is a mixture of good and evil, and the stage of evolution of one's consciousness is attuned to existence in these worlds. But it is possible to regress to animal or subhuman forms of existence by neglecting the development of one's personality or character and becoming a slave to one's passions. It is also exceptionally possible to attain to existence in the deva worlds. In the *Saṅkhārupāpatti Sutta* (MN 120/M III 100), it is said that a person who is possessed of faith (*saddhā*), virtue (*sīla*), learning (*suta*), selflessness (*cāga*), and wisdom (*paññā*) can aspire to and attain better states of existence among human beings or devas.

Intelligibility

The word used to describe the progression from existence to existence is the word "re-becoming" (*punabbhava*). Rebirth is only a special case of re-becoming when a person comes back to an earth-life. Rebirth in this sense takes place until a person attains a spiritual state of "Non-Returner" (*anāgāmi*) or Arahant. If there is any doubt about the interpretation of *punabbhava* as rebirth in these contexts, it may be dispelled by examining similar expressions such as "he does not come back to lie in the womb,"[10] used of an Arahant.

The question has been raised by some philosophers as to whether a conception of survival after death either in the form of rebirth or as a discarnate spirit is at all intelligible. If we preserve someone's heart or kidney in a living condition after his death, we would not say in respect of such an organ that so and so is now alive. It is therefore necessary that there should be some sense in which the re-born person or discarnate spirit should be able to claim identity with the dead person (when he was alive) even though all that can be established is continuity and not identity even in this life. To say that both have the same soul will not help because the existence of such a soul as an unchanging agent or recipient of actions is unverifiable.

10. "*Na punareti gabbhaseyyaṃ,*" Sn 99.

The solution to this problem lies in the criteria that we employ to claim personal identity. In a single human life we normally employ two criteria. One is the spatio-temporal continuity of the body. On the basis of this we can claim that so and so is a person who as a child went to such and such a school, although there may be nothing in common between the two bodies as far as shape and content are concerned. The other criterion is memory on the basis of which someone may claim that he was such and such twenty years ago. When one life is concerned, the two criteria normally support each other.

In the case of the re-born person or discarnate spirit it is the memory criterion alone which can establish the identity. In this case when the body criterion is employed, we have to say that "he is not the same person" but when the memory criterion is employed we would have to say "he is not another person." So according to Buddhism, "he is neither the same nor another" (*na ca so na ca añño*) when we give a strictly accurate description, although in common parlance we may say that he is the same person.

The logical possibility of such personal identity without a soul is granted by Professor A. J. Ayer of Oxford, a logical analyst who says, "I think that it would be open to us to admit the logical possibility of reincarnation merely by laying down the rule that if a person who is physically identified as living at a later time does have the ostensible memories and character of a person who is physically identified as living at an earlier time, they are to be counted as one person and not two." [11]

As for the concept of a discarnate spirit, Professor H. H. Price, following the ideas of some Hindu and Buddhist texts (as he admits) has given an intelligible account of how a "discarnate spirit" may be conceived of, consistent with findings of modern psychology and psychical research.[12]

Although the majority of modern psychologists attempt to explain the functioning of the brain on mechanistic models, they find it difficult to explain away the fact and role of consciousness.

---

11. *The Concept of a Person*, London, 1963, p. 127.

12. H. H. Price, "*Survival and the Idea of 'Another World,'*" in J. R. Smythies, *Brain and Mind*, International Library of Philosophy & Scientific Method, London, 1965, pp. 1–33.

Despite the claim of some philosophers[13] the ghost from the human machine has not been exorcised. Professor Sir John Eccles, who has been described by Sir Cyril Burt as "the most eminent of living neurologists who have specialised in the study of the brain," has made the following statement about the structure and functions of the brain: "the structure of the brain suggests that it is the sort of machine that a 'ghost' might operate," where the word "ghost" is used "to designate any kind of agent that defies detection by such apparatus as is used to detect physical agents."[14] We can do without the concept of a permanent soul, but it is doubtful whether consciousness can be explained away, where it functions as a causal factor in initiating plans, making decisions, etc.

The Buddha did not subscribe to the dualist hypothesis that "the mind and body are different" (*aññaṃ jīvaṃ aññaṃ sarīraṃ*), nor to the identity hypothesis that "the mind and body are the same" (*taṃ jīvaṃ, taṃ sarīraṃ*), but found that there was partial truth in both. Consciousness is partly formed by the impact of the environment on the living body but in turn it determines bodily behaviour.

In rebirth and re-becoming there is continuity of the stream of consciousness (*viññāṇa-sota*) without identity (*anaññaṃ*), making the recall of prior lives potentially possible. It is, however, not a self-identical permanent substance, which is quite independent of the body with regard to its growth and development.

13. E. g. G. Ryle, *The Concept of Mind.*

14. *The Neurophysiological Basis of Mind*, London, Oxford University Press, 1953, pp. 278 ff.

II. The Buddhist Doctrine of Karma

In this talk I merely propose to give a brief account of the Buddhist doctrine of karma, as it is taught in the texts. I do not intend to examine the case for or against it in the light of evidence. I shall undertake this in a later talk.

I refer to this doctrine specifically as the Buddhist doctrine of karma in order to distinguish it from the other non-Buddhist doctrines of karma, which were taught by non-Buddhist thinkers prior to, during and even after the time of the Buddha. In this respect it is important to note the significant differences between the Buddhist doctrine of karma and the doctrines of karma taught in Jainism, by certain Ājīvika thinkers as well as the Brahmins.

Misconceptions

This is particularly necessary since the Buddhist doctrine is often confused with and assumed to be the same as the Brahmanical doctrine of karma. People tend to speak of or criticise the doctrine of karma as though there was only one such doctrine common to different religions such as Hinduism, Jainism and Ājīvikism despite the fact that they profess different teachings about the nature, operations and attitude to the alleged phenomenon of karma.

Another misconception which is partly connected with the above misunderstanding is that the Buddhist doctrine of karma constitutes or implies a fatalist attitude to life and nature, a view put forward by some (not all) Western scholars and even subscribed to by some South Asian intellectuals, both non-Buddhist and even Buddhist.

Yet another source of misunderstanding is the attempt on the part of certain scholars and other individuals to rationalise (quite unnecessarily) the doctrine of karma by interpreting it to mean the social and or biological inheritance of man, or both, ignoring altogether and distorting the authentic teachings of the texts of the Buddhist Canon.

Meaning

In the pre-Buddhist literature the word karma was used mainly in the sense of either religious rituals or the social functions and duties of man. In the latter sense the *Īṣa Upaniṣad* (v. 2) says: "Let a man aspire to live a hundred years, performing his social duties" (*Kurvann eveha karmāṇi jijīviṣet śataṃ samāḥ*). This sense has survived in the Buddhist texts, where the word karma is used in the plural to denote the different professions or occupations of men. Thus, Buddhism recommends people to perform "morally blameless occupations" (*anavajjāni kammānii*).

As a technical term, the word karma is used in the early Buddhist texts to denote volitional actions. These actions may be morally good (*kusala*), morally evil (*akusala*) or morally neutral (*avyākata*). They may be actions which find expression in bodily behaviour (*kāya-kamma*), verbal behaviour (*vacī-kamma*) and psychological behaviour (*mano-kamma*).

The morally good and evil actions are said to be liable to give rise to consequences, individual as well as social, pleasant and unpleasant on the whole as the case may be. The individual consequences may be manifested in this life, the next life or the lives to come, unless their potentialities get extinguished or they do not find an opportunity for fruition.

Conscious volition (*cetanā*) is a necessary condition of such a morally good or evil or neutral act, but does not constitute the whole of it except when it happens to be a purely mental act. Thus, we would not be guilty of the crime of murder merely because we had the intention of murdering somebody. As the *Atthasālinī* (p. 98) points out, "there are five constituent factors in an act of killing: (i) the existence of a living being, (ii) the awareness of the existence of such a living being, (iii) the intention of killing, (iv) the effort or the means employed to kill, and (v) the consequent death of the living being."

The intention is necessary but not sufficient to constitute an act of killing. As the *Vinaya* rules point out, where the intention is absent but one's actions are instrumental in causing the death of a person, one may be guilty of an act of negligence but not of murder.

So the word karma is used to denote volitional acts which find expression in thought, speech or physical deeds, which are good or evil or a mixture of both, and are liable to give rise to consequences, which partly determine the goodness or badness of these acts.

Basis for Doctrine

It is often assumed that the basis for the doctrine of karma in Buddhism is a rational argument implicit in the *Cūḷakammavibhaṅga Sutta*. It is true that in this Sutta the Buddha seems to suggest purely rational grounds for believing in the doctrine of karma, but it would be mistaken to believe that the doctrine is accepted as true or as representing the nature of things as they are on these grounds.

In this Sutta, a Brahmin youth meets the Buddha and asks him for an explanation as to why among human beings some are short-lived while others are long-lived, some are sickly while others are healthy, some are ugly to look at while others are handsome, some have little power or influence while others are influential, some are poor while others are rich, some are of a lower social status while others are of a higher social status.

The question is posed in the form: "What is the reason and the cause for the inequality (*hīnappaṇītatā*) among human beings despite their being human?" The Buddha's reply on this occasion was as follows: "Beings inherit their karma and it is karma which divides beings in terms of their inequalities."

We may argue that this embodies the following rational ethical argument, consisting of an empirical and ethical premise, viz. people are of unequal status; those of unequal status ought to be such only by virtue of their own actions; therefore, since this is not due to their actions in this life, it should be due to their actions in a prior life. This means that both karma and pre-existence are the case.

It is also true that this kind of rational ethical argument has appealed to many thinkers. Maurice Maeterlinck (1862–1949), poet, dramatist and essayist, says: "Let us return to reincarnation ... for there was never a more beautiful, a juster, a purer, a more moral, fruitful and consoling, nor, to a certain point, a more probable creed than theirs. It alone, with its doctrine of successive expiations and purifications, accounts for all the physical and intellectual inequalities, all the social iniquities, all the hideous injustices of fate."[15] Professor Allan G. Widgery also speaks appreciatively of such an argument when he says: "For it affirms that men are not born equal ... and this affirmation appears to be more in accordance with the facts... Men are regarded as different at birth: the differences being due to the manner in which in past lives they have built up their nature through the action of the law of karma."[16]

But it would be mistaken to consider the passage in the above Sutta as presupposing a rational ethical argument with a concealed ethical premise. It is true as Ānanda has said of the Buddha that "so far as anything can be attained by reasoning (*takka*), you have ascertained it,"[17] but the doctrine of karma is not put forward in Buddhism as a product of mere speculative reasoning (*takka*), which is not adequate for the discovery of the facts of nature as the Buddha has elsewhere pointed out. The Buddha's statements even in this Sutta are based on clairvoyant observation and reasoning, and not on mere rational speculation.

It is also mistaken to assume on the ground of the recognition of the fact of the known inequalities among mankind that Buddhism accepted the status quo of a static conception of society or denied the doctrine of what is known as "the equality of mankind."

For as we shall see when we come to the social and political philosophy of Buddhism, Buddhism upholds the biological, social and spiritual equality of mankind and envisages a time in the future when with the economic, moral and spiritual regeneration of man there would come into being a social order in which people would be healthy and long-lived and the inequalities in power, wealth and social status would be greatly diminished.

In this context, we must not forget that one of the central teachings of Buddhism revolves round the conception of the destruction or elimination of the evil effects of karma (*kammakkhaya*) by effecting a change in the basis of human motivation from that of greed (*lobha*), hate (*dosa*) and ignorance (*moha*) to selflessness (*cāga*), compassion (*karuṇā*) and understanding

15. See *Reincarnation: An East-West Anthology*, ed. Joseph Head and S. L. Cranston, New York, 1961, p. 260.

16. Ibid., p. 117.

17. *Yāvatakaṃ takkāya pattabbaṃ anuppattaṃ tayā*, S I 56.

(*paññā*). Even the better social order of the future can be set up only by people who believe in moral and spiritual values and have to some extent cultivated the qualities of selfless service, kindness and wisdom.

Verifiability

As we have said above, the statements about the operations of karma are made by the Buddha on the basis of inferences based on clairvoyant observation. The awareness of the nature of the operations of karma is said to be the second item of knowledge (*dutiya vijjā*) obtained by the Buddha on the night of his Enlightenment.

It is said: "When his mind is thus composed, clear and cleansed without blemish, free from adventitious defilements, pliant and flexible, steadfast and unperturbed, he turns and directs his mind towards an understanding of the death and rebirth (*upapāta*) of beings. Then with his pure, paranormal, clairvoyant vision he sees beings—the high and the low, the beautiful and the ugly, the happy and the wretched—dying and being reborn according to their deeds (*kamma*)."

The three-fold knowledge (*tisso vijjā*) acquired by the Buddha, which is crucial for the attainment of enlightenment consists of the knowledge of pre-existence, of the operations of karma and of the capacity to eliminate the inflowing impulses (*āsavakkhaya*). It is the same knowledge obtained by the Arahants attaining emancipation of mind (*ceto-vimutti*), and in the *Thera-* and *Therīgāthā*, the verses of the elder monks and nuns, we constantly meet with the refrain: "I have attained the three-fold knowledge, I have done the bidding of the Buddha" (*tisso vijjā anupattā, kataṃ Buddhassa sāsanaṃ*).

The operations of karma are therefore personally verified by the Buddha and his disciples. In the *Mahāsīhanāda Sutta*, the Buddha refers to the way he tested the theory of karma as though he was testing scientific hypothesis.

It is said: "There are these five destinies, Sāriputta. What five? The lower worlds, the animal kingdom, the spirit-sphere (*petti-visaya*), human existence and the higher worlds. I know these lower worlds, the path which leads to them or the kind of conduct which takes you to that state of existence at death.... Herein, Sāriputta, I comprehend the mind of a certain individual with my mind as follows: 'This individual is set on behaving in such a manner and follows such a mode of conduct that he is likely to be born in one of the lower worlds at death on the destruction of the body.' I then observe him at a later time by means of clear, clairvoyant, paranormal perception—the same individual born in one of the *lower worlds* at death experiencing *great pain*. Just as if there were a pit of coals and a man were to come along, tired and exhausted, taking a path leading straight to it and a man possessed of sight were to observe him and say to himself 'This man is surely taking a path which will land him in a pit of coals' and later sees him fallen in that pit experiencing great pain; even so ... *the animal world* ... experiencing *much unhappiness*.... Just as if there were a cesspit and a man, tired and exhausted, were to come along ...; even so ... the *spirit-sphere* ... experiencing *more unpleasant than pleasant sensations*.... Just as if there were a tree in a rugged place, with sparse foliage affording scanty shade and a man were to come along, tired and exhausted; even so ... the *human world* ... experiencing *more pleasant than unpleasant sensations*.... Just as if there were a tree with dense foliage in a pleasant spot and a man were to come along, tired and exhausted ...; even so ... in a *higher world* ... experiencing *extremely pleasant sensations*.... Just as if there were a palace with all the comforts and luxuries and a man were to come along, tired and exhausted...."

In the *Mahākammavibhaṅga Sutta*, the Buddha points out that certain yogins who have acquired the capacity for clairvoyant observation, nevertheless, came to false conclusions and denied the fact of karma since they made invalid inferences from the observed data. This is what he says: "Herein a certain yogin, as a result of his efforts and application, attains a certain state of trance, in which he sees with his clear, clairvoyant, paranormal vision a man who has misconducted himself born at death on the dissolution of his body in a happier and better world. He concludes as follows: 'There are no evil actions (*kamma*) and no consequence of misconduct, for I have observed a man....' 'Everyone, whether one misconducts oneself in this life or not, is born at death in a happier and better world.' I do not agree [says the Buddha] with the claim of this yogin that there are no evil actions and no future consequence of misconduct. I am prepared to grant that this yogin has observed a man who has misconducted himself in this life, born at death in a happier and better world. But I do not agree with his conclusion that, therefore, all people, whether they misconduct themselves in this life or not, are born at death in a happier and better world. The knowledge of the Transcendent One (*Tathāgata*) with regard to operations of karma is different.... If a person who has misconducted himself in this life is born at death in a happier and better world, then he has either some time in his past done good deeds, which have resulted in these experiences or at the time of his death has changed his ways and adopted the right view of life."

The mistake that these yogins made, according to the Buddha, was to form generalisations on the basis of one or a few observations without observing a generality of cases and seeing that the apparent exceptions were explicable on other terms. The operations of karma, it is said, are so complex that they are not fully comprehensible (*acinteyya*, A II 80) except to the vision and understanding of a Buddha. Even with regard to the universe (*loka-visaya*), we noted that the Buddha could observe clusters of galaxies and the vast cosmos, while Anuruddha, the specialist in clairvoyance, could observe only a single galaxy.

Relation to Causal Laws

The operation of these laws of karma was only a special instance of the operation of causal laws in nature, in which there were physical laws (*utu-niyāma*), biological laws (*bīja-niyāma*), psychological laws (*citta-niyāma*), karmic laws (*kamma-niyāma*) pertaining to moral acts and their consequences, and laws pertaining to spiritual phenomena (*dhamma-niyāma*). But the patterns of events in nature, according to Buddhism, are neither deterministic nor indeterministic.

Karmic laws, therefore, state tendencies rather than inevitable consequences. Several of these correlations are stated in the *Cūlakammavibhaṅga Sutta*. The general principle is that morally good acts tend to be followed by pleasant consequences and morally evil acts by unpleasant consequences in the long run to the individual. Since it is of the nature of good acts to promote the material and spiritual well-being of mankind, it follows from this general principle that one cannot gain one's own happiness at the expense of others.

Among the specific correlations are the following: Those who harm and hurt living beings tend to be sickly, while those who are compassionate towards them tend to be healthy. Those who are angry and irritable, scowl at and abuse people tend to be ugly, while the others who are not so tend to be beautiful. Those who are envious and jealous of the gain, honour and respect bestowed on others tend to lose respect while the others would tend to command respect.

Medieval Analysis

In the medieval period we find karma classified, firstly, according to function (*kicca*) as what gives birth (*janaka*), what tends to support a tendency (*upatthambhaka*), what tends to obstruct a tendency (*upapīḷaka*), and what destroys (*upaghātaka*). Secondly, according to the manner in which they come into fruition (*pāka-dāna-pariyāya*), they are classified as weighty (*garuka*), proximate (*āsanna*), habitual (*āciṇṇa*), and residual (*kaṭattā*). Thirdly, according to the time of taking effect (*pāka-kāla*) there are four sorts—what is "experiencable" in this life (*diṭṭhadhamma-vedanīya*), in the next life (*upapajja-vedanīya*), some time in the future (*aparāpara-vedanīya*), or never (*ahosi*). Fourthly, according to the locus in which the effects take place there is evil karma finding fruition in the worlds of sense-gratification; similarly it is with good karma; and there is also good karma which becomes effective in the subtle material worlds (*rūpa-loka*) and the immaterial, ideational worlds (*arūpa-loka*).

Distinction

It is necessary to distinguish the Buddhist theory of karma from the other non-Buddhist theories. Firstly, it has to be distinguished from the Jain theory, according to which man could not develop morally and spiritually without undergoing all the consequences of one's previous evil karma. The Jains hoped to achieve this by indulging in ascetic practices, which they believed helped to wear away the evil effects of past karma. The value of a moral act likewise depended on its physical expression rather than the intention, unlike in Buddhism.

The Buddhist theory has also to be distinguished from an Ājīvika theory which asserted that all present actions and experiences are strictly determined by previous karma. Karma, according to Buddhism, while being non-deterministic, was only one among many factors which conditioned the nature of the individual's experiences of pleasure and pain. Among them were the physiological state of the body, which was partly a product of heredity or the biological laws (*bīja-niyāma*) recognised in Buddhism. The other factors were changes in the physical environment (*utu-pariṇāma*), in social vicissitudes (*visama-parihāra*), the intentional activity of the individual (*opakkamika*), and lastly karma. Karma, it would appear, could operate separately in a psychosomatic manner or in cooperation with the other factors.

Since a number of factors operated in conditioning man's experience, it was wrong to say that pleasure and pain were due entirely to one's own actions (*sayaṃ kataṃ sukhadukkhaṃ*). Nor was it due to the action of an external agent like God (*paraṃkataṃ*), nor to a combination of both (*sayaṃ kataṃ ca paraṃ kataṃ ca*), nor was it accidental (*adhicca-samuppanna*). Pleasure and pain were causally conditioned (*paṭicca-samuppanna*), and man by his knowledge of himself and nature could understand, control and master them.

Fatalism, Heredity and Karma

Since karmic correlations were not deterministic, karma was only one of many factors conditioning the nature of experience and past karma was extinguishable and modifiable in the context of one's present actions, it need hardly be pointed out that the Buddhist teaching of karma was not fatalistic. Buddhism, it may be noted, was opposed to all forms of determinism, natural determinism (*sabhāva-vāda*), theistic determinism (*issara-kāraṇa-vāda*), karmic determinism (*pubba-kamma-vāda*) or any combination of them. According to one Brahmanical text, nature (*prakṛti*) compels man to act as he does, while nature itself is under the control or will of God.

According to Buddhism, man is conditioned by his heredity (*bīja-niyāma*), by his environment, physical, social and ideological (*saḷāyatana-paccayā phasso,* etc.), by his psychological past (*citta-niyāma*) including his karmic heritage (*kamma-niyāma*), but he is not determined by any or all of them. He has an element of free will (*atta-kāra*) or personal endeavour (*purisa-kāra*) by exercising which he can change his own nature as well as his environment (by understanding it) for the good of himself as well as of others. In this sense man is master of his fate (*attā hi attano nātho*).

The laws of heredity, likewise, are not to be confused with the laws of karma. Buddhism accepts both. As a result there may be situations in which the causal lines of karma and heredity coincide. A person may have a certain trait because he inherits it from one of his parents and also because he has a particular karmic reason or affinity for it.

Sometimes in the case of mental traits, the origin may be karmic rather than hereditary. As Professor C. D. Broad (Emeritus Professor of Philosophy, University of Cambridge) has stated in his examination of the philosophy of the late Professor John McTaggart of Cambridge University, who urged a belief in rebirth and karma on philosophical grounds in his books *The Nature of Existence* and *Some Dogmas of Religion*: "McTaggart points out that the assumption of selective affinity between certain kinds of mind and certain kinds of organism would explain likenesses in mental characteristics between parents and children which are often ascribed to the direct influence of heredity. Owing to heredity a man's organism will resemble those of his direct ancestors more closely than those of other people. Now, similar organisms will be adapted to similar minds and zygotes which will develop into similar organisms are likely to attract similar minds and unite with them at conception." Professor Broad adds, "I think it must be admitted that this theory is ingenious and plausible."[18] Besides it can be seen how rebirth and karma can explain the (sometimes marked) temperamental differences in identical twins, who when they happen to be "Siamese twins" have an identical and a common environment.

---

18. *Examination of McTaggart's Philosophy,* Vol. II, Part II. Cambridge University Press, 1938, pp. 614–15.

Central Teaching

It must, however, not be forgotten that the central teaching of Buddhism is not that of continuing to perform good karma for the sake of rewards in continued saṃsāric existence (which cannot be enjoyed without the subsequent suffering from the evil which finds fruition), but the elimination of any karmic (i.e. rebirth-producing) action.

The immediate ideal of the Buddhist should therefore be that of attaining the first stage of spiritual development (*sotāpanna*) by the elimination of attachment to notions of ego and ego-centred views (*sakkāya-diṭṭhi*), by elimination of doubts regarding the Buddhist account of the nature and destiny of man in the universe (*vicikicchā*) through examination, inquiry into and partial verification of the truth of the Dhamma, and the realisation that religion is part and parcel of one's daily living and experience, and not of obsessional attachment to rites and rituals (*sīlabbataparāmāsa*). Such a person is "not liable to fall below the status of human existence" (*avinipātadhammo*) and is destined to achieve the goal of enlightenment (*niyato sambodhiparāyano*) before long. This is the path leading to the destruction of karmic bondage (*kammakkhaya*) in which the good life is cultivated with the growth of selflessness, love and understanding, for its own intrinsic worth and not for egoistic rewards.

III. The Case for the Buddhist Theory of Survival and Karma

As we pointed out in the talk on the Buddhist view of survival, it would be incorrect to represent the Buddhist conception of survival as being a simple doctrine of rebirth. If we use the word "rebirth" to denote the view that immediately or some time after death we return to an earth-life, then such rebirth is only a special case of re-becoming.

According to this Buddhist doctrine of re-becoming, there could be continuity of individuality in various planes of existence. We may survive as a discarnate spirit (Pali *gandhabba* = Sanskrit *gandharva*) in the spirit sphere (*petti-visaya*), as a denizen of a subhuman world, or as an angelic spirit in the celestial planes of existence. Such survival, as the *Kathāvatthu* explains, is either in the gross material world (*kāma-loka*), the subtle material world (*rūpa-loka*), or the immaterial world (*arūpa-loka*). There is no intermediate existence (*antarābhava*) apart from existence in one of these three planes of becoming.

Since human existence is a mixture of good and evil, the usual pattern as the texts make out is to survive as a discarnate spirit and come back to a human existence. The practice of Buddhism by the cultivation of faith (*saddhā*), virtue (*sīla*), learning (*suta*), selflessness (*cāga*) and wisdom (*paññā*) makes it possible for a person to determine his future birth on the human or celestial planes. A person who has become a non-returner (*anāgāmi*) need not come back to a human existence and an Arahant will not be born again in the spatio-temporally and causally conditioned cosmos.

Novel Theory

Besides, the Buddhist theory of survival, as we have already shown, is a novel theory which is not to be found in the pre-Buddhist literature. It was a doctrine of survival without the concept of a self-identical substance or soul. The physical form, perceptions, feeling, will or intellect were not the soul, nor did the soul own them, nor was a soul to be found within them, nor again were they to be located in a cosmic soul. There was no self apart from a complex of psychophysical processes and man was defined as a bundle of dispositions (*suddha-saṅkhāra-puñja*). Though there was no self-identical (*anaññaṃ*) substance, there was a continuity (*santati, santāna*) of individuality, sometimes referred to as a stream of consciousness (*viññāṇa-sota*) or a stream of becoming (*bhava-sota*). Associated with a person's present body were the dispositions with potentialities for re-becoming (*ponobhavika bhavasaṅkhāra*).

These planes of existence and the operations of karma were observed by the Buddha on the night of his enlightenment. His knowledge consisting of "the recall of prior lives" (*pubbenivāsānussati-ñāṇa*) is described as follows:

> "When his mind is thus composed, clear and cleansed without blemish, free from adventitious defilements, pliant and flexible, steadfast and unperturbed, he turns and directs his mind to the recollection of his former lives, viz. one life, two lives ... ten lives ... a hundred lives ... through evolving eons, recalling in what place he was born, his name and title, his social status, his environment, experiences and term of life and dying there, in what place he was next born, and so on up to his present existence he remembers the varied states of his former lives in all their aspects and details. Just as a man who has travelled from his village to another and from that to yet another, when he returns to his former village by the same route, remembers how he came from village to village, where he stayed and rested, what he said and what he did; even so, when the mind is composed...."[19]

Since the Buddhist theory of survival is a composite theory, the case in support of such a theory should include at least the arguments for survival as discarnate spirits as well as the arguments for rebirth.

Before we examine such arguments and the evidence, we have to meet the objection that the known facts of science concerning brain-mind phenomena suggest the impossibility of survival.

19. D I 81.

Two Views

There are two classical views regarding the relationship between the mind and the body. One is the identity hypothesis, which either denies the reality of mental experience or holds that such experiences are inseparable from aspects of neural or brain phenomena. The other is dualism, which holds that mental and neural phenomena interact.

The extreme form of the identity hypothesis, called central state materialism, tries to do away with such factors as "experience" or "consciousness" and explains psychological behaviour as being solely the functioning of the central nervous system. This is a purely mechanistic theory.

A less extreme view, which is still monistic, is the psychosomatic theory according to which psychological experience and brain phenomena are merely the two aspects of one reality. According to this theory the brain-mind combination does not function in a purely mechanical manner, but since brain and mind are two aspects of the same process, they both cease to function with the death of the person.

A modern form of the dualist theory would be the instrumental or the transmission theory, according to which the brain would function as the instrument of the mind, being itself affected by it.

Buddhism, which discards the monistic and the dualistic hypotheses, would hold that there is some truth in each without subscribing to either. For Buddhism the human being in normal consciousness is a psycho-physical unit, in which the physical and psychical phenomena are in a state of mutual dependence (*aññamañña-paccaya*). Yet at the same time aspects of will can control, govern and produce mental activity. Also, when the body is brought within control and is in a state of perfect composure with its activities stilled (*kāya-saṅkhāra niruddha*), it can exercise its extrasensory powers of perception.

Buddhism, therefore, while rejecting the identity hypothesis that "the mind and the body are the same" (*taṃ jīvaṃ tam sarīraṃ*) and the dualist hypothesis that "the mind and the body are different" (*aññaṃ jīvaṃ aññaṃ sarīraṃ*), finds partial truth in each and thus puts forward a middle view.

Neurology

The ideal scientist in the field of neurology is not expected to subscribe to any particular point of view. As Dr. Wilder Penfield said in 1957, "Any scientist who looks up from his work to declare, for example, that the truth is to be found in monism or dualism, or that there is a middle ground, ceases to be a scientist."[20]

This does not, however, mean that the findings of scientists have no bearing on these theories. The advances made over the last fifty years are due to new electro-physiological techniques which have made it possible to stimulate single nerve fibres and record responses from single nerve cells; the measurement of the electrical activity of the brain (EEGs); brain surgery; and the study of the chemical basis of neural phenomena. They have shown that it is possible to alter somewhat the state of the personality or consciousness by physical or chemical means.

Consciousness, incidentally, cannot be argued or analysed away to the satisfaction of the extreme monists, for it is a brute fact that certain physiological processes such as aspects of brain phenomena are accompanied by consciousness or self-consciousness, though it could have been otherwise.

Memory

At the same time, this research has also shown that there is no one-to-one correspondence between brain phenomena and mental experience as the psychosomatic theory would like to maintain. Thus, memory is not uniquely located in particular points of the brain. Dr. H. O. Hebb stated in 1953 that "it is very difficult to conceive of memory as a function of a localised region."[21]

Dr. Penfield records that when a specific point in the brain of a woman patient was touched, she heard a mother calling her little boy. But eleven minutes later when the same point was touched with the electrode, the patient no longer heard the mother calling her little boy but instead heard the voices of people calling from

20. Quoted from Professor Hornell, *The Enigma of Survival*, Rider & Co., London, 1959, pp. 218–19.

21. *Brain Mechanisms and Consciousness: A Symposium*, published 1954.

building to building. In another case, the patient heard the same song vividly when each of four different points in the brain was stimulated. Lord Brain F. R. S., the eminent neurologist, states, "Evidently in the brain, memory is not a unitary function nor is there any single part of the nervous system in which all memories are stored." [22]

The lack of specific localisation is not confined to memory but is to be found in other functions as well. In 1912, Yerkes found that habits registered in one part of the nervous system of an earthworm might shift later onto another part, and a similar versatility was to be found in human brains relative to the effects of brain damage in children by Klebanoff, Singer and Wilensky in 1954.

A senior lecturer in zoology, working mainly on the brains of rats, reports as follows: "Three of the preceding sections are headed respectively 'cortex,' 'limbic system' and 'reticular system,' but this anatomical arrangement does not correspond to the facts of function: the study of any of these systems soon becomes meaningless without reference to the others. During every few milliseconds, in the waking brain, information passes to and fro in a network of communication of which only the larger details are yet certainly known.... In such a flux, we cannot, with our present knowledge, properly speak of localisation of function but only of the specific effects of injury or stimulation.... A small injury can influence behaviour which certainly depends also on the functioning of the other parts; by contrast, some substantial injuries leave behaviour largely unaltered; and when behaviour is disturbed by lesions, there may be subsequent recovery due, evidently, to some compensatory process elsewhere. These facts at present defy explanation. All they do is to make accounts of neural function in terms of reflex arcs as absurd as interpretations of learning in terms of conditioned reflexes."[23]

In a recent BBC broadcast, Dr. Grey Walter speaking on *Mind, Matter, and Machines*, confessed the lack of knowledge about

---

22. "Some Aspects of the Brain-Mind Relationship," in *Brain and Mind*, International Library of Philosophy and Scientific Method, London, 1965, p. 69.

23. S. A. Barnett, *A Study in Behaviour*, Methuen & Co., Ltd., London, 1963, p. 238.

the nature of memory. He said: "No sketch of the contemporary world of brain research would be complete without a hue of mystery because this is what catches the mind's eye. For me there are two great obscurities in our picture: memory and sleep."[24] Recently (April, 1968) Dr. Penfield confessed to the limitations of present scientific research. He said: "The more we learn about the mechanisms within the brain, the clearer it becomes that science has not thrown any real light on the nature of the mind.... The only way the neurophysiologist works is to study the action of the brain on one side and the changing stream of mental activity on the other. You can see the parallelism of the activity but you cannot understand the interrelationship."[25]

It is said that a circular stimulus figure that we observe as a circle will be far from circular when it is projected in the occipital lobe of the observer's cortex. So what we perceive as a circle is not circular in outline in the brain. The case is similar with our vision of three-dimensional figures.[26]

Instrumental Theory

The brain functions or is made to function as a whole and there is no one-to-one psychosomatic correspondence between brain phenomena and the concomitant experiences. So despite the recent advance in biochemistry and microbiology, mental phenomena cannot be considered to be just one aspect of a single process in the brain.

Professor Sir John Eccles, who has been described by Sir Cyril Burt as "the most eminent of living neurologists who have specialised in the study of the brain," has observed that "the structure of the brain suggests that it is the sort of machine that a 'ghost' might operate," where the word "ghost" is used "to designate any kind of agent that defies detection by such apparatus as used to detect physical agents." [27]

---

24. "Frontiers of Knowledge," Modern World Series, p. 99.

25. News report from Toronto in *The Times Weekender*, Friday, April 12th, 1968.

26. W. Russell, *Brain, Mind, Perception and Science*, Oxford, 1951, pp. 4–9.

27. *The Neurophysiological Basis of Mind*, London, Oxford University Press,

This suggests that an instrumental theory of the brain cannot be excluded in the light of modern findings. We must not forget in this context that many physiological changes are initiated by the operation of aspects of will, and that many diseases not only have a psychological origin (with or without a discoverable organic condition) but are curable by purely psychological means. We may note that physical pain with an organic basis can be relieved or removed by chemical means (i.e. drugs) or by the suggestions of hypnosis.

When, in addition to all this, we have to take into account the realities of ESP (extrasensory perception), the identity hypothesis becomes almost untenable, although there was much to be said in its favour. Mr. John Beloff, a lecturer in Psychology in the University of Edinburgh, regards the parapsychological evidence as constituting the most damaging objection to any materialist theory of mind as envisaged in the identity hypothesis.

This is what he says: "This [i.e. parapsychological evidence], it seems to me, is the empirical reef on which the identity hypothesis is doomed to founder even if it can survive all other hazards. Most of its supporters do indeed recognise the danger, but like Feigl, pin their faith to the ability of science to explain the ESP phenomena eventually along more or less conventional lines (obscure brain functions, unsuspected sources of energy, etc.). Such faith, though plausible enough twenty or thirty years ago, is now increasingly unrealistic. The choice that confronts us today, I submit, is a very drastic one: either we must blankly refuse to credit the evidence or we must be prepared to accept a radical revision to the whole contemporary scientific world picture on which materialism has taken its stand." [28]

That the parapsychological phenomena constituting ESP have come to stay and are at present accepted as valid by leading scientists, psychologists and philosophers is evident from a recent publication (1967) of a book called *Science and ESP* in the *International Library of Philosophy & Scientific Method.*

1953, pp. 278 ff.

28. *Brain and Mind*, pp. 50–51.

The brain may be compared to a computer, and electronic machines can be constructed to perform certain operations of abstract thinking (such as logical and mathematical calculations) with a greater speed, precision and accuracy than the human mind is capable of. But however much such computers may simulate human behaviour, they cannot have psychological experiences, express personal behaviour as opposed to mere imitation, and have the degree of creativity and spontaneity that a human mind is capable of exhibiting.

Summing up recent scientific findings on the body-mind problem, Professor Hornell Hart states: "To look at the body-mind problem without bias, it is essential that we recognise two pivotal facts: (1) that damage to brain structure may block or distort what the 'I'-thinker wants to transmit and (2) that the chemical condition of the brain has marked effects on the moods and attitudes of the 'I'-thinker himself.... Whatever it is that thinks 'I' in any one of us is not a constant, unchanging reality. Nor is it something which progresses smoothly and consistently along a regular trend." [29]

Buddhist View

All this seems to support the Buddhist theory of the mind, which holds that "conscious mental and cognitive phenomena function in dependence on their physical basis,"[30] that certain aspects of will can direct, govern and produce mental activity as well as verbal and bodily behaviour, and that when the body and the brain are stilled with the attainment of the fourth *jhāna* (and sometimes even otherwise), the mind can exercise its powers of extrasensory perception which are potentially present.

So none of the modern findings with regard to the mind and its relation to the brain, or the assertions of modern brain physiologists, in any way precludes the empirical possibility of survival after death. This does not mean that survival after death

29. *The Enigma of Survival*, p. 219.

30. "*Yaṃ rūpaṃ nissāya manodhātu ca manoviññāṇadhātu ca vattati*"—Paṭṭhāna I.2.

is a fact but that it is an open possibility to be proved or disproved or made probable or improbable in the light of relevant evidence.

Other Objections

There are other objections that are raised specifically against the concept of rebirth. They fall into three categories: (i) that rebirth is a self-contradictory concept, (ii) that it cannot account for the increase in the human population, which is a fact, and (iii) that biogenesis or reproduction by fission at the lowest levels of life is inexplicable on the basis of the rebirth theory.

The first objection is that the concept of rebirth involves the identity of two or more persons, one of whom lives. It is held that the identification of two or more persons regarding them as one and the same person is either meaningless or self-contradictory. This is based on the belief that the identity of the person consists in the identity of the body, which is certainly the case in the law courts. But as the philosopher John Locke pointed out with specific reference to the case of rebirth, we also apply a mental criterion in our identification of persons.

If someone suffers from an attack of total amnesia, which involves a complete blackout of his past memories, resulting in a complete change of life, we would be inclined to say that he is now a new person, that he is not the same person as before. For example, Dr. Jekyll and Mr. Hyde, who have the same body, are regarded as two different persons. This means that as regards the identity of persons, we normally employ two criteria, that of the continuity of the body and that of the continuity of memory and mental dispositions. In the rebirth case all that is claimed is that, in a significant sense, there is continuity (*santati*) of the mind of the individual from one earth-life to another.

This makes it meaningful to say that two persons, historically removed from each other in time, are one and the same individual because they have a continuous mental history. The modern positivist philosopher Professor A. J. Ayer of Oxford, granting the meaningfulness and the logical possibility of rebirth, says: "I think that it would be open to us to admit the logical possibility of reincarnation merely by laying down the rule that if a person who is physically identified as living at a later time does have the ostensible memories and character of a person who is physically identified as living at an earlier time, they are to be counted as one person and not two."[31] The logical objection is, therefore, untenable.

The second objection is that it cannot account for the increase in human population. This objection would be valid if the theory required that any human birth at present presupposes the death of a prior human being on this earth. Such a theory would also make it impossible for human beings to evolve out of anthropoid apes since the first human beings to evolve would not have had human ancestors.[32] But according to the early Buddhist view of the cosmos, there are hundreds and thousands of galaxies spread out in space, containing "thousands of suns, moons, earths and other inhabited spheres." It is also the case according to the Buddhist theory of rebirth that the prior life of a human being may be animal. It is, therefore, possible according to this theory to account for the increasing number of present human births in terms of the deaths of human beings, animals or non-human beings on this as well as on other planets in the universe.

As regards the third objection from biogenesis, it can hardly affect the Buddhist theory. Although according to some Brahmanical theories, rebirth is possible even at the level of plants, it appears to be the case according to Buddhism that rebirth takes place at a higher level of evolution when a "re-becoming mind" has been formed with the persistence of memory. After his Enlightenment, the Buddha refers to some of his Jain practices, as an aspirant to Buddhahood, in the following words: "I used to walk up and down conscientiously extending my compassion even to a drop of water, praying that the tiny beings in it (*khuddake pāṇe visamagate*) may not come to harm."[33] The context seems to suggest that this was a waste of time.

31. *The Concept of a Person*, London, 1963, p. 127.

32. It is of course possible that their saṃsāric ancestors were from other planes of existence.

33. MN 12.47/M I 78.

IV. The Case for the Buddhist Theory of Survival and Karma

In examining the case for the Buddhist theory of survival and karma, we took up for consideration in the last talk certain objections which may be levelled against the Buddhist doctrine of rebirth. The first of these was that modern discoveries about the nature of mental phenomena and the relationship between the brain and the mind ruled out any possibility of a survival hypothesis being true. We pointed out, on the contrary, that in the light of modern findings regarding the brain-mind relationship and the assertions of leading brain physiologists, the empirical possibility of survival after death remained an open possibility.

Body-Mind Problem

The case against the possibility of survival in the light of what we know about the mind is fully stated in a book by Dr. C. Lamont called *The Illusion of Immortality*.[34] A sound criticism of its contents is to be found in Ch. XIII of a book by Dr. C. J. Ducasse, Emeritus Professor of Philosophy, Brown University, called *A Critical Examination of the Belief in a Life after Death*.[35]

The Buddhist theory of the relationship between body and mind can account for the basic facts stated in Lamont's book as well as the criticisms of Ducasse. Lamont's case is based on the following facts:

(a) that "the power and versatility of living things increase concomitantly with the development and complexity of their bodies in general and their nervous systems in particular."

(b) that "the genes or other factors from the germ cells of the parents determine the individual's inherent physical characteristics and inherent mental capacities."

(c) that, during the course of life "the mind and the personality grow and change, always in conjunction with environmental influences, as the body grows and changes."

34. Philosophical Library, New York, 1950.

35. Illinois, 1961.

(d) that "specific alterations in the physical structure and condition of the body, especially in the brain and cerebral cortex, bring about specific alterations in the mental and emotional life of a man."

(e) that "conversely, specific alterations in his mental and emotional life result in specific alterations in his bodily condition."[36]

Ducasse shows that (e) contradicts Lamont's contentions against dualism. He further cites the case of psychosomatic disease to show that, primarily, mental states cause physical changes in the body. Psychosomatic medicine, for example, today recognises the fact that mental states such as anxiety, tension and worry sometimes cause painful stomach ulcers.

Now what is the Buddhist theory? Buddhism clearly holds that conscious mental and cognitive experiences function in dependence on a physical basis. A statement in the *Paṭṭhāna* reads as follows: "That physical basis in dependence on which the category of mental experience (*mano-dhātu*) and the category of cognitive experience (*mano-viññāṇa-dhātu*) function, this physical basis is to the category of mental experience and the category of cognitive experience and to phenomena associated with them, a condition by way of dependence" (*nissaya-paccaya*).

Because of this dependence it is not surprising that (a) is true and (d) occurs, namely, the alterations in the physical basis resulting in alterations in the nature of consciousness.

Yet the dependence is not one-sided. As the Buddhist texts elsewhere state, "the mind follows in the wake of the body" (*kāyanvayaṃ cittaṃ*) and "the body follows in the wake of the mind" (*cittanvayo kāyo*). The relation between the psyche (*viññāṇa*) and its hereditary psychophysical basis (*nāmarūpa*) is one of "mutual dependence" (*aññamañña-paccaya*). The will and other psychological factors can initiate some of the mental and physical changes that take place as suggested in (e).

Again, since according to Buddhism the psychophysical basis of our bodies is partly due to what is derived from mother and father and "biological laws" (*bīja-niyāma*) operate, it is not

36. See Ducasse, op. cit., p. 114.

surprising that (b) is partly true, namely, that genetic factors condition our physical and some of our mental characteristics.

When the Buddha told Sāti that it was wrong to hold that consciousness fares on from life to life without change of identity (*anaññaṃ*), he illustrated this by showing that consciousness was causally conditioned. It is conditioned by the state of our body, which is partly a product of hereditary factors. It is also conditioned by the external environment. On account of the eye and visual phenomena, there arises in us visual consciousness. Similarly in respect of the other senses, there arise forms of consciousness associated with their respective sense objects.

Likewise, it is said that, on account of the impact on the conscious mind (*mano-viññāṇa*) of ideas (*dhamma*), there arise various forms of conceptual consciousness. When these ideas do not come to us through language from our social and external ideological environment, they impinge on the conscious mind from our own unconscious. As a result of this our consciousness changes and grows and this in turn affects our subsequent behaviour. This is how the Buddha explains to Sāti that the psyche (*viññāṇa*) is not an unchanging entity but is in a state of dynamic growth and becoming, in close association with the conditioning of the body.

In the case of visual stimuli, etc., they physically affect the senses in giving rise to their respective impressions (*paṭigha-samphassa*), but in the case of ideas that arise in the mind in remembering, imagining, thinking, etc., the contact with the conscious mind is said to be only conceptual (*adhivacana-samphassa*).

It is these impressions and ideas and their by-products that accumulate in our memory and form part of our mind. So what is stated in (c), namely, that "the mind and the personality grow and change always in conjunction with environmental influences as the body grows and changes," is partly true. As we have seen above, it is stated in the Buddhist texts themselves.

So while Buddhism holds that the person is a psychophysical unit (*nāmarūpa*), it does not subscribe to the identity hypothesis that the mind and the body are one and the same entity, nor to the dualistic hypothesis that the mind and the body are entirely different. Besides, Buddhism holds that if awareness (*sati*) can be retained while the impressions and ideas that impinge on the conscious mind are inhibited, the activity of the body is gradually stilled and the emotions of sensuous desire (*kāmacchanda*) and hate (*vyāpāda*) subside, then the mind being intrinsically resplendent (*pabhassara*) gradually acquires certain extrasensory powers of perception (*abhiññā*).

What we outlined earlier was the relationship of the conscious mind (*mano-dhātu, mano-viññāṇa-dhātu*) to its physical basis, but we must not forget that, according to the Buddhist theory, the "stream of consciousness" has two components without a sharp division between them (*ubhayato abbocchinnaṃ*), the conscious mind and the unconscious, in which accumulate the emotionally charged experiences that we have had, going back through childhood and birth into previous lives. Besides, with the expansion and development of consciousness (*vibhūta-saññi*), it attains a paranormal state.

How much of our memories in the unconscious are associated with the brain? Do they include the memories of prior lives as well? What is the nature of the association between the potentially paranormal mind and the brain? Does the paranormal mind function at its best when the activity of the brain and the body is quiescent (*kāyasaṅkhārā niruddhā*) under its control? The total psyche (*viññāṇa*) of a person, comprising the conscious mind, the memories and dispositions in the unconscious, and the potentially paranormal mind, is said to be "associated with and linked to the body" (*ettha cittaṃ ettha paṭibaddhaṃ*). But it is not clear how close or how loose the association of its several aspects is.

The Buddhist texts speak of two forms of telepathy, direct and indirect. Indirect telepathy, it is said, is had "by attuning oneself with the thought-vibrations of a person as he thinks" (*vitakkayato vitakka-vipphāra-saddaṃ sutvā*). Direct telepathy does not require this mediating process. Is the activity of the brain required for indirect telepathy while it is unnecessary for direct telepathy?

In the previous talk we tried to show that the modern findings in regard to the mind and its relation to the brain do not preclude the possibility of survival after death. While reiterating this point we tried to give a more detailed account of the Buddhist solution to the body-mind problem.

The arguments of the critics from the nature of the mind and its relation to the brain, if valid, would hold against any theory of survival after death including the Buddhist. The other objections which we dealt with in the previous talk could only be levelled against a rebirth theory. They were, that rebirth was a self-contradictory concept in that it claimed that many persons were one and the same person, that it could not account for the increase in the human population, and that biogenesis or asexual reproduction at the lowest levels of life was inexplicable on the basis of a rebirth theory.

Another Objection

If any of the above arguments were valid, they would have shown that a rebirth theory was not merely improbable but impossible. But we saw that the arguments were based on false premises and did not affect the Buddhist theory of rebirth. Where there was continuity of mind in the form of actual or potential memory and mental dispositions, then in popular parlance, we can speak of the many lives of one person. The increase of population would not present a difficulty where pre-existence could be in the form of animal lives or those of non-human beings in this as well as other planets in the universe. Biogenesis ceases to be a problem if rebirth takes place only at a higher level of biological evolution.

One of the commonest objections against a theory of rebirth, which implies pre-existence, is that we do not remember our past lives. The objection may take three different forms. First, that we do not have any memory of prior lives and that, therefore, there is no evidence of our having lived in the past prior to our present birth. Secondly, that memory is indispensable to the identity of a person. Thirdly, that unless we have memory, rebirth is to no purpose, since no moral or other lesson is learnt in the process.

We may first dispose of the third form of this argument. We are concerned only with the question as to whether re-becoming or rebirth is a fact and not whether it is a good thing to be reborn. We cannot argue from what ought to be or what is best, to what actually is the case. It is generally admitted that such an argument has no basis in fact, since if it is true, the world would be very much different from what in fact it is. Besides, there is a variety of rebirth theories and the question as to which one is true cannot be made on the basis of the ethical consideration as to which one is the best to believe in. For, quite apart from differences of opinion as to what is best (whether, for example, it would be better to remember or not to remember), there is no justification, as we have shown, in arguing that what is best is in fact the case.

The second form of the objection is that memory is indispensable to the identity of a person. If by this is meant that unless a person has authentic memories of a past life, we cannot be certain at all that he is the same as one who lived before, there is some substance to this objection. But it would not be necessary to prove that this was so in the case of all people.

If a sufficient number and variety of people can be shown to have such authentic memories, then although we may not be able to identify the prior lives of other human beings, it would be a reasonable presumption that they too had had prior lives and are potentially capable of remembering this at some time or another.

To come back to the first form of the objection, that we have no memory of having lived before, then, if rebirth is a fact, it is certainly not true of all human beings that they do not recollect their prior lives. For there are at least a few who do, while many others could be assisted to recall their previous lives.

It is possible, of course, to argue that the lack of memory regarding prior lives is no proof that we have not lived before, just as the lack of memory regarding the first year of our lives on the part of all or most human beings is no proof that we did not live in the first year of our life. It is true that mere absence of memory of a certain event or phase of life is no proof that such an event did not take place or that we did not live through such a phase of life.

Yet this is an argument from silence. In the case of our present life, we have another criterion to go on, namely, the criterion of bodily continuity and other people can testify to the fact that we existed in the first year of our lives and lived through certain experiences. But in the case of rebirth we have no evidence at all if we do not have actual or potential memories. Memory is, therefore, very relevant to the problem of rebirth.

However, it is necessary to point out that the word "memory" is used in two senses. In a secondary sense, "having a memory" is a matter of retaining a skill or capacity that we acquired. If someone learnt how to swim when he was a child and can now swim very well without having to relearn it and without even being able to recall that he learnt to swim as a child, we still say that he remembers how to swim though he has forgotten that he had learnt it as a child.

If rebirth be the case, is it not likely that some of the capacities or skills we have or acquire without much difficulty in this life may be due to our having learnt them in a prior life, especially where they cannot be fully accounted for in terms of heredity or learning in this life?

The explanation, not only of capacities and skills but of differences of temperament or "weaknesses," which also fall into this category, would have to be the same. Now identical twins (as opposed to fraternal twins) are said to have the same heredity, and when they happen to grow up as "Siamese twins" joined to each other, they have more or less a common environment. Now if individual differences and variations are due entirely to the factors of heredity and environment alone, there should be identity of temperament and character on the part of these twins. At least there should not be marked differences in their dispositions and temperaments. But the facts are otherwise.

Dr. H. H. Newman, Professor of Zoology, University of Chicago, who made a specialist study of twinning, says with regard to the original "Siamese twins," Chang and Eng: "The author of a study made when the twins were in London was impressed with the lack of any strong resemblance between Chang and Eng. Much emphasis was placed on their different dispositions and temperaments. Chang was inclined to drunkenness, while Eng was a teetotaller."[37]

With regard to these identical twins, in general, his observations are as follows: "In describing several pairs of these strange twins, writers have commented upon their lack of close similarity. Such twins have been regarded as the only kind of twins that are beyond question derived from a single egg and therefore surely identical in their hereditary make-up. One would expect such twins, since they have not only a common heredity but a common environment (for they must be in the same environment all the time), to be even more strikingly similar than pairs of separate twins that are not so intimately associated. The fact is, however, that Siamese twins are almost without exception

37. *Multiple Human Births*, New York, 1940, pp. 64–65.

more different in various ways than any but a very few pairs of separate one-egg twins. One of the most difficult problems faced by the twinning specialist is that of accounting for this unexpected dissimilarity of the components of Siamese twin pairs."[38]

Could this difference not be due to a third factor other than heredity and environment, namely, the psychological past of the two individuals? If so, is it not likely that even in other individuals as well there could be capacities, skills, temperaments, weaknesses, etc., which are due to "memories" (in the secondary sense defined above) of prior lives rather than to the factors of heredity and environment? Geniuses or child prodigies, whose extraordinary accomplishments cannot be accounted for in terms of heredity or environment, would only be special cases of such a carry-over of skills from one life to another.

Apart from the use of the word "memories" in the above secondary sense, we use the word in its primary sense to denote the "recall of authentic experiences of one's past." In this sense there are quite a few who have claimed to have remembered experiences of their alleged prior lives. Some of them are spontaneous cases of recall while others are due to the intervention of hypnotists, who have carried out age-regression experiments. How authentic are these memories and what reason have we to believe that they are potentially present in many if not all human beings? These are questions that we shall seek to answer in the subsequent talks on this subject.

38. Op. cit., pp. 67–68.

V. The Case for the Buddhist Theory of Survival and Karma

It may be useful to summarise briefly the argument so far.

The Buddhist doctrine of re-becoming (*punabbhava*) was a novel theory in so far as it spoke of survival without a self-identical soul or substance. There was continuity (*santati*) of personality after death, and rebirth or the return to an earth-life was only a special case of such continuity. The doctrine was propounded after taking into account all the possible theories that could be advanced with regard to the problem of an afterlife.

The Buddhist doctrine of karma merely taught that there was correlation between moral acts and their consequences, without implying any sort of fatalism. In fact, its implications were the very opposite of fatalism in that man by his understanding of his own nature could control his present and determine his own future.

In the two previous talks we examined some of the objections that could be levelled against this doctrine of re-becoming. We investigated the objection against any theory of survival from the alleged state of relationship that exists between the brain and the mind, and found that the evidence against the possibility of survival was by no means crucial. Survival is neither proved nor disproved in the light of the modern findings regarding the brain-mind. Any theory of survival, therefore, stands or falls on the basis of independent evidence.

We also examined some of the objections raised specifically against rebirth. We found that the objection that rebirth was a self-contradictory concept was not valid since we can speak significantly of a single individual having many lives where there is a continuity of memory and mental dispositions. The argument from the increase in the human population could not be levelled against the Buddhist theory of rebirth since Buddhism entertains the possibility of prior lives among animal, human, or non-human ancestors on this or other planets. The objection from bio-geneticists also was not valid since rebirth took place at a higher level of animal evolution.

The objection regarding the lack of memory of prior lives was far from valid. "Memory" may be used in one of two senses: (i) the recall of genuine experiences of one's past and (ii) the presence of capacities and skills acquired in the past. In the second sense we found that there was evidence for the existence of such "memories."

Identical twins when joined together (called "Siamese twins") have a common heredity and common environment. Yet psychologists observed that they differ in character and temperament. It is likely, therefore, that this difference was due to a third factor (other than heredity and environment), namely, the "carry over" of past skills and attitudes from prior lives. Geniuses or child prodigies, whose extraordinary accomplishments cannot be accounted for in terms of heredity or environment, would only be special cases of such a "carry over" of skills from one life to another.

In the former sense of memory, namely, of the recall of genuine experiences in one's past, it is claimed that there is evidence of the recall of genuine experiences from prior lives. Such claims have to be carefully examined.

Unsatisfactory Arguments

Yet, before we proceed to do so, it is necessary to dispose of some unsatisfactory arguments that are sometimes adduced in support of the doctrine of rebirth. They may take many forms.

There is a tendency to urge that some belief is true because almost everybody holds it. Yet the universality of a belief does not entail its truth. Nor at the same time does it entail its falsity. It is sometimes maintained that many primitive peoples of the ancient world believed in survival or the doctrine of rebirth. But this does not imply that the belief is either true or false. Its truth or falsity has to be established independently.

The relevance of the universality of the belief as evidence of its truth becomes more interesting when it is realised that everyone in a state of deep hypnosis gives an account of experiences in alleged prior lives, lived on earth, whatever their conscious beliefs may be. There is evidence that Materialists and Theists holding a variety of views on the subject of survival after death, without subscribing to the doctrine of rebirth or pre-existence, give alleged accounts of prior lives, recounting details of their experiences.

Does this imply the truth of the belief? Not necessarily, for it is possible that all of their beliefs could be illusory, though the universality of such an illusion has to be accounted for. But the experiences they recount certainly constitute evidence for the truth or falsity of the belief in rebirth. We shall carefully examine this evidence later on.

Another form in which an argument for survival is presented is that a human need or want implies the existence of what is needed or wanted. We need or want, for instance, food. Therefore, it is suggested, there must be food. Many people feel the need for immortality or at least survival after death. Therefore, it is suggested, there must be such immortality or survival.

However, this is an argument that cuts both ways. For others may argue that we believe in rebirth or survival because we need to believe or desire to entertain such a belief. But what we like to believe is not necessarily true and, therefore, this is no evidence of the truth of the belief.

Freud in his work called *The Future of an Illusion* tries to show that people entertain certain religious beliefs, like the belief in the existence of God, for instance, because there is a deep-seated craving in us for security amidst the insecurity of life and the uncertainty of the beyond. According to him people believe in God dogmatically because of such a deep-seated craving. It is an object of wish-fulfilment, and, in this special case, an "illusion."

This does not, however, necessarily mean that the belief is false. As Freud himself pointed out, a girl may believe in the existence of a Prince Charming who may, one day, come and propose to her. Because she likes to believe this, it does not necessarily mean that such a person does not exist. So the desire to believe in rebirth or survival does not necessarily show that the belief is false, just as the desire to disbelieve in rebirth does not imply that the contrary belief is false.

The Buddhist view on this material is both relevant and interesting. Our desires influence or condition our beliefs, to which we tenaciously cling (*taṇhā paccayā diṭṭhūpādānaṃ*), but this does not necessarily mean that these beliefs are always false, for when they happen to be "right beliefs" (*sammā diṭṭhi*), they are in fact true.

So although desires affect our beliefs, this fact has no relevance to the truth or falsity of the beliefs. We have, however, because of our emotional involvement with these beliefs, to weigh the evidence for or against their truth or falsity without prejudice. As Buddhists we have to examine the truth even of the belief in rebirth objectively without being prejudiced for (*chanda*), or against (*dosa*), or being affected by fear (*bhaya*) even if it be the fear of the beyond, or being guided by our erroneous beliefs (*moha*). So the desire to believe or not to believe does not affect the truth or falsity of the belief, but we have to guard against the prejudice resulting from these desires in our quest for truth.

Authority and Revelation

Another set of arguments for survival is based on authority. It may be stated that many poets and mystics, as well as rational thinkers brought up in a tradition which condemned the belief, nevertheless professed the belief.

The classic case is that of Giordano Bruno, who is said to have stated in his profession of faith before the Inquisition: "I have held, and hold, souls to be immortal.... Speaking as a Catholic, they do not pass from body to body, but go to Paradise, Purgatory or Hell. But I have reasoned deeply, and, speaking as a philosopher, since the soul is not found without body and yet is not body, it may be in one body or in another, and pass from body to body. This, if it be not (proved) true, seems, at least, likely...."[39] Over two hundred and fifty well-known poets, philosophers and writers of the Western world have either held or professed some sort of belief in rebirth.

All that this seems to suggest is that the belief is worth examining, and it does not in any way imply the truth of the belief.

The argument from revelation is also unacceptable to science and Buddhism. It is true that certain texts in the Vedic tradition, particularly the middle and late *Upaniṣads*, profess a belief in rebirth, but there is a variety of views on the subject of survival in the Vedic tradition itself. In one of the early *Upaniṣads* rebirth

39. *Reincarnation: An East-West Anthology*, ed., J. Head & S. L. Cranston, New York, 1961.

is denied. It is said: "... there are these three worlds, the world of men, the world of departed spirits, and the world of the gods. The world of men is obtained through a son only, not by any other means."[40]

While there are these contradictions within revelational traditions, the different theistic revelations also contradict one another on the problem of survival. So the doctrine of rebirth cannot be established by an argument from authority or revelation, since authority and revelation are not acceptable means of knowledge.

Metaphysical and Ethical Arguments

The metaphysical arguments are no better. Apart from the fact that they make use of unverifiable concepts like "soul," the arguments are of doubtful value and are generally discredited today. One of the traditional arguments for survival has been that the "soul is a substance, substances are indestructible; therefore the soul is indestructible, i.e. immortal." But apart from the difficulty of the concept of a "soul," the notion of an indestructible substance is discredited today.

With regard to rebirth, we have already met with a sample of such a metaphysical argument in that of Giordano Bruno (see above). Such arguments, based on pure reasoning, intended to prove the truth of rebirth, are to be met with, for example, in a work called *Some Dogmas of Religion* (Ch. IV) by Professor John McTaggart of Cambridge. But they have little appeal today since it is recognised that matters of fact cannot be proved by pure reasoning (*takka*), as the Buddha himself pointed out (*mā takka-hetu*).

The ethical argument has a greater appeal, but this is so only for those who accept its presuppositions. We have already stated this in the talk on the Buddhist doctrine of karma. There we pointed out that according to the Buddha karma was one of the predominant factors responsible for human inequalities.

This has often been represented as embodying the following rational, ethical argument consisting of an empirical and ethical premise, viz. "people are of unequal status; those of unequal status

40. *Bṛhad Āraṇyaka Upaniṣad*, 1.5.15.

ought to be such by virtue of their own actions—therefore, since this is not due to their actions in this life, it should be due to their actions in prior lives. This means that both pre-existence and karma are the case."

This is an argument that has appealed to many thinkers down through the ages, but most modern thinkers would not accept the second ethical premise, namely, that "those of unequal status ought to be such by virtue of their own actions." This is because most people believe today that the universe of nature is amoral, and there is no ethical reason why anything should or should not be so. On the other hand many hold that ethical statements are neither true nor false. It is nevertheless a fact that many people brought up in a belief in the inherent justice of nature ask questions of the form, "why should so-and-so be born healthy while I am in a state of ill-health from birth, etc.?"

It is only the modern scholars who have made an argument of this since the Buddha merely stated as an observed fact that the predominant cause of these inequalities was karma. The fact is, in principle, unverifiable, but the argument appeals to one's moral sense, and is of value only if such a moral sense is universally present and shared by all mankind.

The Evidence

The above arguments are, therefore, for one reason or another, unsatisfactory and have little force in proving the truth of rebirth or survival. The truth or falsity of rebirth, therefore, rests on the relevant empirical evidence.

We may classify the main evidence into two sorts: (i) experimental and (ii) spontaneous. The other evidence may be considered separately.

The experimental evidence is based on age-regression. Under hypnosis a subject can recall or relive his past experiences. With regard to this life when regressed to age six, for instance, the subject would behave, write and talk as he or she did at that time and recall the past experiences, which it may not be possible to recall by normal means. The handwriting and the memories could be independently checked. Such experiments have convinced psychologists and psychiatrists today that the authentic buried memories of one's childhood experiences, which cannot be called to mind via normal consciousness, can be unearthed by hypnosis. It may be asked whether the subject is not just responding to the suggestions of the hypnotist and is merely play-acting or shamming. That this is not so has been proved experimentally.

Dr. H. J. Eysenck states that "in one case it was found that when a twenty-year-old girl was regressed to various ages she changed the chalk to her left hand at the six-year-level; she had started writing with the left hand, but had been forced to change over at the age of six."[41]

In another case a thirty-year-old was hypnotised and regressed to a level of about one year of age, on a chair arranged in such a way that with the release of a latch it would fall back into a horizontal position. When the latch was released the behaviour elicited was not that of an adult but of a child. An adult, it is said, would quite involuntarily extend both arms and legs in an effort to maintain balance. Since the subject made no movement of the limbs but screamed in fright and fell backward with the chair, urinating in the process, Eysenck comments, "It is unlikely that such behaviour is simply due to play-acting."[42]

Intelligence and achievement tests have been used to assess the nature of the behaviour of regressed subjects and it has been found that "people tend to behave on tests of this type in a manner roughly appropriate to the given age." Eysenck's observations with regard to the possibility of faking such behaviour are as follows: "Such reactions, of course, could easily be faked, but it has been shown that when, for instance the eye movements of subjects are photographed, a considerable lack of ocular co-ordination and stability is found when regression to a relatively young age occurs. Such physiological phenomena are characteristic of young children and are difficult, if not impossible, to produce voluntarily."[43]

A remarkable fact is that the psychological experiences, when the physiological condition of the body was different, are re-enacted. To quote Eysenck again, "Even more impressive is

41. *Sense and Nonsense in Psychology*, 1961, p. 48.

42. Ibid., p. 49.

43. Ibid.

another case of a subject who had a colloid cyst removed from the floor of the third ventricle. Prior to this removal, the subject had been suffering from blindness in the left half of the right eye: After the operation, vision had become normal, but when the subject was regressed to a time shortly before the operation the visual defect again reappeared during the regression."[44] The expected physiological reaction is not only appropriate to the age but reflects the physiological condition of the body at the time.

In the light of the experimental evidence Eysenck concludes: "Experiments such as those described in some detail above leave little doubt that there is a substantial amount of truth in the hypothesis that age regression does, in fact, take place, and that memories can be recovered which most people would think had been completely lost."[45] This is the consensus of opinion among orthodox psychologists today.

So genuine memories not accessible to normal recall are generally evoked or the experiences relived at the suggestion of the hypnotist in age-regression. So at least as far as this life is concerned, to say that the memories recalled under age-regression are hallucinatory or delusive is not correct. We shall take up for consideration later, in the light of the experimental data, the question as to whether the recall of alleged experiences of prior lives under hypnotic regression is hallucinatory.

44. Ibid.
45. Ibid., p. 51.

VI. The Case for the Buddhist Theory of Survival and Karma

In the preceding talk we stated that the evidence for the doctrine of rebirth was mainly of two sorts. There was (i) the experimental evidence from age-regression and (ii) the spontaneous evidence based on a historical study of people, mainly children, from different parts of the world who claimed to recall their alleged prior lives. There is also a category of evidence which may be considered apart from the above two.

Age-Regression

The experimental evidence is based on age-regression. In this experiment the subject is hypnotised and gradually taken back in time to the past. In the course of this the subject recalls and relives past experiences. Much of these experiences cannot be evoked by normal memory. These experiments have proved to the satisfaction of modern psychologists and psychiatrists that authentic memories of this life, which cannot be called to mind in normal consciousness, can be recalled by these means.

We quoted in the previous talk the view of Dr. H. J. Eysenck, who was Professor of Psychology at the University of London, namely, that "there is a substantial amount of truth in the hypothesis that age-regression does in fact take place, and that memories can be recovered which most people would think had been completely lost." This is in fact the consensus of opinion among orthodox psychologists today on the basis of the experimental findings. Dr. L. M. Wolberg observes: "The consensus at the present time is that 'regression actually does produce early behaviour in a way that obviates all possibility of simulation'; this is the opinion of such authorities as Erickson, Estabrooks, Lindner, and Spiegel, Shor and Fishman. My own studies have convinced me of this fact, although the regression is never stationary, constantly being altered by the intrusion of mental functioning at other levels." [46]

46. *Medical Hypnosis*, Vol. I.

It is a remarkable fact that in the course of these age-regressions even the physiological condition of the body undergoes changes appropriate to the past time at which the subject is having the experiences concerned, even when the present state of the body or the physical environment cannot be responsible for this. Drs. Brennan and Gill report a case where a patient some months after being exposed to a particular situation was regressed back to that time hypnotically. It is stated that "the subject spontaneously began to perspire and complain of the heat: This was rather surprising in view of the fact that this particular phase of the study took place in winter. The experimenters then recalled that on the day to which the patient was now regressed, Kansas had experienced one of its hottest summer days." [47]

Prior Lives

The majority of these orthodox psychologists and psychiatrists, however, are reluctant to concede that the accounts given of and the experiences lived through alleged prior lives are genuine. In such cases they tend to dismiss these accounts and experiences of prior lives as fantasy or a product of dramatisation and role playing based on material derived from the experiences of this life. They are prepared to grant that the subject's behaviour "will give the appearance of reincarnation,"[48] but deny that the reincarnationist interpretation is valid.

So the position is that practically all the modern psychologists and psychiatrists are prepared to concede the fact that under age-regression a hypnotised subject will give detailed descriptions of an alleged prior life; but would not agree with the validity of a reincarnationist interpretation of the data.

The main reason for this seems to be the logical methodological difficulties involved in accepting an explanation in terms of the hypothesis of rebirth rather than a careful

47. *A Scientific Report on "The Search for Bridey Murphy,"* ed. Milton V. Kline, Ph.D., The Julian Press, Inc., New York, 1956, p. 185.

48. F. L. Marcuse, *Hypnosis: Fact and Fiction*, Pelican Books, A 446, Reprint 1961, p. 184.

attempt on the part of these psychologists and psychiatrists to understand or explain the data itself.

In the previous talks we have tried to show that neither these logical nor methodological difficulties are valid. We pointed out that the concept of rebirth does not lead to contradictions. Even a positivist philosopher such as Professor A. J. Ayer of Oxford has stated that the concept of rebirth was meaningful. Besides, there is a growing realisation that the phenomenon of consciousness cannot be explained away purely in terms of physico-chemical phenomena, while the validity of extrasensory perception requires that psychological explanations be contained (where the data require this) within the narrow and limiting framework of mechanistic materialist assumptions. The data therefore require to be examined with an open mind.

There have been however a few psychiatrists who have accepted the reincarnationist explanation as valid. Dr. Alexander Cannon refers to "one thousand three hundred and eighty-two reincarnation sittings to date" in his book *The Power Within*.[49] His own reactions to these and the final conclusion he came to are summed up in the words: "For years the theory of reincarnation was a nightmare to me and I did my best to disprove it and even argued with my trance subjects to the effect that they were talking nonsense, and yet as the years went by one subject after another told me the same story in spite of different and varied conscious beliefs in effect until now, well over a thousand cases have been so investigated, and I have to admit that there is such a thing as reincarnation."[50]

The Evidence

All important is the nature of the evidence and its authenticity, and the legitimate conclusions that we can come to in explaining this evidence with the help of the various hypotheses that may be adduced to explain it. When hypotheses cannot be accepted or rejected outright, they may be held with varying degrees of probability according to relevant criteria.

---

49. Rider & Co., 6th Impression, 1950, p. 183.
50. Ibid., p. 170.

One of the earliest recorded experiments of psychologists was that of Professor Theodore Flournoy, Professor of Psychology in the University of Geneva, who experimented with one of his subjects at the end of the last century and recorded the data and findings in a book published in 1899.[51]

One of the prior lives of his Swiss subject was as an Arab chief's daughter, who married a Hindu prince about four centuries before. The subject spoke and wrote in the language (Arabic and Prākrit), which she knew in the regressed state but not in her normal life, and gave details of experiences in this life, re-enacting and re-living some of the scenes. The facsimiles of the writing are reproduced at pages 289 and 313 of Flournoy's book.

Before we examine this case, we may turn our attention to a more popular work published in 1942. This would enable us to see the issues involved in the interpretation of the data more clearly. Since Buddhists are or ought to be interested only in objective facts or in "things as they are" (*yathābhūta*) it is important that we approach the subject with a critical mind without an initial bias for or against the theory of rebirth.

Researches in Reincarnation and Beyond

The work is by Rev. A. R. Martin, an ordained preacher of the Coptic Church, and is entitled *Researches in Reincarnation and Beyond.*[52] (It is dedicated to "all seekers for truth whether or not it be in accordance with their former teachings or preconceived ideas.")[53] The book records the alleged experiences of people hypnotised by him or trained to recall their prior lives.

His comments with regard to the evidence and the records are as follows: "The questions and their answers thereto were carefully recorded, usually in shorthand, exactly as given. Great care was taken to ask no leading questions, thereby eliminating the possibility of implanting ideas in the mind of the reviewer, thus making certain to bring out only that which was recorded in the reviewer's subconscious mind. These correlations of important persons

51. *Des Indes a la Planete Mars*, Geneva, 1899.

52. First ed., Pennsylvania, 1942.

53. Ibid., p. 11.

and events often occurring hundreds of years ago, were carefully checked in reference books, histories, encyclopaedias, etc., and were found correct as given by the reviewer. This information was known to come solely from the knowledge already in the reviewer's subconscious mind, for it was known that such knowledge was not contained in his intellectual mind of this present life." [54]

He claims that these explorations into the subconscious minds of various people "worked out through powers of mind, absolutely without the use of any kind of drug" was attempted, after a group of about twelve persons of various ages had for years examined various conflicting teachings of speculative philosophy on the subject of an afterlife and were dissatisfied with them.

The author lists a number of beliefs about the nature of an afterlife held by people in the West. The first was that "death ends all ...";[55] the second that "the consciousness-soul dies and is buried with the body and remains there until a time called the resurrection when all persons who have ever lived from the beginning of creation to the time of the resurrection will come forth, from the land or the sea or wherever they may be, to be judged and sent either to an eternal heaven or an eternal hell of fire and brimstone from which there is no escape";[56] the third was the view that there is "an intermediate place of punishment or remorse from which the dead can be released through prayer, and liberated into an eternal heaven...."[57] Several other such views are listed. The author says that he "has lived all of his present life (to this time) in the United States,"[58] and was himself "raised to manhood under the instruction of the second belief,"[59] and that none of these who thus met regularly to investigate these matters "even leaned towards reincarnation."[60]

If this is so, then considering particularly the fact that no "leading questions" were asked, it is all the more remarkable that

54. Ibid., pp. 7–8.
55. Ibid., p. 4.
56. Ibid.
57. Ibid., pp. 4–5.
58. Ibid., p. 3.
59. Ibid., p. 6.
60. Ibid.

they were able to recall prior lives lived on earth. It is a curious fact, which calls for an explanation by itself, that those who in their normal conscious experience are materialists or theists, who do not believe in pre-existence or rebirth, invariably give alleged accounts of prior lives under deep hypnosis. Where the subject is asked to concoct an account of an alleged "prior life," this may be attributed to the suggestion of the hypnotist but where such prior lives are described without any express instructions on the part of the hypnotist to do so, this fact in itself calls for an explanation.

In an article appearing in the magazine *Two Worlds*,[61] the writer states:

> "Sometimes the subject during what is called 'wakeful state' is not a reincarnationist, or even has never heard about such an idea, or else 'belongs to a creed that denies it emphatically.'
>
> "One very intelligent man, a Protestant, asked the hypnotist in a deep, booming, slow voice, 'Why do you ask such a question?' The question was repeated, 'Were you or were you not born for the first time?'
>
> "He still hesitated, as if to conquer a strong inner opposition, and then, began to describe his life a couple of centuries ago in a monastery somewhere in Spain.
>
> "When he awoke slowly and by reversing the age-regression process, the tape was played back to him. He was amazed because he did not know about reincarnation and never thought it possible.
>
> "A bright, beautiful, mature woman talked freely about reincarnation and other related subjects. When she listened to the playback she said, 'I must be crazy to say such things.' She is a diehard Roman Catholic."[62]

Origin of Phobias

Granted that the experiences related in the above mentioned book are authentic and factual, many of our problems in this life can be understood in terms of their causal origins in a prior life.

61. H. C. Miranda, *"Can Reincarnation Be Proved by Hypnotism?"* May 1964, pp. 247–49.
62. Ibid., p. 249.

This is very much like the manner in which the submerged traumatic experiences of this life (as explained in Freudian psychology) are the causal factors which account for symptoms.

Dr. Eysenck records the case of a Mrs. Smith who suffered from recurrent asthmatic attacks. Her work necessitated her going into various hospitals but in doing so she experienced a very strong fear reaction. The sight of a pair of hairy arms, or knives, also produced such a reaction. Under hypnotic age-regression, she was able to recall and relive the incidents which were responsible for this condition. It was the shock caused by an operation for mastoiditis performed on her at the age of sixteen months, which she had forgotten. Dr. Eysenck describes the situation as follows: "During a self-induced trance one day, she was regressed to an early age, when she experienced a previously completely forgotten incident with unusual clarity. She seemed to be lying on a table under brilliant lights. A man was standing beside her holding a small knife. A vague, threatening object was descending from above her head and settled down over her face. She was terror-stricken and tried to rise, but two hairy arms grabbed her and roughly forced her back. She continued to struggle but was violently shaken and slapped repeatedly by someone. Finally, the object came down over her face and smothered her. On inquiry, it was found that at the age of sixteen months a mastoidectomy had been performed on her and that she had been very sick afterwards with complications, caused by severe shock."[63]

The origin of this phobia was traced to a childhood incident in this life. But it is interesting to compare in this connection one of the experiences recorded in the book mentioned above, which locates the origin of a phobia in an incident of an alleged prior life. It is described as follows: "A middle aged woman ... when riding in a car driven twenty miles an hour or more, the motion produced such a fear within her that she would become very nervous and ready to jump out of the car. As a result she could ride only in cars driven around fifteen miles an hour. This fear of speed made it almost impossible for her to travel by train, bus, etc. Upon entering a past-life review, she found herself to be a young girl travelling on a train with her parents, brothers, and sisters.

63. *Sense and Nonsense in Psychology*, 1961, pp. 51–52.

As the train passed over a trestle bridge it was wrecked, killing all the members of the family but herself, along with many others who were on the train. Her injuries were so severe that she was badly crippled and rendered an invalid for the remainder of that life. The speed had been such a dominant factor in this accident and its impression was so deep that the subconscious fixation out-manifested in this life as intense fear whenever any degree of motion was felt by her." [64]

We may recount some of the observations of a like nature made by Dr. Cannon on the basis of his case studies. He says: "The majority of people do not benefit from psychoanalysis because the trauma lies not in this life but in a past life. Let me give you three examples: Mr. A. is a business-gentleman of undoubted capabilities, but all his life he has suffered from a phobia or fear of going down in lifts. He is a common-sensed individual and has studied psychology and psycho-pathology quite seriously and intelligently, and yet he has gained no benefit from it and is at a loss to know why he has this fear of travelling in lifts. Hypnotic experiments reveal that some centuries ago he was a Chinese general who fell from a great height and was accidentally killed. This had resulted in the phobia or fear of descending lifts in this life." [65]

Karma?

If the experiences recounted in Rev. Martin's book, *Researches in Reincarnation and Beyond,* are authentic and factual, they also appear to throw some light on the operations of karma.

In one case five previous lives of a person are recorded. "In the fifth life previous to the present, the person's first recollection was that of awakening as a white baby in a log cabin."[66] The cabin was attacked by Indians, one of whom took her along and brought her up as Indian maiden. Eventually, she was taken away by a British trader "with whom she lived in a small hut" until he decided to leave her and cross the mountains in search of gold. He offered to take her back to the Indian tribe, but conscious of her white parentage

64. Op. cit., p. 44.
65. Op. cit., p. 171.
66. Op. cit., p. 90.

and the coming motherhood she refused. Instead, faced with the prospect of being alone in the hut, it is said that she committed suicide by shooting herself on "the right side of her face."

In the very next birth, she is stated to have been born as a crippled child named Sammy, whose entire right side was paralysed. The subsequent birth is supposed to have been as a U.S. soldier of the South during the Revolution, when he was accosted by a British subject who stabbed him in the right side of the abdomen, causing his death.

In the following birth she was born as a girl named Nancy, whose mother worked for a wealthy family. A son of this family, it is said, fell in love with this girl and wanted to marry her but his parents objected and got her married to a farmhand. She subsequently journeyed West in a covered wagon and settled in Illinois, where two children were born. Nancy died at the age of thirty as a result of abdominal disorders. Her next life was as a person who became well-known as an operatic singer called "Miss Nellie," a daughter of a wealthy family near Baltimore, Maryland. She was happily married but before long her husband was shot dead and it is said that she "died of a broken heart." The author describes and comments on part of her present life as follows: "When she was fifteen years old, the first of these negative conditions resulted in a paralysis of the right side of the face and neck. At this age she knew nothing of reincarnation or of the influence of past lives upon the present. The overcoming of the paralysis, slight traces of which are still apparent, was accomplished in a period of six to seven years through rest and quiet." [67]

If the facts are as stated, are we to attribute her birth as a child paralysed on the right side in her fourth previous life, and her paralysis of the right side of the face and neck in this life, as well as, perhaps, her deaths from abdominal injuries or disorders, as karmic consequences of her suicide while being with child in her fifth previous life?

Taken literally if the experiences recounted here are authentic and true records of prior lives, they exemplify the truths of both rebirth and karma. But what justification have we for accepting these experiences at their face value?

67. Op. cit., p. 94.

Normal Hypotheses

A person with a sceptical frame of mind may very well indulge in doubt and claim that one of several hypotheses other than rebirth could adequately account for the alleged facts. Some may even doubt whether the book I refer to even exists, and whether all of this is not a concoction of mine! This would be the extreme hypothesis of Fraud. The reply to this is that the book is to be found in some libraries, e.g. the library of the University of Ceylon. A less extreme position that one could take would be to doubt whether the author of the book was not merely trying to bring out a sensationalist publication from which he might financially benefit and that the entire account is a concoction of his. One way of verifying this would be to contact the author and through him the people concerned, as the author himself wants those interested to do so. But this is unnecessary, since this kind of evidence can be made available with the help of a suitable hypnotist and hypnotisable subjects.

Once it is established that the book contains an account of authentic experiences accurately recorded, we may still doubt the assumption that they are genuine memories of past lives. We may try to explain them as being due to the role playing of the subject who has proceeded to give dramatised accounts of alleged prior lives the basis of material drawn from this life. We would then resort to the hypothesis of fantasy or self-deception, unless the author can prove to us, as he says he could, that "it was known that such knowledge was not contained in his intellectual mind of this present life."[68] This hypothesis would be difficult to exclude in the present circumstance unless it could be shown that specific items of knowledge later verified from encyclopaedias, etc., were not known to the subject (as the author claims to be the case). However, the fact that some of these alleged experiences solved some of the present psychological problems of some of these subjects is a factor to be taken into consideration in judging the genuineness of these experiences, though this test is by no means conclusive.

Another "normal" explanation would be to assume that such "experiences" can be derived genetically from one's ancestors.

68. Op. cit., p. 8.

Apart from the fact that there is no independent evidence of such hereditary derivation of specific "memory experiences" (leaving out capacities and aptitudes), the hypothesis requires an ancestral link between the two personalities. This is very unlikely at least in those cases in which the prior life is located in such countries as Persia or Egypt.

Paranormal Hypotheses

If the normal hypotheses fail to account for the facts, we have to resort to paranormal hypotheses to explain the evidence.

Granted that the "memories" correspond with historical facts, and knowledge of them is not derived from any experience in this life, it is possible to suggest that they are the product of a telepathic, clairvoyant or retro-cognitive faculty operating along with dramatisation and role-playing. On such a hypothesis, these persons did not actually live in the past but acquired information about past events by paranormal or extrasensory means and dramatised such a past life. Such a hypothesis appears to be more extravagant than a simple hypothesis of "rebirth." For, apart from not explaining all the data (e.g. the claim to identity, the serial nature of the recall in age-regression, etc.), there is little evidence of such wide and penetrative powers of telepathic, clairvoyant or retro-cognitive perception except perhaps in a few extraordinary individuals.

For similar reasons, the hypothesis of spirit-possession appears to be less plausible in accounting for the data. For, in spirit-possession the alleged spirit communicating through the medium claims to be a different person from the personality associated with the body. In the case where a claim to rebirth is made, this is not so.

If a paranormal explanation is to be preferred, "rebirth" therefore appears to be more plausible than the others, the data being what they are. But the data presented in Rev. Martin's book do not clearly rule out the possibility of explanation in terms of fantasy or self-deception, as defined above, unless it can be shown and not merely stated that specific items of knowledge regarding the past were not available to the subject in the course of his present life (for which in this book we have merely to take the author's word). This can be shown to be the case in some of the better-documented case studies, which we shall take up in the next talk.

VII. The Case for the Buddhist Theory of Survival and Karma

We have hitherto examined some of the major problems involved in presenting the case for survival, rebirth and karma. We have also mentioned some of the evidence suggestive of rebirth. It is proposed in this talk to present some typical samples of the authentic evidence available and to indicate some of the conclusions we may draw from them.

As we said earlier, the evidence for rebirth (which is only a special case of re-becoming) falls into three categories: (i) the experimental evidence, (ii) the spontaneous evidence and (iii) the other evidence.

The Experimental Evidence

We have already given samples of the experimental evidence. In the previous talk we gave a brief account of the researches of the Rev. A. R. Martin with his subjects,[69] many of whom, it is said, were able to recall specific details of their prior lives, although they did not start with any preconceptions, presumptions or prejudices about pre-existence being a fact.

However, one may criticise these experiments as not "being conducted under strictly controlled conditions," although the author mentions several precautions he had taken to eliminate subjective bias.

Let us now take examples where the experimental controls appear to have been more satisfactory. In the case investigated by Professor Theodore Flournoy, the account given reads as follows:

> "It appeared that Helene Smith had twice lived upon the earth before her present incarnation. Once, five hundred years ago as an Arab chief's daughter (Simandini by name), she became the favourite wife of a Hindu prince. This prince, Sivrouka, reigned over the kingdom of Kanara, and constructed, in 1401, the fortress of Tchandragiri. This romance was developed

69. *Researches in Reincarnation and Beyond*, first ed., Pennsylvania, 1942.

> with a wealth of detail, and the astonishing features of it were, first, that research in old and little-known books on Indian history confirmed some of the details, such as the names of places and persons described; secondly, that Simandini uttered (in the trance automatisms) many Hindu words and phrases, sometimes appropriately used, sometimes mingled with other words which the experts failed to identify, and wrote also similar phrases in Arabic script. Further, the entranced medium would act the role of Simandini, putting other members of the circle into the vacant places of the drama."[70]

In the Professor's own words: "All this various mimicry and this exotic speech have so strongly the marks of originality, of ease, of naturalness, that one asks with stupefaction whence comes to this daughter of Lake Leman, without artistic training and without special knowledge of the Orient, a perfection of art which the best of actresses might attain only at the cost of prolonged studies or by residence on the banks of the Ganges."[71]

The Professor confesses that he has not been able to resolve the mystery, especially the Hindu language and the historical statements about the kingdom of Kanara, which were verified in an old and rare book to which the subject had had no access. Yet he concludes that the "Hindu drama was a subconsciously elaborated fantasy, incorporating, very skilfully, fragments of knowledge picked up in haphazard fashion."[72]

His explanation is the standard explanation resorted to by most orthodox psychologists when confronted with evidence of this sort, namely, that here we get only dramatisation and roles-playing based on elements of information picked up in this life. Professor Flournoy is however constrained to "admit that some knowledge was displayed, the acquisition of which by normal means would seem to have been well-nigh impossible."[73]

Yet, this does not seem to explain the ease, the spontaneity and accuracy with which she sang Hindi (Prakritic) songs and wrote

70. William McDougall, *An Outline of Abnormal Psychology*, reprint 1952, p. 511.

71. Ibid., pp. 511–512.

72. Ibid., p. 512.

73. Ibid., p. 515.

in a Prakritic script. Nor does it explain the factual information she gave, the claim she made that she was in fact the wife of a Hindu prince in her previous life, and the serial account of the life and the incidents she gave.

Let us take another case, the case of Mrs. Anne Baker reported by Dr. Jonathan Rodney.[74] Mrs. Baker, a Lancashire housewife who has never studied French or been to France and whose education was very ordinary, spoke perfect French under hypnosis, referred to the death of Marie Antoinette as if it had just happened, gave her name as Marielle Pacasse and spoke of a street named Rue de St. Pierre near the Notre Dame Cathedral.

Subsequent investigations revealed that the name Marielle is rare now, but it was much in vogue about 1794, and although there was no such street at present, there was in fact a street of that name in that vicinity one hundred and seventy years back.[75] Here again a normal explanation would not do. Apart from the knowledge of French, one would have to say that the knowledge about the streets of Paris about two centuries back was acquired either clairvoyantly or telepathically from the dead.

An explanation in terms of spirit-possession is also possible though highly improbable. One could say that the discarnate spirit of the dead Marielle Pacasse now inhabits the body of Mrs. Baker. Normally, in the case of spirit-possession, the discarnate-spirit claims to be a separate personality and possession is not continuous, whereas in this case whenever Mrs. Baker was hypnotised she claimed to be Marielle Pacasse in her previous life. So to account for all the facts, "rebirth" is the simpler, paranormal hypothesis.

Another case which cannot pass unnoticed is the famous "Bridey Murphy" case. When Mrs. Virginia Tighe was hypnotised on six occasions between November 1952 and August 1953, she recalled a life as Bridey Murphy in Ireland. It created a wide interest in "rebirth." It will be interesting to see Professor C. J. Ducasse's assessment of the case when it first came into the limelight and later after careful reflection in the light of the verified facts.

74. *Explorations of a Hypnotist*, Elek Books, London, 1955.

75. See pp. 165–66.

In an opinion published in *Tomorrow* in 1956[76] soon after the case became known, Professor Ducasse suggests three hypotheses to account for it: "That the former is a reincarnation of the latter is *one* hypothesis that would account for the veridicality of those details. A *second* hypothesis that would also account for their veridicality is that of illusion of memory, that is, the hypothesis that Mrs. Tighe, in childhood or later, heard or read of the life of an Irish Bridey Murphy and then forgot this, and that, under hypnosis, the ideas so acquired were recalled by Mrs. Tighe but not the manner in which she had acquired them; and hence that they were indistinguishable by her from memories of events of a life of her own. A *third* hypothesis, which would also explain the veridicality of the verified details, is that while in deep hypnosis, Mrs. Tighe exercises powers of paranormal retro-cognition latent at other times, and vastly more far-reaching than those whose reality has been experimentally proved by Rhine, Soal and others." Going on the assumption that Mrs. Tighe's knowledge of Ireland was erroneous (as was thought at the time), Ducasse favoured the *second* hypothesis.

Later, when further investigation vindicated the truth of Mrs. Tighe's statements and the attempts at "debunking" the rebirth theory were seen to be mainly inspired by religious prejudice and based on false assertions, Professor Ducasse changed his views and favoured the first hypothesis (i.e. rebirth) without ruling out the possibility of the third. He does so in his book, *A Critical Examination of the Belief in a Life After Death.*[77]

Here he refers to the items mentioned by Bridey, which could not be easily explained away. One of the most significant was that in her previous life she bought foodstuffs from Farrs and John Carrigan. Extensive research on the part of Mr. John Bebbington, Belfast Chief Librarian, disclosed the fact that these two grocers were found listed in a Belfast city directory for 1865– 66. Bridey died in 1864. Besides, they were "the only individuals of those names engaged in the foodstuffs business there at the time."

Bridey also referred to a rope company and a tobacco house which were in operation in Belfast at the time, and this too was found

76. Vol. 4, No. 4, pp. 31–33.
77. Springfield, Illinois, 1961.

to be correct. Another remarkable fact was that Bridey's statements, which according to experts on Ireland were irreconcilable with known facts, were shown after further investigation not to be so. Ten such facts are listed. To take one example, one of Bridey's statements was to the effect that her husband taught Law at the Queen's University in Belfast, sometime after 1847. *Life Magazine*, on the basis of so-called expert opinion, attacked this on the ground that there was no law school there at the time, no Queen's *College* until 1849, and no Queen's *University* until 1908. However, further investigations showed that this was incorrect. There was documentary evidence to show that on December 19, 1845, Queen Victoria ordained that "there shall and may be erected one College for students in Arts, Law, Physics ... which shall be called Queen's College, Belfast."[78] "The Queen's University in Ireland" was founded by her on August 15, 1850.[79]

Such accuracy may be due either to extraordinary clairvoyant powers on the part of the subject, or to the simple fact that these were genuine memories of her past life. Since she did not display any such clairvoyant powers in other respects during hypnosis, the latter appears to be the more plausible explanation.

Spontaneous Evidence

The spontaneous evidence consists of accounts given by individuals, mostly children, of their alleged prior lives, which when subsequently checked prove to be historical and accurate and could not have been derived from any normal source in this life.

There are several such cases from all over the world and reports of them are to be found in newspapers and magazines. But in coming to valid conclusions on their basis one has to rely on the trustworthy, verified accounts of scientists. The evidence should be first recorded without bias and one should then see what theory best accounts for the data.

In this respect, one of the best studies so far is that of Dr. Ian Stevenson, Professor of Neurology and Psychiatry, School of

78. Op. cit., p. 286.
79. Ibid.

Medicine, University of Virginia. He makes a detailed study and evaluation of twenty cases in one of his books.[80]

Let us briefly review the case of Imad Elawar, as studied and reported in this book. Imad was born on December 21, 1958, at Kornayel and talked of a previous life when he was between a year and a half and two years old. He mentioned a considerable number of names of people and some events in this prior life, as well as certain items of property he claimed to have owned. He said he lived in the village of Khriby and had the name Bouhamzy. He had a woman (mistress) called Jamille, who was beautiful, and a brother called Amin, who lived at Tripoli, etc.

The father, however, discredited the story and scolded Imad for talking about an imaginary past life. Once, it is said, he even recognized a resident (Salim el Aschkar) of Khriby in the presence of his paternal grandmother. The parents attached more importance to Imad's statements after this. But no systematic attempts to verify the authenticity of Imad's statements were made until Dr. Ian Stevenson undertook to investigate the case.

Khriby was situated about 25 miles away from Imad's home. The road from Kornayel was an extremely winding mountain road. The items were carefully recorded prior to the investigations at Khriby. It was revealed that of the fifty-seven items mentioned, fifty-one were correct. In Dr. Stevenson's own words, "Of the fifty-seven items in the first tabulation Imad made ten of the statements in the car on the way nearly all on the first visit to Khriby before we reached that village; but of these ten, three were incorrect. Of the remaining forty-seven items, Imad was wrong on only three items. It seems quite possible that under the excitement of the journey, and perhaps sensing some expectation of hearing more statements on our part, he mixed up images of the "previous life" and memories of his "present life." In any case, his "score" for this group of statements definitely fell below that for the forty-seven made before we left Khriby."[81]

Some of the items were very specific, as when he said that they were building a new garden at the time of his death, and that

80. *Twenty Cases Suggestive of Reincarnation*, New York, 1966.

81. Ibid., pp. 257–271.

there were cherry and apple trees in it, and that he had a small yellow automobile, a bus, etc.

Besides the verification of these items of information, there were significant recognitions of persons and places, sixteen of which are listed; for example, we may note the recognition of the place where Ibrahim Bouhamzy (the previous personality) kept his dog and his gun. He also recognised the sister of Ibrahim, namely, Huda, and the portrait of Ibrahim's brother, Fuad. He was also able to recall his last words before death, which his sister, Mrs. Huda Bouhamzy remembered, and which were, "Huda, call Fuad."

When we consider the above, as well as the similarity in the character traits between the previous and the present personalities, chance or coincidence has to be virtually ruled out. Since neither fraud nor self-deception nor racial memory could account for the evidence, a paranormal explanation is called for. And of all the different paranormal explanations such as telepathy-cum-clairvoyance plus personation, spirit-possession, etc., rebirth appears to be the most plausible. This was, in fact, Dr. Stevenson's own general conclusion after studying several cases of this type.

In the spontaneous case there is no hypnotist to put any suggestions into the mind of the child. We may say, however, that the child's beliefs about a prior life are a product of his fantasy. But such an explanation ceases to be plausible in the above instance when the so-called "fantasies" turn out to be historically true and were not derived from any source in this life.

The Evidence

We have already referred to other evidence for rebirth when we tried to suggest that temperamental differences in identical twins, which cannot be due to heredity and environment, may be accounted for in terms of the impact of the psychological past of the person, which goes back into prior lives. We have also seen how some phobias prevalent in this life have not only been traced to traumatic experiences in prior lives, but have been cured by re-living the experience and discovering its origin.

Although it is possible to give other explanations of the so-called *déjà vu* experiences, the experience of feeling "I have been here before," some of them at least seem to point to or call for an explanation in terms of pre-existence. There is a recorded case of an American couple who found that some parts of Bombay were extremely familiar to them, despite the fact that they were visiting the place for the first time. To test their memories, it is said, they went to a certain spot where they expected to see a house and a banyan tree in the garden. They, however, did not find them but were told by a policeman in the vicinity that he recalled having heard from his father that they had been there, when the house belonged to a family named Bhan. Curiously, this couple had called their son Bhan, because they liked the name.[82] Such stories are however anecdotal and one cannot attach much importance to them. They are of value only when one is certain of their authenticity.

Dr. Raynor C. Johnson suggests that certain recurrent dreams may be memories of experiences "had in prior lives."[83] A brief excerpt from an account of one such dream reads as follows:

> "The dream was of being a prisoner in a place that I knew to be the Tower of London. I had not seen it in real life, but I had no doubt where it was. It was very cold weather (in waking life, a hot summer). I was aware that I had been condemned to death.... This I used to dream over and over again and after being in the dream a vigorous man, to wake up and be a little girl felt rather strange. At last the dream changed, and I was standing on a scaffold which must have been newly erected as it smelt of sawdust. Everything was decorous and decent. The executioner knelt and apologised for what he was about to do. I took the axe from his hand and felt it, and handed it back, bidding him do his duty.... When I woke up I made a drawing of the axe, which was of a peculiar shape. Some time after this I asked to be taken to the Tower of London, and I explained to a friendly gunsmith that I wanted to write history but could not understand the battles perfectly until I understood the weapons. 'You are

82. W. C. White, "Cruise Memory," *Beyond the Five Senses*, ed. E. J. Garrett, J. B. Lippincott, New York, 1957, cited by Dr. Stevenson.

83. *Religious Outlook for Modern Man*, Hodder and Soughton, London, 1963, pp. 184 ff.

right, Missy,' he said, and demonstrated to me the various uses of lance, crossbow, etc. I then asked had he an axe that beheaded people. He said, 'Yes, this certainly beheaded the Jacobite Lords, but it is supposed to be very much older.' Somehow, I was not surprised, for the axe proved to be the exact shape of the axe in my dream." [84]

Here again we can suggest that this is not the only explanation possible, but when one has read about several such dreams one begins to wonder whether they are not hangovers from the person's past-life experiences.

We have further evidence for rebirth from clairvoyants. The best attested case in the twentieth century is that of Mr. Edgar Cayce. A general account of his life and doings is to be found in a book by Dr. Gina Cerminara.[85]

There is good evidence that Cayce had remarkable clairvoyant powers, with which he successfully diagnosed illnesses even without actually seeing the patient. But what is more remarkable is that he went on to give accounts of the prior lives of some of these individuals (some of which were historically verified). He also gave the alleged karmic causes of their present illnesses.

We have already seen how suicide had certain karmic effects in subsequent lives. Cayce in his readings (which are still preserved and are available for study at the Association for Research and Enlightenment, Virginia Beach, U.S.A.) records the different kinds of karmic effects following in the wake of the different kinds of actions done in the past. In one case, it said, a person was born blind in this life because in his third life previous to this, circa 1000 BCE, he was born in Persia as "a member of a barbaric tribe whose custom was to blind its enemies with red-hot irons, and it had been his office to do the blinding." [86]

84. Ibid., pp. 184–185.

85. *Many Mansions*, New York, 1960, pp. 304 ff.

86. Ibid., pp. 50–51.

Schopenhauer and Buddhism

by

Bhikkhu Ñāṇājīvako

WHEEL PUBLICATION NO. 144/145/146

Arthur Schopenhauer (1788–1860)

Works

Year	Title, translated in English	Abbreviations
1813	*On the Fourfold Root of the Principle of Sufficient Reason* (Ph.D. thesis, quoted from 2nd German edition, 1847)	*Über den Satz vom Grunde*
1819	*The World as Will and Representation* (1st edition, volume one)	
1844	2nd edition of the same work (two volumes)	
1859	3rd, final edition of both volumes	W.W.R. I and II
1851	*Parerga and Paralipomena* (two volumes)	P.P. I and II
1836	*On the Will in Nature* (quoted from 2nd German edition, 1854)	*Über den Willen in der Natur*
1841	*The Two Fundamental Problems of Ethics* (quoted from 2nd German edition, 1860)	*Grundprobleme der Ethik*
	Early Manuscripts from: *Der Handschriftliche Nachlass*, Erster Band: *Frühe Manuskripte* (1804 1818), reprinted Frankfurt/M, 1966	F.M.

Source References and Acknowledgements

W.W.R. I and II are quoted from the English translation by Lt. Col. E. F. J. Payne, Dover Publications, New York, 1966. To the page number the paragraph (§) is added for volume I, and the chapter (Ch.) for volume II.

Passages from *Über den Satz vom Grunde* and *Über den Willen in der Natur* are likewise quoted from Col. Payne's translation of these works.

The author and publisher of the present volume are obliged to the aforementioned two publishers for their kind permission to include here extracts from these works.

All other translations have been supplied by Col. E. F. J. Payne from his unpublished manuscripts. Except for the *Early*

Manuscripts, as stated above, references correspond to Paul Deussen's German edition of *Arthur Schopenhauer's Sämtliche Werke*, published by A. Piper, München, 1912–1913. The first number in brackets after the abbreviated title, refers to Schopenhauer's original edition, as indicated above; the second number to Deussen's edition, from which it is quoted here. The text under 0.32 (Ch. II) from *On the Basis of Morality*, pertaining to *Grundprobleme der Ethik*, is quoted from Col. Payne's translation published by Bobbs-Merrill, Indianapolis, 1965.

Particular thanks are due to Lt. Col. E. F. J. Payne, not only for his kind consent to the use of his masterly translations, but also for his friendly help and advice as well as his valuable suggestions for improving on the linguistic form of this volume written by one for whom English is not his mother tongue.

Buddhist Texts and Their Abbreviations

MN	Majjhima-nikāya	AN	Aṅguttara-nikāya
DN	Dīgha-nikāya	Dhp	Dhammapada
SN	Saṃyutta-nikāya	Sn	Suttanipāta

Quotations have been adapted mainly from the editions of the Pali Text Society, *Translation Series* (London). Editions of the Buddhist Publication Society (Kandy) have also been freely used. For the translations from *Dhammapada* the author has consulted various editions and versions. Translations from *Suttanipāta* facing Schopenhauer's texts 5.15–5.18 (Ch. 4) are from E. M. Hare, *Woven Cadences* (P.T.S. ed.).

Numerical Classification of Schopenhauer's Texts

0.10.36	Texts on Buddhism
1.11.5	On the First Noble Truth, Suffering
2.12.14	On the Second Noble Truth, Cause of Suffering
3.13.9	On the Third Noble Truth, Cessation of Suffering
4.14.21	On the Fourth Noble Truth, *"The Road to Salvation"*
5.15.18	Additional analogies

Introduction

"For so long have vain and fruitless attempts at philosophy been made, because men looked for it on the path of science instead of on that of art. Therefore no art boasts of such egregious bungling as does the art of philosophy. Men tried to consider the Why instead of the What; they strove for the distant instead of seizing what is everywhere close at hand; they went outwards in all directions instead of entering into themselves where every riddle can be solved.... The philosopher should never forget that he is cultivating an art and not a science."[1] F.M. (1814) p. 154, §259

Faut-il mourir pour Danzig? ("Do we have to die for Danzig?") exclaimed a French social philosopher in 1939 when the German occupation of this sensitive point on the north-eastern shores of Europe, held at that time by Poland, became the signal for a new world war.

Arthur Schopenhauer, who since the late 19th century has been the most widely read German and European philosopher, was born in Danzig, in 1788. At that time Danzig was a free Hanseatic city, but in 1793 it was captured by the militarist German state of Prussia. Schopenhauer's father, a rich merchant, considering freedom as the best safeguard of prosperity, decided to transfer his business to the still independent Hanseatic city of Hamburg. At the age of nine, Arthur was sent for two years to France, where he stayed at Le Havre with a family of a business friend of his father, who wished to educate his son for an international business career. Arthur, however, since childhood had shown a preference for a study of the classics. To win him over to continue the family business, his father offered him, at the age of fifteen, a choice either of a regular school training in the humanities, or of a pleasure trip through Europe and England with his parents for a few years. Arthur could not resist such a temptation, but he never regretted it, for he considered that "seeing and having experience were just as necessary as reading and study." The journey included a lengthy stay at Wimbledon for the purpose of learning English.

1. Compare the statement of the Buddha, A. IV, 5, 5, facing text 5.10 below.

Soon after, in 1805, his father died in tragic circumstances and his mother, a writer of fiction and fond of an easy way of living, moved to Weimar, then the cultural centre of Germany. There, among other celebrities, Goethe became a friend of the Schopenhauer family. He was best able to discern a touch of genius in the boy's character and the boy on his part remained a lifelong admirer of the poet's penetrating approach to the serious problems of existence.

A deep and ineradicable veneration for his father made him resentful of his mother. Anxious to regain the years lost for a regular secondary course in the humanities, he embarked on an intensive course of study and made good the loss in two years. At the age of twenty he was qualified to enter the university. For the first two years he studied medicine, and then took up definitely the study of philosophy, at the University of Berlin. In 1813, he presented to the University of Jena his dissertation, *On the Fourfold Root of the Principle of Sufficient Reason,* for which he was made a Doctor of Philosophy. Schopenhauer's thesis is based on a critical revision of the theory of categories in Kant's philosophy. Kant's twelve categories (or "pure concept of the understanding") are reduced to only one*: causality.* In his extensive *Criticism of the Kantian Philosophy,* at the end of W.W.R. I, Schopenhauer pointed out that Kant's conception of the whole problem still remained too strongly influenced by the typically European, Aristotelian and Scholastic tradition, and that he was unable to renounce the idea of a "first cause" in the "chain of causes and effects," but still felt tempted to consider this idea in connexion with the ideas of God, of the immortality of the soul, and of the freedom of the will as necessarily innate in the very nature of human Reason. To dispel this error, Schopenhauer, in his main work (W.W.R.), used against Kant the historical argument of Indian philosophies, essential especially to Buddhism (cf. text 0.13 and 5.10 below). This argument was still missing in the dissertation, but the basic idea of an "interdependent arising" is already clearly stated with the words: "Nothing exists for itself and independent, nothing single and detached." From the very beginning this idea is widely elaborated in Schopenhauer's philosophy on the same lines on which he will ultimately identify it explicitly with the Buddhist standpoint.

From 1814 to 1818, Schopenhauer lived in Dresden, where he wrote his main work, *The World as Will and Representation.* Its basic ideas, as far as they pertain to the subject of our comparative study of Schopenhauer from a Buddhist viewpoint, will be singled out in the following chapter, on Schopenhauer's approach to Indian philosophy. As soon as the book was published (and it was to remain unknown and ignored for a long time), Schopenhauer went for a pleasure trip to Italy, but after a year he had to return home on account of unexpected financial difficulties with a firm in which his inherited capital was invested. Afraid that he might suffer a considerable loss, and thus be unable to live as a freelance author, he decided to take the post of lecturer at Berlin University. His financial crisis was soon settled to his advantage. As for his lecturer's career, it turned out to be a complete failure, because he rashly attempted to antagonize Hegel, who at the time was at the peak of his career as "the state's philosopher" in Berlin.

After a second journey to Italy, Schopenhauer returned to Berlin, the city of his most bitter experiences, and stayed there until 1831. Then, as a result of an epidemic of cholera, one of whose victims was Hegel, he left Berlin forever. In 1833, he ultimately settled in Frankfurt am Main, where, living alone "as a hermit" and dedicating the rest of his life to his philosophical meditations and writing, he remained until his death, in 1860.

In 1844, he published the second volume of the W.W.R.; only 15 years later, in the 3rd edition of the complete work, did this bring him well-merited fame. In the meantime the appearance of two volumes of essays, *Parerga and Paralipomena* in 1851, marked the beginning of a wider interest in his philosophy among an increasing number of intelligent and unprejudiced readers, most of whom were not professional philosophers. Outstanding artists were always most appreciative of his ideas on spiritual emancipation through art, and on the art of living.

Though he spent nearly thirty years as a well-to-do man in his house in Frankfurt, his rooms always gave visitors the impression of a wayfarer's temporary residence. And though in his later years the circle of his friends and followers began to grow, his best friend remained his dog, a poodle named Atma (in Schopenhauer's conception the impersonal, eternally renewed primordial force of nature, in the sense so beautifully described in his simile of *saṃsāra* as a waterfall see texts 5.6–5.7, ch. iv, below).

Among the few objects characteristic of the homely atmosphere of his apartment was a small gilded statue of the Buddha. When his housekeeper, a staunch Catholic spinster, first saw it, she asked in astonishment what it was. "It is the Victoriously Awakened One," said Schopenhauer.

With an inquisitive look at the exotic cross-legged posture and the Dhamma-teaching *Mudra* of his fingers, she answered:

"Hm, your Victoriously Awakened One looks rather like a little tailor!"

Unfortunately, introducing Schopenhauer to Buddhist readers nowadays requires in the first place an answer to the "reproach of *pessimism.*" This typical objection is as unjust and misleading as it is shallow and vulgar. Yet it has become a standardized formula defensively applied by some modern Buddhist authors who are not directly acquainted with Schopenhauer's thought and with the extent of his Buddhist inspiration. They state that Schopenhauer, as a "pessimistic" thinker, *did* understand *dukkha,* or the Noble Truth of Suffering, but was ignorant of the teaching of the Buddha to its full and proper extent; that he was not fit to ask the question about the cause of suffering, not to speak of the ultimate question about the possibility of a way out, or a solution to his own pessimistic problem. In simple untechnical terms, this acknowledgement grants to Schopenhauer the privilege of standing at a level of intelligence just above that of an idiot as far as he was able to realize his *own* problem, but not of inquiring about its reasons, or even of looking for help. The criterion of the present selection—Schopenhauer's philosophical analysis of the essential problems regarding all the Four Noble Truths—on whose understanding the teaching of the Buddha is based—was adopted mainly for the purpose of dispelling such prejudices about *the proper meaning of the term "pessimism"* in the philosophy of Arthur Schopenhauer, the "father of pessimism." This documentation is preceded by a chapter containing Schopenhauer's direct references to Buddhism.

From these texts the reader will learn in Schopenhauer's own words to what extent and within what limits his standpoint of pessimism is deduced from the immanent structure of the world, and how it refers to the "worldliness of the world" *exclusively,* or to the nature of *saṃsāra.* This Buddhist term was adopted by

Schopenhauer explicitly in his deduction of the basic idea that pessimism in this connexion is the indispensable motive for urging the human mind on the path of liberation, in the direct, adequate and literal meaning of the term Nibbāna as extinction, and not as a "realm" of "divine" happiness for the hedonist wretch, for whose sake the opposite theory of "optimism" was invented and introduced previously by the European court-philosopher, Leibniz. Schopenhauer's positive intention was also to defend genuine Christianity from such optimistic falsifications which even at that time were detrimental to European civilization that is liable to become a prey to materialism.

With reference to the proper meaning of the term *pessimism* the attention of the reader is drawn particularly to the following texts:

1.4 Basic text for the refutation of the optimistic philosophy of Leibniz. See also 3.2.

4.16 The educational aspect of the problem.

0.16 Schopenhauer's interpretation, in Buddhist terms, of the pessimistic attitude to the world as *saṃsāra*, as the necessary condition for the realization of Nibbāna.

On account of such deep-rooted historical prejudices against the basic tenets of Schopenhauer's philosophy, it might be useful, in connexion with the comparative subject of this essay, to point out yet another danger leading to a misunderstanding of his "single thought" at the very outset as a result of some superficial and negative sources of "general information" in these matters. Such prejudices are more popular with direct reference to Schopenhauer, than is his authentic thought. This refers to the meaning of the basic term *will* in Schopenhauer's philosophy.

It already appears from our text, 1.1, at the beginning of the chapter on *Suffering*, that by this specific term "the-will-to-live" is meant, and that it is identified and explained here and elsewhere as "an unquenchable thirst" whose "basis... is *need, lack and hence pain*." The identity of meaning with the corresponding Buddhist term for "thirst" or "craving"—*taṇhā*— needs no further authentication for our present purpose. That Schopenhauer's negation of the "will-to-live" does not by any means prejudice the injunction of the ascetic ideal of "right effort" (*sammāvāyāmo* on the Noble Eightfold Path of Buddha) will be quite evident from Schopenhauer's texts on that subject (e.g. 4.3, Ch. 3).

The purpose of the present selection is to give *one profile* of Schopenhauer's philosophy in a cross-section through his works. No explicit differential analysis of ideas could be undertaken within this *prima facie* documentary framework, either as regards the delimitation of Buddhist elements of thought in Schopenhauer's system from those closer to his (earlier) Vedantic inspiration (from the Upanishads), or with reference to a delimitation between Indian and European ways of thought in general, or even in the particular case of Schopenhauer's own remarkable comparativistic attempts to coordinate both into a universal whole. The introductory explanation on the development of Schopenhauer's approach to Indian philosophy is meant primarily to facilitate a *historical orientation* throughout his works.

Chapter 1
Schopenhauer's approach to Indian philosophy

Even the first volume of Arthur Schopenhauer's main work, *The World as Will and Representation*, which appeared in 1819 (25 years before the second, supplementary volume), is interspersed from its preface to the last paragraph with quotations from Indian wisdom and reflections on these, almost as profusely as with quotations from "Stoic Sages" and other ancient authors of a kindred inspiration, as to whose oriental provenience Schopenhauer had no doubts. The fundamental ideal of Stoic ethics, "like that of Cynicism from which it sprang," the ideal of *ataraxia* ("imperturbability") or *apatheia* ("apathy," literally, "non-suffering"), as well as the ideal of *epoche*, or "suspension of judgement" in a disinterested contemplation, corresponding to *upekkhā* in Buddhism, brought from India by Pyrrho of Elis, who was in the philosophers' retinue of Alexander the Great—this whole complex of ideas in the later Greek and Roman philosophy appears to Schopenhauer as a "colossal paradox" from any viewpoint except that of Eastern, specifically Indian, asceticism (cf. W.W.R. II, pp. 158–59; pp. 1; 51; 64). Therefore Schopenhauer's references to Indian wisdom often appear alongside those taken from Greek and Roman sources of the closest and most congenial origin.

It is, however, stated quite explicitly even in the preface and first paragraph of *The World as Will and Representation*, that Indian analogies in Schopenhauer's system of thought are not confined solely to this *historical* coincidence. His first reference to India in the preface has been most improperly used by superficial Eurocentrists to deny the importance of Indian influences on his system as a whole. As a matter of fact, Schopenhauer states in this well-known passage that his thought has been shaped first by Kant, then by Plato and finally by Indian philosophy:

"Kant's philosophy is therefore the only one with which a thorough acquaintance is positively assumed in what is to be here discussed. But if in addition to that the reader has dwelt for a while in the school of the divine Plato, he will be the better prepared to hear me, and the more susceptible to what I say. But if he has shared the benefits of the Vedas, access to which, open to us by the Upanishads, is in my view the greatest advantage which this still young century has to show over previous centuries...; if I say, the reader has also already received and assimilated the divine inspiration of ancient Indian wisdom, then he is best of all prepared to hear what I have to say to him."

It appears obvious from Schopenhauer's own delimitation of this last source of his inspiration that it should not be disregarded as the least important:

"Did it not sound too conceited, I might assert that each of the individual and disconnected utterances that make up the Upanishads could be derived as a consequence from the thought I am to impart, although conversely my thought is by no means to be found in the Upanishads."

Within such broad lines of his preliminary orientation, Schopenhauer's estimate of the fragmentary value of the Upanishads for his own systematic purpose has already to be assumed as correct in view of the historical structure of this archaic compilation of Indian wisdom. Apart from this, I propose to show in the following survey that what may be stated more or less correctly concerning the influence of the Upanishads on the shaping of Schopenhauer's philosophical thought *in its earlier stage*, cannot be affirmed with equal right as regards the importance of the Buddhist analogy and the visible expansion of its influence throughout: the further and later elaboration of his system of philosophy in its historical fulfilment.

It seems to me that the longest text on Buddhism, included under 0.22 below, from the 2nd edition (1847) of the *Fourfold Root of the Principle of Sufficient Reason,* beginning with a differentiation from Brahmanism, can be taken as the safest landmark for determining the time when the transition from a predominantly Vedantic to a prevalently Buddhist orientation was accomplished, particularly since this text already comprises the widest scope of Schopenhauer's basic information on both the *Theravada* and *Mahāyāna* sources, including the translation of *Mahāvaṃsa* and other interesting evidence on the earliest confrontation of Buddhism in Ceylon with the alien ideas on religion of colonial conquerors (Dutch period, middle of the 18th century). In the next

15 years, Schopenhauer was to add to his Buddhist bibliography (see 0.9) only a few more works on the Sinhalese *Theravada* with new translations from the same sources.

Unlike the "disconnected utterances that make up the Upanishads," in the case of the teaching of the Buddha the congeniality with Schopenhauer's ideal of philosophy appears in the inner structure of his "single thought" when compared with the "central conception" claimed to be "the peculiar property of the Buddhas," as we shall show.

Schopenhauer's idea of the "construction" of systems in philosophy was in his day still unknown and foreign to modern European thought, and he was fully aware of this difficulty.

"What has to be imparted [by this book] is a single thought.... A *system of thought* must always have an architectonic connexion or coherence, that is to say, a connexion in which one part always supports the other, though not the latter the former; in which the foundation stone carries all the parts without being carried by them; and in which the pinnacle is upheld without upholding. On the other hand, a single thought, however comprehensive, must preserve the most perfect unity. If, all the same, it can be split up into parts for the purpose of being communicated, then the connexion of these parts must once more be organic, i.e., of such a kind that every part supports the whole just as it is supported by the whole; a connexion in which no part is first and no part is last, in which the whole gains in clearness from every part, and even the smallest part cannot be fully understood until the whole has been first understood." (W.W.R. I, Preface to the 1st. edition.)

It has often been noted in the West that the same difficulty is not so evident in earlier Asian attempts at the monolithic and organic forming not only of famous Indian rock and cave temples (see Ajanta and Ellora) but also of philosophical ideas, at least in the pre-scholastic stage. Schopenhauer was also aware of this fact when, with reference to Buddhism, he praised the oldest religions as being, just like the oldest languages, the most perfect. Thus, the confrontation of Schopenhauer's "single thought" with "the teaching which is the peculiar property of the Buddhas" (*yā buddhānaṃ sāmukkaṃsikā dhammadesanā*) or the "central conception" of the Buddha (an expression used ever more frequently even as a typified title for books and articles, since Stcherbatsky coined it) is capable of producing its striking effect on the reader mainly on account of the simplicity of its expression.

Schopenhauer's "*single thought*": "The will-to-live" is "the being-in-itself" of the world. Its nature is "thirst," "craving" and therefore suffering. Consequently, the essential problem of this philosophy is only one: Liberation from suffering by the "denial of the will-to-live." This is "the road to salvation."

The Teaching peculiar to the Buddhas (*"Awakened Ones"*): "I teach only suffering and the liberation from suffering."— Suffering is due to "thirst" for life or "craving."—"As the ocean has only one taste, that of salt, so has my teaching only one taste, that of liberation." Another question of historical importance for our documentation is, how far the translation of the Upanishads was the exclusive "first source" of Schopenhauer's information on Indian philosophical and religious wisdom. It is well known and no longer difficult to verify in the history of European Indology[2] that Schopenhauer, like his older contemporaries Goethe and Schelling, had attended the lectures of Prof. Friedrich Maier, who at the beginning of the 19th century was one of the best known German orientalists. At that time Schopenhauer was writing and submitting to the University of Jena his doctor's thesis. In the same year, 1813, he obtained from Maier his copy of the *Oupnek'hat*, a Latin translation of the Upanishads by Anquetil-Duperron through an excellent and most carefully edited Persian version. (Schopenhauer was always ready to emphasise its superiority to later direct renderings by European scholars, which appeared during his lifetime.)

In 1813, presumably after the work on his doctor's thesis was finished, we find in Schopenhauer's papers the following first intimation of his next and most important work:

"In my hands and still more in my mind there is developing a work, a philosophy, which is to be ethics and metaphysics *in one,* for hitherto these were just as falsely separated as was man into body and soul. The work expands and the parts grow together slowly and by degrees like a child in the womb. I do not know which was the first and which was the last to come into existence.... I who sit here and whom my friends know, do not understand the origin of this work, just as the mother does not understand that

2. Cf. Raymond Schwaab, *La Renaissance Orientale,* Paris, Payot, 1950.

of the child in her womb.... Chance, ruler of this material world, let me live in peace for a few more years, for I love my work as a mother does her child. When it is mature and has been born, you may exercise your right and exact tribute for the reprieve. But if in this stern age I die before my time, then may these immature beginnings, these studies of mine, be given to the world as they are and for what they are. One of these days, perhaps, a kindred spirit will appear who will know how to put the parts together and restore the antique." (F. M. [1813] p. 55, §92)

Later on in the same *Early Manuscripts* we find the first reference to Indian wisdom in 1814, five years before his main work was published. It is a footnote quotation from *Oupnekkhat* in connexion with the central problem of Schopenhauer's philosophy, on the "spectator of that whole tragedy of life." (p. 106, §191)

In the immediately following §192 (p. 107) there is already expressed the thought that is singled out above in the context of the first paragraph of the first volume of *The World as Will and Representation*:

"The wiser Indians started from the *subject*, from *ātmā, jīvātma*. If, after the manner of the Indians, we start from the subject, the world together with the principle of sufficient reason ruling it suddenly stands before us, no matter from which side we begin to consider it. If we start from the object and build, as we must do, one stone on another with the mortar of the principle of sufficient reason, then we are never able to find the foundation on which the building is to rest or the top which is to carry the building's wreath."

In the same year (§213, p. 120) the first mention is made of *māyā,* which is destined to become the technical term for a cornerstone of Schopenhauer's system and thus the first Indian notion to become popular in modern European philosophy. In this first reference the idea of *māyā* appears in contraposition to the ideal of liberation from suffering:

"This release from willing occurs through better knowledge, and so *Oupnek'hat,* vol. II, p. 216, says*: tempore quo cognitio simul advenit amor e medio supersurrexit* ("the moment knowledge appeared on the scene, thence did desire abate"); here by *amor* (desire) is meant *māyā*, which is just that willing, that love (for the object), whose objectification or appearance is the world. As the fundamental error it is at the same time, so to speak, the origin of evil and of the world (which are really one and the same)."

In the next reference (§234, p. 136) *māyā* is defined as the "inward moving force of the corporeal world." In the notes of the following two years (1815 and 1816) this definition is further elaborated in connexion with Kant's philosophy and other basic topics of Schopenhauer's main thought.[3] But these earliest references may suffice to show how deep the first impact of Indian thought was on Schopenhauer at the "very time when the idea of his whole system was beginning to germinate in his mind."

A further critical and differential analysis of the term *māyā* in the early stage of Schopenhauer's philosophy and throughout the first volume of *The World as Will and Representation,* the expansion of its philosophical meaning, would be interesting from our standpoint for yet another reason. At later stages it can be clearly seen how this expansion of the Vedantic idea of *māyā* subsided and its world-creating meaning was taken over by the more explicitly Buddhist connotation of the term *saṃsāra.* It is interesting to note in the index to both volumes of the W.W.R. that sixteen references to the term *māyā* are listed from the first volume, and only two from the second (i.e. 25 years later), while the word *saṃsāra* is mentioned only once in the first volume. All references to it in the Index to both volumes refer to specifically Buddhist contexts which will be quoted in our next chapter.

In addition to the above-mentioned references there are more than 20 to India which are of importance in the formation of Schopenhauer's thought at the same period. The source of most of them is *not* the *Oupnek'hat.* They comprise a much wider area of topics and different layers of historical development, in Schopenhauer's own specific statement with reference to the *Asiatic Researches* of which he was a regular reader, "works of the Saugatas, Buddhas, Arhatas, Jainas and other heterodox philosophers."[4] Besides his earliest references to Buddhism, it is particularly interesting to note also his clear distinction between the Vedantic tradition of the Upanishads and the Saiva religion, where he is particularly

3. Cf. paragraphs 359, 461, 564, 574, 577, 600, 673. See also our text 5.4, in Ch. 4.

4. Cf. *Der Handschriftliche Nachlass*, II, pp. 395–397.

interested in the *Lingam* Cult. Through it he implicitly discovered the deeper Buddhist idea that "not-dying" is not equivalent to the Christian "immortality" (as in the inadequate Nibbāna = *ambrosia* theory of Mrs. C. A. F. Rhys-Davids), but purely and simply a causal correlative to the fact of "no longer being born."[5]

"Dying and generating are inseparable correlatives, merely two aspects of one thing, namely of life, i.e. of the preservation of form and of the giving up of matter. The Lingam is therefore the attribute of Siva. Now just as our life, as a process of nourishment, is a constant generating, a renewal of form, so is it also a constant dying, a throwing off of matter." F.M. (1815) §474, p. 317

"The two opposite views of death and the kinds of immortality have been able to find expression in Europe only at two periods and in two countries very remote from each other. The Indians, however, combined the two views by simultaneously teaching the liberation from life as the supreme good and worshipping the Lingam." F.M. (1815) §499, p. 337

Not much later than these statements, in 1816, we find close to one another a few characteristic observations in which a clear differentiation between "Brahmanism and Buddhism" assumes its first form.

"In Spinoza and Bruno we find no trace of the *denial of life, of not-willing*; we do not find it even in many passages of the Vedas and Purāṇas ..." F.M. (1815) §608, p. 408

A few pages later there follows the first reference to Buddhism at the end of the lengthy and significant paragraph 612, which is reproduced in our next chapter under 0.11. At the beginning of 1817 (§646), a clearer definition of Nibbāna by the Buddha is quoted (0.26, in the next chapter):

"Thou shalt have *Nieban* (*nibbānam*), i.e. a state in which there are not four things, namely, pain, old age, sickness and death."

Though the first reference is rather vague with regard to the importance that the notion of Nibbāna will subsequently acquire in Schopenhauer's system, the source of his information,

5. In the *Avesta*, the Iranian twin of the Veda, there is only the expression "*duryo ziti*" ("to live long") which in the cosmological context could be compared by European scholars to the Christian ideal of a heavenly "immortality." (cf. e.f. YAST 19,11)

as always, is very concisely indicated. It was the *Theravada* Buddhism of the Burmese.

Besides the general prejudice that Schopenhauer's knowledge of Indian religions and philosophies was limited to a few early and unreliable European reports, mainly of Vedantic origin (the Upanishads), it was arbitrarily assumed by earlier uninterested and even hostile historians of philosophy that his acquaintance with Buddhism came late in life and was limited to some second-hand information of the "*Mahāyāna.*" A glance at his own bibliographical *Selection of the Best Books on Buddhism,* among "numerous works on this religion," in 0.9, shows that here again the very opposite of this is the truth.

Besides the *Asiatic Researches* (issues as early as 1799 are quoted by Schopenhauer), it can be seen from the same list that in the middle period of his lifelong and careful studies of these problems there followed a better acquaintance with the Mahāyāna sources, mainly of Tibetan Buddhism, thanks to the outstanding scholarly services rendered to the promotion of Asian studies by the Russian St. Petersburg Academy. The high standard of the internationally organized research work carried out by this Academy and the fundamental importance, even today, of some works, especially the Sanskrit Dictionary (in seven volumes) and the famous series of the *Bibliotheca Buddhica,* should be better known and appreciated by Buddhists in Asia. It should not be forgotten that the first Pali grammar published in Europe was by the St. Petersburg academician L. P. Minayeff (French translation published in 1874), and that Vassilief's book on Buddhism for a long period in the late 19th and early 20th centuries ranked with the best-known sources of general knowledge on the subject in several European languages (particularly in French and German). The books published in the 20th century (down to 1930) by the leading scholar of that Academy, Th. Stcherbatsky, and his collaborators (Rosenberg, Obermüller) on special problems of Buddhist philosophy (Buddhist Logic and Epistemology, Nirvana, and detailed analyses of Abhidhamma terms and implicit philosophical questions) may rightly be considered as the most concise Buddhist studies that the West has produced down to the present time.

As a sample of the high standard of research work on Buddhism at its Asian sources, in Schopenhauer's day, we shall have to be content with the specimen quoted by him from Csoma Korosi's first-hand translations from the Tibetan *Kangyur* (0. 8). It is easy to see that the subject and purpose of that text are the same as are contained in the *Kevaḍḍha Sutta,* DN 11, of the Pali Sutta Piṭaka.

Finally, in the later phase of Schopenhauer's life and work, when he was preparing the 2nd volume of the W.W.R., the influence on him of the Theravada Pali Buddhism, from its *first-hand Sinhalese sources* again became stronger, as can be seen from the note at the end of his bibliographical list (0.9).

Chapter 2

Schopenhauer on Buddhism

0.1 "It almost seems that, as the oldest languages are the most perfect, so too are the oldest religions. If I wished to take the results of my philosophy as the standard of truth, I should have to concede to Buddhism pre-eminence over the others. In any case, it must be a pleasure to me to see my doctrine in such close agreement with a religion that the majority of men on earth hold as their own, for this numbers far more followers than any other." W.W.R. II, 169, Ch. XVII

0.2 "It is a thoroughly established fact that Buddhism in particular, the religion with the greatest number of representatives on earth, contains no theism, indeed rejects it out of hand." W.W.R. I, 486

0.3 In Christianity God comes to the dying, "and likewise in Brahmanism and Buddhism, though in the latter the gods are really exotic." W.W.R. II, 434, Ch. XXXVII

0.4 "... the true spirit and kernel of Christianity, as of Brahmanism and Buddhism also, is the knowledge of the vanity of all earthly happiness, complete contempt for it, and the turning away to an existence of quite a different, indeed, an opposite, kind.... Therefore, atheistic[6] Buddhism is much more closely akin to Christianity than are optimistic Judaism and its variety, Islam." W.W.R. II, 444, Ch. XXXVIII

0.5 "... so for a thorough understanding of Christianity, a knowledge is required of the other two world-denying religions, Brahmanism and Buddhism; moreover as sound and accurate a knowledge as possible. For just as in the first place Sanskrit gives us a really thorough understanding of Greek and Latin, so do Brahmanism and Buddhism enable us to understand Christianity." P.P. II (316) 415, §179

0.6 "The fundamental difference in religions is to be found in the question whether they are optimistic or pessimistic, certainly

6. For Schopenhauer's understanding of the term "a theism," see 0.22 (end).

not whether they are monotheistic, polytheistic, Trimurti, Trinity, pantheistic, or atheistic (like Buddhism)." P.P. II (320) 422, §181

0.7 "These three religions of China, of which the most widespread is Buddhism; this religion subsists merely through its own strength without any protection from the state, a fact which speaks greatly in its favour ... all three are neither monotheistic, nor polytheistic, nor are they pantheistic, at any rate Buddhism is not. For the Buddha did not regard as a theophany a world steeped in sin and suffering, whose beings are all doomed to die and exist for a short time by devouring one another." *Über den Willen in der Natur* (120) 412

0.8 "Up till 1818, when my work appeared, there were to be found in Europe only a very few accounts of Buddhism, and these extremely incomplete and inadequate, confined almost entirely to a few essays in the earliest volumes of the *Asiatic Researches*, and principally concerned with the Buddhism of the Burmese. Only since that time has fuller information about this religion gradually reached us, chiefly through the profound and instructive articles of that meritorious member of the St. Petersburg Academy, I. J. Schmidt, in the records of his Academy, and then in the course of time through several English and French scholars, so that I have been able to furnish a fairly numerous list of the best works on this religion in my book *On the Will in Nature* under the heading Sinology. Unfortunately, Csoma Korosi, that steadfast and assiduous Hungarian who, in order to study the language and sacred writings of Buddhism, spent many years in Tibet and particularly in Buddhist monasteries, was carried off by death just as he was beginning to work out for us the results of his investigations.

"But I cannot deny the pleasure with which I read in his preliminary accounts several passages from the *Kangyur* itself, for example, the following discourse of the dying Buddha with Brahma, who is paying him homage. There is a description of their conversation on the subject of creation. By whom was the world made? Shākya asks several questions of Brahma, whether was it he, who made or produced such and such things, and endowed or blessed them with such and such virtues or properties, whether was it he who caused the several revolutions in the destruction and regeneration of the world. He denies that he had ever done anything to that effect. At last he himself asks Shākya (the Buddha) how the world was made—by whom? Here are attributed all changes in the world to the moral works of the animal beings, and it is stated that in the world all is illusion, there is no reality in the things; all is empty. Brahma, being instructed in his doctrine, becomes his follower." *Asiatic Researches*, Vol. XX, p. 434; W.W.R. II, 169–70; Ch. XVII

0.9 "For the benefit of those who wish to acquire a fuller knowledge of Buddhism, I will here note those works which belong to its literature and are written in European languages and which I can really recommend, as I possess them and am familiar with them ...

[Follows a list of 23 books. The first 5 are works and translations from Tibetan by I. J. Schmidt, published in 1829–1843 in the *Proceedings of St. Petersburg Academy*.]

"... *Asiatic Researches*, Vol. 20, Calcutta, 1839, part 2 contains three very important papers by Csoma Korosi, containing analyses of the books of the *Kangyur*.

10 Burnouf, Introduction *A L'Histoire Du Bouddhisme*, 1844.

11 *Rgya Tsher Relpa*, trad. du Tibetain par Foucaux, 1848. "This is the *Lalitavistara*, i.e., the life of the Buddha, the Gospel of the Buddhists."

15 and 16: two books of Buddhist texts with Latin translations by Spiegel, 1841.

17 *Asiatic Researches*, Vol. 6. Buchanan, 'On the Religion of the Burmans.'

18 Sangermano, *The Burmese Empire*, Rome, 1833.

19 Turner, The *Mahāvamsa*, Ceylon, 1836.

20 Upham, *The Mahavansi, Raja Ratnacari and Rajavali*, 3 vol., 1833.

21 Upham, *Doctrine of Buddhism*, 1829.

22 Spence Hardy, *Eastern Monachism*, 1850.

23 Spence Hardy, *Manual of Buddhism*, 1853.

"These two excellent books, written after a stay of twenty years in Ceylon and from the instruction of the priests there, have given me more insight into the true nature of the Buddhist dogma than have any others." *Über den Willen in der Natur* (119–20) 409–10, Chapter on Sinology

0.10 "As a rule, the death of every good person is peaceful and gentle; but to die willingly, to die gladly, to die cheerfully, is the prerogative of the resigned, of him who gives up and denies the will-to-live. For he alone wishes to die *actually* and not merely *apparently*, and consequently needs and desires no continuance of his person. He willingly gives up the existence that we know; what comes to him instead of it is in our eyes *nothing*, because our existence in reference to that one is *nothing*. The Buddhist faith calls that existence *Nirvana*, that is to say, extinction."

Schopenhauer's footnote to this text: "The etymology of the word *Nirvana* is given in various ways. According to Colebrooke (*Transactions of the Royal Asiatic Society*, Vol. I, p. 566), it comes from *va*, 'to blow' like the wind, with the prefixed negative *nir;* hence it signifies a lull or calm, but as adjective 'extinguished.' Obry, *Du Nirvana Indien*, p. 3, says: '*Nirvanam* in Sanskrit literally means extinction, e.g., as of a fire.' According to the *Asiatic Journal*, Vol. XXIV, p. 735, it is really *Neravana*, from *nera*, 'without,' and *vana*, 'life,' and the meaning would be *annihilatio*. In Spence Hardy's *Eastern Monachism*, p. 295, *Nirvana* is derived from *vana*, 'sinful desires,' with the negative *nir*. I. J. Schmidt, in his translation of the *History of the Eastern Mongolians*, p. 30, says that the Sanskrit *Nirvana* is translated into Mongolian by a phrase meaning 'departed from misery, escaped from misery.' According to the same scholar's lectures at the St. Petersburg Academy, *Nirvana* is the opposite of *saṃsāra*, which is the world of constant rebirths, of craving and desire, of the illusion of the senses, of changing and transient forms, of being born, growing old, becoming sick, and dying. In Burmese the word *Nirvana*, on the analogy of other Sanskrit words, is transformed into *Nieban* and is translated by 'complete vanishing.' See Sangermano's *Description of the Burmese Empire*, transl. by Tandy, Rome, 1833, §27. In the first edition of *Nieban*, I also wrote *nieban*, because at that time we knew Buddhism only from inadequate accounts of the Burmese." W.W.R. II, 508–9, Ch. XLI

0.11 "But now let us turn our glance from our own needy and perplexed nature to those who have overcome the world and have wholly given up the will-to-live, in other words to the saints who, after the will hardly exists any more, only await the dissolution of its phenomenon, the body, and with this the complete decline and death of the will. We then see in them, instead of the restless pressure, the rapturous joy and violent suffering that make up the actions of the man who loves life, an unshakable calm and inner serenity, a state we cannot look at without yearning and which we are bound to acknowledge as infinitely superior and as the only right thing in face of which the emptiness of everything else becomes apparent.... Thus in this way by considering saints, who of course are rarely brought to our notice in real life, but through history and through art with a truth that is better vouched for and manifestly evident, we will banish the sombre impression of that nothingness which stands out as the goal of all virtue and holiness and which we feared as children fear the dark. We shall do this instead of evading it, as is done by the Indians who in its place put meaningless words, such as Brahma, reabsorption in the primordial spirit, or the Buddhist *Nieban* (see *Asiatic Researches* and *Oupnek'hat*). What remains after the abolition of the will is assuredly *nothing* for those who still will; but for those whose will has turned, this very real world of ours with all its suns and galaxies is—nothing." F.M. (1816) 411–12, §612

0.12 "... consequently, with life, the constant suffering and dying of individuals are certain to it. To free it from this is reserved for the *denial* of the will-to-live; through this denial, the individual will tear itself away from the stem of the species, and gives up that existence in it. We lack concepts for what the will now is; indeed we lack all data for such concepts. We can only describe it as that which is free to be or not to be the will-to-live. For the latter case, Buddhism describes it by the word *Nirvana*.... It is the point that remains forever inaccessible to all human knowledge precisely as such." W.W.R. II, 560, Ch. XLIV

0.13 "That the return to an unconditioned cause, to a first beginning, is by no means established in the nature of our faculty of reason [as presumed by Kant. See also note to 3.1 Ch. III] is, moreover, proved in practice by the fact that the original religions of our race, which even now have the greatest number of followers on earth, I mean Brahmanism and Buddhism, neither know nor admit such assumptions but carry on to infinity the series of phenomena that condition one another. On this point ... we can also look up Upham's *Doctrine of Buddhism* (p. 9), and generally every genuine account of the religions of Asia." W.W.R. I, 484

0.14 "Buddhism is free from that strict and excessive asceticism that plays a large part in Brahmanism, and thus from deliberate self-mortification. It rests content with celibacy, voluntary poverty, humility, and obedience of the monks, with abstinence from animal food, as well as from all worldliness.... The moral virtues are not really the ultimate end, but only a step towards it. In the Christian myth, this step is expressed by the eating of the tree of knowledge of good and evil, and this moral responsibility appears simultaneously with original sin. This original sin itself is in fact the affirmation of the will-to-live; on the other hand, the denial of this will, in consequence of the dawning of better knowledge, is salvation. Therefore, what is moral is to be found between these two; it accompanies man as a light on his path from the affirmation to the denial of the will, or, mythically, from the entrance of original sin to salvation through faith in the mediation of the incarnate God (*Avatar*); or, according to the teaching of the *Veda*, through all the rebirths that are the consequence of the works in each case, until right knowledge appears, and with it salvation (final emancipation), *moksha,* i.e., reunion with Brahma. But the Buddhists with complete frankness describe the matter only negatively as *Nirvana,* which is the negation of this world or of *Saṃsāra.* If *Nirvana* is defined as nothing, this means only that *saṃsāra* contains no single element that could serve to define or construct *Nirvana....*

"The holiness attaching to every purely moral action rests on the fact that ultimately such action springs from the immediate knowledge of the numerical identity of the inner nature of all living things. But this identity is really present only in the state of the denial of the will (*Nirvana*), as the affirmation of the will (*saṃsāra*) has for its form the phenomenal appearance of this in plurality and multiplicity. Affirmation of the will-to-live, the phenomenal world, diversity of all beings, individuality, egoism, hatred, wickedness, all spring from *one* root." W.W.R. II, 607–610; Ch. XLVIII

0.15 "In the *Manual of Buddhism* by Spence Hardy, p. 258, the Buddha says: 'My disciples reject the idea that I am this or this is mine.'" W.R.R. II, 614; Ch. XLVIII

0.16 "Therefore *miseria humana, nequitia humana,* and *stultitia humana*[7] are wholly in keeping with one another in this *saṃsāra* of the Buddhists....

"This is *Saṃsāra* and everything therein denounces it; yet, more than anything else, the human world, where morally depravity and baseness, intellectual incapacity and stupidity prevail to a fearful extent. Nevertheless, there appear in it, although very sporadically yet always astonishing us afresh, phenomena of honesty, kindness, and even nobility, as also of great intellect, the thinking mind, and even genius. These never go out entirely, but glitter at us like isolated points that shine out of the great mass of darkness. We must take them as a pledge that, in this *saṃsāra* there lies hidden a good and redeeming principle, which can break through and inspire and release the whole." P.P. II (184) 239, *Senilia* II

0.17 "Obviously these pantheists give to *saṃsāra* the name *God*; the mystics, on the other hand, give the same name to *Nirvana*. Of this, however, they relate more than they can know; this the Buddhists do not do, and so their *Nirvana* is just a relative nothing." P.P. II (86) 108–9, *Senilia* 115

0.18 "In the case of every man with whom we come in contact, we should not undertake an objective examination of his worth and dignity; and so we should not take into consideration the wickedness of his will, the limitation of his intellect, and the perversity of his notions; for the first could easily excite our hatred, and the last our contempt. On the contrary, we should bear in mind only his sufferings, his need, anxiety, and pain. We shall then always feel in sympathy with him, akin to him, and, instead of hatred or contempt, we shall experience compassion; for this alone is the *agape* to which the Gospel summons us.

"In consequence of their deeper ethical and metaphysical views, the Buddhists start not from the cardinal virtues, but from the cardinal vices, as the opposite or negation of which the cardinal virtues first make their appearance.[8] According to I. J. Schmidt's *Geschichte der Ostmongolen*, p. 7, the Buddhist cardinal vices are lust, idleness, anger, and greed. But probably arrogance

---

7. Human misery, human injustice and human stupidity.

8. "For precisely on the strength of this bad element in him, of this evil principle, he was bound to become a human being," ibid, p. (177) 230.

should take the place of idleness; they are stated thus in the *Lettres Edifiantes Et Curieuses* (édit. de 1819), vol. 6, p. 372, where, however, envy or hatred is added as a fifth." P.P. II (169–70) 221–22. §109

0.19 "*Brahmanistic Dogmas* and the distinctions of Brahm and Brahma, of Paramātma and Jivātma, Hiranya-garbha, Prajapati, Purusa, Prakrti, and the like ... are at bottom merely mythological fictions, made for the purpose of presenting *objectively* that which has essentially and absolutely only a *subjective* existence. For this reason the *Buddha* dropped them and knows of nothing except *Saṃsāra* and *Nirvana.* For the more jumbled, confused, and complex the dogmas became, the more mythological they were. The Yogi or Sanyasi best understands who methodically assumes the right posture, withdraws into himself all his senses, and forgets the entire world, himself included. What is then still left in his consciousness is primordial being. But this is more easily said than done." P.P. II (332) 436–37, §189

0.20 "The purpose of the Buddha Sakya-muni, on the other hand, was to separate the kernel from the shell, to free the exalted teaching itself from all admixture with images and gods, and to make its pure intrinsic worth accessible and intelligible even to the people. In this he was marvellously successful, and his religion is therefore the most excellent on earth and is represented by the greatest number of followers." P.P. II (190) 247; §IIS 0.211

0.21 "The world is just a *hell,* and in it human beings are the tortured souls on the one hand, and the devils on the other. ... *Brahma* produces the world through a kind of original sin, an aberration, but himself remains in it to atone for this until he has redeemed himself from it. This is quite a good idea! In Buddhism the world comes into being in consequence of an inexplicable disturbance (after a long period of calm) in the crystal clearness of the blessed and penitentially obtained state of *Nirvana,*[9] and hence through a kind of fatality which, however, is

9. It seems obvious that this interpretation, contrary to any existing Buddhist cosmological tradition, was suggested rather by Brahmanical cosmology with which Schopenhauer had been acquainted earlier than with the respective Buddhist ideas. The idea of *Brahmā-nirvāṇaṃ,* adapted in the later Hinduism, as occurring in the *Bhagavad-Gita* does actually remain

to be understood ultimately in a moral sense; although the matter has its exact analogue and corresponding picture in physics, in the inexplicable arising of a primordial nebula, whence a sun is formed. Accordingly, in consequence of moral lapses, it also gradually becomes physically worse and worse until it has assumed its present sorry state." P.P. II (253–54) 325– 26, §156

0.22 "... the knowledge of God, as the personal ruler and creator of the world who made everything well, is found simply and solely in the religious doctrine of the Jews and in the two faiths derived therefrom, which in the widest sense might be called Jewish sects (i.e. Christianity and Mohammedanism), but it is not found in the religion of any other race, ancient and modern. For it will surely never occur to anyone to confuse Almighty God with, say, the Brahm of the Hindus who lives and suffers in you and in me, in my horse and in your dog, or even with Brahma who is born and dies to make way for other Brahmas and whose production of the world, moreover, is regarded as sin and guilt.... But if we examine that religion which has the greatest number of followers on earth and thus the majority of mankind in its favour, and which in this respect can be regarded as foremost, namely, Buddhism, we can now no longer disguise the fact that it is just as decidedly and expressly atheistic as it is strictly idealistic and ascetic. In fact it is atheistic to the extent that, when the doctrine of pure theism is brought to the notice of its priests, they expressly reject it out of hand. Thus in an article handed to a Catholic bishop by the high priest of the Buddhists at Ava (as reported in the *Asiatic Researches*, Vol. 6, p. 268 and also in Sangermano's *Description of the Burmese Empire*, p. 81), he reckoned as one of the six damnable heresies the doctrine 'that a being exists who created the world and all things and who

---

commingled with the principle of *avidyā* (nescience) in the nature of the divine creator. Cf. *Bhagavad-Gita*, III, 22–24: "I have no duty, nothing that I have not gained, and nothing that I have to gain, in the three worlds; yet I continue in action.... If I did not do work, these worlds would perish..." and IV 6: "Though I am unborn, of changeless nature ... yet I come into being by my own *māyā*." In Schopenhauer's later references to the same problem in Buddhism such inaccuracy does not recur. (See 0.8 above, where an authentic source is quoted, and also the following text, 0.22.)

alone is worthy of worship'.... A hundred such examples could be quoted. But I wish to draw attention to yet another, because it is quite popular and indeed official. Thus the third volume of that very instructive Buddhist work, *Mahāvansi, Raja-Ratnacari and Rajavali,* from the Sinhalese by E. Upham, London, 1833, contains the official interrogatories, translated from Dutch reports, which the Dutch governor of Ceylon conducted with the high priests of the five principal pagodas separately and successively about the year 1766. The contrast between the interlocutors who cannot really reach an agreement is highly entertaining. Imbued with love for all living beings in accordance with the teachings of their religion, even if such beings should be Dutch governors, the priests show the greatest willingness in their efforts to give satisfactory answers to the governor's questions.... But the Dutch governor cannot possibly see that these priests are not theists. Therefore he always asks afresh about the supreme being, and then who created the world, and other such questions. But they are of the opinion that there cannot be any higher being than the triumphant Perfect One, the Buddha Sakya-muni who, though born a king's son, voluntarily lived as a mendicant and to the end of his days preached his sublime teaching for the redemption of mankind, in order to save us all from the misery of constant rebirth. They are of the opinion that the world is not made by anyone; that it is *self-created*; and that nature spreads it out and draws it in again. They say that it is that, which existing, does not exist; that it is the necessary accompaniment of rebirths; but that these are the consequences of our sinful conduct, and so on. And so these discourses continue for a hundred pages. I mention such facts mainly because it is positively scandalous how, even today ... religion and theism are usually regarded without more ado as identical and synonymous; whereas religion is related to theism as the genus to a single species.... Even the other two religions existing with Buddhism in China, those of Laotse and Confucius, are just as atheistic. This is precisely why the missionaries were unable to translate into Chinese the first verse of the Pentateuch, because that language has no expressions for God and creation....

"Incidentally, it should be observed that the word atheism contains a surreptitious assumption, in that it assumes in advance that theism is self-evident *Über den Satz vom Grunde*, 2nd ed. (119–22), 233–37.

0.23 "Therefore we naturally come here on a kind of *metempsychosis*,[10] though with the important difference that this does not affect the whole *psyche*, and hence the *knowing* being, but the *will* alone, whereby so many absurdities that accompany the doctrine of *metempsychosis* disappear.... Accordingly the word *palingenesis*[11] is more correct than metempsychosis for describing this doctrine.... The proper doctrine of Buddhism, as we have come to know it through the most recent researches, also agrees with this view, since it teaches not metempsychosis, but a peculiar palingenesis resting on a moral basis, and it expounds and explains this with great depth of thought. This may be seen from the exposition of the subject, well worth reading and considering, given in Spence Hardy's *Manual of Buddhism*, pp. 394–96 (with which are to be compared pp. 429, 440 and 445 of the same book). Confirmations of it are to be found in Taylor's *Prabodha Chanrodaya*, London, 1812, p. 35; also in Sangermano's *Burmese Empire*, p. 6, as well as in the *Asiatic Researches*, Vol. VI, p. 179 and Vol. IX, p. 256. The very useful German compendium of Buddhism by Koppen is also right on this point. Yet for the great mass of Buddhists this doctrine is too subtle; and so plain *metempsychosis* is preached to them as a comprehensible substitute." [12] W.W.R. II, 502–3, Ch. XLI

0.24 "We might very well distinguish between *metempsychosis* as the transition of the entire so-called soul into another body, and *palingenesis* as the disintegration and new formation of the

10. In 0.26 Schopenhauer translates this Greek word as "the myth of the transmigration of souls." Today the Latin equivalent, 'reincarnation,' is commonly used for this non-Buddhist doctrine (implying the belief in a permanent soul). Schopenhauer is well aware of the difference and tries to explain it within the terms of his own philosophy. His explanation of the difference is contained in the following texts, 0.24 and 0.25.

11. Greek word meaning regeneration and rebirth.

12. At this point, in the last period of his work and life, Schopenhauer's approach is the nearest to the Buddhist doctrine of rebirth. A much earlier formulation of his theory of *palingenesis*, reproduced in our text 0.25 below, seems still clearer in this regard; its second part, if read for itself, sounds almost as an orthodox statement of the Abhidhamma doctrine. However, the wider context shows that at that time Schopenhauer was not yet aware of such closeness of views nor of all the essential implications on the Buddhist side. Therefore Buddhism is not mentioned in 0.25.

individual, since his *Will* alone persists and, assuming the shape of a new being, receives a new intellect....

"From Spence Hardy's *Manual of Buddhism* .... also from Sangermano's *Burmese Empire* ... as well as from the *Asiatic Researches* ..., it appears that there are in Buddhism, as regards *continued existence after death* an exoteric and an esoteric doctrine. The former is just *metempsychosis* as in Brahmanism, but the latter is a *palingenesis* which is much more difficult to understand and is very much in agreement with my doctrine of the metaphysical permanence of the will...." P.P. II (235) 302, §140, *Senilia* 65

0.25 "Now as we have recognized from the results of my philosophy the will's turning away from life as the ultimate aim of temporal existence, we must assume that everyone is gradually led to *this* in a manner that is quite individually suited to him, and hence often in a long and roundabout way. Again, as happiness and pleasure militate against that aim, we see, in keeping therewith, misery and suffering inevitably interwoven in the course of every life, although in very unequal measure and only rarely to excess, namely, in tragic events where it then looks as if the will should to a certain extent be forcibly driven to turn away from life and to arrive at regeneration by a Caesarian operation so to speak.

"Thus that invisible guidance that shows itself only in a doubtful form, accompanies us to our death, to that real result, and, to this extent, the purpose of life. At the hour of death all the mysterious forces (although really rooted in ourselves) which determine man's eternal fate crowd together and come into action. The result of their conflict is the path now to be followed by him; thus his *palingenesis* is prepared together with all the weal and woe that are included therein and are ever afterwards irrevocably determined." P.P. I (211–12), 249–50

Compare the foregoing three texts (0.23–0.25) with the following explanation of the dependent origination (paṭiccasamuppāda) by the Buddha:

> "To believe the doer of the deed will be the same as the one who experiences its results (in the next life): this is one extreme. To believe that the doer of the deed and the one who experiences its results are two different persons: this is the other extreme. Both these extremes the Perfect One has avoided and taught

> the truth that lies in the middle of both, to wit: 'Dependent on ignorance are volitional formations; dependent on volitional formations, consciousness; dependent on consciousness, mentality-materiality; dependent on mentality-materiality, the sixfold base (i.e., the five physical sense-organs and understanding [*mano*] as the sixth); dependent on the sixfold base, contact; dependent on contact, feeling; dependent on feeling, craving (thirst, *taṇhā*); dependent on craving, clinging; dependent on clinging, the process of becoming (rebirth); dependent on becoming, ageing and death, sorrow, lamentation, pain, grief and despair come to pass. Thus does the whole mass of suffering arise.'"

(Cf. Piyadassi Thera, *Dependent Origination*, The Wheel Publication No. 15, Kandy, 1959. Explanations in brackets have been added by the compiler.)

0.26 "The myth of the transmigration of souls teaches that all sufferings inflicted in life by man on other beings must be expiated in a following life in this world by precisely the same sufferings. It goes to the length of teaching that a person who kills only once an animal will be born as just such an animal at some point in endless time, and suffer the same death. It teaches that wicked conduct entails a future life in suffering and despised creatures in this world; that a person is accordingly born in lower castes, or as a woman, or as an animal, as a pariah or *candala*, as a leper, a crocodile, and so on. All the torments threatened by the myth are supported by it with perceptions from the world of reality, through suffering creatures that do not know how they have merited the punishment of their misery; and it does not need to call in the assistance of any other hell. On the other hand, it promises as reward rebirth in better and nobler forms, as Brahmans, sages, or saints. The highest reward awaiting the noblest deeds and most complete resignation can be expressed by the myth only negatively in the language of this world, namely, by the promise so often occurring, of not being reborn any more: 'You will not again assume phenomenal existence' or as the Buddhists, admitting neither Vedas nor castes, express it: 'You shall attain to Nirvana, in other words to a state or condition in which there are not four things, namely, birth, old age, disease and death.'

"Never has myth been, and never will one be, more closely associated with a philosophical truth accessible to so few, than this very ancient teaching of the noblest and oldest of peoples. Degenerate as this race may now be in many respects, this truth still prevails with it as the universal creed of the people.... In India our religions will never at any time take root; the ancient wisdom of the human race will not be supplanted by the events in Galilee. On the contrary, Indian wisdom flows back to Europe, and will produce a fundamental change in our knowledge and our thought." W.W.R. I, 356–57, §63

0.27 "The doctrine that all genuine moral qualities, good as well as bad, are innate is better suited to the metempsychosis of Brahmanism and Buddhism. According to this, 'man's good and evil deeds follow him, like his shadow, from one existence to another.' ... All this I know quite well."[13] P.P. II. (202) 261, §110

0.28 "For example, we can compare the *Lalitavistara* with the Gospel in so far as it contains the life of Sakya Muni, the Buddha of the present world-period. But this remains something quite separate and distinct from the dogma and so from Buddhism itself, just because the lives of previous Buddhas were also quite different and those of future Buddhas will again be quite different .... Therefore *Lalitavistara* is not a gospel in the Christian sense, no glad tidings of a fact of salvation, but the life of him who gave instructions as to how everyone could redeem himself. It is the historical nature of Christianity that makes the Chinese scoff at the missionaries as so many storytellers.

"Another fundamental defect of Christianity, to be mentioned in this connexion, and not to be explained away ... is that it has most unnaturally separated man from the *Animal World*, to which in essence he nevertheless belongs. It now tries to accept man entirely by himself and regards animals positively as *Things*, whereas Brahmanism, and Buddhism, faithful to truth, definitely recognize the evident kinship of man with the whole of nature in general and the animals in particular and represent him, by *metempsychosis* and otherwise, as being closely connected with the animal world." P.P. II (310) 401, §177, *Senilia* 69

13. See analogies under 5.2, Ch. 4, below.

0.29 "In the *Lalita-Vistara,* well known as the life story of the Buddha Sakyamuni, it is related that, at the moment of his birth, all the sick throughout the world became well, all the blind saw, all the deaf heard, and all the insane 'recovered their memory.' This last is even mentioned in two passages." W.W.R. II, 400, Ch. XXXII

0.30 "Meister Eckhart... 'A good man bears to God one creature in the other.' He means that because, in and with himself, man also saves the animals, he makes use of them in this life. ... Even in Buddhism there is no lack of expressions of this matter; for example, when the Buddha, while still a Bodhisattva, has his horse saddled for the last time, for the flight from his father's house into the wilderness, he says to the horse in verse: 'Long have you existed in life and in death, but now you shall cease to carry and to draw. Bear me away from here just this once, O Kantakana, and when I have attained the Law (have become Buddha), I shall not forget you." (*Foe Koue Ki,* transl. by Abel Remusat, p. 233) W.W.R. I, 381, §68

0.31 "Against the Christian doctrine of predestination and grace, as elaborated by Augustine, that guiding star of Luther, the matter assumes, with regard to the fact that genuine moral qualities are actually inborn, quite a different and moral rational significance under the Brahmanic and Buddhist assumption of metempsychosis. According to this, the advantage one man has at birth over another, and thus what he brings with him from another world and a previous life, is not another's gift of grace, but the fruit of his own deeds that were performed in that other world." P.P. II (307) 395–96, §177

0.32 "*The Virtue of Loving-Kindness* ... was first theoretically mentioned, formulated as a virtue—indeed as the greatest of all virtues—and extended even to enemies by Christianity. This is Christianity's greatest merit, although only in respect to Europe; for in Asia a thousand years earlier the boundless love of one's neighbour had been the subject of theory and precept as well as of practice, in the *Veda* and *Dharma-Shastra, Itihasa* and *Purāṇa,* as well as the teaching of the Buddha Sakya-muni, never weary of preaching it." *On the Basis of Morality*, 161–63, §18

0.33 "If we go to the bottom of things, we shall recognize that even the most famous passages of the Sermon on the Mount contain an indirect injunction to voluntary poverty, and thus to the denial of the will-to-live.... Accordingly, they state in an indirect manner just what the Buddha directly commands his followers to do and confirmed by his own example, namely, to cast away everything and become bhikkhus, that is to say, mendicants. ... These precepts afterwards became the foundation of the mendicant order of St. Francis.... I say therefore that the spirit of Christian morality is identical with that of Brahmanism and Buddhism. In accordance with the whole view discussed here, Meister Eckhart also says....: 'Suffering is the fleetest animal that bears you to perfection.'" W.W.R. II, 633, Ch. XLVIII

0.34 "In the same respect, it is noteworthy that the turning of St. Francis from prosperity to a beggar's life is entirely similar to the even greater step of the Buddha Sakya-muni from prince to beggar, and that accordingly the life of St. Francis, as well as the order founded by him, was only a kind of *Sannyasi* existence. In fact, it is worth mentioning that his relationship with the Indian spirit also appears in his great love for animals, and his frequent association with them, when he always calls them his sisters and brothers...." W.W.R. II, 614, Ch. XLVIII

0.35 "... that utterance of the Saviour (Matthew XIX, 24): '*Facilius est, funem ancorarium per foramen acus transire, quam divitem regnum divinum ingredi.*' (It is easier for a camel to go through the eye of a needle than for a rich man to enter into the kingdom of God.) Therefore those who were greatly in earnest about their eternal salvation chose voluntary poverty when fate had denied this to them and they had been born in wealth. Thus Buddha Sakya Muni was born a prince, but voluntarily took to the mendicant's staff; and Francis of Assisi, the founder of the mendicant orders...." P.P. II (266) 346, §170

Chapter 3
The Four Noble Truths

0.36 "In Buddhism all improvement, conversion, and salvation to be hoped from the world of suffering, from this *saṃsāra*, proceed from knowledge of the four fundamental truths: (I) *dolor,* (2) *doloris ortus,* (3) *doloris interitus,* (4) *octopartita via ad doloris sedationem. Dhammapada*, ed. Fausboll, pp. 35 and 347."[14] W.W.R. II, 623, Ch. XLVIII

From the First Discourse of the Buddha (*Dhammacakkappavattana-Sutta*)

The Four Noble Truths

"This, bhikkhus, is the noble truth of suffering: Birth is suffering, old age is suffering, death is suffering, association with the unloved is suffering, separation from the loved is suffering, not to get what one wants is suffering, in short the five constituents of grasping are suffering.[15]

This, bhikkhus, is the noble truth of the origin of suffering: It is the thirst (for existence) which gives rise to rebirth, and, accompanied by pleasure and lust, takes delight in this and that object; namely, thirst for sensuous delight, thirst for being and thirst for non-being.

"This, bhikkhus, is the noble truth of the cessation of suffering: It is the complete cessation, giving up, abandonment of that thirst, liberation and detachment.[16]

---

14. Suffering, origin of suffering, cessation of suffering, the eightfold path to the appeasement of suffering. Schopenhauer quotes Fausböll's Latin translation of the *Dhammapada*, referring to the *gāthā* 190–191 and 273–274.

15. Hence the annihilation, cessation, and overcoming of corporeality, feeling, perception, formations, and consciousness (i.e., *The Five Constituents* of existence)—this is the cessation of suffering, the end of disease, the overcoming of old age and death." (S. XXII, 30)

16. "Be it in the past, present, or future, whosoever of the *samaṇa* or *brāhmaṇa* [the latter are Vedic priests, the former non-Vedic and therefore

"This, bhikkhus, is the noble truth of the way leading to the cessation of suffering: It is the noble eightfold way, namely: right view, right intention, right speech, right action, right livelihood, right effort, right mindfulness, right concentration."

I. Suffering

1.1 "We have already seen in nature-without-knowledge her inner being, as a constant *striving* without aim and without rest, and this stands out much more distinctly when we consider the animal or man. Willing and striving are its whole essence, and can be fully compared to an *unquenchable thirst*. The *basis* of all willing, however, is *need, lack and hence pain*, and by its very nature and origin it is therefore destined to pain." W.W.R. I, 311–12, §5

1.2 "However varied the forms in which man's happiness and unhappiness appear and impel him to pursuit or escape, the material basis of all this is nevertheless physical pleasure or pain. This basis is very restricted, namely, health, nourishment, protection from wet and cold, and sexual satisfaction, or else the want of these things. Consequently, in real physical pleasure man has no more than the animal...." P.P. II (249) 319–20, §153

1.3 "We have ... recognized this striving, that constitutes the kernel and the in-itself[17] of everything, as the same thing that in us, where it manifests itself most distinctly in the light of the fullest consciousness, is called *will*.

"We call its hindrance through an obstacle placed between it and its temporary goal *suffering*; its attainment of the goal, on the other hand, we call *satisfaction*, well-being, happiness. We can also transfer these names to those phenomena of the world-without-knowledge which, though weaker in degree, are identical in essence.

unorthodox or free philosophers, like the Buddhists] regards the delightful and pleasurable things in the world as impermanent (*anicca*), painful (*dukkha*), and without a self (*anattā*), as diseases and cancers, it is he who overcomes the thirst [for existence, *taṇhā*]...." (S. XXII, 66).

17. The radical difference of Schopenhauer's understanding of the connotation "in-itself" as "striving" or *will* from the original meaning of the term *thing-in-itself* in Kant's philosophy is clearly stated in this sentence. See further explanation in the note to 3.1.

We then see these involved in constant suffering and without any lasting happiness. For all striving springs from want or deficiency, from dissatisfaction with one's own state or condition, and is therefore suffering so long as it is not satisfied. No satisfaction, however, is lasting; on the contrary, it is always merely the starting point of a fresh striving. We see striving everywhere impeded in many ways, everywhere struggling and fighting, and hence always suffering. Thus that there is no ultimate aim of striving means that there is no measure or end of suffering.... Therefore, in proportion as knowledge attains to distinctness, consciousness is enhanced, pain also increases, and consequently reaches its highest degree in man. ..." W.W.R. I, 309–10, §56

1.4 "This world is the battleground of tormented and agonized beings who continue to exist only by each devouring the other. Therefore, every beast of prey in it is the living grave of thousands of others, and its self-maintenance is a chain of torturing deaths. Then in this world the capacity to feel pain increases with knowledge, and therefore reaches its highest degree in man, a degree that is the higher the more intelligent the man. To this world the attempt has been made to adapt the system of *optimism*, and to demonstrate to us that it is the best of all possible worlds.[18] The absurdity is glaring. However, an optimist tells me to open my eyes and to look at the world and see how beautiful it is in the sunshine with its mountains, valleys, rivers, plants, animals, and so on. But is the world, then, a peep-show? These things are certainly beautiful to *behold*, but to *be* them is something quite different. A teleologist then comes along and speaks to me in glowing terms about the wise arrangement by virtue of which care is taken that the planets do not run their heads against one another; that land and sea are not mixed up into pulp, but are held apart in a delightful way; also that everything is neither rigid in continual frost nor roasted with heat; likewise that, in consequence of the obliquity of the ecliptic, there is not an eternal spring in which nothing could reach maturity, and so forth. But this and everything like it are indeed *conditiones sine quibus non*. If there is to be a world at all, if its planets are to exist at least as long

18. Thesis formulated by Leibniz in his essay *Theodicee*, or "Glorification of God."

as is needed for the ray of light from a remote star to reach them, ... then of course it could not be constructed so unskilfully that its very framework would threaten to collapse. But if we proceed to the *results* of the applauded work, if we consider the *players* who act on the stage so durably constructed, and then see how with sensibility pain makes its appearance, and increases in proportion as that sensibility develops to intelligence, and then how, keeping pace with this, desire and suffering come out ever more strongly, and increase, till at last human life affords no other material than that for tragedies and comedies, then whoever is not a hypocrite will hardly be disposed to break out into hallelujahs ...

"But against the palpably sophisticated proofs of Leibniz that this is the best of all possible worlds, we may even oppose seriously and honestly the proof that it is the *worst* of all possible worlds. For 'possible' means not what we may picture in our imagination, but what can actually exist and last. Now this world is arranged as it had to be if it were capable of continuing with great difficulty to exist; if it were a little worse, it would be no longer capable of continuing to exist. Consequently, since a worse world could not continue to exist, it is absolutely impossible; and so this world itself is the worst of all possible worlds. For not only if the planets run their heads against one another, but also if any one of the actually occurring perturbations of their course continued to increase, instead of being gradually balanced again by the others, the world would soon come to an end. Astronomers know on what accidental circumstances—in most cases on the irrational relations to one another of the periods of revolution—all this depends. They have carefully calculated that it will always go on well, and consequently that the world can also last and go on. Although Newton was of the opposite opinion, we will hope that the astronomers have not miscalculated, and consequently that the mechanical perpetual motion realized in such a planetary system will also not, like the rest, ultimately come to a standstill. Again, powerful forces of nature dwell under the firm crust of the planet. As soon as some accident affords these free play, they must necessarily destroy that crust with everything living on it. This has occurred at least three times on our planet, and will probably occur even more frequently.... The fossils of entirely different kinds of animal species which formerly inhabited the planet afford us, as proof of our calculation, records of whole worlds whose continuance was no longer possible, and which were in consequence somewhat worse than the worst of possible worlds. ... Powerful as are the weapons of understanding and reason possessed by the human race, nine-tenths of mankind live in constant conflict with want, always balancing themselves with difficulty and effort on the brink of destruction. Thus throughout, for the continuance of the whole as well as for that of every individual being the conditions are sparingly and scantly given, and nothing beyond that. ...

"At bottom, *optimism* is the unwarranted self-praise of the real author of the world, namely, of the will-to-live which complacently mirrors itself in its work. Accordingly *optimism* is not only a false but also a pernicious doctrine, for it presents life as a desirable state and man's happiness as its aim and object. Starting from this, everyone then believes he has the most legitimate claim to happiness and enjoyment. If, as usually happens, these do not fall to his lot, he believes that he suffers an injustice, in fact that he misses the whole point of his existence; whereas it is far more correct to regard work, privation, misery, and suffering, crowned by death, as the aim and object of our life (as is done by Brahmanism and Buddhism, and also by genuine Christianity), since it is these that lead to the denial of the will-to-live." W.W.R. II, 581–84, Ch. XLVI

1.5 "The life of every individual, viewed as a whole and in general, and when only its most significant features are emphasized, is really a tragedy; but gone through in detail it has the character of a comedy. For the doings and worries of the day, the restless mockeries of the moment, the desires and fears of the week, the mishaps of every hour, are all brought about by chance that is always bent on some mischievous trick; they are nothing but scenes from a comedy. The never-fulfilled wishes, the frustrated efforts, the hopes mercilessly blighted by fate, the unfortunate mistakes of the whole life, with increasing suffering and death at the end, always give us a tragedy. Thus, as if fate wished to add mockery to the misery of our existence, our life must contain all the woes of tragedy, and yet we cannot even assert the dignity of tragic characters, but, in the broad detail of life, are inevitably the foolish characters of a comedy.

"Now, however much great and small worries fill up human life, and keep it in constant agitation and restlessness, they are unable to mask life's inadequacy to satisfy the spirit; they cannot conceal the emptiness and superficiality of existence, or exclude boredom which is always ready to fill up every pause granted by care. The result of this is that the human mind, still not content with the cares, anxieties, and preoccupations laid upon it by the actual world, creates for itself an imaginary world in the shape of a thousand different superstitions. Then it sets itself to work with this in all kinds of ways, and wastes time and strength on it, as soon as the real world is willing to grant it the peace and quiet to which it is not in the least responsive. Hence this is at bottom most often the case with those people for whom life is made easy by the mildness of the climate and of the soil, above all the Hindus, then the Greeks and Romans, and later the Italians, Spaniards, and other. ..." W.W.R. I, 322–23, §58

II. Cause of Suffering

(a) The Nature of Knowledge (Avijjā)

2.1 "Thus knowledge in general, rational knowledge as well as mere knowledge from perception, proceeds originally from the will itself, belongs to the inner being of the higher grades of the will's objectification as a mere *mechane* [mechanism], a means for preserving the individual and the species, just like any organ of the body. Therefore, destined originally to serve the will for the achievement of its aims, knowledge remains almost throughout entirely subordinate to its service. This is the case with all animals and almost all men. However, we shall see in the third book how, in the case of individual persons, knowledge can withdraw from this subjection, throw off its yoke, and, free from all the aims of the will, exist, purely for itself, simply as a clear mirror of the world; and this is the source of art. Finally, in the fourth book we shall see how, if this kind of knowledge reacts on the will, it can bring about the will's self-elimination, in other words, resignation. This is the ultimate goal, and indeed the innermost nature of all virtue and holiness, and of salvation from the world." W.W.R. I, 152, §27

2.2 "Therefore, knowledge that serves the will really knows nothing more about objects than their relations, knows the objects only in so far as they exist at such a time, in such a place, in such and such circumstances, from such and such causes, and in such and such effects—in a word, as particular things. If all these relations were eliminated, the objects also would have disappeared for knowledge, just because it did not recognize in them anything else. We must also not conceal the fact that what the sciences consider in things is also essentially nothing more than all this, namely, their relations, the connections of time and space, the causes of natural changes, the comparison of forms, the motives of events, and thus merely relations. What distinguishes science from ordinary knowledge is merely its form, the systematic, the facilitating of knowledge by summarizing everything particular in the universe by means of the subordination of concepts, and the completeness of knowledge thus attained. All relation has itself only a relative existence, for example, all being in time is also a non-being, for time is just that by which opposite determinations can belong to the same thing." W.W.R. I, 177, §33

(b) Life as "Compulsory Service ... for Paying Off a Debt" —Ergasterion (Kamma)

2.3 "... To this, then, false fundamental views lead. Far from bearing the character of a gift, human existence has entirely the character of a contracted *debt.* The calling in of this debt appears in the shape of the urgent needs, tormenting desires, and endless misery brought about through that existence. As a rule, the whole lifetime is used for paying off this debt, yet in this way only the interest is cleared off. Repayment of the capital takes place through death. And when was this debt contracted? At the time of begetting." W.W.R. II, 580, Ch. XLVI

2.4 "We cannot possibly assume that such differences, which transform the man's whole being, which are not to be abolished by anything, and which further determine his course of life in conflict with the circumstances, could exist without guilt or merit on the part of those affected by them, and that they were the mere work of chance. It is at once evident from this that man must be in a certain sense his own work." W.W.R. II, 599, Ch. XLVII

2.5 "To have always in hand a sure compass for guiding us in life and enabling us always to view this in the right light without ever going astray, nothing is more suitable than to accustom ourselves to regard this world as a place of penance and hence a penal colony, so to speak, an *Ergasterion,* as it was called by the oldest philosophers (according to Clement of Alexandria). Among the Christian Fathers Origen expressed it thus with commendable boldness '... This view of the world also finds its theoretical and objective justification not merely in my philosophy, but in the wisdom of all ages, thus in Brahmanism and Buddhism,[19] Empedocles and Pythagoras, and also Cicero mentions ... that it was taught by ancient sages and at the initiation into the Mysteries ...' For one of the evils of a penitentiary is also the society we meet there. What this is like will be known by anyone who is worthy of a better society without my telling him. A fine nature, as well as a genius, may sometimes feel in this world like a noble state-prisoner in the galleys among common criminals; and they, like him, will therefore attempt to isolate themselves. However strange this may sound, it accords with the facts, puts the other man in the most correct light, and reminds us of that most necessary thing: tolerance, patience, forbearance and love of one's neighbour, which everyone needs and each of us therefore owes to another." P.P. II (255–56) 327–28, §156

(c) Will-to-Live (Taṇhā)

2.6 "This great intensity of willing is in and by itself and directly a constant source of suffering, firstly, because all willing as such springs from want, and hence from suffering. ... Secondly, because, through the causal connexion of things,[20] most desires must remain unfulfilled; and the will is much more often crossed than satisfied. Consequently, much intense willing always entails much intense suffering. For all suffering is simply nothing but

19. *Schopenhauer's footnote:* "Nothing can be more conducive to patience in life and to a placid endurance of men and evils than a Buddhist reminder of this kind: 'This is Saṃsāra, the world of lust and craving and thus of birth, disease, old age, and death; it is a world that ought not to be. And this is here the population of Saṃsāra. Therefore what better things can you expect?' I would like to prescribe that everyone repeat this four times a day, fully conscious of what he is saying." *Senilia* 82

20. Compare the formula of the dependent origination (*paṭicca samuppāda*) quoted in addition to the text 0.25, Ch. 2, above.

unfulfilled and thwarted willing. ... Now a person filled with an extremely intense pressure of will wants with burning eagerness to accumulate everything, in order to slake the thirst of egoism." W.W.R. I, 363–64, §65

2.7 "The world is only the mirror of this willing; and all finiteness, all suffering, all the miseries that it contains, belong to the expression of what the will wills, are as they are because the will so wills. Accordingly, with the strictest right, every being supports existence in general, and the existence of its species and of its characteristic individuality, entirely as it is and in surroundings as they are, in a world such as it is, swayed by chance and error, fleeting, always suffering; and in all that happens or indeed can happen to the individual, justice is always done to it. For the will belongs to it; and as the will is, so is the world. Only this world itself—no other—can bear the responsibility for its existence and its nature; for how could anyone else have assumed this responsibility?"[21] W.W.R. I, 351; §63

2.8 "Therefore what is always to be found in *every* animal consciousness, even the most imperfect and feeblest, in fact what is always its foundation is the immediate awareness of a *longing*, and of its alternate satisfaction and non-satisfaction in very different degrees. To a certain extent we know this *a priori*. For amazingly varied as the innumerable species of animals may be, and strange as some new form of them, never previously seen, may appear to us, we nevertheless assume beforehand with certainty its innermost nature as something well known, and indeed wholly familiar to us. Thus we know that the animal *wills*, indeed even *what* it wills, namely existence, well-being, life, and propagation. Since we here presuppose with perfect certainty an identity with ourselves, we have no hesitation in attributing to it unchanged all the affections of will known to us in ourselves; and we speak positively and plainly of its desire, aversion, fear, anger, hatred, love, joy, sorrow, longing, and so on. ... Longing, craving, willing, or aversion, shunning, and not-willing are peculiar to every consciousness; man has them in common with the polyp." W.W.R. II, 204, Ch. XIX

---

21. Compare the statement of the Buddha in *Dhammapada* 160: "One oneself is the guardian of oneself; what other guardian would there be?"

2.9 "All *willing springs* from lack, from deficiency, and thus from suffering. Fulfilment brings this to an end; yet, for one wish that is fulfilled there remain at least ten that are denied. Further, desiring lasts a long time, demands and requests go on to infinity; fulfilment is short and meted out sparingly. But even the final satisfaction itself is only apparent; the wish fulfilled at once makes way for a new one; the former is a known delusion, the latter a delusion not yet known. No attained object of willing can give a satisfaction that lasts and no longer declines; but it is always like the alms thrown to a beggar, which reprieves him today so that his misery can be prolonged till tomorrow. Therefore, so long as our consciousness is filled by our will, so long as we are given up to the throng of desires with its constant hopes and fears, so long as we are the subject of willing, we never obtain lasting happiness or peace. Essentially it is all the same whether we pursue or flee, fear, harm or aspire to enjoyment; care for the constantly demanding will, no matter in what form, continually fills and moves consciousness; but without peace and calm, true well-being is absolutely impossible.

"When, however, an external cause or inward disposition suddenly raises us out of the endless stream of willing, and snatches knowledge from the thraldom of the will, the attention is now no longer directed to the motives of willing, but comprehends things free from their relation to the will. Thus it considers things without interest, without subjectivity, purely objectively; it is entirely given up to them in so far as they are merely representations, and not motives. Then all at once the peace, always sought but always escaping us on that first path of willing, comes to us of its own accord, and all is well with us. It is the painless state, prized by Epicurus as the highest good and as the state of the gods; for that moment we are delivered from the miserable pressure of the will." W.W.R. I, 196, §38

(d) "Endless Flux ... the Essential Nature of the Will" (Anicca)

2.10 "In such a world where there is no stability of any kind, no lasting state is possible but everything is involved in restless rotation and change, where everyone hurries along and keeps erect on a tight rope by always advancing and moving, happiness is not even conceivable." P.P. II (242) 309, §144

2.11 "In fact, absence of all aim, of all limits, belongs to the essential nature of the will in itself, which is an endless striving. ... It also reveals itself in the simplest form of the lowest grade of the will's objectivity, namely, gravitation, the constant striving of which we see, although a final goal for it is obviously impossible. For it, according to its will, all existing matter were united into a lump, then within this lump gravity, ever striving towards the centre, would still always struggle with impenetrability as rigidity or elasticity. Therefore the striving of matter can always be impeded only, never fulfilled or satisfied. But this is precisely the case with the striving of all the will's phenomena. Every attained end is at the same time the beginning of a new course, and so on *Ad Infinitum*. The plant raises its phenomenon from the seed through stem and leaf to blossom and fruit, which is in turn only the beginning of a new seed, of a new individual, which once more runs through the old course, and so through endless time. Such also is the life course of the animal; procreation is its highest point, and after this has been attained, the first individual quickly or slowly fades, while a new life guarantees to nature the maintenance of the species, and repeats the same phenomenon. ... Eternal becoming, endless flux, belong to the revelation of the essential nature of the will. Finally, the same thing is also seen in human endeavours and desires that buoy us up with the vain hope that their fulfilment is always the final goal of willing. But as soon as they are attained, they no longer look the same, and so are soon forgotten, become antiquated and are really, although not admittedly, always laid aside as vanished illusions. It is fortunate enough when something to desire and to strive for still remains, so that the game may be kept up of the constant transition from desire to satisfaction, and from that to a fresh desire, the rapid course of which is called happiness, the slow course sorrow, and so that this game may not come to a standstill, showing itself as a fearful, life-destroying boredom, a lifeless longing without a definite object, a deadening languor." W.W.R. I, 164, §29

(e) Principium Individuationis (Anattā)

2.12 "Just as the boatman sits in his small boat, trusting his frail craft in a stormy sea that is boundless in every direction, rising and falling with the howling mountainous waves, so in the midst of a world full of suffering and misery the individual man calmly sits, supported by and trusting the *principium individuationis*, or the way in which the individual knows things as phenomena. The boundless world, everywhere full of suffering in the infinite past, in the infinite future, is strange to him, is indeed a fiction. His vanishing person, his extensionless present, his momentary gratification, these alone have reality for him; and he does everything to maintain them, so long as his eyes are not opened by a better knowledge. Till then, there lives only in the innermost depths of his consciousness the wholly obscure presentiment that all this is indeed not really so strange to him, but has a connexion with him from which the *principium individuationis* cannot protect him. From this presentiment arises that ineradicable *dread*, common to all human beings (and possibly even to the more intelligent animals) ...." W.W.R. I, 352–53, §63

2.13 "Now *the suffering of wrong* appears as an event in external experience, and, as we have said, there is manifested in it more distinctly than anywhere else the phenomenon of the conflict of the will-to-live with itself, arising from egoism, both of which are conditioned by the *principium individuationis* which is the form of the world as representation for the knowledge of the individual. We also saw above that a very great part of the suffering essential to human life has its constantly flowing source in the conflict of individuals.

"The faculty of reason that is common to all those individuals, and enables them to know not merely the particular case, as the animals do, but also the whole abstractly in its connecxion, has taught them to discern the source of that suffering. It has made them mindful of the means of diminishing, or if possible suppressing, this suffering by a common sacrifice which is, however, outweighed by the common advantage resulting therefrom ... This means is the *State contract* or the *law*. It is readily devised and gradually perfected by egoism which, by using the faculty of reason, proceeds methodically, and forsakes its one-sided point of view." W.W.R. I, 342–43, §62

(f) Death

2.14 "The philosophical wonder is conditioned in the individual by higher development of intelligence, though generally not by this alone; but undoubtedly it is the knowledge of death, and therewith the consideration of the suffering and misery of life, that gives the strongest impulse to philosophical reflection and metaphysical explanations of the world. If our life were without end and free from pain, it would possibly not occur to anyone to ask why the world exists, and why it does so in precisely this way, but everything would be taken purely as a matter of course. In keeping with this, we find that the interest inspired by philosophical and also religious systems has its strongest and essential point absolutely in the dogma of some future existence after death. Although the latter systems seem to make the existence of their gods the main point, and to defend this most strenuously, at bottom this is only because they have tied up their teaching on immortality therewith, and regard the one as inseparable from the other; this alone is really of importance to them. For if we could guarantee their dogma of immortality to them in some other way, their lively ardour for their gods would at once cool; and it would make way for almost complete indifference if, conversely, the absolute impossibility of any immortality were demonstrated to them. For interest in the existence of the gods would vanish with the hope of a closer acquaintance with them, down to what residue might be bound up with their possible influence on the events of the present life. But if continued existence after death could also be proved to be incompatible with the existence of gods, because, let us say, it presupposed originality of mode of existence, they would soon sacrifice these gods to their own immortality, and be eager for atheism. The fact that the really materialistic as well as the absolutely sceptical systems have never been able to obtain a general or lasting influence is attributable to the same reason. Temples and churches, pagodas and mosques, in all countries and ages, in their splendour and spaciousness, testify to man's need for metaphysics, a need strong and ineradicable, which follows close on the physical." W.W.R. II, 161–62, Ch. XVII

III. Cessation of Suffering

(a) The Dilemma

3.1 "He knows *the whole*,[22] comprehends its inner nature, and finds it involved in a constant passing away, a vain striving, an inward conflict, and *a continual suffering* .... Thus, whoever is still involved in the *principium individuationis*, in egoism, knows only particular things and their relation to his own person, and these then become ever renewed motives of his willing. On the other hand, that knowledge of the whole, of the inner nature of the thing-in-itself, which has been described, becomes a quieter of all and every willing. The will now turns away from life; it shudders at the pleasures in which it recognizes the affirmation of life. Man attains to the state of voluntary renunciation, resignation, true composure, and complete will-lessness." W.W.R. I, 379, §68

> "Bhikkhus, I will teach you *The All*. Listen to it. And what, bhikkhus, is the all? It is eye and object, ear and sound, nose and scent, tongue and savour, body and tangible things, mind and mind-states. That is called the all....
>
> "Whoever, bhikkhus, should say: 'Reject this all, I will proclaim another all' it would be mere talk on his part, and when questioned he could not make good his boast, and further would come to an ill pass. Why so? Because it would be beyond his scope to do so.
>
> "I will show you a teaching, bhikkhus, for abandoning the all. Listen to it .... The eye must be abandoned, objects must be abandoned, eye-consciousness must be abandoned, eye-contact must be abandoned. That enjoyment or suffering or neutral state experienced which arises owing to eye-contact, that also must be abandoned.... Mind must be abandoned, mind-states, mind-consciousness, mind-contact must be abandoned....
>
> "This, bhikkhus, is the teaching for the abandonment of the all, by fully knowing, by comprehending it.... Without fully knowing, without comprehending, without detaching oneself therefrom, without abandoning the all, one is incapable of extinguishing suffering." SN 35:23–26

22. See note on the following page. Italics are ours.

Note to 3.1

The stress laid on the meaning of the all, or "the whole," in the two texts compared above, marks with equal clearness the basic difference of both the Buddhist and Schopenhauer's approach to the problem of the ultimate "kernel" of the world "in-itself" from the *opposite* approaches by the *advaita-vedanta* (in the Upanishads and their later interpretation by Sankara) and by Kant's theory of the "thing-in-itself" as a "back-stage" structure of the world.

For the Buddha there is no fixed and permanent cause of being beyond the things as they appear to us, or as *phenomena*, which, according to the interpretation of this Greek word in contemporary philosophy (Heidegger, Sartre), means just the immediate appearance of things "in themselves and by themselves." They are only "aggregates" (*khandha*) in simultaneous "momentary" (*khaṇika*) appearance in their interdependent arising (*paṭicca-samuppāda*). There is no "external cause" to the process of *saṃsāra,* which, in Schopenhauer's words, "is a mere *existentia fluxa*, existing through a continuous change, comparable to a stream of water." (P.P. II (246) 315, §147)

In the same sense Schopenhauer often speaks of the "chain of causes and effects," the knowledge whereof "really knows nothing more about objects than their relations ..." (cf. W.W.R. I, pp. 177, 198). Our existence has no foundation to support it except the ever-fleeting and vanishing present; and so constant *motion* is essentially its form, without any possibility of that rest for which we are always longing" (P.P. II (242) 309, §144).

In his *Criticism of the Kantian Philosophy* (Appendix to W.W.R. I) Schopenhauer rejects Kant's theory of the "thing-in-itself" as being based on a logically incorrect interpretation of the law of causality, in the meaning specified above, and turns Kant's position as follows: "We can arrive at its being-in-itself only on the entirely different path I have followed, by means of the addition of a self-consciousness, which proclaims the will as the in-itself of our own phenomenon ..." (W.W.R. I, 436). By this reversal, however, the "thing-in-itself" loses all attributes of its "transcendent" and "absolute" nature. Instead of being *sat-cit-ānanda* ("being-consciousness-bliss") of Sankara, it becomes the principle of all ill and suffering which therefore should be repudiated and abandoned "all"-together.

The will as the "thing-in-itself," "the inner being of the world and kernel of all phenomena" (W.W.R. II, 294), is nothing more than "a blind will-to-live" (ibid., 579), "groundless" due to its blindness; a principle of metaphysical ignorance (*avijjā*), and thus reduced from a positive principle of *transcendent being* to a negative principle of *merely transcendental* (this word means: *limited* by the structure of the "mind-element") *knowledge,* whose last biological root is traced as far back in our animal nature as the sexual instinct (cf. 5.13). Far from being the ultimate reason of "freedom" or of *sat-cit-ānanda,* one might claim for it only an apparent and contradictory freedom to self-abolition of the will as *principium individuationis* (Buddhist *anattā*): "An actual appearance of the real freedom of the will as thing-in-itself then becomes possible, by which the phenomenon comes into a certain contradiction with itself, as is expressed by the word *self-renunciation,* in fact *the in-itself of its real nature ultimately abolishes itself.* This is the sole and immediate manifestation proper to the will in itself ..." (W.W.R. I, 301).

3.2 "There is only one inborn error, and that is the notion that we exist in order to be happy. It is inborn in us, because it coincides with our existence itself, and our whole being is only its paraphrase, indeed our body is its monogram. We are nothing more than the will-to-live, and the successive satisfaction of all our willing is what we think of through the concept of happiness. So long as we persist in this inborn error, and indeed even become confirmed in it through *optimistic dogmas,* the world seems to us full of contradictions. For at every step, in great things and in small, we are bound to experience that the world and life are certainly not arranged for the purpose of continuing a happy existence. Now, while the thoughtless person feels himself vexed and annoyed hereby merely in real life, in the case of the person who thinks, there is added to the pain in reality the theoretical perplexity as to why a world and a life that exist so that he may be happy in them, answer their purpose so badly.... In addition to this, every day of our life up to now has taught us that, even when joy and pleasure are attained, they are in themselves deceptive, do not perform what they promise, do not satisfy the heart, and finally that their possession is at least embittered by the vexation and unpleasantnesses that accompany or spring from them. Pains and sorrows, on the other hand, prove very real and often exceed all expectation. Thus everything in life is certainly calculated to bring us back from that original error, and to convince us that the purpose of our existence is not to be happy. Indeed, if life is considered more closely and impartially, it presents itself rather as specially intended to show us that we are *not* to feel happy in it, since by its whole nature it bears the character of something for which we have lost the taste, which must disgust us, and from which we have to come back, as from an error, so that our heart may be cured of the passion for enjoying and indeed for living, and may be turned away from the world. In this sense, it would accordingly be more correct to put the purpose of life in our woe than in our welfare.... Now whoever has returned by one path or the other from that error ... will soon see everything in a different light, and will find that the world is in harmony with his insight, though not with his wishes. Misfortunes of every sort and size will no longer surprise him, although they cause him pain; for he has seen that pain and trouble are the very things that work towards the true end of life, namely, the turning away of the will from it. In all that may happen, this will in fact give him a wonderful coolness and composure, similar to that with which a patient undergoing a long and painful cure bears the pain of it as a sign of its efficacy. Suffering expresses itself clearly enough to the whole of human existence as its true destiny. Life is deeply steeped in suffering, and cannot escape from it; our entrance into it takes place amid tears, at bottom its course is always tragic, and its end is even more so. In this there is an unmistakable touch of deliberation.... In fact, suffering is the process of purification by which alone man is in most cases sanctified, in other words, led back from the path of error of the will-to-live.... The completed course of life, on which the dying person looks back, has an effect on the whole will that objectifies itself in this perishing individuality, and such an effect is analogous to that exercised by a motive on man's conduct. The completed course gives his conduct a new direction that is accordingly the moral and essential result of the life.... Because this retrospect, like the distant foreknowledge of death, is conditioned by the faculty of reason, and is possible in man alone, not in the animal, and therefore he alone drains the cup of death, humanity is the only stage at which the will can deny itself, and completely turn away from life. To the will that does not deny itself, every birth imparts a new and different intellect; until it has recognized the true nature of life, and in consequence, no longer wills it." W.W.R. II, 634–37, Ch. XLIX

3.3 "In the hour of death, the decision is made whether man falls back into the womb of nature, or else no longer belongs to her, but: we lack image, concept, and word for this opposite, just because all these are taken from the objectification of the will, and therefore belong to that objectification; consequently, they cannot in any way express its absolute opposite; accordingly this remains for us a mere negation. However, the death of the individual is in each case the unweariedly repeated question of nature to the will-to-live: 'Have you had enough? Do you wish to escape from me?'" W.W.R. II, 609, Ch. XLVIII

(b) The Awakening

3.4 "What is called the awakening of genius, the hour of inspiration, the moment of rapture or exaltation, is nothing but the intellect's becoming free, when, relieved for a while from its service under the will, it does not sink into inactivity or apathy, but is active for a short time, entirely alone and of its own accord. The intellect is then of the greatest purity, and becomes the clear mirror of the world.... Because all suffering proceeds from willing, while knowing on the other hand is in and by itself painless and serene, this gives to their lofty brows and to their clear, perceptive glance, which are not subject to the service of the will and its needs, the appearance of the great, as it were supernatural, unearthly serenity. ..." W.W.R. II, 380, Ch. XXXI

3.5 "Behind our existence lies something else that becomes accessible to us only by our shaking off the world." W.W.R. I, 405, §70

3.6 "... we freely acknowledge that what remains after the complete abolition of the will is, for all who are still full of the will, assuredly nothing. But also conversely, to those in whom the will has turned and denied itself, this very real world of ours with all its suns and galaxies, is nothing.

This is also the *Prajñāpāramitā* of the Buddhists, the 'beyond all knowledge,' in other words, the point where subject and object no longer exist. ..."[23] W.W.R. I, 412, §71

(c) "The Separation of Knowing from Willing"

3.7 "The comprehension of the world now demands more and more attention, and ultimately to such an extent that at times its relation to the will must be momentarily lost sight of so that it may occur the more purely and correctly. This quite definitely appears first in the case of man; only with him does a pure separation of knowing from willing occur." W.W.R. II, 279, Ch. XXII

3.8 "It follows from all that has been said, that the denial of the will-to-live, which is the same as what is called complete resignation or holiness, always proceeds from that quieter of the will; and this is the knowledge of its inner conflict and its essential vanity, expressing themselves in the suffering of all that lives." W.W.R. I, 397, §68

3.9 "As long as no denial of that will has taken place, that-of-us which is left over by death is the seed and kernel of quite another existence, in which a new individual finds himself again so fresh and original, that he broods over himself in astonishment." W.W.R. II, 50I, Ch. XLI

IV. "The Road to Salvation"[24]

(a) Art

4.1 "And we know that these moments, when, delivered from the fierce pressure of the will, we emerge, as it were, from the heavy atmosphere of the earth, are the most blissful that we experience. From this we can infer how blessed must be the life of a man whose will is silenced not for a few moments, as in the enjoyment

23. Compare Dhp 93: "He whose corruptions are destroyed, who cares naught for food, whose abode is emancipation through voidness and unsubstantiality—his path is hard to trace like that of birds in the air."

24. Title of Chapter XLIX of *The World as Will and Representation*, Volume II.

of the beautiful,[25] but forever, indeed completely extinguished, except for the last glimmering spark that maintains the body and is extinguished with it. Such a man who, after many bitter struggles with his own nature, has at last completely conquered, is then left only as pure knowing being, as the undimmed mirror of the world. Nothing can distress or alarm him any more; nothing can any longer move him; for he has cut all the thousand threads of willing which hold us bound to the world, and which as craving, fear, envy, and anger drag us here and there in constant pain. He now looks back calmly and with a smile on the phantasmagoria of this world which was once able to move and to agonize even his mind, but now stands before him as indifferently as chessmen at the end of a game. ..." W.W.R. I, 390, §68

4:2 "The world can appear in its true colour and form, in its complete and correct significance, only when the intellect, freed from willing, moves freely over objects, and yet is energetically active without being spurred on by the will. This is certainly contrary to the nature and destiny of the intellect; thus it is to a certain extent unnatural, and for this reason exceedingly rare. But it is precisely in this that the true nature of Genius lies; and in this alone does that stage occur in a high degree and for some time, whereas in the rest it appears only approximately and exceptionally.

"'What is all this?' or 'How is it really constituted?' If the first question attains to great distinctness and is continuously present, it will make the philosopher, and in just the same way the other question will make the artist or the poet." W.W.R. II 1, 81–82, Ch. XXXI

---

25. From the Buddhist standpoint it should be obvious that there is no proper structure corresponding to Schopenhauer's aesthetical approach to the problem of pure contemplation. On the other hand it is necessary to emphasize the specific position in Schopenhauer's system of both the aesthetic and ethical functions. Just as both the good and the evil have to be transcended in a "deeper" understanding of the ultimate trans-mundane aim pointed out by the Buddha (see fragment added to the text 4.4), so in the analogous structure of Schopenhauer both art and morality obtain their metaphysical value only indirectly, in so far as they guide the capacity that is intended to reveal the ultimate aim of renunciation and "salvation." From the world, not the capacity of enjoyment in it.

(b) Asceticism

4.3 "We therefore find in the lives of saintly persons that peace and bliss we have described, only as the blossom resulting from the constant overcoming of the will; and we see the constant struggle with the will-to-live as the soil from which it shoots up; for on earth no one can have lasting peace.... Therefore we see also those who have once attained to the denial of the will strive with all their might to keep to this path by self-imposed renunciation of every kind, by a penitent and hard life....

"Now, if we see this practised by persons who have already attained to denial of the will, in order that they may keep to it, then suffering in general, as it is inflicted by faith, is also a 'second way' of attaining to that denial. Indeed, we may assume that most men can reach it only in this way, and that it is the suffering personally felt, not the suffering merely known, which most frequently produces complete resignation, often only at the approach of death. For only in the case of a few is mere knowledge sufficient to bring about the denial of the will, the knowledge, namely, that sees through the *principium individuationis* first producing perfect goodness of disposition and universal love of mankind, and finally enabling them to recognize as their own all the suffering of the world....

"Therefore in most cases the will must be broken by the greatest personal suffering before its self-denial appears. We then see the man suddenly retire into himself, after he is brought to the verge of despair through all the stages of increasing affliction with the most violent resistance. We see him know himself and the world, change his whole nature, rise above himself and above all suffering, as if purified and sanctified by it, in inviolable peace, bliss, and sublimity, willingly renounce everything he formerly desired with the greatest vehemence, and gladly welcome death. It is the gleam of silver that suddenly appears from the purifying flame of suffering, the gleam of the denial of the will-to-live, of salvation. Occasionally we see even those who were very wicked purified to this degree by the deepest grief and sorrow; they have become different, and are completely converted. Therefore, their previous misdeeds no longer trouble their conscience, yet they gladly pay for such misdeeds with death, and willingly see the end of the phenomenon of that will that is now foreign to and abhorred by them." W.W.R. I, 391–93, §68

4.4 "Now if we consider the will-to-live as a whole and objectively, we have to think of it, according to what has been said, as involved in a delusion. To return from this, and hence to deny its whole present endeavour, is what religions describe as self-denial or self-renunciation, ... for the real self is the will-to-live. The *moral virtues*, hence justice and philanthropy, spring from the fact that the will-to-live, seeing through the *principium individuationis,* recognizes itself again in all its phenomena; accordingly they *are primarily a sign, a symptom*, that the appearing will is no longer firmly held in that delusion, but that disillusionment already occurs. Thus it might be said figuratively that the will already flaps its wings, in order to fly away from it. Conversely, injustice, wickedness, cruelty are signs of the opposite, that is, of deep entanglement in that delusion. But in the second place, these moral virtues are a means of advancing self-renunciation, and accordingly of denying the will-to-live." W.W.R. II, 606, Ch. XLVIII

> "It is in respect only of such trifling things, of matters of little value, of mere morality, that a worldly man, when praising the Tathāgata (Buddha), would speak. And what are such trifling minor details of mere morality that he would praise? Putting away the killing of living beings, the samana Gotama holds aloof from the destruction of life ... from taking what is not given ... from unchastity ... from lying words ... from wrong means of livelihood. But there are other things, profound, difficult to realize, hard to understand, tranquilizing, not to be grasped by mere logic, subtle, comprehensible only to the wise. ..." D 1

(c) Eudaemonology, or the art of wise living

The way of art, essential also to philosophy, was considered by Schopenhauer as the contemplative way of the genius. On the other hand, the way of asceticism is peculiar to the equally exceptional character of the saint. The third possibility, to be dealt with in the present section, could be considered as a "middle way." The Greek word *eudaemonology,* chosen to characterize it, denotes the classical ideal, which in the later period of Greek and Roman philosophy came to be ever more identified with the popular idea of the philosophical attitude peculiar to "Stoic Sages." This identification remained in popular use until modern times. Schopenhauer was the most vehement critic of the scientific trend in modern philosophy in so far as it was understood to neglect the primary task of interpreting all the problems of the world with reference to, and for the sake of, the human condition in it, problems that arise from the moral commitment of our existence in the world. In other words, his criticism was a protest against the danger of dehumanized philosophy. In this he was a significant forerunner of the philosophy of existence which prevailed in Europe in the middle of the 20th century.

However, Schopenhauer often returned no less critically, from various approaches, to the "Stoical" attitude in its all-too-narrow meaning within the limits of the ideal of a "happy life" or *eudeamonia*. He considered Stoicism historically as a rather decadent derivation from the more rigorous teaching of the Cynics. In order to exclude the danger of a shallow and, above all, hypocritical understanding of a "middle way" in general, it was of critical and vital importance to him clearly to restrict, in each case, the limits of reasonable moral application of the criterion of a "middle way," the more so, as the idea of the "middle way" is usually in its very origin very original, predetermined by specific *historical* circumstances. In the case of Buddhism such circumstances appear very clearly delimited in the first discourse of the Buddha, the *Dhammacakkappavattana-sutta*. In the classical philosophy of Europe the most misused formulation of the principle of a "middle way" was that in Aristotle's *Ethics*:

4.5 "Aristotle's principle of taking the middle course in all things is ill-suited to the moral principle for which he gave it; but it might easily be the best general rule of prudence and wisdom, the best guidance for a happy life. For everything in life is so hazardous and precarious: on all sides there are so many hardships, inconveniences, burdens, sufferings, and dangers, that we have a safe and happy voyage only by steering between the rocks. Usually the fear of a misfortune already known to us drives us to the opposite affliction; for example, the painful nature of loneliness drives us into society, indeed the first being the best;

the troubles and difficulties of society drive us into solitude; we allow a forbidding demeanour to alternate with rash and indiscrete confidence and familiarity, and so on." F.M. (1814) pp. 81–82, §132

4.6 "One cannot serve two masters; and so it must be either one's reason or holy scripture. 'Juste Milieu' [the happy-mean], means falling between two stools. Either believe or philosophize! Whatever is chosen must be entirely accepted. 'To believe' up to a certain point and no farther, and likewise 'to philosophize' up to a certain point and no farther, these are half-measures that constitute 'the fundamental characteristic of rationalism.'" P.P. II (324) 424, §181

In his main work (W.W.R. I) Schopenhauer is particularly strict in criticizing all forms of *eudaemonism* in its primary meaning of a pleasure-seeking attitude, or a yielding to the thirst for life. The influence of the Christian ideal of asceticism was at that time obviously predominant. It was only in a later period (especially, it seems, in the middle period of his life), in *Parerga and Paralipomena,* that he found a more favourable approach, to the entire problem. At the end of the first volume of P.P. he dedicated a section of 200 pages to its re-examination. It seems that, at that time, his attention was again drawn to this aspect of the ancient East-Mediterranean (Hellenistic) philosophy in connection with a deeper progress in his studies of Indian sources and particularly with a progress from the earlier Vedic, or *Brahmanical* trend, as he calls it, towards Buddhism.

The pedagogical interest, if not predominant, undoubtedly became in this context the most characteristic motive of Schopenhauer's inquiry into the problem of *eudaemonology* and of his "hypothesis" on the possibility of striking a balance between "the measure of our pain and our well-being." It would be an exaggeration to call this part of Schopenhauer's philosophy his "optimism," or even to consider it as inconsistent in any respect. But it certainly contains a few characteristic pointers to the limits of his "pessimism." Essentially, such reasonable limits were always and everywhere clearly indicated by him as pertaining to the highest aim and point of orientation of his entire philosophical undertaking, viz. the elucidation of the idea of liberation, or even of "salvation," from the "thirst" by which all "will-to-live" is "fatally" (or karmically) enslaved.

Only a few specimens of Schopenhauer's *eudaemonology* can be added at the end of this section and in the next chapter.

4.7 "Here I take the idea of wisdom of life ... in the sense of the art of getting through life as pleasantly and successfully as possible, the instructions to which might also be called *eudaemonology*...." P.P. II (229) 347

4.8 "I regard as the first rule of all wisdom of life a sentence incidentally expressed by Aristotle ...: 'The prudent man aims at painlessness not pleasure.' The truth of this rests on the fact that the nature of all pleasure and happiness is negative, whereas that of pain is positive.... However, I will here illustrate it by another fact that can be daily observed. If our whole body is healthy and sound except for some sore or painful spot, we are no longer conscious of the health of the whole, but our attention is constantly directed to the pain of the injured spot, and all the comfort and enjoyment of life vanish. In the same way, when all our affairs turn out in the way we want them to go with the exception of one that runs counter to our intentions, this one affair constantly recurs even when it is of little importance. We often think about it and pay little attention to all the other more important things that are turning out in accordance with our wishes. Now in both cases, what is injuriously affected is the will, in the one case as it objectifies itself in the organism, in the other, as it is objectified in man's efforts and aspirations. In both we see that the satisfaction of the will operates always only negatively and therefore is not directly felt at all; but at most we become conscious of it when we reflect on the matter. On the other hand, what checks and obstructs the will is something positive which therefore makes its presence known. Every pleasure consists merely in the removal of this hindrance, in our liberation therefrom, and is in consequence of short duration.

"... Accordingly, whoever wants to assess the result of his life in terms of *eudaemonology* should draw up the account to show not the pleasures he has enjoyed, but the evils he has escaped. Indeed, *eudaemonology* must begin by informing us that its very name is an euphemism and that, when we say 'to live happily,' we are to understand by this merely 'to live less unhappily,' and hence to live a tolerable life. It is quite certain that life is not really given to us to be enjoyed, but to be overcome, to be got over." P.P. I (386–87) 447–49, Ch. I

4.9 "Therefore at the age of adolescence we are often dissatisfied with our position and environment, whatever they may be, because we attribute to them what belongs to the emptiness and wretchedness of human life everywhere, with which we are now making our first acquaintance, after expecting something quite different. Much would have been gained if through timely advice and instruction young men could have had eradicated from their minds the erroneous notion that the world has a great deal to offer them." P.P. I (451) 530, Ch. VI

4.10 "A quiet and cheerful temperament, resulting from perfect health and a prosperous economy, an understanding that is clear, lively, penetrating, and sees things correctly, a moderate and gentle will and hence a good conscience—these are advantages that no rank or wealth can make good or replace. For what a man is by himself, what accompanies him into solitude, and what no one can give him or take away from him, is obviously more essential to him than everything he possesses, or even what he may be in the eyes of others." P.P. I (303) 353, Ch. I

4.11 "When we look at something we do not possess, the thought readily occurs: 'Ah, if that were mine,' and we are made sensible of our privation. Instead of this, we should say more often: 'Ah, if that were *not* mine.' I mean that we should endeavour sometimes to regard what we possess as it would appear to us after we had lost it. Indeed, we should do this with everything, whatever it may be; property, health, friends, those we love, wife, children, horse and dog. For in most cases, the loss of things first tells us of their value." P.P. I (414–15), 482

4.12 "In so far as the feeling of honour rests on this peculiar characteristic (praise), it may have salutary effects on the good conduct of many as a substitute for their morality; but on the man's own *Happiness* and above all on the peace of mind and independence essential thereto, its effect is more disturbing and detrimental than beneficial. Therefore, from our point of view, it is advisable to set limits to this characteristic and to moderate as much as possible, through careful consideration and correct assessment of the value of good things, that great susceptibility to the opinions of other people, not only where it is flattered, but also where it is injured, for both hang by the same thread. Otherwise, we remain the slaves of what other people appear to think.... Accordingly, a correct comparison of the value of what we are In And By Ourselves with what we are in the eyes *of others* will greatly contribute to our happiness.... In their brilliance, their pomp and splendour, their show and magnificence of every kind, the highest in the land can say: 'Our happiness lies entirely outside ourselves; its place is in the heads of others.'" P.P. I (335–36) 390–91, Ch. IV

4.13 "The folly of our nature, here described, puts forth three offshoots, namely, ambition, vanity and pride." P.P. I (341) 396, Ch. IV

4.14 "And so again in a different sense loneliness is not natural to man, in so far as he did not find himself alone when he came into the world, but had parents, brothers and sisters, and was therefore in a community. Accordingly, love of solitude cannot exist as an original tendency, but arises only in consequence of experience and reflection; and this will occur to the extent that our own mental powers are developed, but at the same time with an increase in our age...." P.P. I (405) 470, Ch. IX

4.15 "Thus from all this it follows that love of solitude does not appear directly and as an original impulse, but develops indirectly, preferably in nobler minds, and only gradually. This development is not achieved without our overcoming the natural social urge...." P.P. I (407) 473, Ch. IX

4.16 "Even if he should have gone too far in avoiding them (the evils of life) and have unnecessarily sacrificed pleasures, nothing has really been lost; for all pleasures are illusory, and to grieve about having missed them would be frivolous and even ridiculous.

"The failure to recognize this truth, a failure encouraged by optimism, is the source of much unhappiness. It seems as if an evil spirit with visions of desires always enticed us away from the painless state, from the greatest genuine happiness. The careless and thoughtless youth imagines that the world exists in order to be enjoyed; that it is the abode of a positive happiness; and that men miss this because they are not clever enough to take possession of it. He is strengthened in this view by novels and poems and also by the hypocrisy which the world always and everywhere practises for the sake of appearance.... This hunt for game that does not exist at all leads, as a rule, to very real and positive unhappiness, which appears as pain, suffering, sickness, loss, care, poverty, disgrace, and a thousand other miseries. The undeceiving comes too late. On the other hand, if, by following the rule we are here considering, the plan of life is directed to the avoidance of suffering and hence to keeping clear of want, illness, and every kind of distress, the aim is a real one. Something may then be achieved which will be the greater, the less the plan is disturbed by striving after the chimera of positive happiness." P.P. I (389) 450, Ch. I

4.17 "Moreover, where looking for pleasure, happiness, and joy, we often find instead instruction, insight, and knowledge, a lasting and real benefit in place of one that is fleeting and illusory." P.P. I (393) 456, Ch. III

4.18 "We are accustomed to call youth the happy time of life and old age the unhappy. This would be true if the passions made us happy. Youth is torn and distracted by them and they afford little pleasure and much pain. Cool old age is left in peace by them and at once assumes a contemplative air; for knowledge becomes free and gains the upper hand. Now since this in itself is painless, we are happier, the more conscious we are that it predominates in our nature.... The curious thing, however, is that only towards the end of our life do we really recognize and understand even ourselves, our real aim and objects, especially in our relations to the world and to others." P.P. I (461) 543, 542

4.19 "But possibly to no form of knowledge is experience so indispensable as to a correct appreciation of the instability and fluctuations of things.... The prudent man is he who is not deceived by the apparent stability of things and in addition sees in advance the direction that the change will first take.... On the other hand, men as a rule regard as permanent the state of things for the time being or the direction of their course. This is because they see the effects, but do not understand the causes; yet it is these that bear the seed of future changes...." P.P. I (442– 43) 519–20, 49

Schopenhauer's Characterology

4.20 "On the other hand, everyone has certain *innate concrete principles* that are in his very blood and marrow, since they are the result of all his thinking, feeling, and willing. Usually he does not know them in the abstract, but only when he looks back on his life does he become aware that he has always observed them and has been drawn by them as by an invisible thread. According as they are, so will they lead him to his good or adverse fortune." P.P. I (442) 519, 48

4.21 "Man's character is *empirical.* Only through experience do we come to know it, not merely in others but also in ourselves. Hence we are often disillusioned alike with regard to ourselves and to others, when we discover that we do not possess this or that quality, for example, justice, unselfishness, courage, in the degree we fondly assumed....

"Only a precise knowledge of a man's own empirical character gives him what is called an *acquired character.* It is possessed by the man who has an exact knowledge of his own qualities, both good and bad, and thus knows for certain what he may and may not count on and expect from himself." *Grundprobleme der Ethik* (48–50) 518–523

Chapter 4
Additional Analogies

"Phenomena are preceded by mind, conducted by mind, made by mind. If, therefore, one speaks or acts with impure mind, suffering will follow, even as the wheel the hoof of the draught-ox.

"Phenomena are preceded by mind, conducted by mind, made by mind. If, therefore, one speaks and acts with pure mind, happiness will follow, even as the never departing shadow." *Dhammapada* 1–2

"Just as one would look upon a bubble, just as one would look upon a mirage—if a person thus looks upon the world, the king of death sees him not." *Dhammapada* 170

5.1 "Our own consciousness ... alone is and remains that which is immediate; everything else, be it what it may, is first mediated and conditioned by consciousness, and therefore dependent on it." W.W.R. II, 4

5.2 "As the will is ... the essence of the world, but life, the visible world, the phenomenon is only the mirror of the will, this world will accompany the will as inseparably as a body is accompanied by its shadow; and if will exists, then life, the world, will exist."[26] W.W.R. I, 275, §54

5.3 "However, we continue our life with great interest and much solicitude as long as possible, just as we blow out a soap bubble as long and as large as possible, although with the perfect certainty that it will burst." W.W.R. I, 311, §57

5.4 "For the work of *māyā* is stated to be precisely this visible world in which we are a magic effect called into being, an unstable and inconstant illusion without substance, comparable to the optical illusion and the dream, a veil enveloping human consciousness, a something of which it is equally false and equally true to say that it is and that it is not." W.W.R. I, 419

26. Compare also text 0.27, Ch. 2. above, containing direct reference to Buddhism, with the same motive.

"Let not a man trace back a past or wonder what the future holds.... Instead, with insight let him see each thing presently arisen." MN 131

"How is the solitary life perfected in detail? It is when that which is past is put away; when that which is future is given up, and when, with regard to present states that we have got, will and passion have been thoroughly mastered. It is thus that the solitary life is perfected in detail." SN 21:10

"But do you, reverend Jains, know that you yourself were in the past, that you were not not?

Not so, your reverence.

But do you, reverend Jains, know that you yourself did this evil deed in the past (life), that you did not not do it?

Not so, your reverence.

But do you, reverend Jains, know that so much ill is worn away, or that so much ill is to be worn away, or that when so much ill is worn away, all ill will become worn away?

Not so, your reverence.

But do you, reverend Jains, know the getting rid of unskilled states of mind, *Here And Now,* the uprising of skilled states?

Not so, your reverence." MN 14

5.5 "The present is the only real form of the phenomenon of the will. Therefore no endless past or future in which he will not exist can frighten him, for he regards these as an empty mirage and the web of *Maya.*" W.W.R. I, 284, §54

5.6 "No man has lived in the past, and none will ever live in the future, the *present* alone is the form of all life, but it is also life's sure possession which can never be torn from it. The present always exists together with its content; both stand firm without wavering, *like the rainbow over the waterfall.* For life is sure and certain to the will, and the present is sure and certain to life...." W.W.R. I, 278, §54

5.7 "The will-to-live manifests itself in an endless present, because this is the form of the life of the *Species,* which therefore does not grow old, but remains always young ... Let us now picture to ourselves that alternation of birth and death in infinitely rapid vibrations, and we have before us the persistent and enduring objectification of the will.... *standing firm like a rainbow on the waterfall. This is temporal immortality.* In consequence of this, in spite of thousands of years of death and decay, there is still nothing lost, no atom of matter, still less anything of the inner being exhibiting itself as nature.... Perhaps an exception would have to be made of the man who should once have said from the bottom of his heart to this game: 'I no longer like it....'" W.W.R. II, 479, Ch. XLI

> "Now the question should not be put as you have put it. Instead of asking where the four great elements (earth, water, fire, and air) cease, leaving no trace behind, you should have asked:
>
> "'Where do earth, water, fire, and air,
> and long and short, and fine and coarse,
> pure and impure, *no footing find*?
> Where is it that both name and form
> die out, leaving no trace behind?'
>
> "On this the answer is: ...
>
> "—When consciousness ceases they all also cease." DN 11
>
> "Whoever sees conditioned genesis sees *Dhamma*, whoever sees *Dhamma* sees conditioned genesis. These are generated by conditions, that is to say, the five groups of grasping. Whatever among these five groups of grasping is desire, sensual pleasure, affection, grasping at, that is the uprising of suffering. Whatever among these five groups of grasping is the control of desire and attachment, the objection of desire and attachment, that is the stopping of suffering." MN 28

5.8 "In general, therefore, the law of causality finds application to all things *in* the world, but not *to* the world itself, for this law is *immanent* to the world, not transcendent; *with the world it is established, and with the world it is abolished.* This depends ultimately on the fact that it belongs to the mere form of our understanding and, together with the objective world, that is thus mere phenomenon, is *conditioned by the understanding.* Therefore the law of causality finds complete application, and admits of no exception, to all things *in* the world, in accordance with their form of course, to the variation of these forms, and hence to their changes. It holds good of the actions of man as it does of the impact of a stone, yet, as we have said, always only in reference to events, to *changes....*" W.W.R. II, 43, Ch. IV

5.9 "If, therefore, we have recognized the inner nature of the world as will, and have seen in all its phenomena only the objectivity of the will; and if we have followed these from the unconscious impulse of obscure natural forces up to the most conscious action of the man, we shall by no means evade the consequence that, *with the free denial, the surrender, of the will, all these phenomena also are now abolished.*" W.W.R. I, 410, §71

> "Indeed, friend, I declare there is no world wherein there is no birth, death, decay or repeated deaths and rebirths, the end whereof it is possible to know, see or reach by walking. But, friend, I do not declare that without reaching the end of the world one can make an end of sorrow. My friend, I do proclaim that in this very fathom-long body, with its feelings and mind, is the world, the world's arising, the world's ceasing and the path leading to the world's ceasing." SN 2:26
>
> "For whosoever, bhikkhus, *samana* and *brāhmaṇa* are thus reconstructers of the past or arrangers of the future; or who are both, whose speculations are concerned with both, who put forward various propositions with regard to the past and to the future, they, all of them, are entrapped in the net of these 62 modes (of speculation); this way and that they plunge about; but they are in it; this way and that they may flounder, but they are included in it, caught in it." *Brahmajāla Sutta,* DN 1.3, 72

5.10 "Kant showed that these laws (... according to which all phenomena are connected to one another, and all of which time and space as well as causality and inference—I, comprehend under the expression *the principle of sufficient reason* ...), and consequently the world itself, are conditioned by the subject's manner of knowing. From this it followed that, however far one might investigate and infer under the guidance of these laws; in the principal matter, i.e., in knowledge of the inner nature of the world in itself and outside the representation, no step forward was made, but one moved merely like a hamster in his wheel. We therefore compare all the dogmatists to people who imagine that, if only they go straight forward long enough, they will come to the end of the world; but Kant had then circumnavigated the globe, and has shown that, because it is round, we cannot get out of it by horizontal movement, but that by perpendicular movement it is perhaps not impossible to do so. It can also be said that Kant's teaching gives the insight that *the beginning and the end of the world are to be sought not without us, but rather within.*" W.W.R. I, 420–21

> "Deeds are one's own, brahmin youth, beings are heirs to deeds, deeds are matrix, deeds are kin, deeds are arbiters. Deed divides beings, that is to say by lowness and excellence." MN 135
>
> "By oneself, indeed, is evil done; by oneself is one defiled. By oneself is evil left undone; by oneself, indeed, is one purified: Purity and impurity depend on oneself. No one purifies another." Dhp 165
>
> "In deep insight behold how painful is instability, how void, bereft of own self, and how crime implies the punishment. Break down the mental drive of will." *Theragāthā* 1117

5.11 "But in the light of our whole view, the will is not only free, but even almighty; from it comes not only its action, but also its world; and as the will is, so does its action appear, so does its world appear; both are its self-knowledge and nothing more. The will determines itself, and therewith its action and its world also; for besides it there is nothing, and these are the will itself." W.W.R. I, 272, §53

5.12 "Only this world itself—no other—can bear the responsibility for its existence and its nature; for how could anyone else have assumed this responsibility? If we want to know what human beings, morally considered, are worth as a whole and in general, let us consider their fate as a whole and in general. This fate is want, wretchedness, misery, lamentation, and death. Eternal justice prevails. If they were not as a whole contemptible, their fate as a whole would not be so melancholy. In this sense we can say that the world itself is the tribunal of the world. If we could lay all the misery of the world in one pan of the scales, and all its guilt in the other, the pointer would certainly show them to be in equilibrium." W.W.R. I, 352, §63

"Bhikkhus, I know no other single form by which a man's heart is so enslaved as it is by that of a woman. A woman's form obsesses a man's heart. Bhikkhus, I know no other single sound by which a man's heart is so enslaved as it is by the voice of a woman. A woman's voice obsesses a man's heart. I know of no other single scent ... savour ... touch by which a man's heart is so enslaved as it is by the scent, savour and touch of a woman. The scent, savour and touch of a woman obsess a man's heart. Bhikkhus, I know of no other single form, sound, scent, savour and touch by which a woman's heart is so enslaved as it is by the form, sound, scent, savour and touch of a man. A woman's heart is obsessed by these things." AN 1:1

"Neither through matted hair, nor through clan, nor through birth is one a brahman. In whom there exist both truth and righteousness, pure is he, a brahman is he. He whose knowledge is deep, who is wise, skilled in the choice of the right and the wrong way, has reached the highest goal—him I call a brahman." Dhp 393, 403

5.13 "If in our conception of the world we start from the thing-in-itself, the will-to-live, we find as its kernel and greatest concentration the act of generation. This presents itself as the first thing, the point of departure.... Sexual desire, especially when through fixation on a definite woman, it is concentrated to amorous infatuation, is the quintessence of the whole fraud of this noble world; for it promises so unspeakably, infinitely, and excessively much, and then performs so contemptibly little." P.P. II (263) 343, 166

5.14 "Then, whereas nature has established the widest difference, both morally and intellectually, between one man and another, society, regardless of all this, treats all alike, or rather sets up instead artificial differences and degrees of position and rank, which are often the very opposite of nature's list of precedence. With this arrangement, those whom nature has placed low are in a very good position, but the few who are rated high by her come off badly. The latter, therefore, usually withdraw from society ... for intellectual superiority offends by its mere existence without any desire to do so." P.P. I (401) 464, 9

"Love comes from companionship:
in wake of love upsurges ill.
Seeing the bane that comes from love,
fare lonely as rhinoceros.

In ruth for all his bosom-friends,
a man, heart-chained, neglects the goal.
Seeing this fear in fellowship,
fare lonely as rhinoceros.

The heat and cold, and hunger, thirst,
wind, sun-beat, sting of gadfly, snake:
surmounting one and all of these,
fare lonely as rhinoceros.

Leaving the vanities of view,
right method won, the way obtained:
I know! No other is my guide.
Fare lonely as rhinoceros.

Folk serve and follow with an aim:
Friends who seek naught are scarce today:
men, wise in selfish aim, are foul.
Fare lonely as rhinoceros."

(Sn 36, 37, 52, 55, 75)

5.15 "In accordance with all this, it will be genuine wisdom of life in the man who in himself is worth anything if, in case of need, he limits his requirements in order to preserve or extend his freedom and, in consequence, he has as few dealings as possible with his fellowmen, for relations with them are unavoidable." P.P. I (402) 466, Ch. 9

5.16 "For we cannot with any certainty count on anyone but ourselves; moreover, the difficulties and disadvantages, the dangers and annoyances, that society entails are countless and inevitable." P.P. I (400) 463, 9

5.17 "What a man is and has in himself, that is to say personality and its worth, is the sole immediate factor in his happiness and well-being. Everything else is mediate and indirect." P.P. I (308) 357, Ch. 11

5.18 "I advise a man to learn to be alone to some extent even in company. Accordingly, he should not at once communicate to others what he is thinking; on the other hand, he should not take too literally what they say. On the contrary, he should not expect much from them, either morally or intellectually, and therefore, as regards their opinions, should strengthen in himself that indifference that is the surest way of always practising a praiseworthy tolerance." P.P.I (409) 475, 9

About the Author

Bhikkhu Nanājīvako (Cedomil Veljacic) was born in Yugoslavia in 1915 and has been a Buddhist monk residing in Sri Lanka since 1966. He received his Ph.D. degree in Indian and Greek philosophy and served as a Lecturer in Asian philosophy at the University of Zagreb in Yugoslavia. He is the author of many books on Buddhist and Indian thought in his native tongue. His writings have been published in journals and books in India, Sri Lanka and in many Western countries. His other BPS publications are "Aniccaṃ—The Buddhist Theory of Impermanence" in *Three Basic Facts of Existence, Impermanence I. Collected Essays* (Wheel No. 186/187) and "Karma—The Ripening Fruit" in *Karma and Its Fruit. Collected Essays* (Wheel No. 223/224).

The Wheel of Birth and Death

by

Bhikkhu Khantipālo

WHEEL PUBLICATION NO. 147/148/149

Plate 1

Plate 2

This indeed has been said by the Exalted One:

Two knowable dhammas should be thoroughly known—
mind and body;
Two knowable dhammas should be relinquished—
unknowing and craving for existence;
Two knowable dhammas should be realised—wisdom and
freedom;
Two knowable dhammas should be developed—calm and
insight.

Eight are the bases of unknowing:
Non-comprehension in dukkha,
Non-comprehension in dukkha's arising,
Non-comprehension in dukkha's cessation,
Non-comprehension in the practise-path leading to dukkha's
cessation,
Non-comprehension in the past,
Non-comprehension in the future,
Non-comprehension in past and future,
Non-comprehension in Dependent Arising.

Eight are the bases of knowledge:
Comprehension in dukkha,
Comprehension in dukkha's arising,
Comprehension in dukkha's cessation,
Comprehension in the practise-path leading to dukkha's
cessation,
Comprehension in the past,
Comprehension in the future,
Comprehension in past and future,
Comprehension in Dependent Arising.

Peace it is and Excellence it is, that is to say—the stilling of all conditions, the rejection of all substrates (for rebirth), the destruction of craving, passionlessness, cessation, Nibbāna.

O bhikkhus, there is that sphere where is neither earth nor water nor fire nor air; nor the sphere of infinite space, nor the sphere of infinite consciousness, nor the sphere of nothingness, nor the sphere of neither-perception-nor-non-perception; not this world, nor another world, neither the moon nor the sun.

That I say, O bhikkhus, is indeed neither coming nor going nor staying, not passing-away and not arising. Unsupported, unmoving, devoid of object—that indeed is the end of dukkha.

And this dhamma is profound, hard to see, hard to awaken to, peaceful, excellent, beyond logic, subtle and to be experienced by the wise.

— Translated from the *Royal Chanting Book* (Suan Mon Chabub Luang), compiled by H.H., the 9th Sangharāja of Siam, Sā Phussadevo, and printed at Mahamakut Press, Bangkok).

Introduction

Upon the Full Moon of the month of Visākha, now more than two thousand five hundred years ago, the religious wanderer known as Gotama, formerly Prince Siddhattha and heir to the throne of the Sakyan peoples, by his full insight into the Truth called Dhamma which is this mind and body, became the One Perfectly Enlightened by himself.

His Enlightenment or Awakening, called Sambodhi, abolished in himself unknowing and craving, destroyed greed, aversion and delusion in his heart, so that "vision arose, super-knowledge arose, wisdom arose, discovery arose, light arose—a total penetration into the mind and body, its origin, its cessation and the way to its cessation which was at the same time complete understanding of the "world," its origin, its cessation, and the way to its cessation. He penetrated to the Truth underlying all existence. In meditative concentration throughout one night, but after years of striving, from being a seeker, he became "the One-Who-Knows, the One-Who-Sees."

When he came to explain his great discovery to others, he did so in various ways suited to the understanding of those who listened and suited to help relieve the problems with which they were burdened.

He knew with his great wisdom exactly what these were even if his listeners were not aware of them, and out of his great compassion taught Dhamma for those who wished to lay down their burdens. The burdens which men, indeed all beings, carry round with them are no different now from the Buddha-time. For then as now men were burdened with unknowing and craving. They did not know of the Four Noble Truths nor of Dependent Arising and they craved for fire and poison and were, then as now, consumed by fears. Lord Buddha, One-Attained-to-the-Secure, has said:

> "Profound, Ānanda, is this Dependent Arising, and it appears profound. It is through not understanding, not penetrating this law that the world resembles a tangled skein of thread, a woven nest of birds, a thicket of bamboos and reeds, that man does not escape from (birth in) the lower realms of

existence, from the states of woe and perdition, and suffers from the round of rebirth."

The not-understanding of Dependent Arising is the root of all sorrows experienced by all beings. It is also the most important of the formulations of Lord Buddha's Enlightenment. For a Buddhist it is therefore most necessary to see into the heart of this for oneself. This is done not by reading about it nor by becoming expert in scriptures, nor by speculations upon one's own and others' concepts, but by seeing Dependent Arising in one's own life and by coming to grips with it through calm and insight in one's "own" mind and body.

"He who sees Dependent Arising, he sees Dhamma."

Let us now see how this Teaching is concerned with our own lives. The search of every living being is to find happiness, in whatever state, human or non-human, they find themselves. But what it is really important to know are the factors which give rise to unhappiness, so that they can be avoided; and the factors from which arise happiness, so that they can be cultivated. This is just another way of stating the Four Noble Truths. In the first half of this statement there is "unhappiness" or what is never satisfactory, called in the Pāli language *dukkha.* This dukkha is the First Noble Truth, which we experience all the time, usually without noticing it, which does not make the dukkha any less! First, there is *occasional dukkha:* birth, old age, disease and death, for these events usually do not compose the whole of life. Then we have *frequent dukkha:* being united with what one dislikes, being separated from what one likes, not getting what one wants, and this is everyday experience. Finally, as a summary of all kinds of dukkha there is *continuous dukkha*: the five grasped-at groups, that is to say body, feeling, perceptions, volitions (and other mental activity) and consciousness, the components of a human being. Explanation of these in full would take too long here, but all the readers are provided with these kinds of dukkha in themselves. They should look to see whether these facts of experience are delightful or not. This Dhamma "should be thoroughly known" in one's own person and life, that is where the First Noble Truth may be discovered.

Then the factors which give rise to unhappiness were mentioned. Here again one's person and life should be investigated.

Now when living creatures are killed intentionally by me, when I take what is not given, when I indulge in wrong conduct in sexual relations, when I speak false words and when I take intoxicating drinks and drugs producing carelessness—now are these things factors for happiness or unhappiness? When I covet the belongings of others, when I allow ill will to dwell in my heart, and when I have as the tenants of my heart ignorance, delusion and views which lead astray—is this for my welfare or destruction? There are many ways of describing these factors which make for unhappiness, but all of them derive from unknowing and craving, which are just two sides of the same thing. This is the Second Noble Truth of the Arising of Dukkha. When craving is at work, when unknowing clouds one's understanding, then one is sure to experience dukkha. Lord Buddha instructs us for our own benefit, and for the happiness of others, that this craving "should be relinquished."

Now, the "happiness" in the second half of the statement above can be of many kinds. Two kinds dependent upon conditions can be seen illustrated by the world, while one kind, unsupported by conditions "should be realised" in one's own heart. We are all looking for happiness so let us see what is needed for it. First, there is materially produced happiness. This is born of possessions and jugglery with conditions of life "out there." Called *āmisa-sukha* in Pāli, this happiness is most uncertain; for all the factors supporting it are subject to instability and change. Moreover, they are out in the world and not in one's own heart, so that they call for expert jugglery to save one from dukkha. And failure and disappointment cannot be avoided if one goes after this sort of happiness, so this sort of happiness is short-lived and precarious. A great improvement on this is the happiness which comes from practising Dhamma, called non-material happiness or *nirāmisa-sukha.* This kind of happiness is made sure whenever a person performs wholesome kamma, such as doing the following ten things: giving, moral conduct, mind-development, reverence, helpfulness, dedicating meritorious acts to others, rejoicing in the meritorious acts of others, hearkening to Dhamma, teaching Dhamma and setting upright one's views. People who practise this Dhamma, purifying their hearts in this way, are sure to reap happiness. But this happiness, though more lasting than the first, is not to be relied upon forever. As a fruit of it one may dwell among the gods for aeons, or be born as a very fortunate man, but even the gods have to pass away, let alone man. And the fruits of kamma, good or evil, are impermanent, so it cannot be relied upon to produce a permanent happiness.

Permanent happiness can only be found by removing entirely the cause for dukkha. When craving is uprooted, no growth of dukkha can take place. With purity, compassion and wisdom one can reach the supreme happiness of Nibbāna, which is stable, indestructible and never subject to changing conditions.

This is the Third Noble Truth of the Cessation of Dukkha by the removal of its cause. A good deal of hard work is needed to get to this "which should be realised," and that work must be done along the right lines, hence the Fourth Noble Truth—the Truth of the Path "which should be cultivated." It comprises elements of wisdom—Right View and Right Attitude; elements of moral conduct—Right Speech, Right Action and Right Livelihood; and elements of meditation—Right Effort, Right Mindfulness and Right Collectedness. These will not be explained in detail here.[1] It is certain that any one who practises Moral Conduct, Collectedness and Wisdom in his life has the conditions which sustain happiness. From his practise he may have Dhamma-happiness or the Supreme Happiness, according to the degree he practises, for the latter requires well-developed meditation both in calm and in insight.

These Four Noble Truths—Dukkha, Cause, Cessation and Path—are the heart of the Dhamma and they are in the heart of every man who cares to see them. From their seeing and understanding come happiness, but by trying to escape them only more misery is born.

These Truths are illustrated by the formula of Dependent Arising, which is found elaborated in various ways. The simplest form is:

> "Craving being, dukkha is; by the arising of craving, dukkha arises; craving not being, dukkha is not; by the cessation of craving, dukkha ceases."

1. See Wheel No. 34/35: "The Four Noble Truths."

But Dependent Arising can be given in much more detailed ways than this. The important principle to understand is that whatever is experienced by us, all that arises is due to many conditions. An aspect which will be easy to understand concerns this body which grows in size from birth through youth, which develops certain characteristics in maturity, and as old age creeps on becomes infirm in various ways, and finally dies. The processes which govern this growth and decline are of great complexity and interdependence. The body, to keep going at all, needs clothes, food, shelter and medicines at least. But once the internal chemistry (also dependently originated) starts the process leading to old age and death, none of the exterior supporting conditions can do more than retard the process for a little while. The body, as a whole, does not arise from "no-cause" (the physical particles and kamma being its immediate causes); nor is it derived from *one* cause. If examined, nothing which we experience arises from only one, or no cause at all; on the contrary our experiences all arise dependently. Sight is actually dependent on the eye as base, the object to be seen, and the operation of eye-consciousness. (There are other factors that also contribute: light, air, ...) Similarly, there is ear, sound, ear-consciousness; nose, smell, nose-consciousness; tongue, taste, tongue-consciousness; body, touch, body-consciousness; and mind, thoughts, mind-consciousness. All of our experience falls within these eighteen elements and there is nothing which we know outside them.

It is also important to understand that much of what one experiences arising dependently is the fruit of one's own actions. The happiness one feels and the dukkha one feels, although sometimes brought about by events in the physical world (landslides, earthquakes, a sunny or a rainy day), are very often brought about by one's own past intentional actions or kamma. And in the present time with each deliberate action, one performs more kammas which will come to fruit as experience in the future. So, if one wants to experience the fruits of happiness, the seeds of happiness must be planted now. They may mature immediately, in this life, or in a future existence. We make ourselves, we are the creators of ourselves, no one else has a hand in this creation. And the Lord of Creation is no other than Ignorance or Unknowing. He is the Creator of this Wheel of Saṃsāra, of continued and infinitely varied forms of dukkha. And this Lord resides in the hearts of all men who are called "ordinary-men." We shall return to this in more detail later.

The History of the Wheel

Dependent Arising is explained many times and in many different connections in the Discourses of Lord Buddha, but he has not compared it to a wheel. This simile is found in the *Visuddhimagga* ("The Path of Purification") and in the other commentarial literature. Although Theravāda tradition has many references to this simile, it does not seem to have been depicted at all. But in Northern India and especially in Kashmir, the Sarvāstivāda school[2] was strongly established and besides producing a vast literature upon Discipline and the Further Dhamma (Vinaya and Abhidhamma), they produced also a way of depicting a great many important Buddhist teachings by this picture of the Wheel, which is the subject of the present essay.

In Pāli it is the *bhava-cakka* or *saṃsāra-cakka*, which is variously rendered in English as the Wheel of Life, the Wheel of Becoming or the Wheel of Rebirth.

In their collections of stories about Lord Buddha and his disciples (known as *Avadāna*), there is one which opens with the story of this wheel. Readers will observe that the story refers to Lord Buddha's lifetime and says that he has authorised the painting of this picture, as well as laying down its contents. It is certain that in the Buddha-time painting was well known (it is mentioned several times in the Discourses and the Discipline) while the other facts given in this short introductory story are quite in accord with the spirit of the Pāli Discourses. Even the collection of stories in which this account is contained was, according to some scholars, compiled before the Christian era. So if one does not believe that this painting was ordained by Lord Buddha, still it has an age of two thousand years, a venerable tradition indeed. Of all "teaching-aids" this expression of Buddhist skilful-means (*upaya-kosalla*), must surely be the oldest. Now let us turn to the story.

---

2. One of the eighteen branches of extinct Hinayana.

The Translation

"Lord Buddha was staying at Rājagaha,[3] in the Bamboo Grove, at the Squirrels' Feeding-place. Now, it was the practice of Venerable Mahāmoggallāna to frequent the hells for a certain time, then the animal-kingdom, and also to visit the ghosts, the gods and men. Having seen all the sufferings to be found in the hells, which beings there experience as they arise and pass away, such as maiming, dismembering and so forth; having witnessed how animals kill and devour others; how ghosts are tormented by hunger and thirst; how the gods lose (their heavenly state), fall (from it), are spoiled and come to their ruin; and how men crave and come to naught but thwarted desires—having seen all this he returned to Jambudīpa (India) and reported this to the four assemblies. Whatever (venerable one) had a fellow-bhikkhu or a bhikkhu-pupil leading the holy life with dissatisfaction, he would take him to Venerable Mahāmoggallāna (thinking): 'The Venerable Mahāmoggallāna will exhort and teach him well.' And (truly) the Venerable Mahāmoggallāna would exhort and teach him well. Such (dissatisfied bhikkhus) would again lead the holy life with keen interest, even distinguishing themselves with the higher attainments since they had been taught and exhorted so well by the Venerable Mahāmoggallāna.

"At that time (when the Lord stayed at Rājagaha), the Venerable Mahāmoggallāna was surrounded by the four assemblies consisting of bhikkhus, bhikkhunīs, pious laymen and women.

"Now the illustrious Enlightened Ones who Know (also) ask questions. Thus Lord Buddha asked the Venerable Ānanda (why the second of his foremost disciples was surrounded by the four assemblies). Venerable Ānanda then related Venerable Mahāmoggallāna's experiences and said that he instructed discontented bhikkhus with success.

"(The Lord replied:) 'The Elder Moggallāna or a bhikkhu like him cannot be at many places (at the same time for teaching people). Therefore, in the (monastery) gateways a wheel having five sections should be made.'

3. The familiar Pāli forms of names are used throughout.

"Thus the Lord laid down that a wheel with five sections should be made (whereupon it was remarked:) 'But the bhikkhus do not know what sort of wheel should be made.'

"The Lord explained: 'The five bourns should be represented—the hellish bourn, that of the animal kingdom, of ghosts, of men and the bourn of the gods. In the lower portion (of the wheel), the hells are to be shown, together with the animal-kingdom and the realm of the ghosts, while in the upper portion gods and men should be represented. The four continents should also be depicted, namely, Pubbavideha, Aparagoyana, Uttarakuru and Jambudīpa.[4] In the middle, greed, aversion and delusion must be shown, a dove symbolising greed,[5] a snake representing aversion and a hog, delusion. Furthermore, the Buddhas are to be painted (surrounded by their) haloes pointing out (the way to) Nibbāna. Ordinary beings should be shown as by the contrivance of a water-wheel they sink (to lower states) and rise up again. The space around the rim should be filled with (scenes teaching) the twelve links of Dependent Arising in the forward and reversed order. (The picture of the Wheel) must show clearly that everything, all the time, is swallowed by impermanence and the following two verses should be added as an inscription:

> Make a start, leave behind (the wandering-on)
> firmly concentrate upon the Buddha's Teaching.
> As He, Leader like an elephant, did Nālāgiri rout,
> so should you rout and defeat the hosts of Death.
> Whoever in this Dhamma-Vinaya will go his way
> ever vigilant and always striving hard,
> Can make an end of dukkha here
> and leave behind Saṃsāra's wheel of birth and death.

(= S I 156)

"Thus, at the instance of the bhikkhus, it was laid down by the Lord that the Wheel of Wandering-on in birth and death with five sections should be made in the gateways (of monasteries).

4. These have not been shown in the accompanying drawing and neither does modern Tibetan tradition represent them. They are, respectively, the eastern, western, northern and southern continents of the old Indian geography.

5. In modern representations a cock is always shown.

"Now brahmins and householders would come and ask: 'Revered Sir, what is this painting about?'

"Bhikkhus would reply: 'We also do not know!'

"Thereupon the Lord advised: 'A bhikkhu should be appointed (to receive) visitors in the gateway and to show them (the mural).'

"Bhikkhus were appointed without due consideration (to be guest-receiver), foolish, erring, confused persons without merit. (At this, it was objected:) 'They themselves do not know, so how will they explain (the Wheel-picture) to visiting brahmins and householders?'

"The Lord said: 'A competent bhikkhu should be appointed.'"[6]

The Later History of the Tradition

Tibetan legend says that Lord Buddha outlined the wheel with grains of rice while walking with bhikkhus in a rice field. However this may be, in India, at least in all the Sarvāstivāda monasteries, this painting will have adorned the interior of the gateway, arousing deep emotions in the hearts of those who knew its meaning, and curiosity in others. It is a measure of how great was the destruction of the Buddhist religion in India that not a single example survives anywhere, since no gateways to temples are known to have survived. A solitary painting in Ajanta cave number seventeen may perhaps be some form of this wheel.

In the translation above, the pictures for representing the twelve links of Dependent Arising were not given and it is said that these were supplied from the scriptures by Nāgārjuna, a great Buddhist teacher (some of whose verses are quoted below). From India the pattern of this wheel was taken to Samye, the first Tibetan monastery, by Bande Yeshe and there it was the Sarvāstivāda lineage of ordination which was established. The tradition of painting this wheel thus passed to Tibet, where, due to climatic conditions, it was painted in the vestibule of the temple, there to strike the eyes of all who entered.

Tibetan tradition speaks of two kinds of Wheel: the old-style and the new-style. The old-style is based upon the text translated

6. Translation by Ven. Pāsādiko from the opening paragraphs of the *Sahasodgata Avadāna*, *Divyāvadāna* 21, Mithila Edition, page 185 ff.

above, while the new-style introduces two new features. The great reformer, Je Tsongkhapa (b. 1357 CE), founder of the Gelugpa (the Virtuous Ones, the school of which H.H. the Dalai Lama is the head), gave authority for the division of the Wheel into six instead of five, and for drawing the Bodhisattva Avalokiteśvara in the guise of a Buddha in each of the five non-human realms. Both these features may be seen upon the drawing of the Tibetan-style Wheel. The sixth realm is that of the titans (*asura*) who war against the gods of the sensual-sphere heavens. These troublesome and demonic characters are included in a separate part of the world of the gods in my drawing. The introduction of a Buddha-figure into each realm illustrates the universal quality of a Buddha's great compassion, for Avalokiteśvara is the embodiment of enlightened compassion. The writer has preferred to retain the old-style representation according to the text as it agrees perfectly with Theravāda teachings.

The terrors and violence of saṃsāra, which are with us all the time, may be seen plainly in the ravishment of Tibet by the Chinese invaders. Tibetan artists have kept this tradition alive to the present day and still paint under difficulties as refugees in India. But this ancient way of presenting Dhamma deserves to be more widely known and appreciated. Buddhist shrines could well be equipped with representations of it in the present day, to remind devotees of the nature of this whirling wheel of birth and death.

The Symbolism and Its Practical Meaning

We now turn to the pictures of the Bhavacakka accompanying this book. One is from a Tibetan original after Waddell. The second is a modern version executed by the author, in which the scenes and figures have been given a contemporary colouring.

The Hub

The hub of this painting is the central point for us who live in the realm of saṃsāra, so it is the best point to start a description of the symbolism. In this centre circle, a cock, a snake and a hog wheel around, each having in its mouth the tail of the animal in front. These three, representing Greed, Aversion and Delusion which are the three roots of all evil, are depicted in the centre because they are the root causes for experience in the wandering-on. When they are present in our hearts then we live afflicted in the transitory world of birth and death but when they are not there, having been destroyed by wisdom or *paññā*, developed in Dhamma-practice, then we find rest, the unshakable peace of Nibbāna. It is notable that Tibetan paintings show these creatures against a blue ground, showing that even these afflictions of mind, although powerful, have no real substance and are void, as are all the other elements of our experience.

The cock of fiery yellow-red represents greed (*lobha*). This greed includes every desire for all kinds of "I wish, I want, I must have, I will have" and extends from the violent passion for gross physical form, through attachments to views and ideas, all the way to the subtle clinging to spiritual pleasures experienced by meditators. The colour of the cock, a fiery red, is symbolic of the fact that the passions burn those who indulge in them. Passions and desires are hot and restless, just like tongues of flame, and never allow the heart to experience the cool peace of non-attachment. The cock is chosen as a symbol of greed because as an animal it is observed to be full of lust and vanity.

In the cock's beak there is the tail of a green snake indicating that people who are not able to "satisfy" their ocean-like greeds and lusts tend to become angry. Aversion (*dosa*) of any form springs up when we do not get what we want, or when we get what we do not want. This also can be very subtle, from aversion to mental states ranging through hostile thoughts against other beings, to expressions of inward resentment finding their way out in untruthful, malicious or angry words, or as physical violence. The greenness of the snake indicates the coldness, the lack of sympathy with others, while the snake itself is an animal killing other beings by poison or strangulation, which is exactly what aversion does to those who let it grow in their hearts. Our lives can be corrupted by this venomous beast unless we take very good care to remove it.

At the bottom of the picture there is a heavy hog, the tail of which is chewed by aversion's snake, while in turn it chomps upon the tail feathers of greed's cock. This heavy hog is black in colour and represents delusion (*moha*). This black hog, like its brethren everywhere, likes to sleep for long, to root for food in filth and generally to take no care at all over cleanliness. It is a good symbol for delusion, which prevents one from understanding what is advantageous and what is deleterious to oneself. Its heaviness is that sluggishness of mind and body which it induces in people, called variously stupidity, dullness, boredom; but worry and distraction with sceptical doubt also arise from this delusion-root. One who is overwhelmed by delusion does not know why he should restrain himself from evil, for he can see neither his own benefit with wisdom, nor the benefit of others by compassion—all is blanketed by delusion. He does not know, or does not believe, that kamma (intentional action) has results according to kind. Or he has wrong views which lead him astray from the highway of Dhamma. When people do not get what they want either using greed or aversion, then they turn dull and the pain of their desire is dulled by delusion. From this black hog are born the fiery cock and the cold green snake.

These three beasts, none more dangerous anywhere else, are shown each biting the tail of the other, meaning that really they are inseparable, so that one cannot have, say, greed, without the other monsters lurking in its train. Even characters who are rooted predominantly in one of these three have the other two present, while most people called "normal" have a sort of unhealthy balance of these three in their hearts, ever ready to influence their actions when a suitable situation occurs. These three beasts revolve endlessly in the heart of the ordinary man (*puthujjana*) and ensure that he experiences plenty of dukkha. One should know for oneself whether these beasts control one's own heart, or not.

The First Ring

Out from the innermost circle, the first ring is divided into two (not shown at all upon the Tibetan version illustrated here), one half with a white background and the other having a black background. In the former, four people are seen ascending: the bhikkhu holding a Dhamma-light goes on in front, being followed by a white-robed nun (*upāsikā*), after which come a man and a woman in present-day dress. The four of them represent the Buddhist Community made up of monks, nuns, laymen and laywomen. They are representative of anyone practising the path of good conduct in mind, speech and body. They represent as well two classes of persons: "going from dark to light" and "going from light to light." In the first case, they are born in poor circumstances and have few opportunities due to past evil kamma but in spite of this, they make every effort to practise Dhamma for their own good and others' happiness. Thus they go towards the light, for the fruit of their present kamma will be pleasant and enjoyable. The latter class, "going from light to light," are those people who have attained many benefits with plentiful opportunities in their present life, due to having done much good kamma in the past. In the present they continue with their upward course devoting themselves to further practise of Dhamma in their lives.

What is this Dhamma-practise? There are two lists both of ten factors which could be explained here but the space required would be too great for more than a summary. The first list is called the Ten Skilled Kamma-paths,[7] three of which pertain to bodily action, four to speech and three to mental action. "Paths" here means "ways of action" and "skilful" means "neither for the deterioration of one's own mind nor for the harm of others." The bodily actions which one refrains from are: destroying living creatures, taking what is not given and wrong conduct in sexual desires. In speech, the four actions which should be avoided are: false speech, slanderous speech, harsh speech and foolish chatter. The three actions of mind which should be avoided are: covetousness, ill will, and wrong views. Anyone who restrains himself from these ten, practises a skilful path, a white path which accords with the first steps of training in Dhamma.

The other ten factors are called the Ten Ways of making *Puñña*[8] (meaning actions purifying the heart). They have a different range from the first list of ten, being divided into three basic ways and seven secondary ones. The basic factors are giving (*dāna*), moral conduct (*sīla*), and mind development (*bhāvanā*), while the remaining seven are counted as aspects of these three: reverence, helpfulness, dedicating one's *puñña* to others, rejoicing in other's *puñña*, listening to Dhamma, teaching Dhamma and

7. *Dasa-kusala-kamma-patha.*

8. *Dasa-puñña-kiriya-vatthu.*

straightening out one's views. These actions lead to uprightness, skilful conduct and to the growth in Dhamma of oneself, as well as the benefit of others.

Those who tread upon this white path going towards the light are able to be born in two bourns: either as men or as "shining-ones"—the gods in the three sorts of heavens, of sensuality, subtle form and formlessness. A life of good practice is thus usually followed by a life in one of these two bourns, called *sugati* or the good bourns. But Lord Buddha does not declare that everyone who has led such a life is necessarily born there. This depends not only upon the intensity of their Dhamma-practise but also upon the vision which arises at the time of death. Through negligence at the last moment, one can slip into the three evil bourns difficult to get out of. The round of saṃsāra is very dangerous, even for those who lead almost blameless lives. More of this below. To be born in the two good bourns is the fruiting of *puñña* or skilful kamma and the more purified one's heart, the higher and more pleasant will be one's environment.

In the dark half of the ring, naked beings are tumbling downwards in disorder. Their nakedness symbolises lack of shame in doing evil and their disorder shows the characteristic of evil to cause disintegration and confusion. "Downwards" means that they are falling, by the commission of sub-human actions, to sub-human states of existence. In some Tibetan versions they are chained together and pulled downwards by a female demon who squats at the bottom. This demoness is craving or *taṇhā* (a noun of female gender). This craving is, of course, not outside those who follow the path of evil but in their own hearts. On this path there are two sorts of persons, those "going from light to dark" and those "going from dark to dark." The former have good opportunities in this life but do not make use of them, or else use them for evil ends and thus waste the fruits of their previous good kamma without laying up any further store. Instead, they prefer from delusion to store up evil now for fear and distress in future. Those who go from dark to dark do not have even the advantages of the former group, for they are born in conditions of deprivation due to past evil kamma and then, driven on by the fruits of suffering received by them, they commit more evil.

The ten unskilful kamma-paths are the ways along which they walk: destroying living creatures, taking what is not given, wrong conduct in sexual desires; false speech, slanderous speech, harsh speech, foolish chatter; covetousness, ill will and wrong views. They do not delight in making *puñña* but are by nature mean, immoral, undeveloped in mind, proud, selfish, grasp at possessions, envious, never listen to Dhamma and certainly never teach it, while their hearts are ridden with confused and contradictory views and ideas.

For their pains, having pursued evil, these beings upon their death, already having destroyed "humanness" in themselves, fall down to the three lower states, which are called the Evil Bourns (*duggati*). These are, in order of deterioration and increase of suffering: the hungry ghosts, the animals and the hell-wraiths. Truly a case of "do good, good fruit; do bad, bad fruit"—as the Thai proverb says.

These two half-circles are also an illustration of the refrain which closes every one of the *Avadāna* stories: "Thus bhikkhus, completely black kamma bears completely evil effects; completely white kamma bears completely good effects; and composite kamma bears composite effects. Therefore, bhikkhus, abstain from doing completely black kamma and composite kamma; strive to do kamma completely white. Thus, O bhikkhus, must you train yourselves."

The Five Divisions

The two good bourns and the three evil bourns contain the whole range of possibilities for rebirth. In most Tibetan illustrations, including the one shown here, a sixth bourn is given, by dividing the devas and asuras (the gods and anti-gods or titans). In this section the five, or six, bourns will be described, together with the ways to get to them. Birth in any bourn is a fruit or effect and here we shall see the causes.

A person who has done evil persistently, or even one heavy crime, is likely to see at the time of death a vision, either relating to his past evil actions, or else to the bourn which his past evil actions or kamma have prepared for him. When his physical body is no longer a suitable basis to support life, his mind creates a body ghostly and subtle in substance, which then and there begins to experience one of the evil bourns. But in case his kamma drives him to be born an animal, there is the vision of animals copulating and he is dragged into the womb or egg of those animals.

Kamma which leads to birth as an animal is a strong interest in the things which mankind shares with the animals, that is, eating, drinking and sex. If a man strengthens the animal in himself, to become an "animal-man," he can expect only to be born as an animal. Human beings interested in only these things, strengthening the evil root of delusion in their minds, have already the minds of animals. There is no essential "man-ness" which can prevent such a catastrophe, for no unchanging human soul exists. If a man wishes to guard himself against this, he must protect the conditions for humanity (*manussa-dhamma*), which are the Five Precepts. Sinking below the level of conduct of these precepts is to sink into the sub-human levels. Once rebirth as an animal has taken place it is by no means easy to gain human birth again, as Ācarya Nāgārjuna has written:

> "More difficult is it to rise
> from birth as animal to man,
>
> Than for the turtle blind to see
> the yoke upon the ocean drift;
>
> Therefore, do you being a man
> practise Dhamma and gain its fruits."
>
> — L.K. 59[9]

Kamma dragging one to the hells, which are the most fearful and miserable states, are actions involving hatred, killing, torture and violence generally. People lead themselves to experience hell because they have made the evil root of aversion very strong within themselves.

On the other hand, those who have strengthened the evil root of greed while they were men, having been mean, possessive and selfish, are liable to arise as spirits with strong cravings forever unsatisfied, for which reason they are known as "hungry" ghosts.

---

9. "The Letter of Kindheartedness" by Ācarya Nāgārjuna, in *Wisdom Gone Beyond*, Social Service Association Press of Thailand, Phya Thai Road, Bangkok, Thailand).

However, it does sometimes happen that one who has led an evil life turns sincerely to religion upon his deathbed. When this occurs, with his mind centred upon Dhamma and purified by faith, a person like this may be reborn among men, even arise among the devas. That evil kamma which has been done, though it may have no chance to fructify in those good bourns, remains a potential for creating very unpleasant results whenever conditions are favourable to its fruition. The reverse of this may happen, as when good and noble men become distracted at death and so remember some small evil done, or see a vision of evil done in some past life, the result of which is the arising of unwholesome consciousness leading to the evil bourns.

It is more usual for one who has followed the path of white deeds to be born as a man or among the gods. The basis for the former is the practice of the Five Precepts, which constitute the level of humanness. They are in brief: refraining from destroying living creatures; refraining from taking what is not given; refraining from wrong conduct in sexual desires; refraining from false speech; and refraining from distilled and fermented intoxicants which cause carelessness. Those who refrain from such things, having really lived as men, having strengthened the base of humanness in their own hearts, are born again as men well-endowed with the riches of fine qualities, of varied opportunities, as well as with a wealth of worldly goods.

The path to the heavens is cultivated by those who make special efforts to live with purity and self-restraint, exercising loving kindness towards all beings and so purifying their minds to some extent through meditation. At the time of death, having fulfilled the ten skilful kamma paths and the ten ways of making *puñña*, the heart will be joyful and peaceful to varying degrees, which will result in the experience of arising in one of the many heavenly levels according to the degree of purity and concentration which has been attained.

All these possibilities are within the scope of the mind, the quality of which can be changed in this way or that by kamma, good or bad. From the type of mind which performs the duty of relinking-consciousness at birth, is determined the kind of sense-organs possessed by a being, and hence the kind of world experienced by him. Perception varies—as the famous Buddhist verse puts it:

"As a water-vessel is variously perceived by beings:
Nectar to celestials, is for a man plain drinking-water,
While to the hungry ghost it seems a putrid ooze of pus and blood,
Is for the water serpent-spirits and the fish a place to live in,
While it is space to gods who dwell in the sphere of infinite space.
So any object, live or dead, within the person or without—
Differently is seen by beings according to their fruits of kamma."

From such verses we catch a glimpse of the mysterious depths of the mind, and of the truth of the Exalted Buddha's words which open the Dhammapada:

"Before all dhammas goes the mind;
Mind is the chief, mind-made are they."

To come now to a description of the picture. In the world of *the gods* or "shining-ones" (deva, upper right, but topmost in the Tibetan version), the gilded palaces and glittering jewel trees of the gods of sensuality are shown in the lower part of the drawing. The Tibetan picture shows more details of these superlatively beautiful worlds in which there is also a kind of subtle sexual relationship. Being based upon sensuality, as this world of men is, these devas must also pay the price for this—which is conflict. This conflict is an ever-recurring battle with the asuras, the anti-gods or titans, who have in past times fallen through their quarrelsome nature from the heavens and who now enviously try to invade the celestial realms. In my picture, they share a segment of the world of gods and they are equipped with ancient and modern weapons and are in the dress of soldiers. But they do not only battle with the gods but also among themselves and so a bit of insubordination is depicted as well. The Tibetan picture gives them a world to themselves along the frontiers of which they are fleeing from the victorious heavenly hosts led, upon a very large elephant, by Sakka, the lord of the sensual-realm gods. These titans only understand force, so the Buddha shown in their world bears a sword with which to duly impress them, after which they may be able to hear a little Dhamma. By contrast, the Buddha appearing among the gods bears a lute, in order to lure them into listening to Dhamma sung in exquisite strains, for it was believed that they would not be interested in mere spoken words!

Above the battling of the sensual-realm gods dwell the Brahmas of subtle form and of formlessness, experiencing meditative happiness, serene joy or sublime equanimity. The Tibetan picture also shows a magnificent Brahma world palace in the upper left-hand corner. About all this heavenly splendour, Ācarya Nāgārjuna warns us:

> "Great King, although celestial worlds
> have pleasures great to be enjoyed,
> Greater the pain of dying there.
> From often contemplating this
> a noble person does not wish
> For transient heavenly joys."
>
> — L.K. 98

He goes on to speak of the devas as those

> "Who, dying from celestial realms
> with no remaining merit fruits
> Must take up their abode
> according to the karma past—
> With birth as beast or hungry ghost,
> or else arise in hell."
>
> — L.K. 101

The Brahmas of formlessness dwelling for unthinkable ages in the realms of infinite space, infinite consciousness, nothingness and neither-perception-nor-non-perception being quite without any form, naturally cannot be shown, but even their states are not eternal, but come to an end.

Among men (upper left in both pictures), the progress of the human being is shown: birth (a perambulator); old age, sickness (hospital sign) and death (a bloated corpse in a graveyard), but with this basis of dukkha, men can also understand Dhamma. Lord Buddha, foremost among men, sits highest in the human world teaching Dhamma in a forest grove to his first five disciples. In the original version which my picture follows, he is shown only in the human world, thus emphasising the value of human birth, during which it is possible to gain insight into Dhamma. The religious aspirations of man are represented by a Hindu temple, a Christian church and a Muslim mosque, while a war and a bar show his tendencies towards aversion and greed. The Tibetan picture shows several mundane activities such as ploughing the fields, while people climb towards the top of the picture where there is a temple in which they can listen to Dhamma. In the centre stands a Buddha carrying the alms-bowl and staff, showing to men the way of peacefulness leading to sublime peace of Nibbāna. This is shown in my picture by the sure Dhamma-path which issues from the mouth of the Exalted Buddha. Upon this way a bhikkhu lends a hand to help householders out of the realms of saṃsāra, leading them forward upon the Eightfold Path. Ācarya Nāgārjuna has this to say:

> "Who though he has been born a man
> yet gives himself to evil ways,
> More foolish is he than the fool
> who fills with vomit, urine, dung
> Golden vessels jewel-adorned—
> harder man's birth to gain than these."
>
> — L.K. 60

Hungry ghosts or *peta* (lower right in my picture, lower left in the Tibetan) crave for food and drink but find that it turns to fire or foul things when they are able to get it. I have shown a huge moon and a tiny sun, as the verse says:

> "From want of merit, hungry ghosts
> in summer find the moon is hot,
> in winter sun is cold;
> Barren are the trees they see
> and mighty rivers running on
> dry up whene'er they look at them."
>
> — L.K. 95

Then there is a sky-going *peta* being torn to shreds by birds, as seen by Venerable Moggallāna; one "resting" upon rocks under a leafless tree which is the simile used by the Exalted Buddha in the suttas to symbolise the sole comforts of this realm, and two ghosts sunk in the water up to their lower lips, their gaping mouths just a little too high to get any of it. The state of Tantalus was obviously birth among the hungry ghosts! The ghosts all have bloated bellies, extremely slender necks and "needle-mouths." Their sufferings are illustrated further in the Tibetan. They have to bear the intense cravings for food and drink and then more sufferings when they manage to get a little of it, for it turns to swords and knives in their bellies. The Buddha in this "abundantly painful" realm carries celestial food to allay the ghosts' cravings. In the words of Ācarya Nāgārjuna:

"Lord Buddha has declared the cause
why beings come to birth as ghosts,
torments to endure
For when as men they gave no gifts,
or giving gave with avarice—
They ghostly kamma made."

— L.K. 97

The animals, in the Tibetan illustration, are being encouraged in the Dhamma by a Buddha holding a book, illustrating the point that animals have little ability to understand and are in need of wisdom. My picture illustrates the sufferings of animal-life as described by Ācarya Nāgārjuna:

"Then should you come to birth as beast
many are the pains—
Killing, disease and gory strife
binding, striking too.
Void of peaceful, skilful acts
beasts slay and kill without remorse.

Some among beasts are slain because
they produce pearls, or wool, or bones,
or valued are for meat or hide.
Others are pressed to do men's work
by blows or sticks or iron hook,
by whipping them to work."

— L.K. 89–90

In the animal world, where feelings experienced are "painful, sharp and severe," one can see the dukkha, the hunter and the hunted, in my illustration. The birds of the air are being shot while a vulture is feeding on its prey. A wasp struggling in the net of a spider represents the horrors of life among the insects, while among the larger animals, a buffalo is being forced to work, a deer is being shot and a lion feeds upon its prey. The fish fare no better and are shown being devoured by larger fish, or else hooked and netted by men. Slithering down the division of this world from the hells, there is a gecko. The Tibetan picture illustrates the diversity of animal life and shows, under the waters, the palace of the serpent-spirits or naga, half snake and half man.

The *hells,* which are not permanent states of course, have some new horrors of our day: for railway lines run into a concentration camp from the chimneys of which belches sinister black smoke, while a uniformed member of some secret police force compels a suppliant hell-wraith to swallow molten metal. Towards the viewer flows the river of caustic soda called Vaitarani, which burns the flesh off the bones of those swirling along in it, mingled with a stream of blood from the clashing mountains. Whatever torments hell-wraiths experience, though their bodies are mangled, crushed and ripped apart, yet they survive still for vast ages of time experiencing feelings which are "exclusively painful, sharp and severe," unrelenting and uninterrupted:

> "As highest is the bliss that comes
> from all desires' cessation—
> No higher bliss than this!
> So worst the woe that's known in hell
> Avīci with no interval—
> No woe is worse than this!"
>
> — L.K. 85

In the foreground is the hell of filth where hell-wraiths, who as men had corrupted the innocent, are devoured by gigantic maggots while floundering in a stinking ooze. To the left are the trees of the sword-blade forest which have to be climbed so that hell-wraiths are pierced through and through. This particular aspect of hell is said to be the punishment which adulterers bring on themselves. Various murderers and torturers are impaled upon stakes while a steel-beaked bird rips out the entrails of former cock-fighters. Ācarya Nāgārjuna has some more verses upon these lowest and most-miserable states:

"The criminal who has to bear
throughout a single day
The piercing of three hundred spears
as punishment for crime,
His pain can nowise be compared
to the least pain found in hell.

The pains of hell may still persist
a hundred crores of years—
Without respite, unbearable
So long the fruits of evil acts
do not exhaust the force—
So long continues life in hell."

— L.K. 86–87

Jetsun Milarepa, the great sage and poet of Tibet, who had seen the heavens and hells and other states, once sang this verse:

"Fiends filled with cravings for pleasures
Murder even their parents and teachers,
Rob the Three Gems of their treasures,
Revile and falsely accuse the Precious Ones,
And condemn the Dhamma as untrue:
In the hell of unceasing torment
These evil-doers will be burned...."[10]

Those who now violate the peoples of Tibet and their Dhamma might well take note! This brief survey of the five bourns (*pañcagati*) may be concluded with a verse of exhortation from "The Letter of Kindheartedness":

"If your head or dress caught fire
in haste you would extinguish it,
Do likewise with desire—
which whirls the wheel of wandering-on
And is the root of suffering,
No better thing to do!"

—L.K. 104

10. See *Sixty Songs of Milarepa*, Wheel No. 95/97.

The Rim of the Wheel (Dependent Arising)

The Twelve-linked Chain

Our description has now come to the Rim, or felly of the Wheel, which depicts the Twelve Links of Dependent Arising. It is these links which chain the entire universe of beings to re-becoming and to suffering. It is a well-established tradition to explain this chain as referring to three lives (past, present and future). While the present is the only time which is real, it has been moulded in the past. It is in the present that we produce kamma of mind, speech and body, to bear fruit in the future. In the twelve *nidānas* or "links" around this wheel are set out the whole pattern of life and in it all questions relating to existence are answered.

The teaching of Dependent Arising, central in our Dhamma-vinaya, is not, however, for speculation but should be investigated and seen in one's own and others' lives, and finally it may be perceived in one's own heart, where all the truths of Dhamma become clear after practise. But people who do not practise Dhamma are called "upholders of the world"; they let this wheel whirl them round from unknowing to old-age and death. The Exalted Buddha urged us not to be "world upholders" but through Dhamma-practise to relinquish greed, aversion and delusion so that by the cessation of unknowing there comes to be a cessation of birth, old-age and death.

Now let us have a look at these twelve links in brief.

First Link: Unknowing (Avijjā)

This Pāli word *avijjā* is a negative term meaning "not knowing completely" but it does not mean "knowing nothing at all." This kind of unknowing is very special and not concerned with ordinary ways or subjects of knowledge; for here what one does not know are the Four Noble Truths, one does not see them clearly in one's own heart and one's own life. In past lives, we did not care to see *dukkha* (1), so we could not destroy *the cause of dukkha* (2) or craving, which has impelled us to seek more and more lives, more and more pleasures. *The cessation of dukkha* (3), which perhaps could have been seen by us in past lives, was not realised, so we come to the present existence inevitably burdened with dukkha. And in the past we can hardly assume that we set our feet upon the *practise-path leading to the cessation of dukkha* (4) and we did not even discover stream-entry. We are now paying for our own negligence in the past.

And this unknowing is not some kind of first cause in the past, for it dwells in our hearts now. But due to this unknowing, as we shall see, we have set in motion this wheel bringing round old-age and death and all other sorts of dukkha. Those past "selves" in previous lives who are in the stream of my individual continuity did not check their craving and so could not cut at the root of unknowing. On the contrary they made kamma, some of the fruits of which in this present life I, as their causal resultant, am receiving.

The picture helps us to understand this: a blind old woman (*avijjā* is of feminine gender) with a stick picks her way through a petrified forest strewn with bones. It is said that the original picture here should be an old blind she-camel led by a driver, the beast being one accustomed to long and weary journeys across inhospitable country, while its driver could be craving. Whichever simile is used, the beginninglessness and the darkness of unknowing are well suggested. We are the blind ones who have staggered from the past into the present—to what sort of future?

Depending on the existence of unknowing in the heart, there was volitional action, kamma or *abhisaṅkhāra*, made in those past lives.

Second Link: Volitions (Saṅkhārā)

Intentional actions have the latent power within them to bear fruit in the future—either in a later part of the life in which they were performed, in the following life, or in some more distant life, but their potency is not lost with even the passing of aeons; and whenever the necessary conditions obtain that past kamma may bear fruit. Now, in past lives we have made kamma, and due to our ignorance of the Four Noble Truths we have been "world-upholders" and so making good and evil kamma we have ensured the continued experience of this world.

Beings like this, obstructed by unknowing in their hearts, have been compared to a potter making pots: he makes successful and beautiful pottery (skilful kamma) and he is sometimes careless and his pots crack and break up from various flaws (unskilful kamma). And he gets his clay fairly well smeared over himself just as purity of heart is obscured by the mud of kamma. The simile of the potter is particularly apt because the word *saṅkhārā* means "forming," "shaping," and "compounding," and therefore it has often been rendered in English as "formations."

Depending on the existence of these volitions produced in past lives, there arises the consciousness called "relinking," which becomes the basis of this present life.

Third Link: Consciousness (Viññāṇa)

This relinking consciousness may be of different qualities, according to the kamma upon which it depends. In the case of all those who read this, the consciousness "leaping" into a new birth at the time of conception was a human relinking consciousness arising as a result of having practised at least the Five Precepts, the basis of "humanness" in past lives. One should note that this relinking consciousness is a resultant, not something which can be controlled by will. If one has not made kamma suitable for becoming a human being, one cannot will, when the time of death comes round, "Now I shall become a man again!" The time for intentional action was when one had the opportunity to practise Dhamma. Although our relinking consciousness in this birth is now behind us, it is now that we can practise Dhamma and make more sure of a favourable relinking consciousness in future—that is, if we wish to go on living in saṃsāra.

This relinking consciousness is the third constituent necessary for conception, for even though it is the mother's fertile period and sperm is deposited in the womb, if there is no "being" desiring to take rebirth at that place and time there will be no fertilisation of the ovum.

Appropriately, the picture shows a monkey, the consciousness leaping from one tree, the old life, to another tree. The old tree has died, while the one towards which it jumps is laden with fruits—they may be the fruits of good or evil. The Tibetan picture shows a monkey devouring fruit, experiencing the fruits of deeds done in the past.

Dependent upon relinking consciousness, there is the arising of mind-body.

Fourth Link: Mind-body (Nāma-rūpa)

This is not a very accurate translation but gives the general meaning. There is more included in *rūpa* that is usually thought of as body, while mind is a compound of feeling, perception, volition and consciousness. This mind and body are two interacting continuities in which there is nothing stable. Although in conventional speech we talk of "my mind" and "my body," implying that there is some sort of owner lurking in the background, the wise understand that laws govern the workings of both mental states and physical changes and mind cannot be ordered to be free of defilements, nor body told that it must not grow old, become sick and die.

But it is in the mind that a change can be wrought instead of drifting through life at the mercy of the inherent instability of mind and body. So in the illustration, mind is doing the work of punting the boat of psycho-physical states on the river of cravings. The Tibetan picture shows a coracle, the body, being rowed over swirling waters with three other passengers, who represent the other groups or aggregates (*khandha*) included in *nāma*.

With the coming into existence of mind-body, there is the arising of the six sense-spheres.

Fifth Link: Six Sense-spheres (Saḷāyatana)

A house with six windows is the usual symbol for this link (but the Tibetan shows a house with one window. These six senses are eye, ear, nose, tongue, touch and mind, and these are the bases for the reception of the various sorts of information which each can gather in the presence of the correct conditions. This information falls under six headings corresponding to the six spheres: sights, sounds, smells, tastes, tangibles and thoughts. Beyond these six spheres of sense and their corresponding six objective spheres, we know nothing. All our experience is limited by the senses and their objects with the mind counted as the sixth. The five outer senses collect data only in the present but mind, the sixth, where this information is collected and processed, ranges through the three times adding memories from the past and hopes and fears for the future, as well as thoughts of various kinds relating to the present. It may also add information about the spheres of existence, which are beyond the range of the five outer senses, such as the various heavens, the ghosts and the hell-states. A mind developed through collectedness (*samādhi*) is able to perceive these worlds and their inhabitants.

The six sense-spheres existing, there is contact.

Sixth Link: Contact (Phassa)

This means the contact between the six senses and their respective objects. For instance, when the necessary conditions are all fulfilled, there being an eye, a sight-object, light and the eye being functional, and the person awake and turned towards the object, there is likely to be eye-contact, the striking of the object upon the sensitive eye-base. The same is true for each of the senses and their types of contact. The traditional symbol for this link shows a man and woman embracing.

Where contact arises, feeling exists.

Seventh Link: Feeling (Vedanā)

When there have been various sorts of contact through the six senses, feelings arise which are the emotional response to those contacts. Feelings are of three sorts: pleasant, painful and neither pleasant nor painful. The first are welcome and are the basis for happiness, the second are unwelcome and the basis for dukkha while the third are the neutral sort of feelings which we experience so often but hardly notice.

But all feelings are unstable and liable to change, for no mental state can continue in equilibrium. Even moments of the highest happiness, whatever we consider this is, pass away and give place to different ones. So even happiness, which is impermanent based on pleasant feelings, is really dukkha, for how can the true unchanging happiness be found in the unstable? Thus the picture shows a man with his eyes pierced by arrows, a strong enough illustration of this.

When feelings arise, cravings are (usually) produced.

Eighth Link: Craving (Taṇhā)

Up to this point, the succession of events has been determined by past kamma. Craving, however, leads to the making of new kamma in the present and it is possible now, and only now, to practise Dhamma. What is needed here is mindfulness (*sati*), for without it no Dhamma at all can be practised while one will be swept away by the force of past habits, and let craving and unknowing increase themselves within one's heart. When one does have mindfulness, one may and can know "this is pleasant feeling," "this is unpleasant feeling," "this is neither pleasant nor unpleasant feeling"—and such contemplation of feelings leads one to understand and beware of greed, aversion and delusion, which are respectively associated with the three feelings. With this knowledge one can break out of the Wheel of Birth and Death. But without this Dhamma-practise it is certain that feelings will lead on to more cravings and whirl one around this wheel full of dukkha. As Ācarya Nāgārjuna has said:

> "Desires have only surface sweetness,
> hardness within and bitterness—
> deceptive as the *kimpa*-fruit.
> Thus says the King of Conquerors.
> Such links renounce—they bind the world
> Within saṃsāra's prison grid.
>
> If your head or dress caught fire
> in haste you would extinguish it,
> Do likewise with desire—
> Which whirls the wheel of wandering-on
> and is the root of suffering.
> No better thing to do!"

— L.K. 23, 104

In Sanskrit, the word *tṛṣṇā* (*taṇhā*) means thirst, and by extension implies "thirst for experience." For this reason, craving is shown as a toper guzzling intoxicants and in my picture I have added three bottles—craving for sensual sphere existence and the craving for the higher heavens of the Brahma-worlds which are either of subtle form or formless.

Where the kamma of further craving is produced, there arises grasping.

Ninth Link: Grasping (Upādāna)

This is an intensification and diversification of craving which is directed to four ends: sensual pleasures, views which lead astray from Dhamma, external religious rites and vows, and attachment to the view of soul or self as being permanent. When these become strong in people they cannot even become interested in Dhamma, for their efforts are directed away from Dhamma and towards dukkha. The common reaction is to redouble efforts to find peace and happiness among the objects which are grasped at. Hence both pictures show a man reaching up to pick more fruit, although his basket is full already.

Where this grasping is found, there becoming is to be seen.

Tenth Link: Becoming (Bhava)

With hearts boiling with craving and grasping, people ensure for themselves more and more of various sorts of life, and pile up the fuel upon the fire of dukkha. The ordinary person, not knowing about dukkha, wants to stoke up the blaze, but the Buddhist way of doing things is to let the fires go out for want of fuel by stopping the process of craving and grasping and thus cutting off Unknowing at its root. If we want to stay in saṃsāra we must be diligent and see that our *becoming*, which is happening all the time shaped by our kamma, is *becoming* in the right direction. This means *becoming* in the direction of purity and following the white path of Dhamma-practise. This will contribute to whatever we become, or do not become, at the end of this life, when the pathways to the various realms stand open and we *become* according to our practise and to our death-consciousness.

Appropriately, *Becoming* is illustrated by a pregnant woman. In the presence of Becoming there is arising in a new birth.

Eleventh Link: Birth (Jāti)

Birth, as one might expect, is shown as a mother in the process of childbirth, a painful business and a reminder of how dukkha cannot be avoided in any life. Whatever the future life is to be, if we are not able to bring the wheel to a stop in this life, certainly that future will arise conditioned by the kamma made in this life. But it is no use thinking that since there are going to be future births, one may as well put off Dhamma-practise until then—for it is not sure what those future births will be like. And when they come around, they are just the present moment as well. So no use waiting! Ācarya Nāgārjuna shows that it is better to extricate oneself:

"Where birth takes place, quite naturally
are fear, old age and misery,
disease, desire and death,
As well as a mass of other ills.
When birth's no longer brought about
All the links are ever stopped."

— L.K. 111

Naturally where there is birth, is also old-age and death.

Twelfth Link: Old-age and Death (Jarā-maraṇa)

In future one is assured, given enough of Unknowing and Craving, of lives without end but also of deaths without end. The one appeals to greed but the other arouses aversion. One without the other is impossible. But this is the path of heedlessness. The Dhamma-path leads directly to Deathlessness, the going beyond birth and death, beyond all dukkha.

The Tibetan picture shows an old man carrying off a bundled-up corpse upon his back, taking it away to some charnel-field. My picture has an old man gazing at a coffin enclosing a corpse. We are well exhorted by the words of Ācarya Nāgārjuna:

"Do you therefore exert yourself:
At all times try to penetrate
into the heart of these Four Truths;
For even those who dwell at home,
they will, by understanding them,
ford the river of [mental] floods."

— L.K. 115

This is a very brief outline of the workings of this wheel which we cling to for our own harm and the hurt of others. We are the makers of this wheel and the turners of this wheel, but if we wish it and work for it, we are the ones who can stop this wheel.

The Monster

Both pictures show the wheel as being in the grip of a fearful monster. In my drawing the monster's name is engraved upon his crown so that people should not think of him as a common demon. He is no such thing, for his name is Impermanence and his crown shows his authority over all worlds whatever. He devours them and they are all, heavens and hells together, securely held in the grasp of his taloned hands. The crown upon his head is adorned with five skulls, representing the impermanence of the five groups or aggregates comprising the person. His eyes, ears, nose and mouth have flames about them, an illustration of the Exalted One's Third Discourse in which He says: "The eye is afire..." and so on. Above the monster's two eyes, there is a third one meaning that while for the fool impermanence is his enemy, for the wise man it helps him to Enlightenment. Although the monster has adorned himself with earrings and the like he fails to look attractive—in the same way, this world puts on an outer show of beauty but its beauty fades when examined more carefully.

Below the painting of the wheel, some Tibetan examples show parts of a tiger skin adorning the monster, a symbol of fearfulness. In my drawing I show the monster's tail which has no beginning, looping back and forth. In the same way, we have been born, lived and then died countless times in the whirl of saṃsāra. Sometimes our deeds were mostly good and sometimes mostly bad, and we have reaped the fruit of it all.

Some Other Features

The whole wheel glows with heat and is surrounded by flames burning with the fires of greed, aversion and delusion as the Exalted One has repeated many times in his discourses.

In the upper right corner of both pictures stands the Exalted Buddha shown crossed over to the Farther Shore, meaning Nibbāna. The Tibetan picture shows him pointing out the moon upon which is drawn a hare, the symbol of renunciation, the way to practise Dhamma, and the way out of this wheel.[11] In my picture, he indicates with his hand the nature of saṃsāra and warns us to beware. He is adorned with a radiance about him, symbolising the spiritual freedom and majestic wisdom won by him which can be described in many ways but is finally beyond the limitations of everything known to us.

The Tibetan picture shows in the upper left, a drawing of Avalokiteśvara,[12] the embodiment of compassion, as the way and the goal for those who follow the bodhisattva-path. My picture has the Path of Dhamma of eight lotuses leading to the wheel of Dhamma. The eight lotuses are the eight factors of the Noble Path, the first two—Right View, Right Attitude—being the wisdom-section; the next three—Right Speech, Right Action, Right Livelihood—being the morality section; and the last three—Right Effort, Right Mindfulness and Right Collectedness—being the section of collectedness or meditation. The Wheel of Dhamma has at its centre *suññata*, the Void, another name for the experience of Nibbāna in later Buddhist traditions. Around its hub are the ten petals of a lotus, representing the ten perfecting qualities (*pāramī*) which are necessary for complete attainment: generosity, moral conduct, renunciation, wisdom, determination, energy, patience, truthfulness, lovingkindness and equanimity. Eight spokes radiate from the hub, which stand for the practice by the Arahant, the one perfected, of the Eightfold Path when each factor, instead of being just right, becomes perfect. On the inside of the wheel's nave there are 37 jewels symbolising the thirty-seven factors of Enlightenment, while the outer edge of the nave is adorned with four groups of three jewels showing the Four Noble Truths in each of the three ways wherein they were viewed by the Exalted Buddha when he discovered Enlightenment.[13]

11. Not included in the reproduction given here.
12. Not included in the reproduction given here.
13. See Wheel No. 17: "Three Cardinal Discourses," p. 7f.

Conclusion

This picture teaches us and reminds us of many important features of the Dhamma as it was intended to by the teachers of old. Contemplating all its features frequently helps to give us true insight into the nature of saṃsāra. With its help and our own practice we come to see Dependent Arising in ourselves. When this has been done thoroughly all the riches of Dhamma will be available to us, not from books or discussions, nor from listening to others' explanations...

The Exalted Buddha has said:

"Whoever sees Dependent Arising, he sees Dhamma;
Whoever sees Dhamma, he sees Dependent Arising."

* * *

Aniccā vata saṅkhārā
uppāda-vayadhammino
Uppajjitvā nirujjhanti
tesaṃ vūpasamo sukho.

"Conditions truly they are transient
With the nature to arise and cease
Having arisen, then they pass away
Their calming, cessation is happiness."

Brāhmaṇism, Buddhism, and Hinduism

An Essay on Their Origins and Interactions

by

Lal Mani Joshi

Department of Religious Studies

Punjabi University, Patiala, India

WHEEL PUBLICATION NO. 150/151

Foreword

In the essay that follows Dr. Joshi has set out to reply to certain Indian scholars who have criticised Buddhism, and others who have put forward the theory that Buddhism is simply a form of Hinduism or an offshoot of it. His thesis broadly falls under five heads, namely:

1. The Buddha was not "born a Hindu" because Hinduism in its present form had not emerged at the time of his birth;
2. Before the time of the Buddha the religion of India was *Vedic Brāhmaṇism*, but that alongside the Vedic tradition there was an ascetic (*Śramaṇa*) stream of religious thought and practice having its origin in prehistoric times;
3. That it is to this Śramaṇic culture that Buddhism has its closest affinity;
4. That Hinduism grew out of a fusion of Vedic Brāhmaṇism with Buddhism and other Śramaṇic religious trends;
5. That although Buddhism acknowledges an affinity with the Śramaṇic cults, it is nevertheless a unique product of the Buddha's direct insight.

Dr. Joshi is not the first to have pointed out the more obvious of these facts; but in his essay he has brought to bear on the subject an impressive erudition and has supported his arguments with the result of much painstaking research. We believe that few people will be inclined to question his general conclusions.

Dr. Joshi was Professor at the Department of Religious Studies, Punjabi University, Patiala, India. At present he is serving the Harvard University as a visiting fellow at the Center for the Study of World Religions, Cambridge, Mass., U.S.A. Among other writings, he has to his credit a comprehensive and scholarly work, *Studies in the Buddhistic Culture of India* (New Delhi, 1967, Motilal Banarsidass).

December 1969
Buddhist Publication Society

Brāhmaṇism, Buddhism, and Hinduism

I. Introductory Remarks

Much modern literature in English, French, German, Hindi, and other languages has been produced on early Buddhism and its relation to Brāhmaṇism and Hinduism. It would appear from the apparently settled posture of modern Buddhist scholarship that those problems are settled beyond all doubt and dispute. However, when we reopen these matters with a view to restating them, we record our disagreement with the current theories of the origins of Buddhism, of its early relations with Brāhmaṇism, and of its position with regard to Hinduism.

In India, where the Brāhmaṇical or the traditional standpoint has possessed the scholastic field for about a millennium now, and has been regarded with reverence not only among modern Indian historians and national leaders but also among Western Indologists, for about a century and a half, it would appear almost an impertinence on our part to put forth a view which goes against it.

However, a student of the history of religious traditions of India will have to rise above artificial conventions set by the writings of others should he find that his suggestions would help a better and clearer understanding of some significant facts of the growth of his country's central traditions as "heterodox." This custom is due to our preoccupation with the traditional or Brāhmaṇical point of view. From the Buddhist point of view Brāhmaṇism was a "heresy"; from the Brāhmaṇical point of view Buddhism was a "heresy." When Dr. S. Rādhakrishnan, broadcasting from All India Radio on the occasion of the 2500th Mahāparinirvāna-day of the Buddha, described Buddhism as "an offshoot of the more ancient faith of the Hindus, perhaps a schism or a heresy,"[1] he not only repeated a particular view but perhaps also gave an "official"

---

1. *Occasional Speeches and Writings* (October 1952–February 1959) by S. Rādhakrishnan, Publications Division, New Delhi, 1960, pp. 337–46, p. 323; also *2500 Years of Buddhism,* edited by P. V. Bapat, Publications Division, Govt. of India, New Delhi, reprint 1959, Foreword, pp. v–xvi.

stamp to the Brāhmaṇical standpoint in Indian history. It is no exaggeration to say that whatever has been written on the history of Buddhism in India has been written in modern times largely from this standpoint.

The conflict between Buddhism and Brāhmaṇism, the transformation of the Buddhist heritage in India, and the disappearance of Buddhism as a living faith from Indian soil during the early mediaeval centuries were largely responsible for the growth of misconceptions about Ancient Indian civilization and also for the propagation of the Brāhmaṇical standpoint during mediaeval through modern times. The future of Buddhist studies in India will remain quite doubtful so long as Indian scholars continue to study Buddhism as a "heretical system" and from the "orthodox" standpoint. Buddhism should be studied from the Buddhist standpoint, and its relations with Brāhmaṇism and Hinduism should be studied from the historical standpoint and on scientific lines. The study of Buddhism from the Hindu view would be a study of Hinduism and not of Buddhism.

It was an exceptional thing that a noted British antiquarian, Sir Mortimer Wheeler, actively engaged in digging up India's past, once observed that "it cannot be denied that during the seven centuries between 250 BCE and CE 450 most of the surviving sculpture of the highest quality in India was associated with Buddhism, and it was, above all, Buddhism that during the same period (and particularly the latter part of it) spread Indian art and idiom through the highways and byways of Asia. Archaeologically, at least, we cannot treat Buddhism merely as a heresy against a prevailing Brāhmaṇical orthodoxy, however little its tenets may have affected the routine of village life."[2]

There are about 1200 rock-cut monuments (caves, monasteries, sanctuaries, temples) of ancient India; of these 100 belong to Jainism, 200 to Brāhmaṇism, and the remaining to Buddhism. These three-fourths of ancient Indian rock-cut architecture or the unequalled masterpieces of Buddhist paintings at Ajantā cannot have been due to a heresy.

2. R.E. Mortimer Wheeler, *Romano-Buddhist Art, and Old Problems Restated*, *Antiquity*, Vol. XXIII, No. 89, London, 1949, p. 5. However, the Buddhist sculpture of the Gandhara School can scarcely be called "Romano-Buddhist."

In all fields of the culture and civilization of Ancient India, viz. art, literature, language, ethics, mysticism, philosophy, epistemology, logic, psychology, and social thought, the manifestations of Buddhism in contradistinction to Brāhmaṇism were so great, so profound, so lasting, and so varied that we are not justified in treating it as a "heterodox" episode in the history of "Hindu civilization." It will not be far from the truth to say that the history of Ancient Indian Culture and civilization would not have been worth writing or reading had there been only the Indo-Aryan ideals of the Vedic Saṃhitās and no Buddhism to transform them into the glory that was Ancient India.

Religious harmony is a noble and essential ideal not only for a country like India where many religious communities live together but also for the unity of mankind and peace in the world. Emperor Asoka had taught three and twenty centuries before that harmony among different sects is a good thing.[3] But this harmony cannot be brought about by mystifying or overlooking the distinctive features or by minimising historical manifestations of Buddhism in contradistinction to Brāhmaṇism and its later phase of Hinduism. The Brāhmaṇical authors of the Vaiṣṇava Purāṇas did not bring about harmony between Buddhism and Brāhmaṇism by writing that the Buddha was an incarnation of Lord Viṣṇu that came into existence "to seduce and delude the demons and devils."[4]

On the contrary, this policy brought about the ruin of Buddhism and its effacement in India. Moreover, propagation of the ideal of religious harmony should not come in the way of historical research in religious history. But in modern India it has become a fashion to speak and write that Buddhism is a sect of Hinduism, that the Buddha was a Hindu, that Hinduism is so catholic as to tolerate and worship a heretical and anti-Vedic teacher like the Buddha! The story of the origin and disappearance of Buddhism, told in one sentence, is a matter of street-talk for every grown-up Hindu irrespective of his or her knowledge of ancient Indian religious

3. Asoka Rock Edict No. XII. Samavāyo eva sādhu.

4. See e.g. Bhāgavata Purāṇa, 1.3.24: Kalau saṃpravṛitte saṃmohāya suradviśāṃ / Buddho nāmanā janasutaḥ kikaṭeṣu bhaviṣyāti. Cf. Bhāgavata Purāna, X. 40.22: Namo buddhāya suddhāya daitya-dānava-mohine, Vālmiki, Rāmāyana, II.109.34.

history and archaeology. The story is repeated whenever they happen to visit museums, which are usually crowded by Buddhist antiquities, or when they come across a pilgrim *Bhikṣu* or a *Lama* or hear some news from Buddhist quarters. Just as the Government of India sought to publish all about the history and heritage of Buddhism during the last twenty-five centuries in less than five hundred pages, so the average modern educated Indian seeks to sum up the history of Buddhism by saying that Buddhism grew as a reaction against and reform of Hinduism and it disappeared from India partly due to its *Tāntrika* practices and partly due to the glorious "conquests" of Saṃkarācārya. A few educated Hindus, who have specialised in Buddhist studies or studied something of Buddhism or some book on Buddhism, do concede that Buddhism merged into Hinduism, that the Buddha was the greatest Hindu reformer and that the Buddha was the greatest Hindu Master.

This comfortable doctrine has been so thoroughly propagated in India that it will take great efforts and long years of scholars and historians to sweep away its illusions and clear the way for the growth of Buddhist studies in India. In the following pages we propose to review and restate the origins of Buddhism, its relations with early Brāhmaṇism and with the mediaeval form of the latter called Hinduism. Hence the title of this essay carries the three words in a *chronological order: Brāhmaṇism, Buddhism and Hinduism.* The differences between old Brāhmaṇism and Hinduism are more pronounced than those between Theravāda and Mahāyāna Buddhism.

II. Current Theories of the Origins of Buddhism

Some scholars,[5] under the influence of the materialist interpretation of history popularised by Karl Marx, have sought to correlate the rise of ascetic and intellectual thought-currents of the age of Śākyamuni (624–544 BCE, but the age of Śākyamuni may be extended to 700–500 BCE as the age of philosophers) to the rise

5. Atindranath Bose, *Social and Rural Economy of Northern India*, Vol. II, Calcutta, 1945, pp. 481f.; D.D. Kosambi, *Ancient Kosala and Magadha*, JBBRAS, 1951, pp. 186f.

of capitalism and mercantile middle class economy. This theory, however, is entirely speculative. There is no clear evidence to prove the existence of capitalism, in the Marxist sense, nor of a money-economy controlled entirely by an organised middle class of society in the seventh and sixth centuries BCE. Moreover, it is impossible to demonstrate that the spiritual ideas of a *Bodhisattva* are determined by that social consciousness which is consequent on material progress; indeed a materialist interpretation of the origins of Buddhism or of the events of the life of Siddhārtha Gautama is evidence only of the philosophical crudity of the authors of this theory.

The poet Rabindranāth Tāgore[6] expounded the view that Buddhism and Jainism represented the ideals of the kṣatriyas which conflicted with those of the brāhmaṇas, that the history of ancient India is a record of "the pull of the two opposite principles, that of self-preservation represented by the brāhmaṇa, and that of self-expansion represented by the kṣatriya." This theory, in spite of its striking character, is largely imaginary and cannot be sustained. It is true and is very well known that kṣatriyas were the founders not only of Buddhism, Jainism and Ājīvikism but also of the ascetic and idealistic thought of the early Upaniṣads. But it will be absurd and fantastic to think that supernal teachers like Kapilamuni, Pārśvanātha, Kāśyapa Buddha, Śākyamuni Buddha, Vardhamāna Mahāvīra or even the royal teachers like Aśvapati Kaikeya, Janaka Videha and Pravāhaṇa Jaivali of the Upaniṣads were inspired by a desire to struggle for the supremacy of their supposed ideal of "self-expansion" against that of the priestly "self-preservation."

The Buddha emphasised the ideal of self-abnegation and taught the tenet of "not-self" while some of the greatest teachers and followers of Buddhism came from the caste of the brāhmaṇas. The fact is that, as we shall see below, the history of ancient India is a record of the two opposite ideologies, that of world-affirmation represented by the priestly brāhmaṇas of the Vedic tradition and that of world-denial and world-transcendence represented by the ascetic śramaṇas of non-Vedic tradition. And the conflict antedates the formation of the castes of brāhmaṇas and kṣatriyas. Professor

6. Rabindranāth Tāgore, *A Vision of India's History*, Viœvabharati Publication, 1951.

G. C. Pande has summed up his valuable researches concerning the origins of Buddhism in the following words:

"It has been held by many older writers that Buddhism and Jainism arose out of the anti-ritualistic tendency within the religion of the brāhmaṇas. We have however tried to show that the anti-ritualistic tendency within the Vedic fold is itself due to the impact of an asceticism which antedates the Vedas. Jainism represents a continuation of the pre-Vedic stream from which Buddhism also springs, though deeply influenced by Vedic thought. The fashionable view of regarding Buddhism as a Protestant Vedicism and its birth as a Reformation appears to be based on a misreading of later Vedic history caused by the fascination of a historical analogy and the ignorance or neglect of pre-Vedic civilization."[7]

This most important and epoch-making statement in the history of Buddhist studies in India, in spite of the fact that Prof. Pande thinks that Buddhism was "deeply influenced by Vedic thought" in its origins (a view which is open to doubt and debate), does not seem to have made even the slightest impact on the more recent writings of even the most noted Indologists of India belonging to the traditional approach. The Purāṇic myth still holds ground and flourishes. We shall refer to the views of only two most eminent and living Indian scholars who have been awarded India's highest order of decoration and honour, "Bhārata-ratna," and who might be considered to represent the prevailing Indian standpoint towards the origins of Buddhism and its relation with Brāhmaṇism and Hinduism.

Dr. S. Rādhakrishnan's most mature opinion on this point is summarised in the following statements:

"The Buddha did not feel that he was announcing a new religion. He was born, grew up and died a Hindu. He was restating with a new emphasis the ancient ideals of the Indo-Aryan civilization."[8] In support of this statement he quotes a passage from the *Saṃyutta Nikāya* which will be reproduced below. "Buddhism did not start," he goes on, "as a new and independent religion. It was an offshoot

7. G. C. Pande, *Studies in the Origins of Buddhism*, University of Allahabad, 1957, p. 317.

8. See the two books cited in note no. 1, pp. 341, 344–45 of the first and pp. ix. xiii, xv (of Foreword) of the second.

of the more ancient faith of the Hindus, perhaps a schism or a heresy. While the Buddha agreed with the faith he inherited on the fundamentals of metaphysics and ethics, he protested against certain practises which were in vogue at that time. He refused to acquiesce in the Vedic ceremonialism." Repeating this idea for a third time in the same lecture, Dr. S. Rādhakrishnan goes on to say that "the Buddha utilised the Hindu inheritance to correct some of its expressions."[8]

This scholar is known for his enlightened understanding of different religious traditions and his view deserves careful attention. But as this same view has been reaffirmed with greater emphasis and closer study of Hindu sacred lore by a more recent and very eminent writer, namely, Mahāmahopādhyāya Dr. Pandurang Vāman Kane, it will be convenient to examine this view after setting out the observations and arguments of Dr. Kane. This scholar has written a chapter on the *Causes of the Disappearance of Buddhism from India* in the concluding part of a work which deals with the history of "ancient and mediaeval religious and civil law in India" based entirely on the Brāhmaṇical literature.[9] A noted critic seems to have rightly doubted the desirability of including this unnecessary chapter which contains "some striking passages on Buddhism"[10] and the "protest" and "counterblast" of this National Professor of Indology of India against Buddhism and its modern "encomiasts."[11]

We are not concerned here with the causes of the disappearance of Buddhism from India but only with the origins of Buddhism and its relation with Brāhmaṇism. Curiously enough the origins of Buddhism have been discussed under the causes of its disappearance. "The Buddha was," observes Dr. P. V. Kane, "only a great reformer of the Hindu religion as practised in his time. He did not feel or claim that he was forming a new religion nor did he renounce the Hindu religion and all its practises and

9. P. V. (Pandurang Vāman) Kane, *History of Dharmaśāstra*, Vol. V, Part II, Bhandarkar Oriental Research Institute, Poona, 1962, Chapter XXV, pp. 1003–1030.

10. Cf. J. Duncan M. Derrett, review of Kane's work in the BSOAS, Vol. XXVIII, Part 2, University of London, 1964, p. 461.

11. Cf. L. M. Joshi, op. cit., pp. 146 and 411.

beliefs. The Buddha referred to the Vedas and Hindu sages with honour in some of his sermons. He recognised the importance of Yogic practises and meditation. His teaching took over several beliefs current among the Hindus in his day such as the doctrine of Karma and Rebirth and cosmological theories. A substantial portion of the teaching of the Buddha formed part of the tenets of the Upaniṣadic period."[12] By the "Hindu religion" the author obviously means the religion of the Vedas, Brāhmaṇas and Upaniṣads and the argument is based on the theory that the Upaniṣads are older than the Buddha. Therefore, he goes on to say that "It is generally held by all Sanskrit scholars that at least the oldest Upaniṣads like the Bṛhadāraṇyaka and the Chāndogya are earlier than the Buddha, that they do not refer to the Buddha or to his teaching or to the *piṭakas.* On the other hand, though in dozens of Suttas meetings of brāhmaṇas and the Buddha or his disciples and missionaries are reported, they almost always seem to be marked by courtesy on both sides. No meetings are recorded in the early Pāli Texts or Brāhmaṇical Texts about Śākyans condemning the tenets of ancient brāhmaṇism or about brāhmaṇas censuring the Buddha's heterodoxy. Besides, in all these meetings and talks, the central Upaniṣad conception of the immanence of Brahma is never attacked by the Buddha or by the early propagators of Buddhism."

Besides these arguments based on the supposed pre-Buddhist date of the older Upaniṣads, Dr. Kane seeks to support his thesis by employing a saying of the Buddha. He further observes: "What the Buddha says may be briefly rendered as follows: 'Even so have I, O Bhikkhus, seen an ancient path, an ancient road followed by rightly enlightened persons of former times. And what, O Bhikkhus, is that ancient path, that ancient road, followed by the rightly enlightened ones of former times? Just this very Noble Eightfold Path, viz., right views. ... This, O Bhikkhus, is that ancient path, that ancient road, followed by the rightly enlightened ones of former times. Along that (path) I have gone and while going along that path I have fully come to know old age and death. Having come to know it fully, I have told it to the monks, the nuns, the lay followers, men and women; this *brahmacariya* is

12. P. V. Kane, op. cit., p. 1004.

prosperous, flourishing, widespread, widely known, has become popular and made manifest well by gods and men.'"[13]

This passage is cited by Dr. S. Rādhakrishnan also in support of his view that the Buddha was restating the Indo-Aryan ideals. Commenting on this saying of the Buddha, Dr. Kane says, "It will be noticed that the Noble Eightfold Path which the Buddha put forward as the one that would put an end to misery and suffering is here expressly stated to be an ancient path trod by ancient enlightened men. The Buddha does not claim that he was unique but claimed that he was only one of a series of enlightened men and stressed that the moral qualities which he urged men to cultivate belonged to antiquity."

Having apparently established the brāhmaṇical theory of Vedic origin of Buddhism, Dr. P. V. Kane gives expression to his real intention of incorporating a chapter in his work, *The Crowning Glory of a Life*, at the age of eighty-two years, and makes these remarks, which seem to come from the very bottom of the heart of a staunch Hindu and must be taken to reflect the opinion and attitude of the orthodox majority in contemporary India:

"In these days it has become a fashion to praise the Buddha and his doctrine to the skies and to disparage Hinduism by making unfair comparisons between the original doctrines of the Buddha with the present practises and shortcomings of Hindu society. The present author has to enter a strong protest against this tendency. If a fair comparison is to be made it should be made between the later phases of Buddhism and the present practises of professed Buddhists on the one hand and modern phases and practises of Hinduism on the other. The Upaniṣads had a nobler philosophy than that of Gautama, the Buddha; the latter merely based his doctrine on the philosophy of the Upaniṣads. If Hinduism decayed in the course of time and exhibited bad tendencies, the same or worse was the case with later Buddhism which gave up the noble but human Buddha, made him a god, worshipped his images and ran wild with such hideous practises as those of Vajrayāna."

"As a counterblast to what modern encomiasts often say about Buddhism, the present author will quote a strongly worded (but not unjust) passage from Swāmi Vivekānanda's lecture on *The*

13. Ibid., pp.1004–05 and note no. 1639.

Sages of India (*Complete Works*, Volume III, pp. 248–68, 7th edition of 1953, published at Māyāvatī, Almora): 'The earlier Buddhists in their rage against the killing of animals had denounced the sacrifices of the Vedas; and these sacrifices used to be held in every house. ... These sacrifices were obliterated and in their place came gorgeous temples, gorgeous ceremonies and gorgeous priests and all that you see in India in modern times. I smile when I read books written by some modern people who ought to know better, that the Buddha was the destroyer of Brāhmaṇical idolatry. Little do they know that Buddhism created brāhmaṇism and idolatry in India.... Thus, in spite of the preaching of mercy to animals, in spite of the sublime ethical religion, in spite of the hair-splitting discussion about the existence or non-existence of a permanent soul, the whole building of Buddhism tumbled down piecemeal; and the ruin was simply hideous. I have neither the time nor the inclination to describe to you the hideousness that came in the wake of Buddhism. The most hideous ceremonies, the most horrible, the most obscene books that human hands ever wrote or the human brain ever conceived, the most bestial forms that ever passed under the name of religion have all been the creation of degraded Buddhism' (pp. 264f.)."[14]

III. Criticism of the Current Theory

It might be asked whether such a "protest," "counterblast" and "strongly worded passage" are worthy of the academic spirit? It is for impartial critics to judge whether these passages from the pen of India's National Professor of Indology will contribute anything to the history of *dharmaśāstra* or will explain the causes of the disappearance of Buddhism from India or will promote secularism and religious tolerance in India. The writer of this essay was neither shocked nor pained when he read some of the most striking passages, full of animosity and ignorance, in the criticisms of Buddhism by Uddyotakara, Kumārila, Saṃkara and the Purāṇas, because they belonged to the mediaeval ages when religious feelings and controversies determined the fate of communities and countries and religious wars were common.

14. Ibid., pp. 1029–30.

But he was disturbed for a moment when he read this outburst of Dr. Kane, in the *History of Dharmaśāstra*, because such unjust statements are not expected from so highly respected scholars, especially in twentieth-century India, when an enlightened understanding of different faiths is the need of the nation. With due respect to Swāmi Vivekānanda it should be observed that he was neither a scholar of Buddhism nor a historian of the religious history of India. We can only say that it does not give any credit to Dr. Kane's distinguished scholarship to borrow an ill-conceived verbal explosive from a Hindu sectarian laboratory and explode them on the pages of his lifelong work, which has no direct connection with Buddhism.

Whether the philosophy of the Upaniṣads was nobler than that of the Buddha is a matter of personal opinion and individual interest. That Buddhist philosophy is nobler and profounder than Brāhmaṇical philosophy is the view of some of the most distinguished philosophers and historians of philosophy. The view that the Buddha based his doctrines on the Upaniṣads, however, cannot be proved because the date even of the oldest of Upaniṣads cannot be fixed before the Buddha with any amount of certainty. Let us therefore examine in some detail the views of Dr. P. V. Kane. To begin with the word "Hindu" and its historical perspective:

The term "Hindu" is foreign coinage, of Persian and Arabic origins. The term "Hinduism" is derived from Persian and Arabic words and stands for the mediaeval forms of Indian and Brāhmaṇical religions. Just as Judaism before the birth of Jesus Christ cannot be properly called Christianity though Christianity is founded on pre-Christian Judaism, likewise we cannot use the word Hinduism for pre-Purāṇic Brāhmaṇism of the Vedic and Upaniṣadic age, though mediaeval Hinduism is based to some extent on the Vedic religion. An historical analysis of the elements of Purāṇic Brāhmaṇism or Hinduism shows that more than half of them are of non-Vedic and of post-Buddhist origin.

In modern Hinduism there is so much of Buddhism and Jainism that on the popular level the distinctions between them are blurred. This is not the case with old Brāhmaṇism, which was and still is easily and clearly distinguishable from early Buddhism and early Jainism. We shall point out some of these differences in the course of this essay. We shall see below that even before the oldest

Upaniṣads came into existence and the Buddha taught his gospel, there had been non-Vedic and non-Brāhmaṇic sages (*muni*) and ascetics (*yati*) in ancient India. The culture of these non-Vedic sages and ascetics of pre-Vedic origin may be called Śramaṇism for want of a better word. (This Śramaṇism should not be confused with what in modern times is called "Shamanism.") This pre-Buddhist and non-Vedic Śramaṇic culture was in some ways diametrically opposed to Brāhmaṇism or Vedic-Brāhmaṇic culture.

Although in the older Upaniṣads, due to mutual contact among the upholders of these two seemingly irreconcilable traditions, we find a partial fusion of Brāhmaṇism and Śramaṇism, of sacrificial culture and ascetic culture, of ritual thought and moral thought, yet it took several centuries to bring about this process of mutual contact and fusion. It was left to the Indians of the early centuries of the Christian era to transform the old Buddhism into Neo-Buddhism or Mahāyānism and Vedic Brāhmaṇism into Purāṇic Brāhmaṇism or Neo-Brāhmaṇism, so as to give birth, towards the second half of the first millennium of the Christian era (CE 500–1000) to what are now called Tantra and Hinduism.

When we talk of the continuity and antiquity of Hinduism, we should not forget that from the age of Vedicism (1500–500 BCE) to the age of Tantrism and Hinduism (CE 500–1000 and to our own days) the Brāhmaṇical tradition has grown with all possible vigour and elasticity and under the powerful influence and pressure of non-Āryan and folk cultures, Buddhist and Jaina cultures and more than half a dozen streams of non-Indian or foreign cultures, viz. those of the Persians, Greeks, Sakas, Pārthians, Kusānas, Eurasian Christians, Hūnas, Arabs and the Islamic followers.

It was perhaps Alberuni (circa CE 1030) who first referred to Indians of non-Islamic faiths as the "Hindus" and he meant Indian "infidels." Even this Brāhmaṇism of the first millennium before Christ was not known as Hinduism during this time. There is no authority worth the name, not even an iota of evidence, to support the racial or religious or sectarian or communal sense of the term Hindu before Alberuni's "India." The occurrence of the word "Hindu" in any ancient Indian archaeological or literary source is yet to be discovered.

The term *hidu* (hindu), a form of *sindhu*, was first used by the Persians. It occurs along with the word *Gadara*, a form of

Gandhāra, in an inscription of King Darius of Iran.[15] It is used there in a geographical sense and denotes the people or country on the river Sindhu conquered by that monarch. In old Persian "Sa" is pronounced as "Ha"; "Sindhu" is called "Hindu," from which the Greeks further corrupted it into "Sinthos" or "Indos" from which are derived the Arabic and Persian words Hindu and Hindustan and the English words Indian and India. In mediaeval India the Arabs and early Muslim travellers referred to western India as "Hind" (i.e., Sindha) and the Turks, Afghans and Mongols used this geographical name, Hindustan, for the whole of the country. The word "Hinduism" began to be used for Indian religious traditions usually with a view to distinguishing them from Christian and Islamic traditions in India. What in modern times is called Hinduism is in fact the sum total of the entire religious traditions of India excepting of course, Christian and Islamic, which have retained their individual existence despite mutual contacts. It must be added that Jainism also exists as a separate sect. So does Sikhism. It may be that Buddhism will also reappear again as a distinct faith in the near future. At the present time, the signs are not encouraging.

We are therefore not justified in using the words Hindu and Hinduism in the historical context of the age of the Buddha. Vedic Brāhmaṇism presents the prehistory of historic Brāhmaṇism, and Purāṇic Brāhmaṇism together with Buddhism, have provided the foundations of mediaeval and modern Hinduism. In ancient India, there was no race, no caste, nor any book which could be referred to by the term "Hindu." Therefore the phrase "Hindu religion" in connection with pre-Muslim India is altogether meaningless and misleading. Just as early Buddhism differs from late Lamaism and Vajrayāna, similarly early Brāhmaṇism differs from late Purāṇicism or Hinduism, although Lamaistic Buddhism traces its origin to the Buddha's teachings and Purāṇic Hinduism traces its origin to Vedic doctrines. To describe the religion of the Vedic *Saṃhitās*, *Brāhmaṇas* and *Upaniṣads* as the "Hindu religion" is both historically anachronistic and doctrinally misleading.

To say that the Buddha was a "Hindu" is wrong. To say that "the Buddha was only a great reformer of the Hindu religion as practised in his time" is doubly incorrect, since there was no

15. Cf. W. Crook, *Hinduism*, in ERE, Vol. VI, ed. by J. Hastings, pp. 686f.

"Hindu religion" in his time but only primitive Brāhmaṇism or Vedicism; and to call the Buddha "only a great reformer" of Vedicism is also incorrect. The Supernal Teacher was a Seer, an Awakened One, who broadcast a teaching so original, so profound and universal as to become the powerful and creative matrix of a distinct civilization which is yet unsurpassed in some respects.

His teachings, no doubt, reformed many of the debased practises of Vedic religion. But he did not claim to be a reformer; neither Hindu scriptures nor Brāhmaṇical texts recognise him as a reformer. The Purāṇas recognise him only as a "seducer." As for his admission to the rank of "incarnation," this is no special tribute to the Buddha, because all sorts of beings and beasts, e.g., a fish, a tortoise, a boar, a dwarf, a half-man-and-half-lion, etc., are also given that position. Dr. Rādhakrishnan says: "For us, in this country, the Buddha is an outstanding representative of our religious tradition.... In a sense the Buddha is a maker of modern Hinduism."[16] But this is a modern and partially enlightened view unknown to Brāhmaṇical antiquity and orthodoxy.

There was a constant struggle between Brāhmaṇism and Buddhism right from the days of the Buddha to the time of the effacement of Buddhism towards the beginning of the second millennium. This struggle is proved by the Pāli Texts, the Sanskrit Buddhist Texts, the Upaniṣads, the Dharma Sūtras of the Brāhmaṇas, the Purāṇas, the philosophical treatises of both traditions, and it is confirmed in some cases by archaeological evidence and foreign notices. This struggle ended only with the exit of the professed Buddhism from the Indian scene. The rapprochement that began to take place between Brāhmaṇism and Buddhism from the early centuries of the Christian era was in spite of this struggle between the two: "In the twofold process of assimilation and condemnation of Buddhism, the Brāhmaṇical priests sacrificed at the altar ... of mythical Viṣṇu even the most historical and overwhelmingly non-brāhmaṇical personality of the Buddha and mystified the historical existence of Buddhism as a delusive trick of a Purāṇic God."[17]

It is only in these Purāṇic tricks and myths that the ninth Avatāra of the Bhāgavata God "was born, grew up, and died a

16. *Occasional Speeches and Writings* (1960), p. 345.
17. L. M. Joshi, op. cit., p. xiii.

Hindu." In the history of ancient India, however, the Buddha Śākyamuni lived, taught and died as a non-Vedic, non-brāhmaṇic and non-theistic "teacher of gods and men" (*satthā devamanussānaṃ*), though regularly criticised, condemned and insulted by the most noted teachers and texts of the Vedic-Brāhmaṇic tradition.

In the opinion of the most distinguished modern historian of India, Dr. R. C. Majumdār, the admission of the Buddha as an Avatāra of God by the orthodox tradition was a "well-conceived and bold stroke of policy which cut the ground from under the feet of Buddhism, which was already steadily losing ground, and the ultimate result was the complete effacement of Buddhism from India as a separate sect."[18] It seems to us that it was with a view to destroying the very ground of Buddhism, to overpowering the very crown of Buddhism, the Buddha, that Brāhmaṇical priestly authors of the post-Gupta age went so far as to accept the same Śākyamuni who had been despised as a *vasalaka*, a *muṇḍaka*, a *śramaṇaka*, a *nāstika* and a *śūdra* by the brāhmaṇas of the pre-Christian era.

Two most fundamental elements of pre-Buddhistic Vedic Brāhmaṇism are the doctrine of sacrifice (*yajña*) and the doctrine of four castes (*varṇas*). Dr. Kane ignores the fact that both are criticised and rejected by the Buddha. By rejecting the sanctity and authority of the Vedas, the Buddha rejected all that was in pre-Buddhist Vedic culture. The anti-Vedic and anti-sacrificial ascetic thought of the old Upaniṣads does not belong to Vedic Brāhmaṇism or the Indo-Aryans because it cannot be traced to the early and middle Vedic culture.

Buddhism and the non-Brāhmaṇic thought of the Upaniṣads belong to a non-Āryan and pre-Vedic Indian cultural tradition. The Buddha referred to the Vedas and Vedic sages with honour not because he accepted their teachings but because he found some items of value in the faith of even those who did not follow and who opposed his doctrine. He was neither a brāhmin by caste nor a teacher of Brāhmaṇism. He was never recognised as a teacher or seer or reformer in Brāhmaṇism prior to the age of the Purāṇas. The Mahābhārata, for example, was compiled during the period when Buddhism flourished most in India, during circa 400 BCE to

18. *The Cultural Heritage of India*, 2nd ed., Vol. IV, Calcutta, 1956, p. 48.

CE 400 and though it is full of Buddhist influence, yet its authors carefully avoided the name of the Buddha even from its list of Avatāras.[19] The present form of the Mahābhārata, with its ethics and philosophy, would have been impossible without Buddhism. Its silence about the Buddha only speaks of the deliberate attempt to disguise the originality of Buddhist tenets and to mythologize the non-Vedic influences. The Rāmāyaṇa (II.109,34) recalls the followers of the Tathāgata only for their atheism and quietly incorporates the fundamentals of Buddhist ethics in its better parts. The entire corpus of Brāhmaṇical literature before the rule of the Gupta Kings (CE 400–500) is clearly against the theory of Drs. Rādhakrishnan and Kane.

The partial similarity between the Buddha's teachings and the teachings of the older Upaniṣads cannot by itself prove the assumption that these so-called Vedic texts are older than the Buddha. The hypothesis that Buddhism was influenced by the Upaniṣads rests entirely on the belief that the oldest Upaniṣads must be pre-Buddhist in date. In fact neither of these assumptions can be supported by clear evidence. The only evidence is the traditional view that Vedic literature is older than Pāli literature. But Vedic literature includes some texts which were composed long after the age of the Buddha, and so-called Vedic texts continued to be composed down to the beginning of the Christian era. The chronology of the oldest Vedic texts has to be revised in the light of the date of the Indus Valley Civilisation. However, the assumption that the older Upaniṣads are earlier in date than the Buddha has been one of the fundamental arguments of the upholders of the theory of a Vedic origin of Buddhism. Let us, therefore, turn our attention to the chronological position of the oldest Upaniṣads.

19. In the Bhagavadgīta, which forms part of the Mahābhārata, it is the Buddhist teaching of the wickedness of warfare which is implicitly opposed. Though Buddhism is not mentioned, Arjuna's initial objections to war are couched in typically Buddhist terms. The doctrine of the "imperishable ātman" is used to combat his scruples—Editor.

IV. Date of the Oldest Upaniṣads

There are more than 110 texts called Upaniṣads. Some of these Upaniṣads, e.g., the Allah Upaniṣads, were written in the reign of the Mughal King Akbar in the 16th century CE and some even later. About a dozen Upaniṣads seem to have been in existence in the 9th century CE when Śaṃkara (CE 788) wrote comments on some of them. Sāntirakṣita (CE 800) has critcised the *Ātman* doctrine of the Upaniṣads. The Bhagavadgītā (CE 200) calls itself an Upaniṣad and contains Upaniṣadic passages from about eight of the oldest Upaniṣads.

It is likely that about one dozen Upaniṣad texts were in existence about the beginning of the Christian era. A. B. Keith has divided the fourteen so-called older Upaniṣads into three groups in the following chronological order:

1. *First group*, oldest Upaniṣads: 1. Aitareya 2. Bṛhadāraṇyaka 3. Chāndogya 4. Taittirīya 5. Kauṣītaki 6. Kena.
2. *Second group*: 7. Kaṇha 8. Iṣa 9. Śvetāśvatara 10. Muṇḍaka 11. Mahānārayaṇa.
3. *Third group*: 12. Praśna 13. Maitrāyaṇīya and 14. Māṇḍūkya.

With regard to the date of the Upaniṣads of the first and oldest group, Keith observes that, "it is wholly impossible to make out any case for dating the oldest even of the extant Upaniṣads beyond the sixth century BCE and the acceptance of an earlier date must rest merely on individual fancy."[20]

S. N. Dāsgupta, A. A. Macdonell, Max Müller, Winternitz, Jacobi and a few other scholars usually place the older Upaniṣads in the sixth and fifth centuries BCE. The Kaṭha, Maitrāyaṇīya and Śvetāśvatara Upaniṣads were placed by E. W. Hopkins in the fourth century BCE. Buddhist and Jaina impact on the Muṇḍaka Upaniṣad was demonstrated by J. Hertel. M. Walleser was of the view that the illusion theory of the Upaniṣads was derived from the early Mādhyamika thought and he placed the Māṇḍūkya Upaniṣad in

20. A. B. Keith, *Religion and Philosophy of the Veda and Upaniṣads*, Vols. I–II, HOS, Vols. 31–32, 1925, pp. 498–502.

the sixth century CE.[21] According to Dr. Kane the Bṛhadāraṇyaka and the Chāndogya Upaniṣads are generally held to be "earlier than the Buddha." There is no general agreement on this point. The view entertained by Walleser, Rāhula Sāmkṛtyāyana and others that the Tevijjā Sutta of the *Dīgha Nikāya* refers to the Aitareya, Chāndogya and Taittirīya Upaniṣads is quite wrong. As Keith said, "the definite use of any particular Upaniṣad by any Buddhist sutta has still to be proved." Dr. O. H. de A. Wijesekera has observed that "the older Suttas of the *Dīgha Nikāya* were composed before the end of the Brāhmaṇa period when the Upaniṣads had not come to be regarded as independent texts."[22]

The Brāhmaṇa period of the Vedic age came to an end towards the third century BCE. This is true especially of the Śatapatha Brāhmaṇa of which Bṛhadāraṇyaka Upaniṣad forms the concluding part. According to Pāṇini and Kātyāyana, the Brāhmaṇa texts of the Vājasaneyins or Yājñavalkyas were contemporary with them.[23] Pāṇini has been placed in the 5th century BCE by some and in the 4th century BCE by others. Kātyāyana should belong to the fourth or even to the third century BCE.

The only argument for placing the oldest Upaniṣads in the 6th century BCE. is the archaic character of their language. But their language can be compared only with the Mahābhārata and Rāmāyaṇa, which are very late composite compilations, or with the language of Pāṇini and the Bṛhad-devatā which have been placed in the fourth and third centuries BCE. There is thus no sound linguistic evidence to consider the Bṛhadāraṇyaka and Chāndogya Upaniṣads as pre-Buddhist in origin. The Tevijjā Sutta does not know the way of the Upaniṣads. But it refers to the Brāhmaṇa-caraṇas such as those of Adhvaryu, Taittirīya, Chāndogya, and Bahuvṛca Brāhmaṇas.[24] T. W. Rhys Davids and George Buhler were of the view that the oldest Pāli Suttas are "good evidence,

---

21. Ibid., pp. 501–503; S. N. Dasgupta, *History of Indian Philosophy*, Vol. I, London, 1957 (reprint), p. 28; A. A. Macdonell, *History of Sanskrit Literature* (1899, reprint 1962, Delhi), pp. 171 f.
22. O. H. de A. Wijesekera, "A Pāli Reference to *Brāhmaṇacaraṇas*," *Adyar Library Bulletin*, Vol. XX, 1956, pp. 254 f.
23. Max Müller, *History of Ancient Sanskrit Literature* (1960), p. 363.
24. DN 13.10/Dīgha Nikāya, Vol. I 237.

certainly for the fifth, probably for the sixth century BCE."[25] In our opinion, the bulk of the oldest Upaniṣads including the Bṝhadāraṇyaka and the Chāndogya should be placed between the age of the Buddha and that of Aśoka. None of the Upaniṣads can be dated before the age of the Buddha (624–544 BCE).

There is strong evidence of Buddhist influence in the language as well as in the doctrines of the oldest Upaniṣads. Doctrines characteristic of early Buddhism, which are quite foreign to pre-Upaniṣadic Vedicism, are found in the Upaniṣads. This point needs emphasis because it at once establishes the *heterogeneous character and hybrid origin* of these texts and their doctrines. It will be absurd to hold that any of these Upaniṣads was composed at one time or by one person. They are compilations and represent many contradictory doctrines. R. E. Hume has discussed some Buddhist impact on the older Upaniṣads in the following words: "Evidence of Buddhist influences are not wanting in them."[26] In Bṝh 3.2.13 it is stated that after death the different parts of a person return to the different parts of Nature from whence they came, that even his soul (*ātman*) goes into space and that only his karma, or effect of work, remains over. This is a clear reflection of the Buddhist doctrine.

Connections in the point of dialect may also be shown. *Sarvāvat* is "a word which as yet has not been discovered in the whole range of Sanskṝit literature, except in Śatapatha Brāhmaṇa 14.7.1.10 (= Bṝh 43.9) and in Northern Buddhist writings" (Kern, SBE, 21, p. xvii). Its Pāli equivalent is *sabbavā*. In Bṝh 4.3 to 2.6 *r* is changed to *l*, i.e., *paly-ayate* for *pary-ayate*—a change which is regularly made in the Pāli dialect in which the books of Southern Buddhism are written. It may be that this is not direct influence of the Pāli upon the Sanskṝit, but at least it is the same tendency which exhibits itself in Pāli, and here the two languages are close enough together to warrant the assumption of contact and synchronous origin.

Somewhat surer evidence, however, is the use of the second person plural ending *tha* for *tā*. Müller pointed out in connection

25. T.W. Rhys Davids, *Dialogues of the Buddha*, Part I (SBB Vol. II, reprint 1950), p. xx.

26. R. E. Hume, *The Thirteen Principal Upaniṣads*, 2nd edition, OUP, 1958 (reprint), pp. 6–7.

with the word *ācaratha* (Muṇḍ 1.2.1) that this irregularity looks suspiciously Buddhistic. There are, however, four other similar instances. The word *saṃvatsyatha* (Praśna 1.2) might be explained as a future indicative (not an imperative), serving as a mild future imperative. But *pṛcchatha* (Praśna 1.2), *āpadyatha* (Praśna 1.2.3) *jānatha* and *vimuñcatha* (Muṇḍ 2.2.5) are evidently meant as imperatives, and as such are formed with the Pāli instead of with the regular Sanskrit ending. It has long been suspected that the later Śiva sects, which recognised the Atharva-Veda as their chief scripture, were closely connected with the Buddhistic sects. Perhaps in this way the Buddhistic influence was transmitted to the Praśna and Muṇḍaka Upaniṣads of the Atharva-Veda. This alone shows that the Upaniṣads are not unaffected by outside influences. Even irrespective of these, their inner structure reveals that they are heterogeneous in their material and compound in their composition. Keith's criticism of Hume's view is not convincing. Some names of Vedic persons mentioned in the Āraṇyakas, Sūtras and Upaniṣads are known to the Pāli Suttas, where they are mentioned as contemporaries of the Buddha.

The Sāṃkhyāyana or Kauṣītaki Āraṇyaka mentions Guṇākhya Sāṃkhyāyana as a pupil of Kahola Kauṣītaki.[27] This Sāṃkhyāyana was a contemporary of Āśvalāyana as is clear from the fact that Āśvalāyana honours Kabola as a guru.[28] This Āśvalāyana is called Kauśalya in the Praśna Upaniṣad—that is a resident of Kosala. As Rāychaudhuri has pointed out, this Āśvalāyana Kauśalya is identical with Assalāyana of Sāvatthī mentioned as a great Vedic teacher of Kosala in the Assalāyana Sutta. He was a contemporary of the Buddha and also of Kabandhi Kātyāyana.[29] It is possible that this Kabandhi Kātyāyana was identical with Kakudha Kaccāyana or Pakudha Kaccāyana mentioned as a noted teacher and contemporary of the Buddha in the Sāmaññaphala Sutta (DN 2). Two famous brāhmaṇas of the later Vedic age, Pauṣkarasādi and Lauhitya, mentioned in the Sāṃkhyāyana Āraṇyaka, are also mentioned as contemporaries of the Buddha in the Ambaṭṭha and

---

27. Sāṃkhyāyana (Kauṣitaki) Āraṇyaka, *Adhyāya* 15; cf. H. C. Raychaudhuri, *Political History of Ancient India*, 6th ed. (1953), p. 33.
28. Āsvalāyāna Gṛhyasūtra II. 4.4.
29. Praṣṇa Upaniṣad, I; Assalāyana Sutta, MN 93/M II 147ff.

Lohicca Suttas (DN 3 and 12).[30] This evidence thus clearly places the older Pāli suttas in the sixth century BCE. Thus the Āraṇyaka and the Sūtras associated with Sāṃkhyāyana and Āśvalāyana cannot be placed before the age of the Buddha.

The Upaniṣads are posterior to the Āraṇyaka texts. Pāṇini, the author of the *Aṣṭādhyāyī*, who cannot be placed before BCE 500–400 BCE, does not know the Vedic texts called *Āraṇyakas*; but Kātyāyana (400–300 BCE) knows the use of the word *āraṇyaka* both as a "forest dweller" and as a "forest treatise." This means that the Āraṇyakas cannot be earlier than the Aṣṭādhyāyī. It is well known that Yājñavalkya was a contemporary of Kahola, the teacher of Guṇākhya Sāṃkhyāyana. As already noted, Pāṇini does not recognise Yājñavalkya's works among the older (*purāṇaprokta*) Brāhmaṇas.[31] Śvetaketu, the famous person in the Bṛhadāraṇyaka (VI.2.1f.) and Chāndogya (VI.1f.) Upaniṣads, is mentioned in the *Āpastamba-Dharmasūtra* as an *avara* or modern scholar.[32] Śvetaketu was a contemporary of Kahola, and therefore a contemporary of Guṇākhya Sāṃkhyāyana and Āśvalāyana of Sāvatthī.

The royal philosopher, Ajātaśatru, mentioned in the Kauṣītaki (IV.1) and Bṛhadāraṇyaka (II.I.1) Upaniṣads, was evidently King Ajātasattu of Magadha, a contemporary of the Buddha. In the Upaniṣads he is called a king of Kāsi (Vārāṇasī) and a contemporary of Drīptabālāki Gārgya, Janaka Videha and other noted Upaniṣadic personages. In the time of the Buddha, Kāsi was under the control of Bimbisāra and his son Ajātasattu; the small territory of Kāsi had come to the Magadhan monarch as a dowry and Ajātaśatru inherited his father's kingdom. There is no reason to think that the Upaniṣadic Ajātaśatru of Kāsi was different from the Magadhan Ajātaśatru known to Buddhist and Jaina literature. It would be absurd to think that the Upaniṣads have preserved the names of noted brahmins and kṣatriyas in a chronological order. These texts are composite in character and contain the names of

30. For Vedic references to these teachers see *Vedic Index* by Keith and Macdonell, Vol. II (Delhi, reprint 1967), pp. 27, 235.

31. Pāniṇi, *Aṣṭādhyāyī* IV, 3. 105; cf. Goldstucker, *Pāṇini, His Place in Sanskrit Sanskrit Literature*, (1914), p. 106.

32. Āpastamba Dharmasūtra, I, 2. 5, 4–6; see also H. C. Rāychaudhuri, op. cit., pp. 34–35.

persons who flourished before the Buddha (e.g., Janaka), in the age of the Buddha, and perhaps also of persons who flourished in the fifth and fourth centuries BCE.

The dialogues in the Upaniṣads were recorded long after the age of persons figuring in these dialogues and hence the mixing of names of persons of early and late ages. Kings of Videha lineage ruled over Kāsi as is clear from the Saṃbula and Mātuposaka Jātakas. Brahmadatta was the generic or family name of the rulers of Kāsi (Vārāṇasī) (*Jātaka*, Nos. 519, 455, 421). King Ajātaśatru, a contemporary of the Buddha, is called Vedehaputta as well as a Kāsva (of Kāsi); this is because his mother came from Videha and his stepmother came from Kāsi. He is claimed by the Upaniṣads as an Upaniṣadic teacher, by the Jaina Sūtras as a follower of Jainism and by the Buddhist sources as a devout follower of the Buddha.

A person called Bhadrasena Ajātasatrava, who was a contemporary of Uddālaka Āruṇī, is referred to in the Śatapatha Brāhmaṇa.[33] Raychaudhuri thinks that he may have been a successor of Ajātaśatru. It is possible that Bhadrasena was an epithet of the latter. We know that Uddālaka was a contemporary of Pravāhaṇa Jaivali and father of Śvetaketu. The Upaniṣads contain names of such persons who were contemporaries of the Buddha, even of followers of the Buddha, like Ajātaṣatru, Āśvalāyana, Lauhitya and Pauṣkarasādi (and his pupil Ambaṭṭha). There is therefore no reason to think that the Chāndogya and Bṛhadāraṇyaka Upaniṣads are later than these two. The very name of the Muṇḍaka Upaniṣad, "the Upaniṣad of the shaven-headed ones," suggests its post-Pāli origin. *Muṇḍaka*, *samaṇaka* and *vasalaka*—these were the words of abuse which were used as such for the Great Ascetic (*mahā śramaṇa*) Buddha by the brāhmaṇas (Vasala Sutta, Sn I.7). Moreover, this Upaniṣad approves the monastic way and is most vociferous in criticising Vedic ritualism; it thus indicates the Buddhist influence in Brāhmaṇical circles.

The Kaṭha Upaniṣad criticises the Buddhist doctrine of the plurality of elements (*dharmas*). It says, "Just as the water fallen over rocks is scattered and lost among the hills, likewise, *he who holds the existence of separate dharmas* is lost after them" (*Kaṭha Upaniṣad*, IV. 14). The term "*dharma*" in the phrase *pṛthag-dharmān*

33. Śatapatha Brāhmaṇa, v. 5.5.14; SBE, Vol. XLI, p. 141.

does not mean "quality" as Hume has translated. The theory of dharmas, or elements of mind and matter, was a Buddhist theory taught by the Buddha. The fact that the Kaṭha Upaniṣad is aware of it and criticises its expounders proves that this old Upaniṣad cannot be earlier than the fifth century BCE.

The word *śramaṇa* occurs for the first time in the Bṛhadāraṇyaka Upaniṣad and it never became a word of respect in Brāhmaṇical literature. Apart from the evidence discussed by Hume, the occurrence of this word shows that this Upaniṣad knows Buddhist and Jaina śramaṇas.

The older Upaniṣads thus should be placed in between 500 and 300 BCE. The approval of asceticism (*yoga* and *dhyāna*) and criticism of sacrificial ritualism characteristic of the older "Upaniṣadic period" therefore means the period between the Buddha and Asoka.

The argument of Dr. Kane that the Upaniṣads do not refer to the Buddha's teachings is thus wrong. If the absence of any reference to the Pāli Piṭakas in the older Upaniṣads were to prove that the Upaniṣads are earlier than the Piṭakas, then the absence of any reference to the Upaniṣads in the Pāli Piṭakas should prove that they are earlier than the Upaniṣads. This argument of Dr. Kane thus does not help his thesis. He is not correct when he says that no meetings are recorded in the Pāli Suttas in which hostility between brāhmaṇas and śramaṇas or the Buddha and his pupils is reflected.

There are many reports in the Pāli Suttas which demonstrate the hostile attitude of the brāhmaṇas of Vedic tradition towards the Buddha, his pupils and his doctrines. Thus the Vasala Sutta of the Suttanipāta records how brāhmaṇas disliked and abused the Buddha (Sn I.7). The Piṇḍa Sutta of the Saṃyutta Nikāya records that the Buddha was not given even a meal in a village of the brāhmaṇas (SN 4:18). A noted brāhmaṇa named Soṇadaṇḍa, we are told in the Dīgha Nikāya (DN 4), hesitated to pay homage to the Buddha in the presence of other brāhmaṇas lest his community would excommunicate him. The demeanour of Kasibhāradvāja, as reported in the Kasibhāradvāja Sutta (Sn I.4), can hardly be called courteous. The heretics who, according to the commentary on the Dhammapada, killed the Arahat Moggallāna were probably Vedic brāhmaṇas.[34] In many Suttas the Buddha

34. *Dhammapada-Aṭṭhakatha*, II, 65; cf. Malalasekera, DPPN, Vol. II, p. 546.

says that some brāhmaṇas and śramaṇas misrepresented his teachings and gave publicity to ill-conceived theories wrongly attributed to the Buddha.

Dr. Kane's view that the Buddha and his early pupils did not attack the central Upaniṣad conception of the immanence of Brahmā is ill conceived. As a matter of fact, this conception of a neuter Brahman or absolute Ātman of the Upaniṣads had not come into vogue in the time of the Buddha. No Pāli Sutta refers to the theory of Upaniṣadic Brahman as the ultimate reality and the question of its criticism does not arise at all. As pointed out above, this Upaniṣadic idea of an absolute Brahman had not come to overwhelm the central Vedic ideas of god Brahmā or Prajāpati. And the ideas of supremacy of god Brahmā over the creatures and of the desirability of trying to obtain his supposed heaven by performing Vedic rituals are repeatedly ridiculed by the Buddha. The greatest Vedic gods, Indra and Brahmā Prajāpati, appear as humble disciples of the Buddha in many Pāli Texts (SN 6:1; DN 21).

The fact that the Buddha praises an ideal *brāhmaṇa*, in many of his discourses,[35] and uses the words *brahmacariya*, *brahmakāya* and *brahmadhūta* in some of his discourses should not mislead us. The word *brahma* was not a monopoly of the Vedic brāhmaṇas; it was a word of common usage among the people in the age of the Buddha. In the Brāhmaṇa Vagga of the Dhammapada, the word *brāhmaṇa* does not mean a Vedic priestly brāhmaṇa. In Buddhism the concept of a true brāhmaṇa means the concept of an Arahat or a Buddha. The word *brāhmaṇa* is a synonym of *muni* or śramaṇa. *Brahmacariya* means *dhammacariya*. In the Pāli Texts *brahmacariya* means what Śāntideva calls *bodhicaryā* in his *Bodhicaryāvatāra*. Since Brahma, Bodhi, Dhamma and Buddha are here used as synonymous words, *brahmakāya* means *dhammakāya*, i.e., the Absolute Element (*dhammadhātu*) or *nirvāṇa-dharma*. *Nirvāṇa* is the peace that passes understanding. The word *brahmabhūta* means *nibbuta* or *sitibhūta*, an epithet of the Tathāgata.

The venerable antiquity of the older Upaniṣads is thus a matter of mere traditional belief. Scholars heretofore have been persuaded to believe that the Buddha's teachings are partly presupposed by the older Upaniṣads. Our contention, however, is

35. E.g., Dhammapada, Brahmaṇa Vagga.

that the Upaniṣads have been greatly influenced by the Buddha's teachings. The Buddha's date (624–544 BCE) is certain; the date of the Upaniṣads, on the other hand, is a matter of traditional bias.

V. Early Brāhmaṇical Ideals Contrasted with Early Buddhist Ideals

Dr. P. V. Kane says that "the moral qualities which he (Buddha) urged men to cultivate belonged to antiquity." By "antiquity" he means the pre-Buddhist Vedic age. Dr. Rādhakrishnan has also referred to the Buddha's teachings as a restatement of "the ancient ideals of the Indo-Aryan civilization." Let us therefore briefly discuss the ancient ideals of the Indo-Āryans and examine the "moral qualities" of old Vedic religion.

The doctrine of Karma and rebirth, the practice of meditation and Yoga for seeking the final goal, and the idea of the futility of rituals and sacrifices, which begin to appear in old Brāhmaṇism or Vedic religion in the age of the early Upaniṣads were not the creations of the Indo-Āryans. These doctrines and practices do not represent a linear or inner evolution of the old Indo-Āryan ideology.[36] The Upaniṣads are a continuation of the older Vedic tradition of the Brāhmaṇa texts, but for the most part, their spirit is decidedly antagonistic to the doctrinal tradition of the Vedas and the Brāhmaṇas.[37] Though the Upaniṣadic thought has been preserved in these texts of Brāhmaṇical tradition and all followers of Brāhmaṇism and Hinduism are rightly proud of it, yet the fact remains that it had no roots in the philosophy of the pre-Buddhist Brāhmaṇical texts.

Buddhism is especially famous for its stern ethics and high moral ideals. The moral and spiritual ideals and ideas of *Ahiṃsā, Mokṣa*, Karma and Rebirth were entirely unknown to pre-Upaniṣadic Vedic religion or Indo-Āryan civilisation.

According to A. B. Keith, the Brāhmaṇas do not know the doctrine of transmigration, "have no conception of pessimism,

36. G. C. Pande, op. cit., p. 285.

37. Cf. R. D. Ranade, *Constructive Survey of Upaniṣadic Philosophy* (1926), p. 6.

and therefore seek no release from the toils of life."[38] The ethical content of the Upaniṣads, he says, is "negligible and valueless."[39] It is a mis-search (*vippallāsa*) to try to find out anything of morality in Vedic religion. "The failure to rise to the conception even of a system of ethics," observed Keith, "is a sign ... of the lack of ethical sense. On the part of the brāhmans ... in truth, the aims of the brāhmans were bent on things which are not ethical at all."[40]

In the opinion of Sylvain Levi, "It is difficult to imagine anything more brutal and more material than the theology of the Brāhmaṇas.... Morality finds no place in this system."[41]

The divine stories of "Indra overcome with drink," says W. Crooke, "and committing adultery with Asura women, of the incest of Prajāpati, are in contradiction with the ethical elements of faith."[42] "The Brāhmaṇa texts," says H. Jacobi, "are almost entirely concerned with sacrifice."[43]

The *Purohita* or priest, and not the liberated saint, points out Bloomfield, was supreme in Vedicism, and his supremacy rested merely on his skill in magic.[44] According to E.W. Hopkins, "the priest performs the sacrifice for the fee alone, and it must consist of valuable garment, kine, horses or gold ... gold is coveted most, for 'this is immortality, the seed of Agni,' and therefore, peculiarly agreeable to the pious priest."[45]

The greatest principle of Vedic thinkers was the principle of sacrifice (*yajña*); sacrifice was the hallmark of ancient Indo-Āryan civilisation. The origin and end of this culture of the Indo-Āryans lay in the idea of *yajña*. Though much violence and cruelty to living beings were involved in the multifarious sacrifices of the Indo-Āryans, yet it was the chief end and means in the

---

38. A. B. Keith, *Religion and Philosophy of the Veda and Upaniṣads*, pp. 441–42.
39. Ibid., pp. 585–86.
40. Ibid., pp. 585–86.
41. Sylvain Levi, *Doctrine du sacrifice chez les Brahmanas*, Paris, 1898, p. 9. Quoted by T. W. Rhys Davids, *Buddhist India*, p. 108.
42. W. Crooke, "*Hinduism,*" in ERE, Vol. VI, p. 648; A. Lang, *Myth, Ritual and Religion*, Vol. I, London, 1891 p. 9.
43. H. Jacobi, *Brahmaṇism*, in ERE. Vol. II, p. 800.
44. Bloomfield, in *Sacred Books of the East*, Vol. XLIII, introduction.
45. E. W. Hopkins, *Religions of India* (1902), p.192.

Brāhmaṇical philosophy of pre-Buddhist India. To quote Dr. G. C. Pande, "The chiefest idea which the priests repeatedly stress is the majesty of sacrifice. Sacrifice is indeed identified with Viṣṇu, and with Prajāpati? and through its help the sacrificer was assured not only a celestial after-life, but safety, longevity, progeny, prosperity and fame in this life."[46]

The doctrine of sacrifice, the heart and soul of Vedic culture,[47] was the one and sufficient element or "ideal" which at once distinguished Brāhmaṇism from Buddhism. In the latter system it is attacked because it did not help liberation, prolonged saṃsāra, and involved violence to living creatures.[48] Yet this gospel of violence was sought to be justified as late as the time of Manusmṛti (CE 200). According to this sacred text of old Brāhmaṇism, "since the Dharma has originated from the Vedas, that violence, which is prescribed in the Veda in this living and non-living world, is indeed non-violence" (V. 44).

The moral doctrine of *ahiṃsā* (non-violence or inoffensiveness) is unknown to the old Vedic texts. The idea of *ahiṃsā* in Vedicism occurs first in the Chāndogya Upaniṣad as a thing to be given to the priest (or teacher) in the form of "gift" (*dakṣiṇa*).[49] The text, however, declares that *ahiṃsa* towards all beings should be observed "at places other than the sacred spots" (*anyatra-tīrthebhyaḥ*). The *tīrthas* or "sacred spots" of Indo-Āryan ("Hindu"?) people of Vedic age were the places where the slaughter of living beings at sacrifice was prescribed.[50] Deliberate killing of living beings was thus an integral part of "the Hindu religion" and "the Hindu inheritance" of the Upaniṣadic period. In other words, the doctrine of non-violence, which is based on the idea of the sanctity of all forms of life and implies a positive notion of kindness (*karuṇā*) towards all living beings, was in direct contradiction with the central philosophy of the Vedic Āryans.

46. G. C. Pande, op. cit., and footnotes 141, 149.

47. Vide Śatapatha Brāhmaṇa, XI.1.8.2–4; Pañcaviṃsa Brāhmaṇa, VII. 2. 1; cf. Keith, op. cit., pp. 454–455.

48. Vide e.g., DN 5, Kuṭadanta-Sutta, where an ideal sacrifice is also alluded to.

49. Chāndogya Upaniṣad, III. 17.4 f; cf. ERE, Vol. I. "Ahiṃsa" p. 230.

50. Chāndogya Upaniṣad, VIII. 15; cf. Hume, op. cit., p. 274, note 1.

The ideal of final liberation (*mokṣa, nirvāṇa*) was quite unknown to the priests or "seers" (of the gods and demigods) of the Vedas. Vedic "seers" endeavoured for the attainment of heaven, "a glorified world of material joys as pictured by the imagination not of warriors, but of priests."[51] The way to this heaven was the sacrificial ritualism, *yajña*.

The idea of transmigration appears only in the latest of Vedic texts which, as we have seen above, cannot be older than 5th century BCE.[52] The doctrine of karma and transmigration is clearly said to be of non-Vedic and non-Āryan origin. Thus the legend of the dialogue between the tempter or death (*Mṛtyu, Māra, Yama*) and Naciketas shows that Naciketas learnt the ideas of moral karman, yoga and transmigration from some non-Āryan sage who is here mystified and mythologised as Mṛtyu or Yama.[53] The later texts, e.g., the Mahābhārata and the Purāṇas, likewise mythologised the historical and human teachers of non-Vedic tradition, the founders of the Sāṃkhya (*Kapilamuni*) and Buddhism (*Śākyamuni*) who had taught the doctrines of karma, rebirth, immortality and freedom.

The ideal of renunciation or the homeless holy life was not known to Vedic culture. The legend of Yājñavalkya's decision to abandon his wives to seek the welfare of his own soul and go to the forest is perhaps based on the example of Siddhārtha Gautama, who left his wife and royal household. Not a single characteristic teaching of the Buddha can be traced to any pre-Buddhist Vedic or Brāhmaṇical text. The early Indo-Āryan or old Brāhmaṇical ideals were diametrically opposed to the early Buddhist ideals.

To say that the Buddha's teachings were based on the ancient ideals of Indo-Āryans is an example of *suggestio falsi suppressio veri*;

---

51. A. A. Macdonell, *Vedic Mythology*, Varanasi (reprint), 1963, p. 168.

52. Śatapatha Brāhmaṇa, I. 5.3; this text contains materials of as late a date as the third century BCE according to H. Kern. The Bṛhadāraṇyaka, the Chāndogya and the Kaṭha Upaniṣads, which know this doctrine, cannot be dated before the older Pāli suttas for reasons discussed above.

53. Kaṭha Upaniṣad relates the legend of Naciketas' visit to the realm of Death. The origin of this legend is to be seen in the *Taittreya Brāhmaṇa*, III. 11. 8. 1–6, a text generally dated in the sixth century BCE, but may be placed even later.

for this amounts to condemning the Buddha to the category of those primitive Vedic priests who were neither ascetic in outlook nor monks in practise, who neither knew the moral doctrines of karma and rebirth nor sought Nirvāṇa as a release from saṃsāra. The historic founder of Buddhism was a *muni*, a *yati*, a *śramaṇa*, a *bhikṣu*, whereas the founders of old Indo-Āryan culture were warlike chiefs and householder priests. The Indo-Āryan leaders and teachers fought battles, propitiated gods through rituals and spells, and craved for the riches and joys of the world whereas the teachers and leaders of Buddhism practised compassion and non-violence, renounced the world with all its joys and sought transcendental peace. The greatest teacher of old Vedic or ancient Indo-Āryan civilisation, Yājñavalkya, had two wives, and though he parted with his wives, he still continued the acquisition of wealth and fees.[54]

The true Indo-Āryan ideal, that of a prosperous worldly life with continued progeny, is expressed in the following lines of the Aitareya Brāhmaṇa:

Kin nu malaṃ kiṃ ajinaṃ kimu śmasrūṇi kiṃ tapaḥ
Putraṃ brāhmaṇa icchadhvaṃ sa vai loko vadāvadaḥ

That is to say, "What is the use of wearing dirty (*kāsāva*) garments, what use of antelope's hide, what use of (growing) a beard, what use of austerity? Desire a son, O brāhmaṇa; that is the only praise-worthy thing in the world."[55] It is erroneous to trace here the theory of the fourth stage (*āśrama*) of life known to post-Vedic texts. Even the Chāndogya Upaniṣad (II.23.1), for the first time, refers only to three classes of duties (*trayo dharmaskandhāḥ*) and it does not know the fourth stage of life and its duties. The theory of four *āśramas* (stages) of life is decidedly posterior to Buddhism.[56] In the earliest *Dharmasūtras*, those of Gautama and Baudhāyana, which cannot be earlier than the third century BCE, though the theory of four *āśramas* (*brahmacarya*, *gṛhastha*, *vanaprastha*, and

54. Bṛhadāraṇyaka Upaniṣad, IV.1.2 and IV. 5.2.

55. Aitareya Brāhmaṇa, VII. 13.7; Sāṃkhyāna Śrauta Sūtra XV. 17; Bloomfield, *A Vedic Concordance*, HOS, X, Delhi, p. 327;

56. See the detailed discussion on this point in G. C. Pande, op. cit., pp. 323, 326.

parivrājaka or *sanyāsī*) is expounded, the idea of ascetic life, the stage of a mendicant, is not approved. It is clearly stated in these texts that there is really only one stage (*eka-āśramyaṃ*), the stage of a householder (*gṝhastha*) which is prescribed.

Baudhāyana's view on this point deserves special notice. He says that all the other three stages are an obstruction to progeny; the stage of a householder, which is conducive to procreation and continued progeny, is the only prescribed stage. He says that there was "a demon named Kapila" (*Kapilo nāma asura-āsa*) who introduced the stages other than that of the householder because "he was jealous of the gods" (*devaiḥ spardhamān*). "The wise should not honour his scheme."[57] What does this statement amount to? It amounts to the facts that the institution of *sanyāsī* or *parivrājaka* is of non-Āryan and non-Vedic origin; that early Brāhmaṇism disapproved the ascetic or monastic life and discipline; that the brāhmaṇas, gods on earth (*bhūdevas*), held the life of a householder as the best life and that this ideal was opposed to the monastic ideal of the *śramaṇas*, *yatis* and *munis*—in one word, ascetics. We shall see below who this Kapila Asura, the father of the monastic way of life, was. From Bādarāyaṇa's *Brahmasūtras* (III 4.18) we learnt that Jaimini, the author of the *Mīmānsāsūtras*, held, like Gautama and Baudhāyana, that all the other stages were an obstacle to the stage of the householder, which is the only stage sanctioned in the Vedas.

The way of the *śramaṇas* or *bhikṣus* of the age of the Buddha was clearly opposed to the way of the Vedic and Upaniṣadic brāhmaṇas. Not only Kapila but also the Buddha is described as an Asura in early Brāhmaṇical scriptures. The idea that the supreme bliss consists in the destruction of craving and the renunciation of attachment to worldly affairs is essential for success in Yoga and meditation, and the ideal of obtaining immortality through the extinction of saṃsāra are foreign to the Hindus of Vedic age; the old Indo-Āryan ideals were thoroughly materialistic.

The priests of the Ṛgveda prayed thus: "May we, O Fire, attain immortality through children" (*prajābhir agne amṝtatvamasyām*). This was the highest form of thought reached in the Vedic culture

57. Gautama Dharmasūtra, III. 1 and 35–36; Baudhāyana Dharmasūtra, II, 6. 29–31.

and this passage is repeated in the Taittirīya Saṃhitā and the Baudhāyana Dharmasūtra[58] as scriptural authority against the ascetic and monastic way.

Upaniṣadic brāhmaṇas, who regularly kept wives, produced children and maintained cattle, never failed to admonish their students "not to cut off the line of progeny" (*prajā tantuṃ mā vyavacchetsiṃ*).[58] This was meant to exalt the householder's life and to denounce the homeless life. It was the acknowledged view in Vedic culture that a brāhmaṇa is born involved in debts including a debt to his fathers (*pitṛs*) which he cannot repay except by producing children, especially a son (Taittirīya Saṃhitā, VI.3.10.5). Hence one must marry and beget progeny. There was no awareness of *saṃsāra* or *dukkha,* hence no thought of any transcendental goal nor of any spiritual endeavour in this primitive Āryan way of life. It is perfectly in keeping with the central current of Vedic Brāhmaṇism that the Śatapatha Brāhmaṇa (XII.4.1.1) declares that "Agnihotra is the only session (of duty) which must be continued till old age and death" (*etad vai jarā maryaṃ satraṃ yad-agnihotraṃ*). This is possible only in the life of a householder. That is why the Dharmasūtras of Gautama (III.35), Manu (VI.89–90; III.77–80), Vasiṣtha (VIII.14–17), Viṣṇu (59.29), and Dakṣa (II.57–60) have praised the stage of a householder as the best stage of life.

Even when the brāhmaṇas of Vedic tradition in the Maurya and post-Maurya periods (300 BCE–CE200) began to talk of the stages (*āśrama*) other than that of the householder, they kept the stage of a mendicant (*bhikṣu, parivrājaka*) at the very end of the scheme, the last choice to be made in old age when no moral or spiritual virtues can be observed. The highest spiritual goal of freedom or peace was relegated to the background as if it was the concern of men only in decrepitude and on their death-bed. Indeed, there is evidence to prove that Brāhmaṇical teachers actually held this view. The continued exaltation of the life of a *gṛhastha* to the exclusion of other modes of life is in itself the strongest evidence. From the *Mitākśarā* commentary on the *Yājñavalkyasmṛti* (III.56) we learn that according to the orthodox section of Brāhmaṇical lawgivers the *gṛhastha-āśrama* was the rule of life and other *āśramas* were for

58. Ṛgveda, V. 410; Taittirīya Saṃhitā, I.4 46.1; Baudhāyana Dharmasūtra, II, II.6.29.42–43.

the blind and other incapable persons. Though the author of the *Mītākśara*, Vijñāneśvara (CE 1100), rejects this view as he flourished at a time when the way of the Buddha had transformed the way of the Vedas and the Buddha had been transformed into a form of Viṣṇu of Purāṇic mythology, yet his commentary reflects the old Vedic notion of materialism and hostility to ascetic philosophy.

The historic founder of Buddhism had challenged the two foundations of Vedic culture: the doctrine of sacrifices and the institution of social classes or castes. He observed a way of life and taught a doctrine which were not only unknown to the teachers and authors of Vedic texts but which continued to be resisted by the brāhmaṇas of Vedic tradition for centuries after the age of Śākyamuni. The resistance lessened only with Saṃkara (CE 781–820), who based his Advaita doctrine on Buddhist teaching and took over the monastic organisation from the Buddhist institution of monks. The Purāṇas further sought to bridge the gulf between the two traditions by accepting the Buddha as an Avatāra of Viṣṇu and his moral legacy as the highest Dharma. It would be instructive to refer to a few sayings of the Buddha at this juncture and contrast them with the Vedic viewpoint discussed above.

We read in the Dhammacariya or Kapilasutta (Sn II.6 v. 1) the following: "A life of purity is indeed the supreme life; this is called the excellent gem, if one has left the home for a homeless life." Here *brahmacarya* as against *gṛhastha* is exalted as the best way of life and this could be observed only through leading a monk's life. The Buddha says, in another place (A I 80/AN 2:61), the following: "There are, monks, these two pleasures. What two? That of the home-life, and that of the homeless (ordained) life. Of these two, the pleasure of the homeless life is the pre-eminent." Elsewhere (A I 93), the Teacher contrasts the spiritual quest (*dhamma-pariyesanā*) with the worldly quest (*āmisa-pariyesanā*) and says that of these two, the former is the superior. The same is the message of the Ariyapariyesanā or *Pāsarāsi Sutta* (MN 26). Here the Tathāgata has taught that there are two quests: the "noble quest" and the "ignoble quest." Search after the undecaying and incomparable Peace or Nibbāna is the noble quest. Search after the son (*putta*), wife (*bhariyaṃ*) and other domestic things is the ignoble quest. The Vedic ideal is thus called an ignoble quest. The *Pabbajjā Sutta* (Sn III.1) tells us why Bodhisattva Siddhārtha renounced the home-life, the stage of a *gṛhastha*: "This house life is an oppression, the seat of impurity" and "an ascetic life is like the open sky." So considering, he embraced an ascetic life. We shall reproduce here only two more verses, one each from the Pāli and Sanskrit versions of the celebrated *Khaggavisāṇa Sutta* (Sn I.2), to point out the early Buddhist attitude towards the ideals of a householder's life and that of an ascetic's life. The evils and dangers of the worldly life are summed up thus:

Iti ca gaṇḍo ca upaddavo ca
Rogo ca sallaṃ ca bhayaṃ ca metaṃ,
Etaṃ bhayaṃ kāmaguṇesu disvā
Eko care khaggavisāṇakappo.

"These (pleasures) are to me calamities, boils,
misfortunes, diseases, sharp pains, and dangers;
seeing this danger (originating) in sensual pleasures,
let one wander alone like a rhinoceros." (Sn I.2 v. 17)

Saṅdārayitvā grihivyāñjanāni
Sikhir yathā bhasmāni ekacārī,
Kāsāyavastro abhini.skramitvā
Eko care khaḍgaviṣāṇakalpo.

"Removing the characteristics of a householder,
like lonely (Buddha) Sikhī,
clothed in yellow robe, having left the home,
let one wander alone like a rhinoceros."[59]

Contrary to the Brāhmaṇical ideals of seeking immortality through progeny, the Buddha taught "sons are no help, nor a father, nor relations; there is no help from kinsfolk for one whom death has seized" (Dhp 288). The Vedic brāhmaṇas sacrificed to the gods and muttered hymns in their praise with a view to gaining health, wealth, victory, sons, cattle and so on; the *śramaṇas*, on the other hand, endeavoured through Yoga and meditation to transcend the world and destroy the passions.

In short, the declared ideal of early Buddhism was the attainment of an utterly tranquil (*upasama*), deathless (*amata*) state

59. *Mahāvastu*, ed. by R. G. Basak, Vol. I. Calcutta, 1963; cf. p. 468; *Khaggavisāṇa Sutta*, verse 30.

of peace (*santi*) and supreme bliss (*parama-sukha*). Destruction of impurities (*āsavakkhayā*) such as desire, ignorance, and will-to-be, etc., and the extinction of all attachment to worldly things were the most important aims cherished by the non-Brāhmaṇical and non-Vedic monks of the age of the Buddha.

The pursuit of early Indo-Aryan ideals required just the opposite of these things. The old Vedic world-affirming Dionysian and Olympian philosophy stood in sharp contrast to the early Buddhist philosophy of ultimate peace and transcendental good.

Early Buddhist culture aimed at obtaining the Deathless State (*amata-padaṃ*) by the extinction (*nibbāna*) of the fires (*aggi*) that are craving (*taṇhā*) and attachment (*rāga*). The early Vedic culture aimed at kindling "the fires of male and female" (*puruṣagni* and *yoṣāgni*).[60] We have already referred to some passages in the Aitareya Brāhmaṇa and the Taittirīya Upaniṣad which teach men to desire a son above everything else and never allow the line of progeny to be stopped. There is thus no correspondence or agreement between the basic views of early Brāhmaṇism and early Buddhism. The two religious traditions had different backgrounds in the prehistoric Vedic epoch, and in the age of the Buddha and the older Upaniṣads some thinkers of Brāhmaṇical tradition seem to have been deeply influenced by non-Brāhmaṇical, non-Vedic and non-Āryan thoughts and ideals. The earliest leaders of this hybrid Brāhmaṇical culture were, for the most part, kṣatriyas, the royal philosophers called Rājarṣis, and brāhmaṇas learnt this higher philosophy (*Brahmavidyā*) for the first time from these kṣatriya teachers.

This stage of the development of Brāhmaṇism is reflected in the older Upaniṣads in which kings like Janaka Videha, Aśvapati Kaikeya, Ajātaśatru, Pravāhaṇa Jaivali, etc., figure as the foremost teachers of brāhmaṇas.[61] Although there is a partial similarity between early Buddhism and the teachings of some of the older Upaniṣads, yet the old Brāhmaṇical or Indo-Aryan ideas are quite

60. Chāndogya Upaniṣad. V. 7.1; V. 8.1.

61. See Chāndogya Up. V. 3.7, where King Pravāhaṇa Jaivali says to Gautama that 'this knowledge has never yet come to brāhmiṇs before you; and therefore in all the world has the rule belonged to the Kṣatriya only.' R. E. Hume, op. cit., p. 231.

prominent in the latter texts. The contrast or conflict between Brāhmaṇism and Buddhism pointed out above is to be seen to some extent in the older Upaniṣads which have preserved for us the fundamental discord between the ideals of brāhmaṇas and those of śramaṇas and yatīs. This conflict in these Vedic texts of post-Buddhist date cannot be explained without acknowledging the influence of the Buddha's teachings among the royal authors of the philosophy of the Upaniṣads. Moreover, the Upaniṣads show the influence of certain doctrines which are neither Brāhmaṇical nor Buddhist, doctrines which in later literature are attributed to the Sāṃkhya and the Yoga traditions. Not only the oldest Upaniṣads but also a few Pāli Suttas are perhaps aware of the primitive Sāṃkhya-Yoga. There is no evidence in Vedic literature to prove that Buddhism and the Sāṃkhya-Yoga tradition are of Vedic or Brāhmaṇical origin. It must therefore be admitted that before the age of the Buddha and before the compilation of the earliest Upaniṣads there must have existed in India some *yatīs* and *munīs*, the ascetic and silent or meditative teachers of non-Vedic and non-Aryan cultural tradition who held non-Brāhmaṇical or Śramaṇic ideas and ideals such as are found in Sāṃkhya-Yoga, Jainism and Buddhism.

In historic times, the brāhmaṇas of Vedic tradition had accepted the Sāṃkhya and the Yoga as their own systems of thought so that it has become customary to count these two systems in the "six systems" of Hinduism, but originally both these systems were of non-Vedic and non-brāhmaṇical tradition. Just as at a later stage the brāhmaṇas of Vedic tradition accepted asceticism, some characteristic doctrines of Jainism, Ājīvism and nearly the whole of Buddhism including the Buddha as an Avatāra of Viṣṇu, they had also accepted the dualistic Sāṃkhya system and the technique of ascetic Yoga.

In Patañjalī (CE 200), Yoga is turned into a theistic system and in early mediaeval days the Sāṃkhya also was sought to be interpreted on theistic lines of Śiva (Puruṣa) and Śakti (Prakṛti). But before the compilation of the Mahābhārata and the main classical Purāṇas, the Sāṃkhya, the Yoga, Jainism, Ājīvaka teachings and Buddhism were held by the brāhmaṇas to be anti-Vedic and belonging to demons or non-Āryans. The Brāhmaṇical ideology was held to be of divine origin; the strictly Brāhmaṇical systems seek to trace their origin to the Śruti, the sacred revealed texts, the Vedas. Jainism, Buddhism, Ājīvikism and the Sāṃkhya-Yoga do not recognise the Veda and do not have their roots in the Brāhmaṇical theories of pre-Upaniṣadic and pre-Epic origin.

The Mahābhārata, that growth of centuries, that gigantic mass of heterogeneous cultural lore of ancient India, which started its career towards the third century BCE and stopped the growth of its unwieldy volume towards the end of the fourth century CE, seems to have begun the great Vaiṣṇava processes of assimilation of non-Brāhmaṇical and non-Āryan culture-currents, of a systematic mystification of older historical personalities and of a carefully planned mythology of fancifully conceived sages and satans, gods and demons, of Indo-Āryan war-lords and priestly bards, of Indianised barbaric Āryan races and indigenous pre-Āryan races, of what are called the Dāsas, Dasyus, Niṣādas, Rākṣasas, Nāgas, Daityas and so on.

Although the fusion of Indo-Āryan races from beyond north-western India and the indigenous pre-Āryan races of India must have started in the middle Vedic age so that the older Upaniṣads already bear the fruits of a mixed culture, their racial and cultural differences seem to have persisted for several centuries afterwards. In particular we must mention a few important pieces of evidence which prove the existence of a basic rift or a fundamental gulf between the ideologies of divine and human origins, between the ideologies of the brāhmaṇas of Vedic tradition and the śramaṇas or *munis* of non-Vedic tradition. As noted above, the Baudhāyana Dharmasūtra condemns Kapilamuni (the author of the institution of *sanyāsa*) as an Asura, a "demon." The Vedic brāhmaṇas in the age of the Buddha reviled Śākyamuni as a *vasalaka*, an "outcaste." At many places in the Pāli Suttas the way of the Vedic brāhmaṇas is shown to be in sharp contrast with that of the Śākya śramaṇas.

The Jaina Sūtras also refer to the cleavage between the ways of the brāhmaṇas (*baṃbhaṇṇayesu*) and the śramaṇas or wandering monks (*paribbāyayesu*). Even the Macedonian envoy, Megasthenes (circa 310 BCE), was able to mark the differences between "*sarmanai*" (*śramaṇas*) and "*brāchmanai* (*brāhmaṇas*). Emperor Aśoka (circa 273–233 BCE) repeatedly refers to the brāhmaṇas and śramaṇas in his inscriptions and admonishes them to live in harmony. Patañjali, the grammarian (circa 150 BCE) refers to the brāhmaṇas and the śramaṇas as constant opponents.[62] This conflict was based on the mutually opposed philosophies of the brāhmaṇas and śramaṇic teachers.

VI. Pre-history of Śramaṇism

We have seen above that the older Upaniṣads are not earlier than the Buddha and that the non-Brāhmaṇical ideas and ideals of the Upaniṣads and the Pāli Suttas are not known to the Vedic Āryan culture. What then was the original source of the thoughts of the historic munīs, *yatīs* and śramaṇas? It would be absurd to think that Buddhism and Jainism or the Sāṃkhya and Yoga or the anti-Vedic spiritual thoughts of the older Upaniṣads appeared suddenly in the sixth and fifth centuries BCE. The fashionable theories of "revolt" or "reaction" and "reform" within the Vedic Brāhmaṇism are gratuitous, wholly conjectural and without any evidence. The Upaniṣads themselves prove that non-Vedic, non-brāhmaṇical and non-Āryan influences were at work; the pre-Upaniṣadic Vedic texts prove that there were in prehistoric India non-Āryan and non-Vedic *munīs* and *yatīs* or "ascetics." Finally, the archaeological remains of Mohenjodāro and Harappa prove that there were ascetics or *yatīs* and yogins in India in the second millennium before Christ. There is thus literary as well as archaeological evidence to furnish the prehistoric background of the origins of the Upaniṣads, Buddhism, Jainism and other forms of śramaṇism. It is a well-known fact that the older Upaniṣads are aware of the historic *śramaṇas, yatīs, munīs* and *muṇḍakas*.[63]

62. See Baudhāyana Dharmasūtra, II. 6.29.31; Vasala Sutta, Sn; Brahmajāla Sutta, Ambaṭṭha Sutta, Soṇadaṇḍa Sutta, DN; Kalpa Sutta, I. 9; *Jaina Sūtras*, SBE, XXII, p. 128; AN Vol. I (Nālanda Ed.) p. 155; J. W. McCrindle, *Ancient India as Described by Megasthenes and Arrian*, Calcutta, 1928, p. 97f.; 104f.; Asoka Rock Edict XII; cf. E. Huṭzsch, *Corpus Inscriptionum Indicarum*, Vol. I. (1925, p 20f.); *Mahābhāsya on Pāniṇi*. II. 2. 9. For a detailed modern discussion, see G. C. Pande, op, cit. p. 324f.

63. Bṛhadāraṇyaka Up. III. 4 1; iv, 3.22; iv. 4.25; Taittreya Āraṇyaka, II. 71, IT. 20; Svet. Up. is full of reference to yatīs and ascetics; likewise the Muṇḍaka Up. is a creation of monks. Cf. Tait. Upa. I. 9.1.

Their evidence on śramaṇism, therefore, is of no value for the background of the origins of Buddhism. On the other hand, words such as *bhikṣu, tāpasa, nirvāṇa, pratītyasamutpāda* are known neither to these texts nor to the older Vedic texts. But pre-Upaniṣadic Vedic literature contains some casual references to the *munīs, yatīs, vaikhānasas* and *vṛātyas*. The references show that these sages or tribes with ascetics as their teachers were not of Vedic cultural stock but belonged to non-Āryan or non-Vedic cultures of India. It is most unfortunate that pre-Buddhist literature of the Śramaṇic culture has altogether disappeared. But it is most likely that there must have been some non-Vedic pre-Buddhist literature which is now lost forever. It is quite possible that this literature was destroyed partly through human violence and partly through the ravages of time. We must remember in this connection the story of the gradual disappearance of Pāli, Sanskrit and Prākrit versions of Buddhist scriptures from the land of Buddhism. Let us briefly review the pre-Upaniṣadic Vedic evidence on the culture of the munīs or ascetics in prehistoric India.

The Ṛgveda (X. 163. 2–4) describes a *munī* who practised meditation and led an austere life. He is said to be "long-haired" and probably wore a beard. The *munīs* either lived naked (*vātarasanā*, wind-girt?) or wore tawny-coloured or dirty (*mala*) garments and were experts in techniques of silent ecstasy. Macdonell and Keith say that the Ṛgvedic *munī* was "an ascetic of magic powers with divine afflatus, the precursor of the strange ascetics of later India."

"The *munīs* must have been quite well known in Vedic times but they were probably not respected in Vedic circles. A *munī* was probably not approved by the priests who followed the ritual and whose views were essentially different from the ideals of a *munī*, which were superior to earthly considerations, such as the desire for children and Dakśiṇā." [64]

The Aitareya Brāhmaṇa (VI.33.3) mentions munī Aitasa who was also known for his strange "ecstasy" (or trances). We have seen above that this text (VII.13.7) refers to such ascetics who wore tawny robes, deer skin, wore beards and performed austerities, and these practices are condemned as useless compared to the ideal of

64. A. A. Macdonell and A. B. Keith, *Vedic Index of Names and Subjects*, Vol. II, Delhi, 1958, pp. 167–68.

having a son. At one place the Ṛgveda (VIII.17.14) refers to Indra as the "friend of munīs" (*munīnām*), showing that there were many munīs or ascetics. But the mention of Indra's friendship with these ascetics is rather curious, for, in other texts, Indra is the declared enemy of the *yatīs* or ascetics. The Atharvaveda (VIL 74.a) refers to a "divine munī." The Śatapatha Brāhmaṇas (IX.5.2.15) also mentions a *munī* while the Pañcaviṃsa Brāhmaṇa (XIV.4.7) refers to a place called "ascetic's death" (*munī-maraṇa*) where the Vaikhānasa ascetics were killed, obviously by Brāhmaṇical followers of Indra.

The Vedic literature knows persons called *yatīs*. *Yatī* means an ascetic. Modern scholars think that *yatīs* were a tribe, real or mythical. In Vedic myths they are mythologised and connected with Bhṝigus.[65] Indra is said to have caused the death of the *yatīs*. In the Ṛgveda (VIII.3.9) Indra is hostile to them. In the Taittirīya Saṃhitā (II. 4.9.2; VI.2. 7.5) and in other texts Indra is said to have thrown the *yatīs* to wolves or hyenas (*vyālavṝikebhyaḥ*) [66] The *yatīs* and *munīs* of the Vedic age were non-Vedic ascetics. A third word denoting ascetics in the Vedic age was *vaikhānasa*. That a *vaikhānasa* was called a *muni* is clear from the Pañcaviṃsa Brāhmaṇa (XIV.4.7), which refers to the slaughter of these ascetics. The Taittirīya Āraṇyaka (I.23.3; IV.9.29) knows the Vaikhānasas and mentions a Vaikhānasa sage called Puruhanman.

A very late Brāhmaṇical commentator of *Gautama Dharmasūtra* (on III.2), Haradatta by name, states that Vaikhānasa and Bhikṣu refer to the third and fourth stages (*āśramas*) respectively. The term *bhikṣu*, "mendicant monk," a characteristic Buddhist term, is, however, "not found in the Vedic literature." Likewise the term *āśrama*, "resting place" or a stage of life, "does not occur in any Upaniṣad which can be regarded as pre-Buddhistic." The word *śramaṇa*, "mendicant monk," "is first found in the Upaniṣads."[67] The Buddha was known as a *mahāśramaṇa* before the Upaniṣads were compiled.

---

65. Ibid., Vol. II, p. 185; Macdonell, *Vedic Mythology* (Varanasi, 1963), p. 140; P. V. Kane, op. cit., Vol. V, Part II, p. 1386.

66. For details see *Vedic Index*, II, p. 185.

67. Ibid., Vol. II, pp. 104, 401; Vol. I, p. 68; P. V. Kane admits, op. cit. Vol. II, Part 1. p. 418, that the word *āśrama* does not occur in the Saṃhitās and the

We shall note one more Vedic term which refers to non-Vedic people who had some ascetic ideology. This word is *vrātya*, which occurs in the Vājasaneyi Saṃhitā (XXX.8), Taittirīya Brāhmaṇa (III 4.5, 1), Atharva Veda (Kāṇḍa XV), Pañcaviṃsa Brāhmaṇa (XVII.1–4), and in the latest Vedic texts, the Śrauta Sūtras, Kātyāyana, Lātyāyana and Āpastaṃba. The Yajurveda (Vājasaneyi Saṃhitā, XXX.8) includes the *vrātya* among the victims of "human sacrifice" (*puruṣamedha*). This evidence alone is enough to prove that the *vrātyas* were non-Āryan and non-Vedic people and that the Vedic Āryans of Brāhmaṇical tradition were hostile to them.

The *St. Petersburg Dictionary* defines the term *vrātya* as "belonging to a roving band (*vrāta*), vagrants; member of a fellowship that stood outside the Brāhmaṇical pale." In the Brāhmaṇical Sūtras on Śrauta and Dharma, the son of an uninitiated man is considered a *vrātya*; those who were not consecrated in accordance with the Vedic rituals were deemed to be "depressed" or "degraded" (*hīna*). The Manusmṛti regarded the Licchavīs as *vrātya-kṣatriyas*. It has been suggested by older writers that the fifteenth book of the *Atharvaveda* represents the "idealisation of the pious vagrant or wandering religious mendicant."[68] This book is captioned *vrātyakāṇḍa*.

The word *vrātya* seems to be connected also with *vrata*, vow; the *vrātyas* were possibly ascetics who kept certain pious vows. That they were wandering religious mendicants is quite in keeping with their tradition of ascetic life. It is not suggested here that all the people called *vrātyas* were ascetics; but that ascetic or śramaṇic ideas were popular among the teachers of the *vrātya* community admits of no doubt. The fact that Brāhmaṇas or Vedic priests composed "*vrātya stomas*" and prescribed formal ritual for the admission into the Brāhmaṇical fold of persons who were of non-Āryan origin or belonged to a non-Brāhmaṇical cultural stock confirms the fact that the *vrātya* culture was different from the

---

Brāhmaṇas and that there is nothing in the Vedic literature corresponding to *vanaprastha*.

68. *St. Petersburg Dictionary*, VI. 1503; W.D. Whitney, *Atharva Veda Saṃhitā* Vol. II, HOS, VIII, pp. 769–70; cf. *Vedic Index*, Vol. II. pp. 343–44; A. Weber, *History of Indian Literature*, p. 112; R. R. Bhagavat in JBBRAS, Vol. XIX, p. 357.

Vedic culture. According to J. W. Hauer, the Vedic *vrātyas* were related to Kṣatriya *yogins* or *yatīs*.[69] It is generally believed that the *vrātyas* were a people of eastern India, the region of Kosala and Magadha. It may be noted that the leader of the *vrātya* community wore a headdress which is called "*uṣṇīṣa*," one of the thirty-two marks of a "great man" (*mahāpurisa*) in the Pāli and Buddhist Sanskrit texts. Keith and Macdonell admit that the principles of the *vrātyas* "were opposed to those of the Brāhmaṇas."[70]

A synonym of *vrātya*, "wandering religious mendicant," is *parivrājaka*, a mendicant monk, a religious wanderer. The word *parivrājaka* (Pāli *paribbājaka*) is unknown to Brāhmaṇical literature prior to the Nirukta of Yāska, which is usually dated at 400 BCE. It must be observed that the mystical and ritualistic picture of Vrātya culture recorded in the Atharva Veda (Book XV) is a Brāhmaṇical version of a non-Brāhmāṇical fact. Likewise, the information about *munīs*, *yatīs*, *vaikhānasas* and *śramaṇas* given in Vedic texts is coloured and reflects considerable mixing of non-Āryan and Āryan cultures. At any rate, the evidence discussed above shows that there was what may be called a prehistoric form of the culture of munīs and there were before the sixth century BCE its teachers called munīs, *yatīs*, *vrātyas*, *vaikhānasas*, etc. The texts of the Vedic age show that the Vedic Indo-Āryans had been deeply influenced by the non-Āryan and pre-Āryan culture of India at the time of the composition of the Saṃhitās and Brāhmaṇas. The Upaniṣads reveal the profound and enduring impact on Vedic priests of the non-Vedic ascetics. Dr. H. Zimmer observes that "Following a long history of rigid resistance, the exclusive and esoteric Brāhmaṇ mind of the Āryan invaders opened up, at last, and received suggestions and influences from the native civilisation. The result was a coalescence of the two traditions."[71]

Apart from this old Vedic evidence, there is the evidence of the literary traditions preserved not only in Pāli and Sanskrit Buddhist sources, the Prākrit and Sanskrit Jaina sources, but also in some Brāhmaṇical sources which are datable between the

69. See A. B. Keith, op. cit., Vol. I, p. 148 note I; Vol. II, p. 337 note 2.

70. See *Vedic Index*, Vol. II, p. 343.

71. H. Zimmer, *Philosophies of India*, ed. by Joseph Campbell, Meridian Books (1960), p. 281; cf. G. C. Pande, op. cit. p. 261.

fourth century BCE and fourth century CE, which strongly suggest the existence of saints or ascetics such as are conceived in the traditions of Jainism, Buddhism and Sāṃkhya-Yoga.

Most of the older writers have held the view that these systems arose within Vedicism as a reaction against Vedic sacrificial ritualism. Drs. G. C. Pande, H. Zimmer and H. L. Jain have pointed out that Buddhism, Sāṃkhya-Yoga and Jainism were of non-Vedic and non-Āryan origin. John Marshall had demonstrated the non-Āryan and Harappan origin of Yoga while Dr. H. Jacobi had shown the great antiquity of the Jaina tradition. But the credit of making a detailed and critical study of the prehistoric background of the rise of Buddhism and suggesting Harappan influence in the culture of the *munīs* and *śramaṇas* goes to Dr. G. C. Pande.[72] However, none of these scholars seems to have taken into account the Buddhist tradition of six "past Buddhas" who are believed to have flourished before Śākyamuni Buddha in prehistoric ages.

The most important epithets of the historic founder of Buddhism, Gautama Buddha, were Munī, Śramaṇa and Tathāgata. Although he is also called Yatī, Jina, Āṅgirasa, Ādiccabandhu, etc.[73] and although the epithets Munī and Śramaṇa are also given to many sages of the Jaina tradition, the epithet Tathāgata, "One who came thus," or "One who had arrived (at Truth; Bodhi) in the same way," is a peculiar epithet, the very meaning of which essentially implies the existence of the Buddhas before Gautama Buddha.

Tathāgata (*tathā*+ *āgata*) means "One who has arrived (*āgata*) at the timeless Nibbāna in the same way (*tathā*) just as the Enlightened Ones of former ages (*pubbakehi sammāsambuddhehi*) had attained to it."

In our opinion, it is in this context, with reference to the Buddhas of prehistoric India, the enlightened munīs and *yatis* of pre-Upaniṣadic and non-Vedic Śramaṇic antiquity, that Gautama

72. G. C. Pande, op. cit., pp. 251 ff.; Zimmer, loc. cit.; H. L. Jain, "Bhāratīya Sanskriti Main Jaina Dharmaka Yogadana," Bhopal, 1962, pp. 1–18; John Marshall (ed), *Mohenjodaro and the Indus Civilization*, Vol. I, London, 1931, pp. 48f.; H. Jacobi in ERE, Vol. VII, p. 466; ibid., Vol. II, p. 799; SBE, XLV, pp. XXI ff.

73. See *Mahāvyutpatti*, edited by Sasaki (1928), first section, where 80 names of the Buddha are listed.

Buddha referred to himself as a Tathāgata. It is not our view that all the Buddhas and Pratyeka-Buddhas known to Buddhist tradition (e.g., the Buddhavaṃsa and the Mahāvastu know more than 25 Buddhas and in Mahāyāna myths they are numberless) were historical and human sages. But we strongly believe that the six Buddhas: 1. Vipassī, 2. Sikhī, 3. Vessabhū, 4. Kakusandha, 5. Koṇāgamana and 6. Kassapa, mentioned in the Dīgha and the Saṃyutta Nikāyas as immediate predecessors of Gautama, were most likely real human Śrāmaṇic teachers whose historicity has been shrouded in the myths and legends so universally found in the Buddhist literature and art of Asia.[74]

Besides the evidence of the Dīgha and Saṃyutta Nikāyas, the Majjhima Nikāya knows at least Kakusandha and Kassapa, while an inscription of Aśoka mentions Kanakamuni or Konāgamana.[75] Whatever be the Brāhmaṇical theory of the mythical incarnation of Viṣṇu in the form of the historic founder of Buddhism, and whatever be the views of modern Buddhists and Buddhist scholars regarding the origin of Buddhism and the antiquity of the gospel of Śākyamuni, the latter himself and his ancient followers including the two most famous of them, Aśoka and Hsuan Tsang, had a firm faith in the historicity of the six aforesaid "former" Buddhas. The present writer shares this faith of ancient Buddhists.

---

74. Editorial Note: According to Buddhist tradition, only the last three Buddhas of the past (Kakusandha, Koṇāgamana, Kassapa) belong to the present world period (*kalpa*, Pāli *kappa*) which is called a fortunate one (*bhadda-kappa*) as five Buddhas appear in it. In addition to the aforementioned three, the Buddha of the present age, Gotama śakyamuni, is the fourth to be followed by Metteyya (Maitreyya) Buddha in a distant future. But also the appearance of the Buddhas within a single Kalpa has to be thought to be separated by cataclysmic changes which entirely interrupt cultural continuity so that the characteristic Teaching of all Buddhas (i.e., the Four Truths) is entirely lost to the age of a subsequent Buddha, who has to rediscover it by his own effort. The Buddhas prior to Kakusandha are said to belong to different Kalpas. Śrāmaṇic sages of the past who had not the knowledge of the Four Truths, however spiritually advanced they may have been otherwise, would never be called Buddhas in any Buddhist tradition.

75. Vide Mahāpadānasutta, DN 14; Nidānasaṃyutta, SN 12; Māratajjanīyasutta, MN 50; *Nigalisagar Pillar Inscription of Aśoka*; T. Watters, *Yuan Chhwang's Travels*, Delhi, 1961, Vol. I, p. 400; Vol. II, pp. 1–9, 58, 124, 141.

The famous *ipse dixit* of Gautama Buddha, which has been cited as an authority in support of their hypothesis of Hinduistic origin of the Buddha's teachings by Drs. Rādhakrishnan and P. V. Kane, has to be interpreted, in our view, in the context of the Buddhist tradition of the existence of the Buddhas before Gautama Buddha. The passage quoted by these scholars occurs in the Nagarasutta (SN 12:65). It has been wrongly employed to support the modern Hindu view that the Buddha himself claimed to teach the path of the ancient "Hindu" sages and to show that the Buddha did not feel that he was announcing a new religion. The word "Hindu" does not occur in the statement of the Buddha; nor does he refer to Vedic sages or Indo-Āryan seers or brāhmaṇas or priests as the teachers of that ancient path which he followed and preached. It has been our contention that his teaching was connected with the ancient ideals of the munīs, *yatīs* and *śramaṇas* who were neither "Hindu" nor Brāhmaṇical or Vedic; nor even Indo-Āryan.

The antiquity of the Śramaṇic, as distinguished from the Brāhmaṇic, path (*magga*), affirmed by Śākyamuni, must be accepted as a fact. It is impossible to trace in the Vedas and Brāhmaṇas any one single element referred to in that statement attributed to the Buddha which is quoted by these scholars and which should be summed up as follows: The Buddha gives an example of an ancient city (*nagara*) and an ancient road (*magga*) leading to that city. Just as a man wandering in a forest sees an ancient road and following that road arrives at an ancient city which was established by men in ancient times, in a like manner, the Buddha says, when he had been a Bodhisattva wandering in quest of the Supreme Peace, he saw and followed an ancient path and arrived at the highest goal. What was that path and what that goal?

The answer is contained in these lines: "Even so (*evameva*)," says the Buddha, "monks, I have seen an old path, and an old road, traversed by the Supremely Enlightened Ones of yore. What, monks, is that old road, traversed by the Supremely Enlightened Ones of yore? Just this noble Eightfold Path, to wit, Right Views, Right Aims, Right Speech, Right Actions, Right Livelihood, Right Endeavour, Right Mindfulness, Right Concentration. This, monks, is that old path, that old road, traversed by the Supremely Enlightened Ones of yore. Along that I have gone. Going along that I have fully known old age and death; I have fully known the end of old age and death; I have fully known the path leading to the end of old age and death, I have fully known birth, I have fully known becoming (*bhava*), I have fully known the path leading to the end of volitional formations (*saṅkhārā*)."[76]

In this statement the "Eightfold Path" is called an "Ancient Path" (*purāṇaṃ maggaṃ*). Nobody can maintain that the Eightfold Path is known to the Vedic literature; it is unknown even to the Upaniṣads. In later Yoga texts a theory of "eight limbs" of Yoga was advanced apparently after the old Buddhist theory of an eightfold way. Likewise, the theory of "Four Truths" concerning the origin and end of ills (*dukkha*) is unknown to the entire range of Vedic literature, though the Buddha says that it also belonged to antiquity.

In later texts on medicine and Yoga we find that a similar view of four facts concerning origin and end of disease is expounded, obviously on the model of the Buddhist theory of the Four Truths. Not only are the "Eightfold Path" and the "Four Truths" related to antiquity but also the doctrine of "conditioned origination" (*paṭiccasamuppāda/pratītyasamutpāda*) is said to be ancient. This doctrine is quite unknown to the Vedas, Brāhmaṇas and Upaniṣads. The idea of *nirodha* of saṃsāra, i.e., the conception of Nibbāna or Nirvāṇa, the highest goal referred to here, is quite unknown to the Vedic tradition. Yet the Buddha was quite right in saying that these cardinal doctrines of his Dhamma or Buddhism belonged to antiquity. They belonged to the Buddhas of former ages, to the Supremely Enlightened Ones of ancient times. The six "Seers" (*isīs, ṛṣīs*) or "Past Blessed Ones" (*pubba bhagavanto*), namely, Vipassī, Sikhī, Vessabhū, Krakucchanda, Kanakamuni and Kāsyapa, are called "Supremely Enlightened Ones of Yore" by the Buddha. Śākyamuni trod their ancient path and arrived at the highest "Sphere" (*āyatana*) or "City" (*nagara*) known to these ancient seers. Hence he referred to himself as Tathāgata, and hence also he was called "the seventh Seer among the Seers" (*isīnam isī sattamo;* SN 8:8).

76. Mrs. Rhys Davids and F. L. Woodward, *The Book of the Kindred Sayings (Saṃyutta Nikāya)*, Part II, PTS, London, 1952, pp. 74–75. We have modified the translation in our text.

The six seers or Buddhas of Yore must have belonged to the tradition of *munīs* and *yatīs* whose existence in prehistoric India is attested by the Vedic Saṃhitās and Brāhmaṇas. Nothing more than their names is known to us. Their biographies in extant sources are quite mythical but there seems to be some historical basis of facts underlying so ancient and so universally accepted a Buddhist tradition as that concerning these past Buddhas.

A. S. Geden observes, while commenting on the evidence of the Nigālīsāgar pillar inscription of Aśoka referring to the stupa of Kanakamuni Buddha, that "of the numerous Buddhas whose names are recorded in the Buddhist books as predecessors of Gautama, it would seem therefore historically probable that a real basis of fact underlies the name and personality of Kanakamuni; and also of his successor Kāśyapa."[77]

Confirming the interpretation offered here of the Saṃyutta Nikāya passage quoted above, the *Mahāvastu Avadāna*[78] records the following relevant lines addressed to Bodhisattva Siddhārtha:

Yena gato krakucchando kanakamuni ca kāsyapo
Etena tvaṃ gaccha vīra adya buddho bhaviṣyasi.

These lines obviously refer to that path which had been traversed by former Buddhas called Krakucchanda, Kanakamuni and Kāśyapa, and Siddhārtha is being advised to go along that path so as to become a Buddha soon.

It may be noted that the Jaina tradition also seems to be older than is generally believed. It will be difficult to maintain that all the twenty-three Jinas whose legends are found in Jaina books as predecessors of Nigaṇṭha Mahāvīra were historical teachers. But the historicity of some of them,[79] for example, of Pārśvanātha, is now an acknowledged fact. The *siṣṇadevas* or naked teachers known to Vedic literature may have been prehistoric predecessors

---

77. A. S. Geden on *Kanakamuni* in ERE, Vol. VII, p. 644; cf. V. Smith, *Asoka*, Oxford, 1901, p. 146; J. J. Legge, *Fa-Hian Records of Buddhist Kingdoms*, Oxford, 1886, p. 64; H. Jacobi in *Ages of the World* in ERE, Vol. I, p. 202.

78. *Mahāvastu Avadāna*, ed. by R. G. Basak, Vol. II, Calcutta, 1964, p. 541 verse 5; see also pp. 366–67, 413, 415; Vol. I, Calcutta, 1963, pp. 377, 411–12, 468.

79. See H. Jacobi, *Mahāvīra and His Predecessors*, *Indian Antiquary*, Vol. IX, Bombay, pp. 158 ff.; H. Zimmer, op. cit., pp. 181–82, 281.

of historic ascetics of Jaina and Ājīvika traditions. Dr. Jacobi, relying on Jaina sources, placed Pārśvanātha in circa 750 BCE.

We should now briefly consider the origins of the Sāṃkhya and Yoga. In later Brāhmaṇical tradition these two systems are generally mentioned together. Yoga as a way of religious perfection is older than the Yoga system of thought now associated with Patañjalī's *Yogasūtras* (circa CE 300). Yoga as a way was an essential element of Śramaṇic culture. Yoga is therefore of non-Brāhmaṇical and non-Āryan origin. The *munīs* and *yatīs* of Vedic age practised Yoga and *dhyāna*. This is clear from the Ṛgveda (X.136.1–3) and the Aitareya Brāhmaṇa (VII.13.7). The early Yoga was possibly identical with Buddhist Yoga or the way of meditation. As it belonged to the non-Vedic Śramaṇic tradition, the early Yoga was possibly non-theistic and ascetic. Even in the Yoga system of Patañjalī, God (Īśvara) does not seem to be an essential element in the system.

In later Brāhmaṇical myths known to the Mahābhārata and the Purāṇas, Yoga is said to be of divine origin and is usually interpreted on theistic lines. The older Upaniṣads were deeply influenced by Yoga. From the time of the Svetāsvatara Upaniṣad onwards, Rudra-Śiva seems to have been associated with Yoga. Śiva is now known as Yogīśvara. Kṛṣṇa in the Bhagavadgīta is called Yogeśvara. It is characteristic of this text to praise not only Yoga but also the Sāṃkhya, and the two are identified as one.

There is strong evidence to prove the great antiquity of Sāṃkhya and its non-Vedic or Śramaṇic origin. This system remained anti-Vedic, non-theistic, dualistic and ascetic till as late as the *Sāṃkhyakārikā* of Iśvarakṛṣṇa (circa CE 300). The Upaniṣads and the Mahābhārata, including the Gīta, have been greatly influenced by the Sāṃkhya system. It is wrong to suppose, as Dr. R. Garbe has done, that the Sāṃkhya originated as a reaction to Upaniṣadic idealistic monism.[80] The system is almost certainly of pre-Upaniṣadic origin. The Brahmajāla Sutta "probably refers to the Sāṃkhya dualism at one place when it refers to the view that the soul and the world (*attānaṃ ca lokaṃ ca*; cp. *puruṣa* and *pṛkṛti* or matter) were held to be real by certain śramaṇas."[81] From other

80. ERE, Vol. XI, p. 189.

81. DN 1; cf. T. W. Rhys Davids, *Buddhism, Its History and Literature*, 2nd ed. (1901), pp. 24–26.

Buddhist sources we know that Ālāra Kālāma, a contemporary and teacher of Siddhārtha, was possibly a Sāṃkhya teacher. The partial similarities between early Sāṃkhya and Theravāda theories are due, in our view, to the fact that the Sāṃkhya belonged to the same tradition to which early Buddhism belonged and the practice of Yoga was a common bond between these two sister traditions of non-Brāhmaṇical origin.

The founder of the Sāṃkhya system was, according to all accounts, Kapilamuni or Ṛṣi Kapila. He was a historical teacher and may be placed in the 9th century BCE. So many are the legends in the Great Epic and Purāṇas woven around his name that he was completely mythologised and deified. But before the Brāhmaṇas or Vaiṣṇavaite Hindus accepted him as an Avatāra of Viṣṇu, his doctrine as a way to the Highest Good, and his institution of the ascetic stage as the fourth Āśrama, he was held to be a "demon" (*asura*), and his teachings were treated as heterodox.[82] For old Brāhmaṇism, Kapilamuni was as good or bad as Śākyamuni; in Hinduism, however, both are revered as gods.

The Mahābhārata (*Vanaparva* 221.26) as well as the Sāṃkhya-kārikā (verses 70–71) recognise Kapila as the founder of the Sāṃkhya; Āsuri and Pañcaśikha were the two most important teachers after Kapila. The Śvetāśvatara Upaniṣad (III.4, IV.12, V.2, VI.13) knows the Sāṃkhya, Yoga and Kapila and identifies the latter with the Golden Germ (*hiraṇyagarbha*). The Atharvaveda (X.8.43) knows three "qualities" (*guṇas*), and the Ait. Upa. (III.3), the Praśna Upa. (VI.4), and the Kaṭha Upa. (III.15) refer to five great elements and their five qualities. The Mahābhārata mystifies Kapila with Vāsudeva, Agni and Prajāpati, but gives a detailed account of the Sāṃkhya doctrine and the ascetic culture called Yoga. The great Sāṃkhya teacher Pañcaśikha is called in the Epic a "*bhikṣu*," "*kāpileya*," and is said to have belonged to Pārāsarya gotra. It is important to note here that Pāṇinī (IV.3.110) seems to attribute a text called "*Bhikṣu Sūtra*" to a Pārāsarya. Thus two sources tell us that Kapila and his pupil, Pañcaśikha, were associated

82. Cf. Baudhāyana Dharmasūtra, II. 629–631; Bādarāyana treats Sāṃkhya as a heterodox system, *Vedāntasūtra*, I.1.5 and II.I.1 and II.21–10 with Saṃkara's commentary; Ālāra Kālāma, a Sāṃkhya teacher, is found criticising Vedicism in *Buddhacarita* XII, 30–32.

with the institution of *saṃyāsa* and its organisation or rules. We have already noted that Baudhāyana makes Kapila responsible for the introduction of the stage called *pravrajyā* or *saṃyāsa*. This authority refers to Kapila as "Asura" and asks people not to respect his teaching. This is clear proof of the non-Vedic origin of Kapila, his Sāṃkhya and his fourth Āśrama.

Indeed, Kapila is mentioned in the Ṛgveda (X. 27.16: *dasānāṃ ekaṃ Kapilaṃ samānaṃ taṃ hinvanti kratave pāryāya*) as one among the ten (*Āngīrasas*). The Āngīrasas were connected with the *yatīs*. The Buddha is sometimes called an Āngīrasa. In a Sri Lankan tradition Kapila is known as "Isuru-munī" which is identical with Kapila-munī who is called an Asura. Dr. G. C. Pande thinks that Kapila in Baudhāyana Dharma Sūtra (II.6.29–31) "may be merely eponymous for the Kapilas or the tawny-clad ascetics." This should not mean that a Kapila was not a real teacher called Kapilamuni. Dr. Zimmer says that "Kapila, who stands outside the traditional assembly of Vedic gods and goddesses as an Enlightened One in his own right, must have lived before the sixth century BCE."

Something should be observed about the term *ārya* (Pāli: *ariya*). It will be argued that the word Ārya or Ariya is of such frequent occurrence in Buddhist literature, both Pāli and Sanskrit, that to trace Buddhist origins to a non-Āryan and pre-Āryan source is rather difficult to appreciate. The word *ārya* or *ariya* means "noble," "honourable," "respectable," "one who is faithful to the religion of his country," etc. Modern researches have shown that there was no human race called the Āryan race. Archaeologists and philologists now use the word *āryan* for those peoples who spoke a dialect belonging to the family of Indo-European, Indo-Āryan and Indo-Iranian group of languages. In ancient India the word *ārya* or *ariya* was a word of common use among educated people. It was often used to show respect for a person or a group of persons or a doctrine. We have used the word Āryan for the Vedic or Brāhmaṇical culture following this convention.

The word perhaps originated among the victorious barbarians, who came from beyond the northwestern border of India in about 1500 BCE and who referred to the autochthonous people in contemptuous terms such as *dāsa*. We have a similar case in later Buddhist history when the followers of the Mahāsāṅghikas and Sarvāstivādins coined the word Mahāyāna for their own doctrine and described the older schools as belonging to the Hīnayāna. The word *ārya* or *ariya* has no racial or linguistic sense attached to it in Buddhist literature. *Ariya-puggala* means "a noble person"; *ariya-sacca* means "noble truth" and so on.

Before we conclude this section we must say a few words about the ascetics of the pre-Vedic culture of the Indus Valley. Archaeological evidence is more reliable and authentic than literary evidence. It has been rightly acknowledged by antiquarians like Marshall, Mackay, Piggot and Wheeler that some of the basic elements of the historic religious beliefs and practices of India go back to the Harappan culture or Indus civilization of the third millennium BCE.[83] For example, we find the holy animals like deer, lion, horse, elephant, bull, rhinoceros and the sacred snake represented in the plastic art of Mohenjodāro and Harappa. These creatures are often given an important place in Buddhist art and literature of historic times. The sacred *Ficus religiosa*, the *Asvattha* or the Pipala tree is already a religious article in this prehistoric civilization. In Buddhism this becomes the symbolic *Bodhi-rukkha*, the Tree of Enlightenment. More significant than these is the discovery of at least four sculptures which show ascetics or munīs in ascetic and meditative posture establishing thereby the existence of Yoga and those who practise it in pre-Vedic India.

A steatite seal from Mohenjodāro, discovered by E. Mackay, and described by John Marshall as the prototype of historic Śiva, "Trimurti," and "Paśupati," deserves special mention. Long before the ideas of Śiva, Mahādeva, Trimurti and Paśupati had come into existence in historic Brāhmaṇism and Hinduism, there had been in prehistoric India and in Buddhism and Jainism what are called *munīs*, *yatīs* and *śramaṇas*. The Indus seal therefore should be looked upon as the figure of an ascetic of pre-Vedic Indian culture. The figure shows a human ascetic, seated cross-legged on a pedestal, around him are figures of a lion and an elephant on his right, and a buffalo and a rhinoceros on his left while below the pedestal are figures of a pair of deer. The ascetic wears a headdress resembling the symbol of the Buddhist *Triratna* as found in the art of Bhārhut and Sāñchī. The figure is probably four-faced.

---

83. John Marshall, op. cit., Vol. I, pp. 44ff.; Mortimer Wheeler, *The Indus Civilization,* Cambridge, 1953, pp 78–80, 95; Stuart Piggott, *Prehistoric India*, pp. 957ff., 286ff.

Another figure on a seal is supposed to be that of a "priest." This human figure shows only the upper half of the body, the eyes are almost closed, seemingly in meditation; he wears a beard and long hair; the cloth on his body is thrown in a peculiarly Buddhist monk's manner, keeping the right arm uncovered. Here is the prototype of a historic *bhikkhu* or monk in concentration. There is then a stone figure of a man clearly seated in meditation, dating from the second millennium BCE. Last, we may mention the figure of another *muni* or ascetic found on a steatite seal from Mohenjodāro, depicting a man seated in a cross-legged yogic posture. He is flanked by two human worshippers with raised and folded hands apparently in adoration: behind each of these worshippers is a snake (*nāga*) in half-rearing posture.[84] There are some more Harappan figures depicting ascetics which have not been considered here due to lack of space.

VII. Concluding Remarks

We have seen that Jainism, Sāṃkhya and Yoga constituted Śramaṇism, which was an altogether different culture from Brāhmaṇism. Śramaṇism means that culture of ancient India in which spiritual and moral "exertion" (*śrama*) was the dominant ideal; its teachers were ascetics called śramaṇas or munīs who believed in moral karma and practised concentration and austerities. It was a mixture of atheistic, anti-ritualistic, ascetic and pluralistic ideologies. Buddhism was more nearly related to this Śramaṇic stream of thought which had its origin in prehistoric times. In later day India this Śramaṇic culture and Buddhism were assimilated by the Brāhmaṇical culture and the result was what is now called Hinduism. Thus Brāhmaṇism, plus elements from Buddhism, Jainism, Yoga and Sāṃkhya make the Hindu religion.

What we have discussed above is primarily intended for students of the history of Indian religious ideas but it also has a practical importance for those who are followers of Buddhism today.

84. See the figures of ascetics of prehistoric India in *Mohenjodāro and the Indus Civilization*, Vol. I (1931), plates XIII, 17a; XVI, 29; CXIVII, 11; H. Zimmer, *The Art of Indian Asia*, Vol. II (1955), plate 2e; for E. Mackay's views on Indus statuary, see Marshall, op. cit., Vol. I, pp. 356–57.

The comparative or synthetic study of different religious traditions should not lead us to overlook the different origins and distinctive elements of the different religious thought-currents.

With respect to the question of comparison between Buddhism and Hinduism raised by Dr. P. V. Kane, it should be observed that nobody has made "unfair comparisons between the original doctrines of the Buddha with the present practices and shortcomings of Hindu society." His "protest" against such comparisons is therefore quite uncalled for. His view that a comparison between "the later phases of Buddhism" and "modern phases and practices of Hinduism" will be a "fair comparison" is untenable. In such a comparison one should compare early Brāhmaṇism with early Buddhism, Mahāyāna Buddhism with Purāṇic Brāhmaṇism (Vaiṣnavism and Śaivism), Tāntrika Buddhism with Tāntrika Brāhmaṇism, and modern Buddhism with modern Hinduism. What he has called the "hideous practices" of "degraded Buddhism" should be compared with similar practices of the Śāktas, the Śaivas, the Kaulas, the Kāpālikas and the Kālāmukhas of early mediaeval Hinduism.

A scholar of early mediaeval Indian religious practices and beliefs will not find any difference between the Tāntrika Buddhists and the Tāntrika Hindus. The contents of the *Śaiva-Śākta-Vaiṣṇava Tantras* are quite as bizarre as those of the *Vajrāyana* and *Sahajayāna Tantras*.[85] The strange rites of early mediaeval Hindu sects of Śaivasa Śāktas and Bhāgavatas will be found also in the *Purāṇas*, the *Āgamas*, the *Harṣacarita*, the *Gauḍavaho* and the *Rājataraṅgini*. These texts do not belong to a degraded phase of Hinduism, for Tāntricism has been an essential element of Hinduism or Purāṇic Brāhmaṇism from the earliest times.

In fact, Brāhmaṇism rarely declined; it went on growing with the growth of centuries, and it retained its original Indo-Āryan character in some form or another even when it had been refined and transformed by non-Brāhmaṇical doctrines and practices. The divinely ordained system of *varṇa* (castes and classes) and their *dharmas* (duties, vocations and privileges), the gospel of producing many sons, the doctrine of untouchability, the customs

85. Cf. L. M. Joshi, *Studies in the Buddhistic Culture of India* (1967), p. 153 note 223.

of *devadāsi, sati*, etc.—these features which have been criticised by some educated and advanced modern Indian leaders as well as by European scholars—have been regular features of Brāhmaṇism and Hinduism right from the days of the Vedic Dharma Sūtras and the Mahābhārata. They are present even now.

Neo-Brāhmaṇism or Hinduism is, in the present writer's opinion, superior to the Vedic Brāhmaṇism from which it came; there are many points of agreement between this Neo-Brāhmaṇism or Hinduism and Buddhism. But there are also some vital differences. The differences are due to the persistence of Indo-Āryan Brāhmaṇism while the agreements come from the fact that something of Buddhism survives in Hinduism. A comparison between the two would be the task of another essay.

ABOUT PARIYATTI

Pariyatti is dedicated to providing affordable access to authentic teachings of the Buddha about the Dhamma theory (*pariyatti*) and practice (*paṭipatti*) of Vipassana meditation. A 501(c)(3) nonprofit charitable organization since 2002, Pariyatti is sustained by contributions from individuals who appreciate and want to share the incalculable value of the Dhamma teachings. We invite you to visit www.pariyatti.org to learn about our programs, services, and ways to support publishing and other undertakings.

Pariyatti Publishing Imprints

Vipassana Research Publications (focus on Vipassana as taught by S.N. Goenka in the tradition of Sayagyi U Ba Khin)

BPS Pariyatti Editions (selected titles from the Buddhist Publication Society, copublished by Pariyatti)

MPA Pariyatti Editions (selected titles from the Myanmar Pitaka Association, copublished by Pariyatti)

Pariyatti Digital Editions (audio and video titles, including discourses)

Pariyatti Press (classic titles returned to print and inspirational writing by contemporary authors)

Pariyatti enriches the world by

- disseminating the words of the Buddha,
- providing sustenance for the seeker's journey,
- illuminating the meditator's path.

www.ingramcontent.com/pod-product-compliance
Lightning Source LLC
Chambersburg PA
CBHW020345170426
43200CB00005B/57
* 9 7 8 1 6 8 1 7 2 1 6 0 6 *